I0814525

"Mark Lindsay has finally given us his much-awaited biography of Markus Barth. Markus Barth—though often overshadowed by his father, the great theologian Karl Barth—was an amazing theologian in his own right. Barth the younger was way ahead of the curve on so many topics of New Testament scholarship that are only now becoming mainstream. Lindsay's biography of Markus Barth shows the life, story, and scholarship of a truly amazing figure in Christian scholarship of the twentieth century. A must-read book!"

Michael F. Bird, deputy principal at Ridley College in Melbourne, Australia, and author of *A Bird's-Eye View of Luke and Acts*

"In this captivating and meticulous biography, Mark R. Lindsay offers a window into the life of a theologian who is often overlooked. As someone guilty of neglecting Markus Barth, despite hearing many wonderful things about him, I found this book eye-opening. It is also beautifully written and accessible, making it not simply an academic treatise but a read that will be enjoyable for a broad audience."

Andrew B. Torrance, director of impact and senior lecturer in theology at the University of St Andrews

"Mark Lindsay has written an invaluable and engaging portrait of Markus Barth in which we meet the person, the scholar, and the Christian. The key elements of Barth's lifework—his contributions to New Testament exegesis (most especially to the study of Paul), his passionate commitment (both theological and personal) to the importance of Jewish-Christian relations, and his provocative ecumenical contributions to rethinking the nature and practice of baptism and the Lord's Supper—are all insightfully examined on the basis of careful archival research. The result is a fine account of Barth's life and legacy that also affords important perspectives on the history of theology in the twentieth century."

Philip G. Ziegler, professor of Christian dogmatics at the University of Aberdeen

"Mark Lindsay's book on Markus Barth is a well-articulated and valuable contribution, not just in lifting up Markus' life and scholarship in biblical studies and theology but also as a helpful resource for the study and discussion of the issues that were central to Markus' work and thought."

David MacLachlan, associate professor of New Testament studies at the Atlantic School of Theology in Halifax, Nova Scotia

"Mark Lindsay's long-awaited book on Markus Barth is a fascinating study of Karl Barth's eldest son, a theologian and provocative thinker in his own right. Markus Barth's commitment to doing theology 'in the service of the church' shaped his understanding of the inherently political aspects of faith and ministry. Lindsay's discussion of Barth's often contentious engagement in Jewish-Christian relations is particularly thoughtful. This is a remarkable and rich study, with insights not just into Barth's life and scholarship, but into the major theological and political discussions of his times."

Victoria J. Barnett, former director of programs on ethics, religion, and the Holocaust at the US Holocaust Memorial Museum and general editor of the Dietrich Bonhoeffer Works series, English edition

MARKUS BARTH

HIS LIFE & LEGACY

MARKUS BARTH

HIS LIFE & LEGACY

MARK R. LINDSAY

An imprint of InterVarsity Press
Downers Grove, Illinois

InterVarsity Press
P.O. Box 1400 | Downers Grove, IL 60515-1426
ivpress.com | email@ivpress.com

InterVarsity Press® is the publishing division of InterVarsity Christian Fellowship/USA®. For more information, visit intervarsity.org.

Cover design: David Fassett
Interior design: Jeanna Wiggins
Image: © kundoy / Moment / Getty Images

ISBN 978-1-5140-0162-2 (print) | ISBN 978-1-5140-0163-9 (digital)

Printed in the United States of America ♾

Library of Congress Cataloging-in-Publication Data
Names: Lindsay, Mark R., 1971- author.
Title: Markus Barth : his life and legacy / Mark R. Lindsay.
Description: Downers Grove, IL : IVP Academic, [2024] | Includes bibliographical references and index.
Identifiers: LCCN 2024017914 (print) | LCCN 2024017915 (ebook) | ISBN 9781514001622 (hardcover) | ISBN 9781514001639 (ebook)
Subjects: LCSH: Barth, Markus. | Theologians–Switzerland–Biography. | BISAC: BIOGRAPHY & AUTOBIOGRAPHY / Religious | RELIGION / Christian Theology / History
Classification: LCC BX4827.B32 L56 2024 (print) | LCC BX4827.B32 (ebook) | DDC 230/.42092 [B]–dc23/eng/20240628
LC record available at https://lccn.loc.gov/2024017914
LC ebook record available at https://lccn.loc.gov/2024017915

31 30 29 28 27 26 25 24 | 13 12 11 10 9 8 7 6 5 4 3 2 1

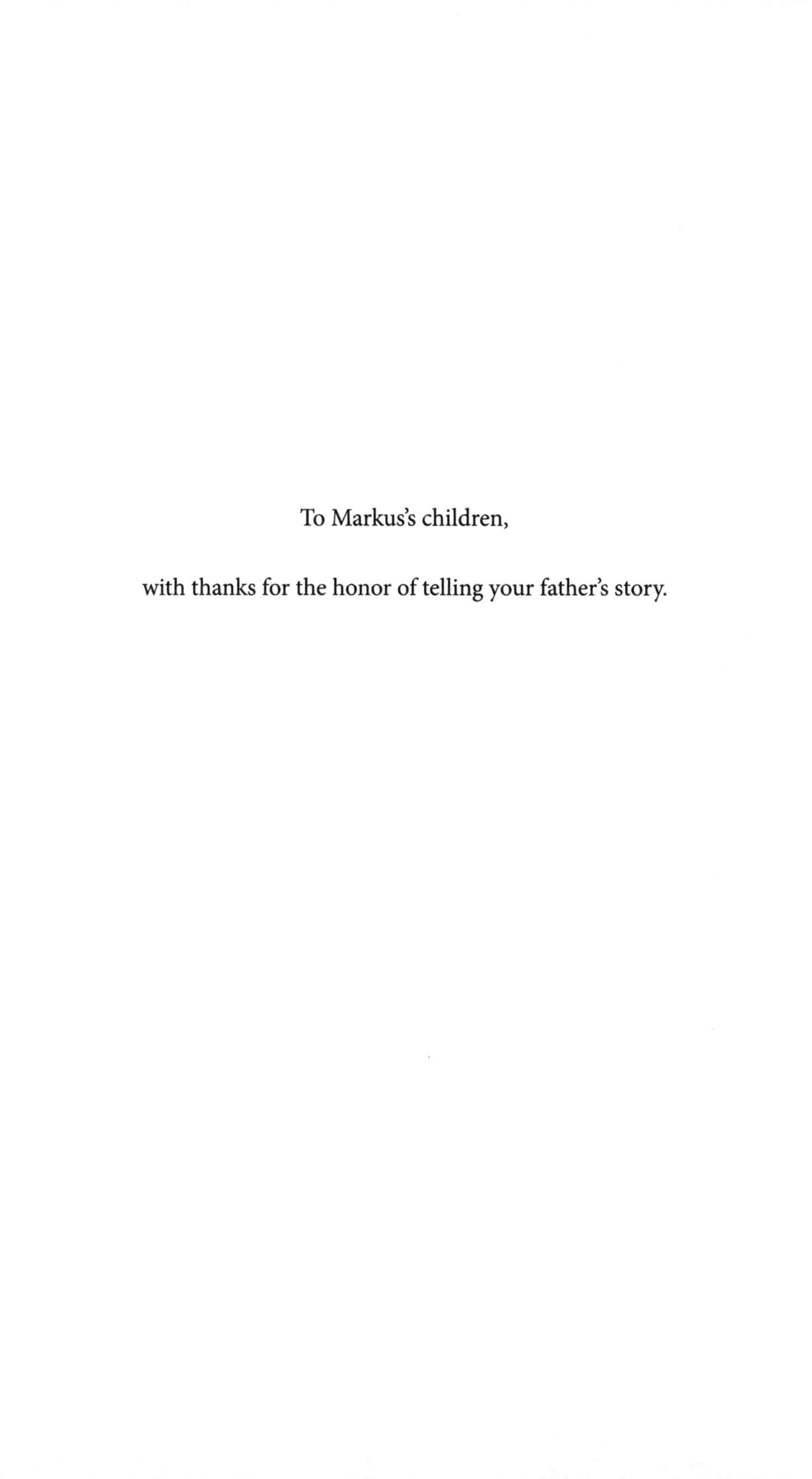

To Markus's children,

with thanks for the honor of telling your father's story.

CONTENTS

PERMISSIONS

THE AUTHOR GRATEFULLY acknowledges receipt of the following:

Durham County Record Office (Durham, UK): letter, M. Barth to Lt. Col. H. McBain. Reproduced by permission of the trustees of the former Durham Light Infantry and the Durham County Record Office.

The Markus Barth Manuscript Collection. Special Collections, Princeton Theological Seminary Library (White Library).

Peter Barth, Anna Barth, Ruth Naveau, Rose-Marie Barth Häfeli, and Shabnam Edith Barth, for permission to use the photographs reproduced herein, and the unpublished documents that are not part of the Princeton collection.

All translations of German source material are mine, unless otherwise specified.

PREFACE

I **FIRST ENCOUNTERED** Markus Barth in 2009. It was, frankly, an accidental meeting. Hoping to have a paper accepted for that year's Karl Barth conference in Princeton, the theme of which was "Karl Barth on Religion and the Religions," I offered up instead a presentation on Markus Barth and Jewish-Christian relations as the after-dinner talk on the opening night.[1] I was at that stage hardly an expert on Markus Barth—though I was somewhat more knowledgeable about Jewish-Christian dialogue and about Karl's theology of Israel—and so offered the paper as a tentative exploration of the ways in which the son had built upon, and then extended in his own particular way, the teachings of his father. The results of that study so intrigued me that I decided to take the project further. This I did by spending three months over 2016–2017 as a visiting scholar at Princeton Theological Seminary, working with the Markus Barth Papers that were held in the special collections section of Princeton's White Library.[2] Again, my fascination grew. I was astonished, however, to find not only that no one had ever really explored in depth Princeton's collection of Markus Barth's letters and papers, but also that no one had undertaken a full-length biography of him. Surely, here was a subject deserving of a book.

---

[1]Published as "The Identity of the People of God: Israel and the Church in the Theology of Markus Barth," *Colloquium* 43, no. 1 (2011): 3-16.

[2]The results of this research were published as "Jewish-Christian Relations from the Underside: Markus Barth's Correspondence with Michael Wyschogrod (1962–84) and Emil Fackenheim (1965–80)," *Journal of Ecumenical Studies* 53, no. 3 (2018): 313-47.

After several conversations with Kait Dugan and Bruce McCormack, in which I tentatively proposed the possibility of writing a biography, it was my privilege in 2019 to be put in touch with Markus Barth's children. They were overwhelmingly supportive of the idea and generous in their assistance. Since then, it has been my great joy to work on this project. As I have read, researched, and written—and discussed the work and witness of Markus Barth with his family, friends, students, and colleagues—I have come to appreciate and marvel at the extent of his contributions to the church, Jewish-Christian relations, the theological academy, and civic life more generally. In doing so, it has surprised me constantly that no one has hitherto told his story. And I continue to wonder whether his family name served or hindered him. No doubt, opportunities were afforded to Markus because he was a Barth. By the same token, his work and witness have for decades been overshadowed by the towering figure of his father. Had Markus been someone other than Karl's son, perhaps his theological and ecclesial contributions would have been better known before now. Or perhaps he would have remained even less known than he already is.

In either case, it has been an honor to write this account of his life and his work. There is, of course, more to do. No biography can ever be the final word on anyone. As Mark Twain once memorably put it, "Biographies are but the clothes and buttons of the man."[3] Others will, I'm sure, see Markus Barth dressed in clothes different from the ones in which I have portrayed him. My aim here is, thus, quite modest: to bring Markus Barth's extraordinary legacy to a wider readership and to instill and inspire a new form of "Barth studies" that looks beyond Karl to a more recent Barthian contribution—a contribution that built upon the father's foundation but that then developed it in fascinatingly complex directions.

---

[3]Mark Twain, *Autobiography of Mark Twain*, vol. 1, *The Complete and Authoritative Edition*, ed. H. E. Smith (Berkeley: University of California Press, 2010), 221.

ACKNOWLEDGMENTS

I OWE SINGULAR DEBTS OF GRATITUDE to a number of people, without whose generosity and assistance this book would not have come to fruition. First, to Kait Dugan and Bruce McCormack, both of Princeton Theological Seminary, who encouraged me in my first dreamings about this project and who have remained invaluable supporters throughout.

Second, to my editors at IVP Academic, David McNutt and Jon Boyd. This is the second book on which David has worked with me. I am indebted to him for his care and counsel, his willingness to contract the book in the first place, and his sharp eye for details that would otherwise have escaped me. I am grateful also to Jon Boyd, who took over the project late in the process and brought it to fruition. It would be an honor to work with him in the future—and indeed, I hope to do so.

To those among my colleagues at Trinity College Theological School who have asked probing questions along the way and whose interest in the progress of the project has been greatly encouraging, I am deeply thankful: Bob Derrenbacker, Scott Kirkland, Dorothy Lee, Fergus King, Rachelle Gilmour, and Chris Porter. It is the great privilege of my working life to have such people as my most immediate colleagues, and from whom I am delighted and honored to learn every day.

I am grateful, of course, also to the University of Divinity and the Governors of ARTFInc, who awarded me a number of grants, without which I would not have been able to undertake the necessary primary source research in Princeton and Basel.

Once again, and as always, to my family—Sonia, Jack, Tom, and Elijah. My thanks to them for their patience and forbearance of me will always be insufficient. In particular I am grateful to Tom, who at the end of his high school years chose not to party with his friends but instead work as my research assistant in Princeton and Basel as we pored over papers, trying to decipher that notoriously tiny Barthian handwriting. And yes, Markus's is just as illegible as Karl's! Thank you, Tom—your help was above and beyond.

Finally, I wish and need to thank the Barth family themselves: Peter, Anna, Ruth, Rose-Marie, and their sister-in-law, Shabnam. Throughout this project, they have been unfailingly supportive and overwhelmingly generous in providing access to documents, letters, and photos that would otherwise have remained unknown to me. Their keen questions, timely and thorough advice, and always-helpful feedback on draft chapters have been an immense privilege to receive. I will forever be deeply grateful that they were willing to entrust their father's story to me. I only hope that this book, in which I have tried to do justice to their father and his work, is something of a satisfactory repayment to them for all that they have given me. And so it is with heartfelt and humble gratitude I dedicate this book to them.

A CHILDHOOD OF "PARTICULAR AFFECTION"

The Early Years, 1915–1930

Karl Markus Barth was born on Wednesday, October 6, 1915, in the small, semi-industrial town of Safenwil in the Aargauer Canton, where his father had been pastor to the Reformed community since 1911. The second of Karl and Nelly Barth's five children,[1] Karl Markus—known from birth by his middle name—was welcomed into the family with much rejoicing. His godfather, Karl's great friend Eduard Thurneysen, greeted Markus's birth as an occasion of "great joy."[2] But while his arrival was a source of undeniable happiness, he was, in truth, born during a period of considerable upheaval. North over the borders, the First World War had been raging for just over a year. The devastating effects of the Gallipoli campaign, the battle for Ypres, and the Artois-Loos Offensive were still being felt across Europe and even beyond.

The Barths themselves were out of harm's way in Switzerland, but they were not for that reason isolated from the war or its effects. While Switzerland itself was neutral, its borders were not entirely secure. Certainly, the executors of Germany's Schlieffen Plan had, in the end, opted to attack

---

[1]Franziksa (April 13, 1914–January 11, 1994); Karl Markus (October 6, 1915–July 1, 1994); Christoph Friedrich (September 29, 1917–August 21, 1986); Robert Matthias (April 17, 1921–June 21, 1941); and Hans Jakob (April 6, 1925–July 25, 1984).

[2]E. Thurneysen to K. Barth and N. Barth, October 8, 1915, in Karl Barth, *Gesamtausgabe*, 56 vols., ed. Hinrich Stoevesandt, Hans-Anton Drewes, and Peter Zocher (Zurich: TVZ, 1971–2022), V.3, 90 (hereafter *GA*).

France through Belgium instead of through the more mountainous Switzerland. Nevertheless, a tactical violation of Switzerland's border had been considered, even if momentarily, meaning that Swiss citizens could not take their security for granted. As it was, there were occasional attacks on Swiss territory throughout the war, particularly in the Porrentruy region, some 85 kilometers from Safenwil, and only 45 kilometers from Basel. While such attacks were uncommon, they did serve as constant reminders of how close Switzerland was to the fighting. As Markus recalled in an interview toward the end of his life, "When the wind came from the West or North West, we could hear the sound of guns coming from the Alsace region . . . and we thought: 'Oh, they're shooting at each other again.'"[3]

Just nine days after Markus's birth, his father, Karl—at this time, still a largely unknown pastor, and very far from the towering theological figure he was later to become—told his congregation that the darkness of the coming winter would coincide with the dreadful consequences of the war's "great foolishness," and that only a very few would not be affected.[4] Karl himself chose to be affected quite personally. He joined the Swiss home guard and—when time permitted and duty called—put aside his pastoral duties to patrol the fields around Safenwil with a rifle, a task to which he would return in 1940 with equally unbridled enthusiasm (if not, perhaps, skill!).[5] With somewhat greater regularity than his soldiering duties, Karl also found himself drawn at this time—and as he would be, time after time, throughout his career—into the battles for the church's own conscience. During World War I, this fight increasingly took place

[3]"Conversation with Dr Markus Barth," 1. M. Barth interview in Tokyo, May 1987. MBMC. Subject Correspondence 3. Box 7. In the same interview, Markus noted that Safenwil garrisoned a company of Swiss soldiers.

[4]"Dieses Jahr wird es der Winter wohl auch bei uns an den Tag bringen, was die große Narrheit des Krieges für Folgen haben muß; nur ganz Wenige werden nichts davon merken." K. Barth, sermon, October 24, 1915, in *GA* I.27, 422.

[5]E. Busch, *Karl Barth: His Life from Letters and Autobiographical Texts*, trans. J. Bowden (Grand Rapids, MI: Eerdmans, 1994), 81, 305-6. By his own admission, Karl was not an especially good soldier, but he relished the opportunity to don the uniform and share in the collegiality of his Sentry Company V. Perhaps this is not surprising; much earlier, during his student days, Karl had gained something of a name for himself for his "passionate involvement in the exercises and route marches of the Bern cadet corps." See Busch, *Karl Barth*, 26. Even then, though, he displayed only "modest talent" with his rifle. See C. Tietz, *Karl Barth: A Life in Conflict*, trans. V. Barnett (Oxford: Oxford University Press, 2021), 17.

in heated conversation with the Swiss Religious Socialists, among whom the sharply divergent opinions about the church's proper stance toward the war—between a prophetic quietism on one hand, and a radical activism on the other—were personified by Herrmann Kutter and Leonhard Ragaz, respectively.[6]

In large part because of the war, these were also theologically tumultuous years. There was, especially but not only in Germany, the dominating presence of an ardently nationalistic "war theology" (*Kriegstheologie*), by which all manner of heresies could be, and were, justified. The Marburg theologian Martin Rade—under whom Karl Barth had studied in 1908, and with whom he worked in 1909 as editorial assistant for *Die Christliche Welt*—famously insisted that God was "the only possible ground and author" of the German people's enthusiasm for the war.[7] Rade's belief in the providential nature of the German war effort paled, though, in comparison to the sentiments expressed by some others. Dietrich Vorwerk, for example—a Lutheran pastor from Pomerania—"praised the God of the cherubim, seraphim, and Zeppelin," and even saw fit to rewrite the Lord's Prayer along distinctly German lines: "Thine is the Kingdom, the German land; may we through Thy mailed [armoured] hand, come to power and glory."[8]

When, therefore, in October 1914—almost exactly one year before Markus's birth—Karl Barth recognized a number of his former professors among the signatories to a pair of manifestos defending Germany's war aims, he could do nothing other than diagnose the complete bankruptcy of modern liberal Protestantism.[9] Behind it all, of course, was the

---

[6]B. L. McCormack, *Karl Barth's Critically Realistic Dialectical Theology: Its Genesis and Development, 1909-1936* (Oxford: Clarendon, 1997), 117-25.

[7]M. Rade to K. Barth, October 1, 1914, in C. Schwöbel, ed., *Karl Barth—Martin Rade: Ein Briefwechsel* (Gütersloh: Gütersloh Verlagshaus, 1981), 101.

[8]"Dein ist das Reich, das deutsche Land; uns muss durch deine gepanzerte Hand, Kraft und Herrlichkeit werden!" D. Vorwerk, *Hurra und Halleluja: Kriegslieder* (Schwerin-in-Mecklenburg: Verlag von Friedrich Bahn, 1914), 31. See also P. Jenkins, *The Great and Holy War: How World War I Became a Religious Crusade* (New York: HarperCollins, 2014), 13.

[9]Traditional historiography, including that presented in Busch's seminal biography, has assumed that the trigger for Karl Barth's break with his liberal Protestant heritage was the so-called Manifesto of the 93 from October 4, 1914—*Der Aufruf der 93 an die Kulturwelt*. While that was certainly a significant document for Barth's growing disaffection with his theological forebears, it was not the only, nor even the most decisive, one. In his magisterial book on Rudolf Bultmann,

ever-present figure of Friedrich Schleiermacher. "He was unmasked," said Barth. "In a decisive way all the theology expressed in the manifesto and everything that followed it . . . proved to be founded and governed by him."[10] And so with nothing left of his theological schooling to fall back upon, Barth, together with his friend—and Markus's godfather—Eduard Thurneysen, from the neighboring parish of Leutwil, began "learning [their] theological ABCs all over again."[11] It was this venture that would eventually culminate in that "bomb on the playground of the theologians,"[12] the much-vaunted *Römerbrief*.

In the Barth household itself, life in Safenwil was busy and at times difficult. Bruce McCormack has detailed some of the more obvious consequences of the war by which Switzerland, even in its neutrality, was impacted. There was a doubling of the cost-of-living index during the years 1914–1918, a 30 percent drop in real wages, the institution of food rationing in 1917, and the first ever direct national tax as an emergency response to skyrocketing national debt.[13] Within such strains of those war years, Nelly Barth gave birth to three children. The Barths' fourth child, Matthias, was born little more than two years after the Armistice, at a time when Switzerland's economy was still in the doldrums and its political stability was in consequence under threat from widespread strikes and civil

David Congdon has shown that Barth was just as, if not more, profoundly shaken by a similar manifesto that had been published exactly one month prior to the *Aufruf der 93*; a manifesto written not by the intelligentsia in general but specifically by Christian pastors and professors. *Der Aufruf deutscher Kirchenmänner und Professoren: An die evangelischen Christen im Ausland*—published on September 4, 1914—not only theologically legitimized Germany's wartime objectives but did so on the basis of Germany's distinctive missiological task. See D. W. Congdon, *The Mission of Demythologizing: Rudolf Bultmann's Dialectical Theology* (Minneapolis: Fortress, 2015), 243-44, 838-43. Barth preached intentionally against the sentiments of this manifesto in, among others, his sermon on September 6, 1914, when he declared—against the "German people, who said from the beginning: we will conquer or perish"—that in fact "God does not want this war!" In the face of those among his former professors who were seeking to claim God's justification for Germany's wartime victories, Barth instead insisted: "Wartime successes are—like everything in human life—transient and provisional [*Vorübergehenden, Vorläufigen*]." Sermon, September 6, 1914, in *GA* I.5, 457-62.

[10]K. Barth, "Nachwort," in *Schleiermacher-Auswahl* (Munich: Siebenstern-Taschenbuch, 1968), 293. Cited in Busch, *Karl Barth*, 82.

[11]Barth, "Nachwort," 113-14. Cited in Busch, *Karl Barth*, 97.

[12]K. Adam, "Die Theologie der Krisis," *Hochland* 23 (1926): 271-86.

[13]McCormack, *Karl Barth's Critically Realistic Dialectical Theology*, 137-38.

disturbances.[14] In this challenging economic climate, Karl Barth's vigorous advocacy on behalf the town's factory workers caused Safenwil's industrialists considerable irritation.[15] Like most young Swiss families during these years, the Barths had therefore to live under considerable pressure. As was recalled at her funeral, it was often hard for Nelly Barth "to have an open house despite [in view of] the required frugality."[16]

Figure 1.1. Barth family portrait, 1921. Left to right: Karl, Matthias, Christoph, Markus

To compound the difficulties, a young Markus contracted scarlet fever in early 1921 while Nelly was pregnant with Matthias. To keep both mother and baby safe, Markus was hospitalized 100 kilometers away in the lakeside town of Stäfa, where Nelly's widowed mother, Anna, lived. With the risk of infection so great, Nelly was, of course, unable to check up on Markus herself. She relied instead upon her mother to visit him and to provide reports on his

[14]Switzerland's inflation peaked in 1918 at 25 percent, which coincided—unsurprisingly, perhaps—with a national strike in 1918 and a severe recession in the early 1920s. C. Stohr, "Trading Gains: New Estimates of Swiss GDP, 1851-2008," London School of Economics and Politics, Working Papers, No. 245 (June 2016), 18.

[15]The story of Barth's campaign for workers' rights in Safenwil—and his subsequent nicknaming as "the Red Pastor"—has been told in considerable detail by both Busch and McCormack. See Busch, *Karl Barth*, 68-72; McCormack, *Karl Barth's Critically Realistic Dialectical Theology*, 86-104, 184-95. As Busch records, "Already as a 25-year old, he had declared . . . [that]: 'For 1800 years, the Christian church has always looked to heaven in the face of social distress. She has preached, converted, comforted—but she has not *helped*. She probably recommended good works of Christian charity, but she did not say that "this should not be," and then use all her strength to make sure that this *would not* be. Such is the great, heavy apostasy of the Christian church.' But *he* [Barth] campaigned for the 'this should not be.'" Busch, *Glaubensheiterkeit. Karl Barth—Erfahrungen und Begegnungen erzählt von Eberhard Busch* (Neukirchen: Neukirchener Verlag, 1994), 33.

[16]F. Zellweger-Barth, "Lebenslauf," in *Nelly Barth-Hoffman 26. August 1893–23. Oktober 1976* (n.d.), 6. MBL. Series I. Box 25.

condition. The strain of not only of Markus's sickness but also of her separation from him must have been heart-wrenching for Nelly. Thankfully, though, Markus was lucky. Whereas in Aargau alone there were 134 deaths from scarlet fever in 1921, with 3,733 deaths across Switzerland as a whole, Markus himself made a full recovery.[17] In mid-February, "the young doctor" was able to inform Anna that "the disease [was taking] an entirely normal course, and that even a little fever was completely usual."[18] Nevertheless, Markus remained in the hospital until the first week of April, and even then Nelly's sister Hedwig[19] was concerned that he stay quarantined, lest the other children become sick. "You [Anna] should keep Markus away from [Nelly's] house . . . as it may be that he is still infectious." "It seems to me," Hedwig cautioned, "that a child should not be released from hospital if there is still the possibility of infection."[20] Yet despite all these concerns—the post-war economic downturn, the challenges of three young children, a new baby, and Markus's serious illness—Nelly could still find reason for joy. On Easter Day 1921 she wrote to her mother that "they are all so dear to me—Karl, and each of the children—I am so lucky as a mother, and so happy!"[21]

It would not only be regrettable, but indeed a falsification of the record, if Nelly's declaration of her own happiness at this time were to be glossed over or interpreted as something less than sincere. The longer history of the Barths' domestic arrangements—including the indispensable role played by Charlotte von Kirschbaum, to which we shall have to attend in due course—renders this, of course, a conclusion at which one might reasonably, if inaccurately, arrive. It is certainly the case that even in the early years of their marriage, Karl and Nelly's relationship was not without its tensions. There was a certain territoriality to this. Christiane Tietz, in her biography of Karl Barth, has drawn attention to the fact that Nelly was determined not to be subsumed entirely by her husband's work but worked

[17]"Gemeldete Fälle von Scharlacherkrankungen nach Kantonen 1901-1930," Historische Statistik der Schweiz, accessed May 8, 2024, https://hsso.ch/de/2012/d/26.

[18]A. Hoffmann to N. Barth, February 14, 1921. MBL. Series II. Box 4.

[19]Hedwig Kisling-Hoffmann (1888–1957).

[20]H. Kisling-Hoffmann to A. Hoffmann, late March 1921. MBL. Series II. Box 4.

[21]N. Barth to A. Hoffman, Easter 1921. MBL. Series II. Box 4.

hard to retain her own sense of identity. As she informed Thurneysen, a wife should not "self-evidently" give up or postpone "her own deepest interests . . . in order to be filled post-haste with Kutter etc." In Nelly's case, those deeper interests often revolved around taking time to practice her violin, at which she was highly proficient.[22] Barth, responding occasionally out of jealously, admitted that he sometimes "allowed stupid complexes to arise against the violin—the violin teacher, the violin case, violin virtuosos."[23]

It is equally clear that the causes of that friction were more than simply the economic and political pressures occasioned by the war and its aftermath, or the very natural negotiations around role expectations that form part of any new marriage. At least according to Suzanne Selinger's account, the young Barth's wedding in 1913 had been engineered in part by Karl's mother, Anna, who had been adamantly opposed to her son marrying his first love, Rösy Münger.[24] The match with Nelly was, therefore, at least in part an attempt to move Karl on toward a more appropriate partner.[25] Nevertheless, despite the occasional tensions between them—not to mention the catastrophe into which Europe had been plunged throughout these years—Nelly was unmistakably still able to find great joy in her marriage, her husband, and her children.

---

[22]K. Barth to E. Thurneysen, July 14, 1915, in *GA* V.3, 64. See also Tietz, *Karl Barth*, 75-76. Nelly had taken her first violin lessons at the age of ten and continued with formal tuition at the Geneva Conservatory until her withdrawal from those studies following her engagement to Karl.

[23]K. Barth to E. Thurneysen, July 14, 1915, in *GA* V.3, 64.

[24]Karl and Rösy had met in Bern in 1907, and the two had fallen deeply in love. Karl's parents, however, were opposed to the marriage on account of Rösy's family belonging to a more liberal-minded church. The result was that Karl ended his relationship with Rösy in May 1910, apparently breaking it off in writing, so that he did not have to look her in the eye. Selinger records that Barth "never got over this love and kept a picture of Rösy till the end of his life." As he wrote to her sister in 1943, "I cannot imagine my life without her." Five years later, he told a friend that he had "never been able to forget" his first love. Rösy and Karl met only once more after their breakup in 1915. According to Selinger, Rösy died of leukemia ten years later, in 1925. Rösy's older sister, however, has a different recollection, namely that Rösy, too, never fully recovered from the end of her relationship with Karl and died "of a broken heart." For these two contrasting accounts, see S. Selinger, *Charlotte von Kirschbaum and Karl Barth: A Study in Biography and the History of Theology* (University Park: Pennsylvania State University Press, 1998), 5-6. See also Tietz, *Karl Barth*, 32-33.

[25]While the marriage was largely arranged by Karl's parents, he and Nelly were far from strangers. They had met first in Geneva in 1909, when Karl was working under Adolf Keller as an assistant pastor in the German-speaking Reformed Church, and of which Nelly and her parents were members. Nelly also attended Karl's confirmation classes, and the following year was confirmed by him. For a brief period between October 1909 and February 1910, Karl had pastoral oversight of the congregation, following Keller's relocation to Zurich and before the arrival of his successor.

Markus's own early childhood in Safenwil was also, by all accounts, a happy one. Eberhard Busch has noted that for the rest of their lives, the entire Barth family "remembered Safenwil with particular affection" (*besonderer Anhänglichkeit*).[26] That having been said, it was a family life that was nonetheless increasingly punctuated by a very specific set of challenges and circumstances. Being part of this particular family meant being intricately connected with, and understanding and accepting of, Karl Barth's sense of purpose and his feelings of responsibility to God and to the world. Thus, for Markus, while the Safenwil years were very happy, they were also transformative. While he could not have been aware of it at the time, the contours of his own theological career would be decisively shaped by his experiences there. In 1961, Rose Marie Barth penned a curriculum vitae of sorts for her husband, in which she recounted that "one of his earliest memories was that, from time to time, he was allowed to nestle silently in the attic, and watch while his father, at his little standing desk, would pore over Paul's letter to the Romans." Neither father nor son, Rose Marie noted, "was aware of just how explosive that material would prove to be."[27] Notwithstanding, then, that Karl's first pastorate was characterized by pressures and strains within the family home, the parish, as well as within the town itself, the children at least seem not only to have been sheltered from the more robust aspects of those years but indeed—at least in Markus's case—significantly and positively influenced by them.

NORTH TO GÖTTINGEN

Things were not to stay so simple. No matter how pleasant Safenwil might have been, it was not to be Markus's home for long. Just one week after his sixth birthday, Markus and his family moved 600 kilometers north to the Lower Saxon city of Göttingen, where Karl had been appointed honorary professor of Reformed dogmatics. Not only was this a radical new beginning for Karl—from the pastorate to the academy—it also required a very great deal from each family member. For Nelly, there was a significant reduction

---

[26]Busch, *Karl Barth*, 125; E. Busch, *Karl Barths Lebenslauf* (Munich: Christian Kaiser Verlag, 1975), 138.

[27]R. M. Barth, "Markus Barth CV," January 1961, 1. MBL. Series II. Box 10.

in the household budget, occasioned less by a lower salary for Karl and more by Germany's postwar skyrocketing inflation.[28] The difficulties of these circumstances were not lost on Markus despite his youth. As he later recalled, "Our arrival in Göttingen [coincided with this] inflation. There were many unemployed people around, many younger men still in uniform. Their uniforms were in rags . . . but they had no other clothes."[29] For Markus and his siblings, the move to Germany also meant adapting from one day to the next to a new school system in a different language. To have roots both in Switzerland and in Germany could, and would, be enriching, but it was also a challenge to everyone's sense of identity.

For the next four years, Markus was to live in what his father described as the "better quarter" of the city,[30] in Nikolausberger Weg 66. The businessman Rüdi Pestalozzi—who Karl had met through Eduard Thurneysen and who would, for many years to come, be a friend, sponsor, and host at the "Bergli"—had been able to secure the purchase of a house from the systematic theologian Arthur Titius, whose fortunes had risen with his appointment to Schleiermacher's chair in Berlin.[31] The house, however, was both a boon and a burden, and Nelly was not shy in expressing her apprehension that it might prove too expensive for them. As she wrote to her mother, "It's now ours—but it also exceeds our credit!"[32] Moreover, and despite its cost, it was more than a little dilapidated. While the rooms were considerably larger than those they had enjoyed in the Safenwil vicarage,

---

[28]Because the position was only an honorary professorship, its stipendiary conditions could be negotiated, meaning that Barth's salary was approximately the same as that of a pastor. As it was, though, Karl and Nelly had been used to fairly meager salary provisions in Safenwil. According to Karl's grandchildren, his pastoral stipend was consistently reduced over the years of his ministry there by the town's industrialists, who he angered through his advocacy of workers' rights and who themselves sat on the local church council. Thus, Nelly was not unused to the difficulties of managing a tight budget. Nevertheless, Germany's economic woes hit the family budget harder than any churlish Swiss industrialist could! Correspondence with Rose-Marie Barth, Anna Barth, and Ruth Naveau, July 20, 2019.

[29]"Conversation with Dr Markus Barth," 2.

[30]K. Barth to W. Spoendlin, December 21, 1921. Cited in Busch, *Karl Barth*, 126.

[31]Arthur Titius (1864–1936) had already made a name for himself in church politics, as well as in the academy. In November 1918, Titius had founded the *Volkskirchenbund*, a grassroots movement that sought to unify the disparate strands of German Protestantism that had been left foundering in the political chaos of the immediate post-war months. K. Scholder, *The Churches and the Third Reich*, vol. 1, *1918–1934*, trans. J. Bowden (Philadelphia: Fortress, 1988), 10.

[32]N. Barth to A. Hoffmann, September 27, 1921. MBL. Series II. Box 4.

Figure 1.2. Barth family portrait, 1922. Left to right: Markus, Christoph, Matthias, Franziska

only the kitchen and two of the bedrooms were presentable; according to Nelly, the rest of the house was most definitely not. "You wouldn't believe it," she wrote to her family. "The house was just not in a suitable condition."[33] She noted, too, that to begin with, they would have to do without the use of some of the rooms to accommodate both a janitor who lived on the top floor and some of Titius' furniture, for which he was unable to find space in Berlin.[34] On the other hand, despite these irritations, the house was conveniently located just 1.5 kilometers from both the Botanical Gardens and the Georg-August University, where Karl was to teach.

The move to Germany coincided with the start of Markus's schooling, with his older sister, Franziska, having begun her formal education the previous year in Safenwil. This may well have been regarded as serendipitous timing by their parents; Safenwil had, after all, boasted only a single school, which had itself been in operation for only a decade. Göttingen, on the other hand, being considerably larger, had plenty of schooling alternatives available to the Barth children. Markus himself

[33]N. Barth to her family, October 28, 1921. MBL. Series II. Box 3. Markus's memories were, perhaps unsurprisingly, somewhat more positive. "It was a very stately house which my father had been able to buy because my mother had received an inheritance. For a ridiculously small Swiss sum, which in comparison to the grossly inflated German mark represented a fortune, he got a marvelous three storey house. . . . I remember that other professors were very envious of it." "Conversation with Dr Markus Barth," 3.

[34]N. Barth to A. Hoffmann, September 27, 1921. It is worth noting that Karl Barth finished the second edition of his *Romans* commentary the very day that Nelly wrote this letter to her mother. As she said in the letter—"*Der Römerbrief ist heute fertig.*"

notes that he completed both his *Volksschule* and the *Sexta* (the equivalent of American fifth grade) in Göttingen.[35] While there are no records to indicate precisely where he might have done this, Nelly's letters suggest that it was a semi-private school—that is, most likely a confessional school that was partially funded by the state.[36] Franziska, on the other hand, most likely attended the Hainberg-Gymnasium, a girls-only school that was situated a little over one kilometer from the family home. Nevertheless, despite its apparent advantages over the limited educational possibilities that Safenwil had been able to offer, Karl was not immediately encouraged by the quality of Göttingen's school system. It was utterly perplexing to him that even after the war, children (such as his eldest daughter, Franziska), could still be taught the song: "Der Kaiser ist ein lieber Mann, er wohnet in Berlin, / und wär es nicht so weit von hier, so ging ich selber hin."[37]

Karl was convinced that Markus also was ill-served by the local school. His son, he complained, had fallen into the hands of a "modern teacher," from whom, week after week, the students would learn nothing but useless games instead of the serious business of reading and writing.[38] Markus himself did not share his father's concerns. As he was later to recall, "I had an excellent teacher [Lüderitz] . . . and it was a pleasure to be in school."[39] In any event, regardless of the quality of schooling Markus received, his mother continued to tutor him. On their walks to and from the markets, Markus and his mother would converse in "Deutsch"—that is, *Hochdeutsch*, as opposed to the *Schweizerdeutsch* with which he had been brought up—and according to Nelly, he was "alert and eager to learn."[40] These impromptu

---

[35]M. Barth, "Eigener Lebenslauf," unpublished, April 3, 1945. MBL. Series II. By *Volksschule*, Barth was probably referring to the "compulsory *Grundschule* [elementary] schooling."

[36]Nelly writes of Markus being enrolled in "*eine halbe Privatschul*," that is, a semi-private school. N. Barth to her family, October 28, 1921.

[37]K. Barth, circular letter, January 22, 1922, in *GA* V.4, 28. "The Kaiser is a lovely man, he lives in Berlin; and if it weren't so far from here, I would go there myself." This was a song written in honor of Kaiser Wilhelm I, but taught to children in Prussia during the First World War as a propaganda device in support of Wilhelm II.

[38]K. Barth, circular letter, May 9, 1922, in *GA* V.4, 70.

[39]"Conversation with Dr Markus Barth," 3.

[40]N. Barth to A. Hoffmann, November 20, 1921. MBL. Series II. Box 3. It is worth noting that these were not the only language lessons Markus received. Due to a curricular change, he entered the *Gymnasium* at age nine, and immediately began studying Latin. According to his recollections,

language classes evidently paid off. One day toward the end of their first year in Germany, Karl was relieved to see that Markus had at last been able to come home from school and "read and write nicely." It was, he said, enough to make him "revoke the accusation he had made against [Markus's] kindergarten."[41]

Alongside these new school routines, the move to Göttingen brought about other significant changes to the family's daily schedule, with Karl forced to spend long hours adjusting to the rhythm of academic life. Lamenting what he saw in retrospect as his own lost opportunities for further study, Karl warned his friends in a circular letter that they "should let no hour pass fruitlessly in [their] rectories or be spent on the newspaper *as happened unfortunately only too often with me in Safenwil*."[42] While he was almost certainly overstating the extent to which he had wasted his time in the pastorate, Barth was nonetheless acutely conscious of what he called his "horrible theological ignorance," not least in comparison to his faculty colleagues, and so worked assiduously to prepare himself for every lecture. As Bruce McCormack has put it, the task of filling in the gaps in his theological learning was "a traumatic one."[43] Possibly, this sense of unpreparedness for life in the academy had roots as far back as his student days in Tübingen in 1908. On receiving a "Zwei" (roughly equivalent to a B) for his final thesis—prepared for Hermann Lüdemann on the topic "The Concept of Christ's Descent into Hell in Church Literature up to Origen"—Karl confessed in a letter to his parents that "academic work in a narrow sense is not for me. . . . I have come to see that with growing clarity."[44] In light of all this, it is no wonder that in

he then began taking French classes at eleven, Greek at twelve, and, during the final three years of schooling in Bonn, Hebrew. "Conversation with Dr Markus Barth," 4.

[41]K. Barth, circular letter, December 19, 1922, in *GA* V.4, 125.

[42]K. Barth, circular letter, March 26, 1922, in *Revolutionary Theology in the Making: Barth-Thurneysen Correspondence 1914-1925*, trans. J. D. Smart (London: Epworth, 1964), 93 [hereafter *RevTh*]. Emphasis added.

[43]McCormack, *Karl Barth's Critically Realistic Dialectical Theology*, 293-94. According to Barth's own estimation of his lecture schedule in Basel, each fifty-minute lecture—of which he delivered four per week—required as much as ten hours' preparation. If this was the investment of time needed once he was an experienced scholar of twenty years' standing, the burden of lecture preparation in his very first academic post must have been even weightier. See Busch, *Karl Barth*, 373.

[44]Letter, K. Barth to F. and A. Barth, December 14, 1908, *GA* III.21, 247.

one of his letters to friends back in Switzerland, Markus's father confessed to his own sense of inadequacy: "I have to build my own scholarly structure, achieve a 'thorough mastery,' as they say, in something. How does one do it? Will they ever be able to say that of me? Or shall I always be this wandering gypsy among all the honourable scholars by whom I am surrounded, one who has only a couple of leaky kettles to call his own, and who occasionally sets a house on fire?"[45]

Barth's colleagues did not make it easy for him to overcome his feelings of self-doubt. Emanuel Hirsch, quite aside from his increasingly zealous nationalism, was a "know-it-all" (*Alleswisser*), while Carl Stange, as dean of the faculty, led the "hateful piece of mischief-making" by which Barth's curricular freedom was severely curtailed.[46] Symbolizing the contempt with which they regarded him, the faculty even posted Barth's announcements about his lectures next to those of the harmonium teacher![47] It is little wonder, then, that Karl Barth's early years in the academy were overshadowed by a profound sense of inferiority and an urgent need to improve his own theological education. As he recalled in 1935,

> I shall never forget the spring vacation of 1924. I sat in my study at Göttingen, faced with the task of giving lectures on dogmatics for the first time. No one can ever have been more plagued than I then was with the problem, could I do it? And how? My Biblical and historical studies to date had more and more expelled me from the goodly society of contemporary, and, as I began to realise ever more clearly, of almost the whole of more recent theology; and I saw myself, as it were, alone in the open without a teacher.[48]

The upshot was that whereas Karl had been an ever-present figure at the family's vicarage in Safenwil, in Göttingen he would begin teaching at 7:00 a.m., having frequently only finished writing the lectures between two or three hours beforehand. For the first few months in the new job, Karl

---

[45]K. Barth, circular letter, December 11, 1921, *GA* V.4, 20-21.

[46]K. Barth to E. Thurneysen, January 22, 1922, *GA* V.4, 29; K. Barth to E. Thurneysen, December 27, 1923, *GA* V.4, 213. See also *RevTh*, 162. During the Nazi years, Emanuel Hirsch was an outspoken advocate for Adolf Hitler, joining the Nazi Party in 1937 and even becoming a patron member (*Förderndes Mitglied*)—that is, a financial supporter—of the SS.

[47]Busch, *Karl Barth*, 133.

[48]K. Barth, "Foreword," in H. Heppe, *Reformed Dogmatics: Set Out and Illustrated from the Sources*, trans. G. T. Thomson (London: George Allen & Unwin, 1950), v.

was, by his own admission, "almost always on night shift," and consequently often unavailable to the rest of the family.[49] Thus, Nelly's accompanying of Karl to his lectures on Tuesdays, Thursdays, and Fridays—while it was certainly borne of her own genuine interest in the subject matter, and her desire to learn more about her husband's way of thinking—had the additional pragmatic benefit of allowing her time to spend with him.[50]

In other ways, too, Karl was less accessible to Nelly and to his children than he had been in Switzerland. Deeply aware that the recent war had upturned most of the long-held and cherished assumptions about Christianity and its God, and that many of his students felt a consequent and urgent need "to put questions and register objections," Barth—in addition to his regular lecturing schedule[51]—held "open evenings" in his house each Wednesday night, during which lengthy conversations could be had.[52] On Saturday afternoons, too, he took interested students on walking tours, thus providing yet further opportunities for discussion and debate.[53] Such commitment to his students' education must have been a godsend to them, yet the pressures of this workload would inevitably have been felt not only by Karl himself but also Nelly and the children.

And of course, the frequency of these absences was simply exacerbated by the traveling to which Karl was more and more committed. The immense interest in his *Romans*, which had been the reason for his call to Göttingen in the first place, led to an increasing number of invitations to speak at conferences and pastors' meetings throughout the country—from

---

[49]Busch, *Karl Barth*, 127.

[50]"It's a lot [of extra work] that I go with Karl to his lectures. . . . But I want to do it [*Aber ich möchte das durchführen*]." N. Barth to A. Hoffmann, November 20, 1921. Note that Karl typically also read his sermons to Nelly before delivering them—demonstrating both her interest in his work and his reliance on Nelly as a sounding board.

[51]Bruce McCormack provides an overview of Barth's lecture cycles during his years in Göttingen. During each semester (with the exception of summer 1922), he would teach two courses—one on theology, and one exegetical course on a New Testament epistle.

[52]This was something that Barth had perhaps learned from his father, Fritz. Almost immediately after his marriage to Anna, and while still a pastor, Fritz made a habit of inviting students over to his house, one evening a week, for conversation. Tietz, *Karl Barth*, 12. As shall be seen, the practice would pass also to Markus, in the next generation.

[53]Busch, *Karl Barth*, 128-29. See also Nelly Barth's letter to A. Hoffmann, November 20, 1921. "Samstag Nach[mittag] spaziert Karl mit Studenten."

Wiesbaden to Lüneberg, and from Bochum to Elgersburg. "Good heavens," Karl wrote to Thurneysen, "how huge and varied Germany is!"[54]

Despite all this, the Barths were content with their life in Göttingen. Karl and Nelly would occasionally tour the surrounding countryside on bicycle and in the summers would participate in the International Handel Festival that had been founded in 1920.[55] "Everything is going well for us here," wrote Nelly to her mother. "We are happy, and have no wish to return to Safenwil."[56] They were not, of course, sheltered from the effects of the economic downturn by which Germany was crushed in the early 1920s. Nelly wrote frequently to her family about how exorbitant prices were for the most basic of items and was keenly aware that there was significant poverty in the suburbs surrounding them. But in their part of the city, the Barths were separated from the most obvious signs of it. Indeed, Nelly could even foresee "a rich life" for them in Göttingen.[57]

The one darker cloud that appeared over the Barth family during these years concerned Nelly and Karl's marriage. Strains between the pair—some of which, as has been seen, had been present from the earliest days of their marriage—began to re-emerge. Stephen Plant suggests that contributory factors included the inevitable upheaval of moving from Switzerland to Germany—and thus to a place where family support was harder to access—the stress on Nelly of having to provide for a growing family within straitened economic circumstances, Karl's increasing absence from family

[54]K. Barth to E. Thurneysen, October 26, 1922, in *RevTh*, 115. It is worth noting that broader interest in, and even awareness of, Karl Barth was occasioned only after his Tambach lecture—"Der Christ in der Gesellschaft" ("The Christian in Society")—of September 1919. The first edition of his *Romans* commentary, published at the beginning of 1919 by the Bern-based company G. A. Bäschlin, had a print run of only one thousand copies, of which only about three hundred were actually sold, almost exclusively within Switzerland. In other words, it was not, in the first instance, the commentary itself that secured Barth's reputation in Germany. That shift happened more as a consequence of his presentation to the Religious Socialist conference in Tambach, where he was a very late replacement for Leonhard Ragaz. Attending the conference put Barth in contact with a wider network of German pastors and scholars than he had previously known—including Hans Ehrenburg, Friedrich Gogarten, and Gunther Dehn—and also enabled publishing and distribution rights for *Romans* to be transferred from Bäschlin to the much larger Christian Kaiser Verlag. See Busch, *Karl Barth*, 112-13.

[55]A celebration of the music of G. F. Handel (1685–1759), the festival celebrated its centenary in 2021—a year late due to the COVID-19 pandemic.

[56]N. Barth to A. Hoffmann, November 20, 1921.

[57]N. Barth to A. Hoffmann, December 7, 1921. MBL. Series II. Box 3.

life on account of his work pressures, and Nelly's own sense of being looked down upon by Karl's faculty colleagues.[58] Whatever the causes, it would seem that Nelly had begun considering the possibility of seeking a divorce from Karl from as early as 1923.[59] The situation was evidently still tense between them the following year and was compounded when Nelly, sick with what Plant describes as "nervous exhaustion," sought respite in a sanitorium.[60] During these middle months of 1924, when they were apart from one another during Nelly's treatment, Karl expressed an anxiety that his wife had seemingly stopped communicating with him. "How are you?" Karl wrote to her at the end of July. "You are not writing to me at the moment, and yet I love you so much."[61] The second half of 1924 was hardly any happier. Nelly, by this time pregnant with Hans Jakob, was hospitalized in Stäfa, on the Zürchsee. Following a summer vacation together, Karl—"with a heavy heart"[62]—had to leave her in Switzerland, together with Christoph and Matthias, while he returned to Göttingen with Franziska and Markus. Back at their home in Germany, he wrote frequently to Nelly, updating her on the activities of her two eldest children. "Fränzeli [has been] practicing her English this morning, [while] Markus worked on a jigsaw from the Church."[63] Both of them were, he told her, "marching now to school healthy and happy."[64] And then, in early October, Karl could report that "today, Markus won 'first-prize' in a big scooter race with the rest of the neighborhood lads, and is now planning on building a 'car' so that he can compete in another race in four weeks' time!"[65]

While he was evidently trying to keep things as normal as possible for Franziska and Markus throughout this time, Karl was nevertheless clearly

---

[58]S. Plant, "When Karl Met Lollo: The Origins and Consequences of Karl Barth's Relationship with Charlotte von Kirschbaum," *Scottish Journal of Theology* 72, no. 2 (2019): 132.

[59]Tietz, *Karl Barth*, 245n123.

[60]Plant, "When Karl met Lollo," 132. It is worth remembering that Nelly, who was a physically slight woman, had given birth to four children in just seven years. One can hardly be surprised if this took a physical toll on her.

[61]K. Barth to N. Barth, July 28, 1924. MBL. Series II. Box 3.

[62]K. Barth to E. Thurneysen, September 13, 1924, *GA* V.4, 274.

[63]K. Barth to N. Barth, September 17, 1924. MBL. Series II. Box 3. "Fränzeli" was the diminutive name by which Franziska was known in the family, from her birth until her death in 1994.

[64]K. Barth to N. Barth, September 22, 1924. MBL. Series II. Box 3.

[65]K. Barth to N. Barth, October 11, 1924. MBL. Series II. Box 3.

bereft. His letters went either unanswered—"Again, no news from you today"[66]—or, when Nelly did write, it caused him only sorrow. Certainly, much of the distress was occasioned by Nelly's poor health and exhaustion. However, there were also subterranean tensions within the marriage that went beyond her periods of sickness, and even beyond the two of them. On one hand, there were angry exchanges between Karl and Anna Hoffmann, who accused Karl of placing her daughter under too much stress and of not doing enough to help with the children. On the other hand, the relationship between Karl's mother and Nelly was similarly bitter. Indeed, there had been a history of suspicion and animosity between them both that had played out since Karl and Nelly had first married. Karl, apparently, tried to mediate: "I have been writing letters to mama . . . all evening, imploring her on all sides to take it easier on you. . . . It just cannot go on like this." As he put it in another of his letters, "Oh, these 'in-law relationships'—how the devil has his fingers in this game!"[67]

It would, of course, be easy to interpret these difficulties retrospectively—through the prism of the later history between Karl, Nelly, and Charlotte von Kirschbaum—and to read into the Barths' marriage both an unhealthiness and an unhappiness that made Karl's relationship with Charlotte somehow inevitable. Indeed, this is the conclusion at which Stephen Plant seems to arrive when he contends that neither the conception of Hans Jakob in August 1924 "[nor] anything else" could mend the fatally broken marriage.[68] Yet such a conclusion would be far too simplistic. In spite of all the stresses and intrafamily conflicts with which the Barths had to deal throughout the latter months of 1924, the epistolary evidence demonstrates unequivocally that Nelly and Karl continued to be close, loved each other deeply, and worked hard to build a happy home for their children.

INTO THE CATHOLIC HEARTLAND

With Nelly having returned from Stäfa, Hans Jakob was born in Göttingen in April 1925. The family was, for a time, reunited. Again, however, their

---

[66]K. Barth to N. Barth, September 22, 1924. MBL. Series II. Box 3.
[67]K. Barth to N. Barth, September 22, 1924; October 11, 1924; October 14, 1924. MBL. Series II. Box 3.
[68]Plant, "When Karl Met Lollo," 132.

domestic situation was not to stay the same for long. In late October 1925, three weeks after Markus had turned ten, the family was on the move again, this time to the predominantly Catholic city of Münster, in Westphalia. Markus's father had been appointed professor of dogmatics and New Testament exegesis by the Protestant faculty at the university there. Given that the new post was offered without the restrictions under which he had to teach in Göttingen, and was being made at the rank of *ordentlicher Professor*,[69] it represented a significant promotion for Karl and one not to be dismissed. There were also monetary benefits. As Karl wrote to his friend Thurneysen, "The financial improvement which I need for my five [children] to be educated is considerable. The provision in case of death is also worth something."[70]

In the first instance, however, Karl made the move to Münster alone, with the sale of the family house in Göttingen taking longer than anticipated. And so, aside from some rare holiday visits, from October 1925 to March 1926 the family was divided "into two groups: the better part, Nelly and the five children [in Göttingen]; the lesser part, [Karl] in Münster."[71] During these months, Karl "lived a bachelor existence" in a room that he rented from a widow in Warendorferstraße 23. Karl's loneliness during this time was at least temporarily alleviated when he was able to return to Göttingen for Christmas. Even this visit, however, was bittersweet. As he put it in letters to Charlotte von Kirschbaum and various other friends, "the 'Papa' . . . was more an object of entertainment and amusement"; indeed Nelly seemed to have everything under control in his absence, with "everything [going] very well even without me."[72] The family was together again in Göttingen for New Year's celebrations,

---

[69]In Göttingen, Barth was permitted to teach *Reformed* theology only—a restriction which did not apply to the Münster position. Moreover, even though the post Barth was being offered was normally appointed at the level of *extraordinarius Professor* (*außerordentlicher Professor*)—that is, a senior lecturer, or perhaps associate professor—the Münster faculty was willing to appoint him to the rank of full professor. While this was procedurally unusual, the fact that Münster had already bestowed upon Barth an honorary doctorate in February 1922 perhaps renders this less surprising. As a "thank you" to the faculty for the honor, Barth dedicated to them his 1924 book, *Die Auferstehung der Toten: Eine akademische Vorlesung über 1 Kor. 15*. He may have come to regret that decision—in 1939, the University rescinded the honorary doctorate on account of Barth's vocal opposition to the Nazi regime. The award was reconferred only in 1946. See Tietz, *Karl Barth*, 280.

[70]K. Barth to E. Thurneysen, July 22, 1925, in *RevTh*, 235.

[71]K. Barth, circular letter, January 17, 1926, *GA* V.4, 396.

[72]K. Barth to C. von Kirschbaum, February 5, 1926, *GA* V.45, 15; K. Barth, circular letter, January 17, 1926, *GA* V.4, 400.

albeit this time with von Kirschbaum, of whom we will speak again shortly, also present. Unsurprisingly, after seven months spent largely apart, the family reunion—when they were all finally able to move into their new house in Himmelreichallee 43—was a happy occasion.

Once the family was together again, the children's most immediate priority was to familiarize themselves with a new home in a new city. Their house was ideally situated—particularly for the three older children—between the cemetery on the one side, from which came the daily serenade of trombone-led funeral processions, and the zoo on the other, with its own distinct soundtrack—the "roar[ing] of the predators."[73] Both the zoo and the cemetery provided ample green space to play and explore. Not everything, however, was to the children's taste. According to Franziska, at first—and compared to the hilly surroundings in which they had been raised—they did not much like the flatter land of Westphalia. The purchase of new bicycles, though, proved a happy consolation. Not only were the children able to ride to school along the walls of the old city, they were set free to discover various landmarks, including the Wasserburg Hülshoff—birthplace of the nineteenth-century writer Annette von Droste-Hülshoff (1798–1848)—which lay ten kilometers west of the city.[74]

As it had in their early days in Göttingen, school again posed fresh challenges. Markus went to the *Schillergymnasium*,[75] a five-minute bike ride from home. Its convenient proximity notwithstanding, however, the school was governed by a very different curriculum (*ein anderes Schulsystem*) from that which had prevailed in Göttingen. As a result, Nelly was obliged to take on the role of tutor (*Nachhilfslehrerin*) to both Franziska and Markus, particularly in French, in which they were three years behind.[76]

As for Markus's father, his own academic environment proved significantly more amenable than it had been in Göttingen. There, the theology faculty had been populated, at least in Karl's experience, by "backbiters and poison-spreaders."[77] And so even though he did not find his Protestant colleagues in Münster to be especially academically stimulating, he at least

[73]F. Barth, October 1992. MBL. Series II. Box 5.
[74]F. Barth, October 1992.
[75]M. Barth, "Eigener Lebenslauf." MBL. Series II.
[76]F. Barth, "Nelly Barth Gedenkbüchlein," 1976. MBL. Series II. Box 5.
[77]Busch, *Karl Barth*, 167-68.

got along well with them socially—something which had never been possible in the toxic culture of Göttingen. His encounter with north German Catholicism, on the other hand, was a breath of fresh air and a source of considerable stimulus for him. Notwithstanding that Catholicism's "attempt to claim control over God's grace" was its "one, fundamental error," Karl's engagement with the Westphalian Catholic community "became very important to [him]"[78] and was far more intellectually satisfying than any conversations he was able to have with his Protestant colleagues.[79]

Karl's students in Münster were also a constant source of delight. They were "rather a rough crowd," and Karl was initially scandalized by the (in his view) woefully low academic expectations that his faculty colleagues had of them.[80] Nonetheless, "their openness, their delight in telling stories, their capacity to keep up with the professor and, once aroused, to spur him on to new heights," was a tonic.[81] One of his students, in particular, caused Karl great joy during these Münster years; in the winter semester of 1928–1929, a thirteen-year-old Markus attended his first set of theology lectures, on the epistle of James.[82] While they were the first, they would not be the last of his father's classes that Markus would take.

NEW CITY, NEW RELATIONSHIPS

It was noted above that when Karl Barth first moved to Münster in late 1925, delays in the sale of the Göttingen house meant that he had to make the move alone, with the remainder of the family joining him only in March 1926. The narrative would be incomplete, however, if it were not

---

[78]Busch, *Karl Barth*, 168, 178. The Jesuit theologian Erich Przywara (1889–1972) was particularly stimulating for Barth. Having invited him to Münster to present a guest lecture in February 1929, Barth said of Przywara afterwards that, after teaching a "masterclass" (*Meisterstück*) on the church, "he shone for another two hours in my seminar . . . and finally 'overwhelmed' (*überströmt*) me for two whole evenings here. In this way he was an illustration of the way in which, according to his doctrine, the good God (at least within the Catholic Church) overwhelms men with grace." K. Barth to E. Thurneysen, February 9, 1929, *GA* V.4, 651-52.

[79]Busch, *Karl Barth*, 168. Conversely, these years in Münster were the very ones during which Barth's relationship with his erstwhile "dialectical" colleagues—Bultmann, Gogarten, Merz, and (to a much lesser extent) Thurneysen—began, finally, to fracture into distance, disagreements, and even hostility.

[80]See Tietz, *Karl Barth*, 156.

[81]Busch, *Karl Barth*, 167.

[82]Busch, *Karl Barth*, 181.

also noted that by the time that they arrived, Charlotte von Kirschbaum was already there.[83] Karl and Charlotte had first been introduced by a mutual friend, George Merz, in 1924. Within the space of a year, Charlotte had been drawn and accepted into that somewhat exclusive group of close friends—Barth, Thurneysen, Merz, and Rüdi and Gerty Pestalozzi—who regularly vacationed in the Pestalozzi's summer retreat, the "Bergli."[84] In September 1925, Barth and von Kirschbaum visited the Bergli together.[85] By February 1926, Karl and Charlotte were close enough friends for Charlotte to visit him for a month in Münster, while he was living his self-described "bachelor existence" in the Warendorferstraße. In a letter to Charlotte from this time, Barth openly acknowledged "all the difficulties" (*allen Schwierigkeiten*) that were part and parcel of his marriage.[86] Thus it is perhaps not surprising that it was also during this time that the two first declared their love for each other. Charlotte, Barth would say, not only brought to an end his terrible loneliness but was at last a woman who understood him.[87] While she would not move into the Barth family home until October 1929, her time with Karl in early 1926 established three things that would remain in place until 1966, when her deteriorating health necessitated that she be moved to a sanatorium: first, that Karl both wanted and needed Charlotte's help with his theological work; second, that they loved each other deeply enough to refuse to be separated; but third, that Karl also loved Nelly enough that he did not wish to cause her the pain of a divorce.[88]

---

[83]Busch, *Karl Barth*, 165.

[84]It is worth noting that Nelly Barth never felt included within this circle—"sie stand allenthalben außerhalb." M. Flesch-Thebesius, "Nelly Barth," in *Ich bin was Ich bin: Frauen neben grossen Theologen und Religionsphilosophen des 20. Jahrhunderts*, ed. E. Rohr (Gütersloh: Gütersloher Verlagshaus, 1997), 230.

[85]Busch, *Karl Barth*, 164.

[86]K. Barth to C. von Kirschbaum, February 28, 1926, *GA* V.45, 24. It should be appreciated, however, that in the same letter, Barth told von Kirschbaum that his marriage was, nonetheless, "happy" ("*glücklich*").

[87]Selinger, *Charlotte von Kirschbaum*, 6, 82-83.

[88]For fuller histories of the relationship between Karl, Nelly, and Charlotte, see Selinger, *Charlotte von Kirschbaum and Karl Barth*, 1-20; C. Tietz, "Karl Barth and Charlotte von Kirschbaum," in *Theology Today* 74, no. 2 (2017): 86-111; S. Hennecke, "Biography and Theology: On the Connectedness of Theological Statements with Life on the Basis of the Correspondence Between Karl Barth and Charlotte von Kirschbaum (1925–1935)," *International Journal of Philosophy and Theology* 77, nos. 4-5 (2016): 324-36.

And thus it was that during these years in Münster, Charlotte von Kirschbaum became a more regular member of the Barths' household. In August 1927, the family vacationed in Nöschenrode, at the foothills of the Harz mountains. Von Kirschbaum traveled with them to help Karl prepare for publication the book that would, in time, come to be known as Karl's "false start"—his *Christliche Dogmatik*.[89] In Selinger's words, by this time "a rhythm and sense of normalcy in working together [had] been established."[90] Karl himself said much the same thing in a letter to Thurneysen: "Lollo and I have our hands full with the *Dogmatics*, so all our days are passed in the same tranquil tempo—interrupted by pleasant late walks, evening visits to the inn, and so on."[91]

In autumn of the same year, Karl was offered a job at the University of Bern.[92] In a letter to Thurneysen, Karl noted that "the children rejoice at the idea of moving back to Switzerland."[93] Karl's description of why his children were keen to make the move is perhaps slightly uncharitable. In his view, they had "high hopes for something like an eternal vacation stay with snowy mountains and the ringing of cowbells and among people who 'don't talk and cackle so loud.'"[94] In reality, however, there was likely more to their desire than simply this. As already mentioned, the family's memories of Safenwil were happy. Moreover, given the (almost-certainly obvious) tensions that were now re-emerging between Karl and Nelly in Münster—not least on account of the growing love between Karl and Charlotte—it is hardly surprising that Switzerland beckoned as an attractive option. In the end, however, the demands made by both Bern and Barth upon each other proved irreconcilable, and so the family remained in Germany.[95]

---

[89]Busch, *Karl Barth*, 174.

[90]Selinger, *Charlotte von Kirschbaum*, 56.

[91]K. Barth to E. Thurneysen, August 21, 1927, *GA* V.4, 515.

[92]The offer was precipitated by the retirement of Hermann Lüdemann (1842–1933), who in 1884 had been appointed professor of church history in Bern, and then professor of theology in 1891.

[93]K. Barth to E. Thurneysen, August 21, 1927, *GA* V.4, 517.

[94]K. Barth to E. Thurneysen, August 21, 1927, *GA* V.4, 517.

[95]The University of Bern insisted that, were Barth to be appointed, the next chairs in the faculty would have to go to more liberal theologians. Karl, for his part, refused to accept the offer unless the university rescinded this insistence. Busch, *Karl Barth*, 175.

As it turned out, though, Nelly and the three youngest children—Christoph, Matthias, and Hans Jakob—did return to Switzerland for five months the following year, from May to September 1928. Throughout this time Karl's mother, Anna, looked after the rest of the family, including Markus, in their Münster home.[96] While Busch does not give any reason for Anna's presence in Germany, Selinger claims that von Kirschbaum herself was the cause. In May 1928, Karl's relationship with Charlotte had provoked "a terrible quarrel" with his brothers and mother. Apparently taking advantage of Nelly's extended summer holiday in Switzerland with the younger children, it would seem that Anna traveled to Münster, ostensibly to keep house, but rather more probably to have it out with her son.[97] The situation was, understandably, profoundly painful for everyone concerned. While Karl, Nelly, and Charlotte were—each and together—burdened by "unspeakably deep suffering" and the presence of tensions that "shook them to the core," the "intimacy" of Karl's relationship with Charlotte placed "particularly heavy demands" on Nelly.[98]

But the circle of those affected was far wider than these three. Marlies Flesch-Thebesius has argued that Nelly was so determined to provide a normal home for her children, albeit a home that included "Aunt Lollo," that the children "did not feel the tension." Markus was able, she says, to recall his childhood, even in this strange context, as being "peaceful." "Only later did the Barth children discover that not everything was the same as other families."[99] Eberhard Busch, however, offers a different and rather more credible suggestion that each of the five Barth children—Markus included—"faced the burden of this difficulty at home and suffered under it."[100] While direct evidence is scant, it stretches credibility to believe that either Franziska or Markus, both of whom had stayed in Germany with their father during the summer of 1928, would have been unaware of the tensions or indeed their underlying cause.

---

[96]Busch, *Karl Barth*, 180.

[97]Selinger, *Charlotte von Kirschbaum*, 7. Busch records that "many people, even good friends, *and not least his mother*, took offence at the presence of 'Lollo' in [Karl's] life, and later even in his home." Busch, *Karl Barth*, 185.

[98]Busch, *Karl Barth*, 185-86.

[99]Flesch-Thebesius, "Nelly Barth," 234.

[100]Busch, *Karl Barth*, 185-86.

Precious little else is recorded about Markus's time in Münster. In late 1928, Karl wrote with undisguised pride to Eduard Thurneysen about how well Markus was doing in his Latin and Greek lessons, noting with some wryness that his eldest son was better at them than he himself had been. Nonetheless, Karl could not resist a slight quip at Markus's expense—he was still somewhat willful and was likely, in his father's opinion, to remain so for some time![101] Then, just before Christmas of the same year, Markus was diagnosed with galloping myopia, a side effect of having earlier contracted measles. While poor eyesight was to follow him throughout his life, the immediate consequences of the diagnosis were particularly difficult to bear, as Markus's doctors forbade him to read for an entire year.[102] "The poor thing!" wrote Thurneysen. "It won't be easy for him to keep up, if he isn't allowed to read."[103] As she had previously done with her children's language instruction, Nelly again stepped in to take control, reading to Markus every day so that he would not fall behind in his schoolwork.

One other key event in Markus's life during these years, around which there was some consternation, was his decision not to follow his sister Franziska in being confirmed. Fränzeli had been confirmed on March 17, 1929, in rather strange circumstances, the pastor having been dressed in the brown uniform of a SA (Sturmabteilung) member.[104] Markus, on the other hand—his own confirmation having been scheduled for the following year, on March 27, 1930—refused to go ahead with it. As he told his father in a "solemn conversation," his instruction had been less than impressive—the pastor lacked discipline, and his lectures were confused (*verworrene Reden*). Moreover, Markus was not even certain that he believed in the rite itself.[105]

---

[101]"Ist es mir ein Vergnügen zu sehen, wie gediegen Markus im Lateinischen und Griechischen unterrichtet wird, besser als ich seinerzeit. Aber er ist doch auch noch ein rechtes Kalb und darf es wohl auch noch eine Weile sein." Letter, K. Barth to E. Thurneysen, September 9, 1928, in *GA* V.4, 616.

[102]Personal correspondence with the Barth family, August 2019.

[103]E. Thurneysen to K. Barth, December 14, 1928, in *GA* V.4, 633.

[104]F. Barth, October 1992. The *Sturmabteilung* was the Nazi Party's original paramilitary organization that had been formed over the course of two years, between 1920 and 1921. Known colloquially as the "Brown Shirts," on account of the color of their uniforms, the SA was led by Ernst Röhm until the infamous "Night of the Long Knives" in late June 1934, which severely curtailed its power. From then on, the SA was overshadowed by the *Schutzstaffel* (SS).

[105]K. Barth to E. Thurneysen, February 8, 1930, in *GA* V.4, 715.

Shortly after having this discussion with Karl, Markus—having been instructed by his father to do so—provided a fuller written explanation for his refusal, which Karl then forwarded to Markus's godfather, Thurneysen. In it, Markus outlined the reasons for his decision in the following way. "Why do I not want to be confirmed? Because: A. I am unsatisfied with the [catechetical] instruction. B. I do not believe [in] confirmation, as I understand it to be, to be able to participate in it honestly."[106]

Markus's reasoning is instructive for understanding who and what he was like as a fourteen-year-old. While it might be tempting to put this episode down to simple adolescent contrariness, there was clearly more than that going on here. Far from this being an open rebellion against his parents, Markus was, on the contrary, seeking to exercise some independence of thought.[107] When pushed by his father for a more fulsome explanation of his convictions, Markus showed himself capable of offering his own type of theological critique. It would appear, in fact, that his negative assessment of both the catechesis and the pastor by whom it was offered was shared by his father: on witnessing the public examination of the confirmands, Karl was horrified by what he saw. As he described it to Thurneysen, the spectacle was "a gruesome impression" (*schaurigen Eindruck*) of what those students had been taught![108]

---

[106]A written report of these reasons, dated February 16, 1930, is held by the Thurneysen estate. For details, see K. Barth to E. Thurneysen, March 23, 1930, in *GA* V.34, n6.

[107]That Markus was not stubbornly refusing on principle to go ahead with his confirmation *at some stage* is demonstrated by Karl's comment to Thurneysen: "In any case, I will now make up for those unsuccessful lessons [i.e., by providing personal instruction to Markus]—whether for the sake of making his confirmation possible in a hurry, or whether to have it go ahead afterwards in Bonn, in peace and quiet, remains to be seen. Markus himself wants the latter." K. Barth to E. Thurneysen, February 8, 1930, in *GA* V.4, 715.

[108]K. Barth to E. Thurneysen, March 23, 1930, in *GA* V.34, 8.

2

"YOU CAN STILL LEARN SOMETHING FROM SOMETHING FALSE"

The Student Years, 1930–1939

The Barths stayed in Münster for almost exactly four years. In March 1930, they were on the move again, this time in response to Karl's call to a professorship in systematic theology at Bonn. For the next five years, the family lived in a "stately house" at Siebengebirgstraße 18. It may indeed have been imposing; indeed, it was large enough to host as many as eighty-eight people who came to one of Karl's regular "open evenings" (*offenen Abends*).[1] However, the house was not quite so conveniently located as their previous homes had been, lying on the opposite side of the Rhine—and a good ten kilometers—from both the University, where Karl now worked, and the Beethoven-Gymnasium, where Markus was enrolled to complete his schooling.

In any case, Markus's mother did not have much time to enjoy it. Within a month of arriving in their new home, Nelly fell ill with chest pains and traveled alone to the Bergisches Land region for recuperation. Charlotte—whose letters most likely did very little to ease Nelly's angina—wrote to keep her in touch with events at home. Matthias's injured foot, she reported, was

[1] N. Barth to A. Hoffmann, May 15, 1930. MBL. Series II. Box 2.

"much better"; meanwhile, Markus and Franziska had again made good use of their bicycles to explore the nearby Siebengebirge.[2] Indeed, all five children evidently adjusted to life in Bonn quickly. In May, Nelly told her mother that Hans Jakob was "flourishing and sparkling"; Matthias was either devouring books or building models with his Meccano set;[3] while Christoph and Markus were enjoying cycling to school and resuming their piano lessons.[4] Even Franziska—by now nearing the end of her schooling—had settled in well to the new routines and was finding lessons (even Latin!) easy.[5]

That the children had been able to adapt so easily is remarkable given the turmoil and tension in the family home. Quite aside from the busyness and demands of Karl's new appointment, the move to Bonn coincided with a fresh round of animosity between Nelly, Karl, and Charlotte. It also coincided, perhaps not surprisingly, with the first of Nelly's demands for a divorce.[6] Throughout this time, notes Stephen Plant, Nelly's family—in particular her mother, Anna—sought to bring the situation to a head, reckoning it to be both unsustainable and intolerable, not least for Nelly's health.[7] The situation was so tense that by August 1930, barely five months after their arrival, Nelly had moved out of their home. "It's time," she wrote to Karl's mother, Anna, "for you to know where I am." She continued:

> Since the day before yesterday I have been staying with [my sister] Anny[8], while Hans Jakob has been with my sister Gritti.[9] Berti[10] is with Matthisli

[2]C. von Kirschbaum to N. Barth, April 23, 1930. Series II. Box 2.

[3]Matthias was not the only one to enjoy building Meccano models. Sometime in 1930, presumably—given the detailed writeup of it—as part of a school project, Markus constructed a Meccano model of the Dornier Do X flying boat. At the time, this particular flying boat was very much in the news; the largest such aircraft ever built, the first Do X had been completed in June 1929. While its size and weight prevented it from being commercially viable—indeed, only three Do X's were ever built—it clearly captured the public's imagination, including Markus's.

[4]A short item in the local paper listed "Barth" as the pianist for Chopin's *Nocturno für Cello und Klavier* in a concert put on by the Beethoven-Gymnasium. "Schülerkonzert im Beethoven-Gymnasium," in *General-Anzeiger für Bonn und Umgegend*, February 26, 1931, 4. The article does not specify which Barth it was. However, Christoph preferred the cello to the piano, and so the pianist was almost certainly either Markus or Franziska, who was herself an accomplished pianist throughout her life.

[5]N. Barth to A. Hoffmann, May 15, 1930. MBL. Series II. Box 2.

[6]M. Flesch-Thebesius, "Nelly Barth," in *Ich bin was Ich bin: Frauen neben grossen Theologen und Religionsphilosophen des 20. Jahrhunderts*, ed. E. Rohr (Gütersloh: Gütersloher Verlagshaus, 1997), 236.

[7]S. Plant, "When Karl Met Lollo: The Origins and Consequences of Karl Barth's Relationship with Charlotte von Kirschbaum," *Scottish Journal of Theology* 72, no. 2 (2019): 135.

[8]Anny Schuler (1889–1964).

[9]Nelly's sister, Franziska Margarita Knauer (1886–1956), who lived in Zürich.

[10]Bertha Bultmann (1913–1987) was the Barths' housekeeper from March 1930 to February 1931.

> [Matthias] in Stäfa. You have my three big ones with you. . . . I have just written to Karl at the "Bergli" that, until I have learned how to walk this path or another, I must remain alone. I'm not coming to Adelboden, and perhaps also not Bonn. I cannot find the courage, with no new or different inner strength, to return to that existence.[11]

The very next day, Nelly wrote again to her mother-in-law, this time expressing her belief that Karl and Charlotte would continue on their way together without her (*Karl werde mit Lollo ohne mich weiter seinen Weg gehen*). Even though she stood "to lose everything," she felt that she could not continue with the way things were.[12]

As for Markus, his own maturation continued within this strained and complicated environment. In late March 1931, having previously resisted doing so, Markus was finally confirmed following some much needed "catch-up" catechesis from Karl.[13] On Palm Sunday of that year, Nelly traveled with her eldest son to Duisberg—an industrial city about 100 kilometers to the north of Bonn—where superintendent Fritz Horn, a friend of Karl's, conducted the service. Whether Markus was himself by now fully convinced of the sacramental need for the rite—and, as we shall see, he was later to express grave reservations about it—his confirmation served at least one important practical purpose: it kept open the possibility of theological studies. As Nelly explained to her mother a week before the service, "If he would like to study theology later on, it is a prerequisite."[14]

There were other causes for familial celebration too. A year after Karl and Nelly's separation, Nelly threw a joint birthday party for Christoph and Markus, noting in a letter to her own mother that Karl, too, had been

[11]N. Barth to A. Barth, August 4, 1930, in *GA* V.34, 31. While Nelly speaks of being alone—and no doubt she must have felt so—she was nonetheless supported by Eduard and Marguerite Thurneysen, who also took a great interest in the children's welfare. See, for example: "Nelly and the children have arrived. We were over there and saw each other. . . . [Nelly] didn't say much, just hinted that difficult days lay behind her. We'll see each other again tomorrow. The children are happy, and came with us to our little house." E. Thurneysen to K. Barth, August 8, 1930, in *GA* V.34, 66-67.

[12]N. Barth to A. Barth, August 5, 1930, in *GA* V.34, 32.

[13]See K. Barth to E. Thurneysen, February 8, 1930, in *GA* V.4, 715. It will be remembered that the woeful nature of Markus's earlier catechesis had been one of the main reasons why he had initially decided not to be confirmed.

[14]"Wenn er Theologie studieren möchte später, ist das erforderlich." N. Barth to A. Hoffmann, March 22, 1931. MBL. Series II. Box 2.

there—*alone*![15] That Karl was evidently at the party without Charlotte allowed him and Nelly to talk properly for the first time in a long while, about how the situation with Charlotte—what Karl referred to as their "emergency community" (*Notgemeinschaft*)[16]—could be endured better on all sides. And perhaps to Nelly's astonishment—but certainly to her great joy—the party demonstrated that as a family they *could* be happy together. "Yesterday was so good, so refreshing, once again after a long, long time." Moreover, "the children also felt it, sitting around the smaller table, only talking Swiss German—it was as intimate as it used to be."[17]

At the same time, contentment was able to be found in those parts of family life that were significant precisely because of their normalcy. In April 1932, Charlotte wrote to Nelly—who was, at the time, in Switzerland—of the children's delight in their own, very ordinary activities: Hans Jakob was cheery, despite a persistent cold; Christoph had (once again) redesigned his bedroom; Markus was happy and planning a solo trip to Paris; and Franziska had, as always, her "joyful plans and intentions."[18]

Within this atmosphere, Markus began to find his own way. Just before Christmas 1932, Karl informed Thurneysen of Markus's most recent exploits: "He has started to move within a circle of . . . Communists, and has been joyfully initiated into the *Communist Manifesto*, and other secrets of our Soviet future."[19] This political commitment took shape in written form as well. In April 1933, as a seventieth birthday present to his grandmother, Anna Barth-Sartorius, Markus wrote a ten-page booklet titled "Attempts to Solve the Social Questions from the Pre-Marxist Period: A Partial Description of Utopian Socialism Between 1800–1840."[20]

Beginning with the claim that any attempt to discern "the nature and aims of socialism" (*dem Wesen und dem Ziel des Sozialismus*) must start by

---

[15]N. Barth to A. Hoffmann, September 28, 1931. MBL. Series II. Box 2. In the original letter, "allein" is underlined, highlighting Charlotte's absence from the celebrations.

[16]*GA* V.45, 287n3.

[17]N. Barth to A. Hoffmann, September 28, 1931.

[18]C. von Kirschbaum to N. Barth, April 23, 1932. MBL. Series II. Box 2. Markus spent fourteen days in Paris in late May, immediately after Pentecost.

[19]K. Barth to E. Thurneysen, December 23, 1932, *GA* V.34, 430.

[20]M. Barth, "Versuche zur Lösung der soziale Frage aus vormarxistischer Zeit: Eine auszugsweise Darlegung des utopischen Sozialismus der Zeit 1800–1800," April 1933.

recognizing that its necessary precondition was the development of modern capitalism,[21] Markus continued by explaining to his grandmother how dependent early socialism was on eighteenth-century philosophy. Those first proponents of socialist thought, he said, were indebted to the Enlightenment vision of the perfection and goodness of humankind (*die Vollendung und Güte des Menschen*) and of the goodness and reasonableness (*die Güte und Vernünftigkeit*) of God (or nature).[22] While Markus recognized that their ideals were frequently at odds with the reality of the world around them—he gives as examples the plight of mine workers in English collieries[23]—he argued that their philosophic convictions nevertheless compelled them to believe fervently in the inherent goodness of the world "and all its institutions" (*Einrichtungen*).[24] After discussing two specific examples—Robert Owen[25] (1771–1858) in England and Henri de Saint-Simon (1760–1825) in France—Markus concluded his paper by comparing the somewhat naive sentiments of those early socialists with the more sophisticated form of socialism advanced by Karl Marx. Despite acknowledging its occasional problems (*die marxistiche Lehre an manchen Stellen noch entscheidende Fehler bringt*), Markus ended his booklet by arguing that Marx's teaching had "meant great progress for the development of socialism, and was perhaps the only right thing for the labor movement."[26]

This short paper, written when Markus was only seventeen years old, not only paints a fascinating picture of his early political thinking but also illustrates his preparedness to venture into risky territory. In April 1933, precisely at the time when Markus penned these thoughts in Bonn, Adolf Hitler's newly formed National Socialist government was ramping up its

---

[21]Barth, "Versuche zur Lösung der soziale Frage," 1.

[22]Barth, "Versuche zur Lösung der soziale Frage," 3.

[23]"When one hears, for example, of eight-year-old children, weak women, and grown-up girls having to work fourteen hours a day in the mines and that men were, on average, unfit to work beyond forty, then we can understand why—even before the middle of the nineteenth century—people who were aware of their responsibilities toward their fellow men and women began to work their hardest (*mit aller Macht*) to improve the lot of the poorest and most numerous class (*der ärmsten und zahlreichsten Klasse*). Barth, "Versuche zur Lösung der soziale Frage," 2.

[24]Barth, "Versuche zur Lösung der soziale Frage," 3.

[25]Markus mistakenly refers to him as Richard Owen.

[26]Barth, "Versuche zur Lösung der soziale Frage," 9-10.

persecution of political enemies, with communists being chief among them. Repressive action against leftist political groups had been commonplace since Hitler's seizure of power in January but had escalated in violence and scope in the lead-up to the passing of the "Enabling Act" of March 23 and the "Law for the Reconstruction of the Professional Civil Service" of April 7. The former effectively voted the Reichstag—the parliamentary site of democratic governance—out of existence, while the latter removed Jews and political opponents, especially on the left of the ideological spectrum, from the state's administrative machinery.[27] During March and April, ten thousand communists and social democrats had been arrested in Bavaria alone.[28] It was, in other words, an acutely dangerous time in Germany in which to express any socialist sympathies; for Markus not only to harbor those views but to put them in writing was both brave and reckless. Eventually, Karl was able to dissuade his son from joining the communist cell, about which he had spoken to Thurneysen.[29] Nevertheless, he could not entirely suppress a certain paternal pride in Markus's ambitions, no matter how potentially dangerous they might be. As Karl said to Thurneysen, "He [Markus] is the closest to me of all my children, and the one I understand best."[30]

Despite the increasingly obvious and potentially calamitous risks, Markus's fledgling political activity was not restricted to paper alone for very long. On the contrary, he became progressively more engaged in his own forms of subversion and resistance. As a seventeen-year-old, Markus had been required to attend a *Hitler Jugend* camp.[31] But his attendance

---

[27]Members of the Social Democratic Party and the Communist Party within the Reichstag were not even allowed to vote in the debate on the Enabling Act. Hitler told them that, as members of "the International," they were cognitively incapable of grasping the nuances of the Enabling Act. While he was prepared to offer his hand of friendship to those whose views differed from his, "this did not apply to the Social Democrats." "Germany will become free, but not through you." See I. Kershaw, *Hitler, 1889–1936: Hubris* (London: Penguin, 1998), 468.

[28]Kershaw, *Hitler*, 463.

[29]Personal correspondence with the Barth family, August 2019.

[30]K. Barth to E. Thurneysen, December 23, 1932, in *GA* V.34, 334-35.

[31]While the Hitler Youth (HJ) had been founded at the Nazi Party Congress in Weimar in 1926, it was not until June 24, 1933—the launch of the Party's "Youth Festivities"—that the HJ was deployed nationwide. By this time, HJ membership numbered two million—up from 100,000 at the start of the year—though a significant part of that increase was due to coercion. But Markus's security was fragile. As André Postert notes, "The Social Democrat and Communist youths of

was out of compulsion, not conviction, with his real political sympathies on display shortly afterward. In the months immediately following Hitler's seizure of power, Markus and some of his school friends staged daring, if foolish, protests against the new regime. On at least two occasions, they tore down the Nazi flag from the school roof, all the while shouting, "Death to Hitler!" (*Hitler verrecke!*). After the second such incident, some of the students involved were arrested by the Gestapo. Markus himself managed to get away on his bicycle, which he had hidden nearby.[32] The family home on Siebengebirgstraße was itself also the site of increased political activity. Throughout the *Kirchenkampf*,[33] Karl used the home for meetings with other leading figures of the church opposition. The meetings themselves took place behind closed doors, but it seems that they were not quite as secretive as might have been hoped. According to his own recollections, Markus was able to recognize many of his father's visitors during this time, and he would then tell his mother about who it was who had just arrived.[34]

Such, then, was the Barths' home environment for much of the time they spent in Bonn. Alongside periods of stability, and even great happiness, the strangeness of the domestic situation remained, with 1933 being a year of particular familial crisis. In that year—as well as the many pressures brought about by the Nazis' *Machtergreifung*,[35] and the consequent beginnings of

---

Germany had already been forced into the underground." A. Postert, "German Youth Between Euphoria and Resistance: Political Coercion and the Coordination of German Youth," in *From Weimar to Hitler: Studies in the Dissolution of the Weimar Republic and the Establishment of the Third Reich, 1932-1934*, ed. H. Beck and L. E. Jones (New York: Berghahn, 2019), 366-67.

[32]Personal correspondence with the Barth family, August 2019. See also "Lebenslauf," in Markus Barth's funeral booklet, 21. MBL. Series V, file 13.

[33]The *Kirchenkampf*—literally, "church struggle"—was the fight between the Nazi-aligned German Christian Movement (*Deutsche Christen Bewegung*) and those pastors, theologians, and parishes who sought to resist the imposition of National Socialist ideology onto the doctrine and polity of the German Protestant churches. Karl Barth was a leading figure in the church opposition that came to be known as the Confessing Church (*Bekennende Kirche*), not least through his authoring of the Barmen Declaration of 1934. For the best histories of this time, see V. Barnett, *For the Soul of the People: Protestant Protest Against Hitler* (New York: Oxford University Press, 1992); K. Scholder, *The Churches and the Third Reich*, 2 vols. (London: SCM Press, 1987–1988); J. S. Conway, *The Nazi Persecution of the Churches 1933–1945* (London: Weidenfeld & Nicolson, 1968).

[34]M. Barth, interview, February 14, 1994. Flesch-Thebesius, "Nelly Barth," 236.

[35]Literally, "seizure of power," *Machtergreifung* quickly became the standard way of referring to Hitler's accession to the chancellorship on January 30, 1933. Hitler himself, however, preferred

what would be a drawn-out *Kirchenkampf*—the relationship between Karl, Nelly, and Charlotte became so strained that divorce was once more openly canvassed. Were such a thing to eventuate, it was Karl's belief that Franziska and "the two little ones" (Matthias and Hans Jakob) would return to Switzerland with Nelly, while Markus and Christoph would stay—"if it was their will"—with Karl in Germany.[36]

As it happened, a divorce was avoided, though not without continuing distress to the three people most closely involved. Nonetheless, the family was split up, albeit for very different reasons. By Eastertide 1934, Markus had finished his schooling and was ready to commence university studies. In a move that perhaps surprised his father, Markus chose not to stay in Germany but decided instead to return to Switzerland and begin his theological studies at the University of Bern. The reasons for this decision were many and complex, but in all likelihood included a very natural desire to return to the country of his birth, an equally natural wish to remove himself from the ongoing (if often unstated) tensions between his parents and Charlotte von Kirschbaum, and (given his previous close shaves with the authorities) a recognition of his need to escape the dangers of Nazism. As a consequence of Karl's increasingly prominent role in the church struggle, his own recent association with communist groups, and those rather brazen schoolyard protests, Markus's future in Germany was far from secure. The decision to return to Switzerland was, therefore, both understandable and wise. It was also almost certainly made easier by the fact that his older sister, Fränzeli, with whom he had always been very close, was already in Basel studying music and education.[37] As will soon be seen, Markus's brother, Christoph, also returned to Switzerland in the same year, having himself run afoul of the authorities.[38]

---

the term *Machtübernahm*—the "take-over of power"—as it better reflected the reality that the transfer of authority was entirely legal and constitutionally valid.

[36]K. Barth to N. Barth, April 5, 1933, in *GA* V.34, 484. For further details of the domestic stresses and strains of this year, see C. Tietz, *Karl Barth: A Life in Conflict*, trans. V. Barnett (Oxford: Oxford University Press, 2021), 214-20.

[37]E. Busch, *Karl Barth: His Life from Letters and Autobiographical Texts*, trans. J. Bowden (Grand Rapids, MI: Eerdmans, 1994), 81, 245.

[38]In a letter to a friend—possibly in England—Christoph had been sufficiently critical of the German political situation that, following a three-hour interrogation by the police, his case had been forwarded to the senior prosecutor in Leipzig. Christoph's move to Switzerland was thus a precautionary move by the family to keep him safe from further judicial action. See Tietz, *Karl Barth*, 237.

Figure 2.1. Holidays in Rome, September 1934. Left to right: Peter Barth, Karl, Markus, Ernst Wolf

In the weeks between finishing school and starting university, though, Markus journeyed by himself to Rome, full of "youthful freshness" (*jugendliche Frische*)—his father "almost" envying his freedom to "plunge himself into the discovery of the wide world."[39] Then, during the summer of the same year—immediately after the decisive Barmen Synod—Markus traveled again to Rome, this time in the company of his father, his uncle Peter (Barth), and the young theologian Ernst Wolf. He could hardly have wished for a more intense and formative introduction to his formal theological education. Not only would those Roman conversations have delved deeply into the various church-political machinations by which the First Confessing Synod, held a few months earlier in Barmen, had been riven, but it was also during this vacation that Karl composed his polemical *Nein!* to his former colleague Emil Brunner.[40] With this as his preparation, Markus launched into his own theological studies.

[39]K. Barth to N. Barth, March 22, 1934. MBL. Series II. Box 2.

[40]K. Barth, "Nein! Antwort an Emil Brunner," *Theologische Existenz heute* 14 (1934): 1-63. See Busch, *Karl Barth*, 248.

THE UNIVERSITY STUDENT

In the spring of 1934, Markus began his university education back in Bern, the town in which his father had spent most of his youth, and in which his grandfather, Fritz Barth, had worked from 1889 to 1912.[41] He matriculated in the theological faculty almost exactly thirty years after Karl had commenced his own studies in the same place. Unlike Karl, however, who, in beginning his university education "entered into a territory which was still largely unknown to him,"[42] Markus joined a world of academic theology with which he was already deeply familiar. Such familiarity, though, could cut both ways; while the university environment itself was quite normal for him, Markus could not escape the dominating legacy of his father. Later in life, Markus recounted that his professors simply expected that he would know more than his fellow students. Such a weight of expectations was not, he recalled, always easy to bear.[43] Nevertheless, Markus was far from overawed by such assumptions. As his father had before him, Markus joined the student fraternity "Zofingia," for which, in the winter of 1937, he wrote an article on the church's political message of peace. With civil war raging in Spain, the Second Sino-Japanese War just five months old, and military tensions rising throughout Europe, Markus wrote,

> The [Christmastide] announcement of peace to the world seems now more problematic than ever. . . . The justification for, and way in which, the church must proclaim its message of peace cannot depend on the attitude of Christians to the problems of the world. . . . World peace *per se* is not the content of the church's message. But, the members of the church are united in prayer and wish, that God wants them to really be witnesses of Christ in word and deed. [And so] your message about him should be heard as a message of political peace. This political peace may not be visible—but the church must bring the good news of the peace that really exists in Christ.[44]

---

[41]Busch, *Karl Barth*, 9. Fritz Barth was appointed successor to Adolf Schlatter as professor of early and medieval church and New Testament.

[42]Busch, *Karl Barth*, 33.

[43]Markus Barth to Ruth Naveau-Barth, personal correspondence with the Barth family, August 2019.

[44]M. Barth, "Der politische Friede in der Botschaft der Kirche," *Zentralblatt des Schweizerischen Zofingervereins* 78 (Zürich: Zofingia, 1937–1938), 133, 137.

This article typified Markus's preparedness to offer his frank assessment on any and all matters and to enter, often quite bluntly, into politically sensitive areas. Perhaps not surprisingly, whereas Karl's Zofingian nickname had been "Finch" (*Fink*)—which carried connotations of cheerfulness—Markus was soon known as "Sparrow" (*Spatz*), a word which, in German, connoted cheeky boldness![45] Before long, he and Franziska were joined in Bern by their younger brother, Christoph. The reason for his relocation from Bonn to Bern was political. Christoph had a pen-pal in Palestine, to whom he had made some critical comments about the Hitler regime. Unfortunately, the letter in which those criticisms had appeared had been intercepted by the censor. Given that, at this time, Karl Barth himself was under "city arrest," Christoph's own security was therefore clearly at risk. In late May, and following the advice of a lawyer friend to "send that boy to Switzerland immediately," Christoph was dispatched forthwith to Bern for his own safety.[46]

Markus himself did not remain in Bern for long. In 1935, he transferred his theological studies to Basel where, from late October, Karl was now also teaching.[47] Before long, father and son were reunited in the classroom, fulfilling what had long been anticipated since Markus's first foray into Karl's lectures on the epistle of James in 1928. Markus followed

---

[45]Personal correspondence with the Barth family, August 2019. Note that while Busch records Karl Barth's nickname as *der Fink*, the editor's preface to Barth's 1906 paper "Zofingia und soziale Frage" suggests that his "association name" (*Vereinsnamen*) was in fact *Sprenzel*, connoting either "lightweight" or "puny." See Busch, *Karl Barth*, 29; cf. Tietz, *Karl Barth*, 27; editor's introduction to "Zofingia und soziale Frage," *GA* 3.21, 61.

[46]Busch, *Karl Barth*, 245; personal correspondence with the Barth family, August 2019. Christiane Tietz says that Christoph's offending letter was to his English pen pal. Tietz, *Karl Barth*, 237. However, Marie-Claire Barth—Christoph's widow—told Markus Barth's children in August 2019 that the letter had been written to a Palestinian Jewish friend of Christoph's. It is always possible that Christoph wrote similarly dangerous letters to more than one person!

[47]Having fallen foul of §4 of the "Gesetz zur Wiederherstellung des Berufsbeamtentums" ("Law for the Reconstruction of the Civil Service," April 7, 1933)—the law which, inter alia, had introduced the infamous "Aryan Paragraph"—Karl Barth had been dismissed from his teaching post in Bonn on June 22, 1934, and expelled from Germany in July. Barth's "crime" was his refusal to commence his lectures with the Hitler salute. Thus, while Busch records that it was §6 of the law according to which Barth was disciplined—a section which permitted the retirement of public officials without the need to demonstrate incapacity—it is more likely that it was §4—which required all public servants to "wholeheartedly" (*rückhaltlos*) and "at all times" (*jederzeit*) guarantee their loyalty to the National Socialist State. See Busch, *Karl Barth*, 261.

in his father's steps outside the classroom as well. In March 1937, seventeen years after Karl had last attended, Markus went to the Aarau Student Conference. There he heard lectures on the cross and resurrection (Pastor Zindel, from Canton Graubünden), on the distress of being isolated from one's community (Prof. Jakob, from Zürich), and on the church's mission to the world (the German missiologist, Karl Hartenstein). Unlike Karl's first impressions of the Aarau Conference, Markus was less than impressed. "I can't help but give you a brief report of the conference that I have just now survived. I don't regret having gone, despite the anticipated unpleasantness. After all, you can still learn something from something false." The lectures themselves, however, "were very bad—except [Hartenstein's], and unfortunately extraordinarily below the academic level that one might expect." In Markus's opinion, Zindel especially "did not know what to say." At Aarau, he also ran into Karl Schmidt, dean of theology at Basel, with whom he would later have a very bitter conflict. Schmidt, Markus had to admit, spoke well on a number of occasions. It would appear, however, as though Markus, and some of the other student delegates, discovered—and exploited—one of his weaknesses. "We did not fail to foster a little 'cult following' with [Schmidt]—to 'fawn over him,' as they say here—which increased his self-confidence, and made him very happy."[48]

Markus remained in Basel until the spring of 1937. His time there as a student was rich and rewarding not only intellectually but also personally. He remained life-long friends with many of his fellow theological students from those days, not least with the church historian Martin Schmidt, with whom Markus had gone to school in Bonn. Thirty years later, they would find themselves working together, back at the same university.[49] Much more significant than even his friendship with Schmidt, though, was the

---

[48]M. Barth to K. Barth, March 18, 1937, 2. MBL. Series V, file 5.

[49]Martin Anton Schmidt was born in Germany in 1919 and studied theology at Basel. Under threat of conscription to the *Wehrmacht* at the start of World War II, Schmidt declared himself stateless and was given protection by the Canton of Basel. After completing his *Habilitation* in 1951, he taught at Emory University, and then the San Francisco Theological Seminary from 1955–1967. In 1967, Schmidt returned to Basel to take up a chair in church and dogmatic history. Six years later, in 1973, he was reunited with Markus Barth, who by then had also been appointed to a professorship back in Basel.

relationship he forged in the final year of his studies with a young woman who was also studying theology, occasionally even with Markus in his father's classes, named Rose Marie Oswald.

ROSE MARIE AND A RETURN TO GERMANY

Born in 1913 in Basel, Rose Marie had taken confirmation classes with Markus's godfather, Eduard Thurneysen, and by the age of fifteen had already worked her way through Karl Barth's *Römerbrief*. After completing her initial training in Geneva as a nurse, Rose Marie was determined to pursue her theological education, and so enrolled for three semesters at the University of Basel. There she took classes with Karl Barth himself, the Old Testament scholar Wilhelm Vischer—whom the elder Barth described with imaginative wit as "a free, childlike troubadour of the Good God"[50]—and Oscar Cullmann, whose chair in New Testament would in fact, on his retirement in 1972, pass to Markus.

Rose Marie's own recollections of this time are worth noting, for it seems that, at least initially, she was befriended by someone from the Barth household other than Markus. Having enrolled in Barth's course on 1 Peter, Rose Marie

> liked to sit down behind a sympathetic little woman, a good ten years older than myself, hardly a student, but an intense listener. When I approached her after a few weeks, asking her whether, after having completing training as a nurse, I would now be better off training to be a church assistant or really get stuck into theology, her answer was: "If you really are interested in how theology *develops* from here, then you must study theology." . . . Soon afterwards, as Markus' fiancée, I found myself in the Barths' house, where I encountered her again, but this time as "Aunt Lollo."[51]

It did not take long for Markus and Rose Marie to get engaged. Before getting married and settling into a country rectory, however, Markus decided to spend his final semesters abroad.[52]

---

[50]K. Barth, "W. Vischer zum 60. Geburtstag," *Kirchenblatt für die reformierte Schweiz*, April 28, 1955, in Busch, *Karl Barth*, 269.

[51]R. M. Barth, "Zum Geleit," in R. Köbler, *Schattenarbeit. Charlotte von Kirchsbaum—Die Theologin an der Seite Karl Barths* (Cologne: Pahl-Rugenstein, 1987), 7.

[52]R. M. Barth, *Markus Barth CV*, January 1961, 2. MBL. Series II. Box 10.

In the first instance, "abroad" meant heading back to Germany. In a short resume that he wrote in 1945,[53] Markus says that he spent his "seventh semester, in the summer of 1937, as a student at the theological training center [*Theologischer Ausbildungsstätte*] of the Confessing Church in Berlin, where [he] attended lectures by G. Dehn, H. Vogel, H. Asmussen and W. Niesel"—key figures in the Confessing Church's struggle against Nazism.[54] His experience in this environment was both formative and challenging. In a letter to his parents from May 1937, Markus commented that in contrast to the difficulties he had sometimes experienced in Switzerland—especially in Zofingia—he was getting on remarkably well with his peers.[55] Many of them certainly appreciated his theological acuity, not least his exegesis of Romans 13. "My interpretation [of Paul] from the *taxis* to *ypo* to the final judgment and the like, was considered to be right, and they want to use it as the basis for further exploration."[56] Exactly what his interpretation was remains unknown. However, it seems likely that Markus was presenting a politically provocative exegesis of Paul's teaching on Christian responsibility to and under the state.[57] In any event, his peers

[53]This was part of a submission that Markus made to the faculty of theology at the University of Basel to complement his application to progress to the final examinations for his doctorate.

[54]M. Barth, "Lebenslauf," 1. MBL. Series I. Box 6. It has been suggested by some who were close to him that during this period in Germany, Markus attended Bonhoeffer's Finkenwalde seminary. While certainly an intriguing possibility, it seems, on the whole, to be unlikely. For a start, the fifth and final teaching session at Finkenwalde lasted from April 18 to September 11, 1937, before the seminary was forcibly closed by the Gestapo in accordance with the so-called Himmler Decree of August 1937. Markus's summer semester in Berlin would therefore have overlapped with the majority of the fifth Finkenwalde session—so while he may possibly have *visited* the seminary, he could not have studied there for the entirety of that final teaching session. Second, neither Markus nor Rose Marie, in their respective *Lebensläufen*, make any mention of him being a student at Finkenwalde during this period—if he had been, it seems inconceivable that they would have omitted reference to it. Third, Markus is not mentioned as being a student or member of the House of Brethren in the extant lists. Certainly, none of this precludes him having visited Bonhoeffer at Finkenwalde while he was studying in Berlin. But there is no extant evidence that he studied there, or indeed under Bonhoeffer anywhere, in any formal sense.

[55]M. Barth to K. Barth and N. Barth, May 21, 1937, 2. MBL. Series I. Box 3.

[56]M. Barth to K. Barth and N. Barth, May 21, 1937, 2.

[57]It is instructive that in this letter, Barth did not translate the Greek words τάξις and ὑπο- (transliterated as *ypo*) into German. In the context of Romans 13, these words can only refer to the verb ὑποτάσσω, which Paul uses to speak of (the limits of) subjection to the state. Moreover, Barth separates the prefix from its main verb, making his verbal reference point less obvious. Why might he have done so, given that he retains reference to "the last judgment" (*jüngsten Gericht*) in German? It seems probable that Barth's interpretation of Romans 13—long the standard text for determining a Christian's rightful attitude to political authorities—was critical

who heard it were evidently both astonished and grateful—"they sat with their mouths open," Barth recalls. That what he was suggesting was potentially politically dangerous, however, is suggested by his further comment that "they dare not say more" (*sie sich nichst mehr zu sagen getrauen*). This is an indication, perhaps, that Markus's willingness to theologically criticize the Nazi regime (of which we have already seen evidence) went a step further than the local German students were prepared to go, no matter how much they may have agreed with him on theological grounds.[58]

Of equal interest is the keenness with which Markus sought to extend his stay in Germany in order to continue his studies at Marburg. As he expressed it to his parents, he was "reluctant to take my exams next spring, as my peers will do in Basel. . . . Wouldn't it be possible to postpone this matter for a year . . . ?" His reasoning was simple: "I would like to go to Marburg, in order to see for myself what is actually going on with Rudolf [Bultmann]."[59]

According to Rose Marie's own recollection of this time, it was "a short, interrupted semester."[60] It was not, however, uneventful. On one occasion, two Gestapo officers raided Markus's room, searched it, and pored over his

---

of the Nazi regime. This would make sense of both his own political views and prior actions, the positive reception of his exegesis by his peers, but also their reticence to speak about it openly. It would also help explain why he pulled apart verb and prefix and left them in Greek—such a device would have confounded any censors who may have intercepted the letter between Germany and Switzerland. It is perhaps useful to note that thirty-seven years later, in his commentary on Ephesians for the Anchor Bible series, Barth wrote an extended excursus on ὑποτάσσω in the context of Ephesians 5:21. There, he notes that "the translation 'be submissive' is alien to the sense and intent of the verb . . . used by Paul. . . . The participles or imperatives calling for subordination may well contain an appeal to free and responsible agents that can only be heeded voluntarily, but never by the elimination or breaking of the human will, not to speak of servile submissiveness." He goes on to say that, even in the case of the submission owed by Christians to the state, as in Romans 13:1, Paul insists on "a corresponding obligation of those in the superior position." See M. Barth, *Ephesians: Translation and Commentary on Chapters 4–6*, The Anchor Bible 34A (New York: Doubleday, 1974), 609, 610n10. All of this suggests that the reason why Barth's exegesis of Romans 13 in 1937 was politically subversive—and thus why he would have thought it prudent to disguise his views from the possible scrutiny of Nazi censors through the retention of the Greek and the separation of the verb ὑποτάσσω into prefix and stem—is because he understood a Christian's subjection to the (Nazi) state to be an act of voluntary agency and not an intrinsic obligation that could be unreservedly demanded by the state.

[58]M. Barth to K. Barth and N. Barth, May 21, 1937, 2.

[59]M. Barth to K. Barth and N. Barth, May 21, 1937, 3-4.

[60]Barth, *Markus Barth CV*, 1.

letters for three hours, later interrogating him at the local police station. They were, Markus recalled, trying to find evidence that he was acting on Karl's orders, whom they suspected of being the leader of an anti-Hitler movement. There were also, however, allegations that Markus himself was engaged in subversive activities. These had originated from his landlady, who had twice found that the obligatory portrait of Adolf Hitler, hanging beside Markus's desk, had been turned around to face the wall![61]

Aside from Markus being personally of interest to the Nazi authorities, the lectures that he was attending in Berlin were, by the late summer of 1937, now also illegal. Heinrich Vogel's school, in which Barth was enrolled—as well Bonhoeffer's Finkenwalde and the other seminaries of the Confessing Church—had been considered unlawful by the official church authorities from the first days of their establishment immediately after the Dahlem Synod of October 1934. It was not, however, until the infamous "Himmler Decree" of August 29, 1937 (S–PP (II B) 4431/37), according to which almost all activities of the Confessing Church were banned, that these Confessing seminaries became technically illegal. Once they were, and as soon as the teaching venues had been identified by the Gestapo, the lecturers were forced to continually relocate their classes to a series of different places outside the city, "sometimes here, sometimes there" (*einmal da, einmal dort*).[62]

One day toward the end of his time in Berlin, Markus received a letter ordering him to appear again at the same police station in which he had previously been questioned. Taking this as his cue to flee Germany, he hosted a farewell party with his fellow seminarians, then boarded an express train away from Berlin. After sheltering in a farmhouse owned by the father of one of the other students, he made his way over the course of the next month to Basel, staying with friends along the way. His journey was longer and more circuitous than it should have been, as he was forced to take multiple detours to avoid running into the Gestapo.

[61]Recollections from P. Barth, "Reisetagebuch, Sommer 1954," July 20, 1954. MBL. Series II. Box 7.

[62]Barth, "Reisetagebuch, Sommer 1954." These memories are confirmed by the recollections of Markus's fellow student in Berlin, Annemarie Grosch, and the seminary's director, Heinrich Vogel. See Barnett, *For the Soul of the People*, 86-87.

A YEAR ABROAD

Safely out of Germany, Markus spent a further two semesters in Basel, at the end of which, in October 1938, he sat and passed his final theology exams. With these out of the way, and having received a very generous scholarship from the Faculty of Divinity at the University of Edinburgh, Markus traveled to Scotland to conclude his theological studies. There he began to develop themes that would become characteristic of his later scholarship. In March 1939, for example, he presented a seminar paper on the topic, "The Seat of Authority in Religion: The Bible as the Word of God." In it he showed himself to be very much indebted to his father's teaching—and consistent with the declaration from Barmen—on the doctrines of revelation and Scripture. "Jesus Christ alone is the Word of God."[63] What, then, of the Bible? In a passage reminiscent of Karl's dogmatic lectures on the doctrine of the Word of God, Markus insists that "the Bible as such, unless the Holy Spirit gives us open eyes, is not the word of God, but a human book like many others."[64] Therefore, to say that the Bible is inspired "does not mean that the words and thoughts and theological meanings of the Bible are infallible, and free from error."[65] What the Bible does, though, is bear *witness*. In speaking to this idea, Markus not only rested his argument upon his father's teaching but also gave notice of a theme that was to become critical in his first major publication.

Rose Marie, having already pursued her own theological studies in Basel, visited Markus in Edinburgh for three months. There she enrolled as an audit student in some of his classes and assisted him in the research that would eventually become Markus's doctoral dissertation. "In the mornings, when I am at College, she is sitting at my desk . . . and furthering my thesis by some minute and subtle enquiries. . . . She is comparing the utterances of the synoptics as to the disciples, and attempting to point out [what their] respective characteristics might be."[66] Markus and Rose Marie also took the opportunity

---

[63]M. Barth, "The Seat of Authority in Religion: The Bible as the Word of God," March 1939, 3. MBL. Series V, file 8.

[64]Barth, "Seat of Authority in Religion," 5; see also, for example, K. Barth, *Church Dogmatics*, vol. 1, part 1, *The Doctrine of the Word of God*, 2nd ed. (Edinburgh: T&T Clark, 1975), 111 [hereafter *CD*].

[65]Barth, "The Seat of Authority in Religion," 5.

[66]M. Barth to K. Barth, April 26, 1939. MBL. Series I. Box 3.

that Edinburgh presented to prepare themselves for a shared life of ministry, making pastoral visits both separately and together. "Such visits, though supposed in the first rank to [en]gender and to keep upright a sort of general friendship with people, can be used for more earnest purposes. . . . The whole business may be for us a profitable training for the later call."[67]

Their time in Scotland was not, of course, without its difficulties, not least the tensions that can so often attend an engaged couple. "We are living so obviously under the auspices of the 'not yet,' it is of course sometimes hard to bear for each—she [Rose Marie] for instance must leave this house each night before half past ten." Nonetheless, they thought it a precious opportunity, with Markus even declaring that "the fellowship" that they would have "when once we shall be married—it cannot be much nicer" than what they were able to enjoy in Edinburgh![68]

But Markus did more in Scotland than simply study and prepare for the pastorate. With Karl having recently visited Scotland himself—he traveled to Aberdeen twice between 1937 and 1938 to deliver the Gifford Lectures[69]—so now Markus also was called upon to speak publicly. Most of his addresses dealt explicitly with the German *Kirchenkampf* between the Nazi-aligned German Christian Movement (*Deutsche Christen*) and the Confessing Church, of which his father had been such a prominent founder. Two weeks after his arrival, he noted in his first public engagement that the Scottish church "is not so troubled with quarrels and dissentions as in other countries. . . . To be a Christian is still here an easy and natural thing."[70] In an unambiguous reference to the situation in Germany, Markus urged his hearers to be grateful for this blessing. "Thank God that your Churches are not destroyed, and that you are not hindered by the state."[71] Later in the talk, Markus made the point with even greater clarity.

> You know that in Germany to-day it is different. When Hitler came to power, he and his party tried to get the Church also in their power. And in the Church

---

[67]M. Barth to K. Barth, April 26, 1939.

[68]M. Barth to K. Barth, April 26, 1939.

[69]Published as *The Knowledge of God and the Service of God*, trans. J. L. Haire and I. Henderson (London: Hodder & Stoughton, 1938).

[70]M. Barth, untitled address (nd), 1. MBL. Series I. Box 2.

[71]Barth, untitled address (nd), 1.

> itself there were people demanding that Hitler should be honoured as a second Christ, that his picture should be placed on the altar [and they] set beside Holy Scripture Hitler's book "Mein Kampf," and preached that these two books were of equal value for the Church. They preached, that not Christ alone, but Hitler and Christ are our redeemers. So they attempted to destroy the Church from her foundations.[72]

In detailing the rise of the Confessing Church, Markus noted that the leaders and members of it were not seeking to establish a "Free Church" (*freie Kirche*) and that "their aim was not political agitation against Hitler." Nevertheless, said Markus, "they were [deemed] enemies of the state, guilty of high treason."[73]

With the disastrous Munich Agreement and the inevitable annexation of the Sudentenland[74] that had followed soon after, Markus clearly recognized how hard it was for his listeners to see anything good in the German nation at the present time. "It is hard for us to pray for German men and women, and for the German Church. For Germany is doing so much injustice to the world and we all dislike its present government. But just for that reason we must pray for the Confessing Church. See, the

---

[72]Barth, untitled address (nd), 1-2.

[73]Barth, untitled address (nd), 2-3. This point is illuminating on two counts. First, it was Karl Barth who, in the wake of the disastrous "Brown Synod" of September 1933, urged an impetuous Bonhoeffer to resist the temptation to form a *Freie Kirche*; thus in this respect, the younger Barth was reflecting his father's views, and not what had been a unanimous opinion within the church opposition. See D. Bonhoeffer to K. Barth, September 9, 1933; K. Barth to D. Bonhoeffer, September 11, 1933 in *Dietrich Bonhoeffer Works*, vol. 12, *Berlin: 1932–1933*, ed. Larry L. Rasmussen (Minneapolis: Fortress, 2009), 165-67 [hereafter *DBWE*]. Second, Markus Barth's contention that the members of the Confessing Church were not seeking to act politically against Nazism as such is one of the enduring grounds for criticism of the *Bekennende Kirche*. As Matthew Hockenos has said, "The . . . conflict between the Confessing Church and the Nazi state . . . often erroneously conceived as the primary (even the only) struggle . . . was [in reality] occasional critiques by a small group of churchmen against particular state policies." It was never understood, except by a tiny minority within the Confessing Church, as being a struggle against the Nazi regime in and for itself. See M. D. Hockenos, *Church Divided: German Protestants Confront the Nazi Past* (Bloomington: Indiana University Press, 2004), 16.

[74]The Sudetenland was populated predominantly by German-speaking people who, in the aftermath of World War I and the dismemberment of the Austro-Hungarian Empire, had found themselves living in the newly created Czechoslovakia. The 1919 Treaty of Saint-Germain-en-Laye affirmed the inclusion of these German-speaking territories within the Czech state. For the next two decades, there was a strong secessionist movement that sought the independence of these German-speaking lands from Czechoslovakia, and their reintegration with the German lands to the west. Nazi Germany's occupation of the Sudentenland in October 1938 could thus be justified by Hitler as merely the fulfilment of the Sudeten Germans' own long-standing wishes.

European powers cannot bar Hitler's desire for expansion . . . How much harder therefor [*sic*] is it, to resist Hitler in Germany?" Nevertheless, he closed his speech with this plea: "Consider that not all Germans are Nazis, help with your prayers those who *in* Germany are resisting Hitler's cunning and power. . . . Do not in the quietness of your Scottish Church forget, that in Germany the Church is persecuted and opposed. Pray God that he will help the Confessing Church and its members in their struggle."[75]

On February 21, 1939, he again described the perilous situation of the German church to a gathering of the League of Nations Union in Edinburgh. After outlining the theological presuppositions of the *Deutsche Christen*—"I believe in Germany, the country of which . . . is the source of our new humanity . . . [and that] through Hitler came Christ. . . . Therefore is [National Socialism] the positive and practical Christendom"—he noted, significantly, that such ideas were not in fact new in Germany. "Throughout the 18th and 19th centuries there were people in the German Church, who have not been so far from such beliefs."[76] He also noted, however, that the early days of the church struggle, when the *Deutsche Christen* were in the ascendancy, were also the *good* days of the Confessing Church. At that time, when Nazism and German Christianity seemed to be in lockstep, "There was something so strong and real and brave in the faith of the [Confessing Church] members."

But, he said, "The German Christians blew themselves up" by presuming a greater synchronicity with National Socialism than the state was prepared to accept.[77] The situation now, claimed Markus, was far more

[75]Barth, untitled address (nd), 5.

[76]M. Barth, typescript of "The Religious Situation in Germany Today," 1. MBL. Series I. Box 2.

[77]Barth, "The Religious Situation in Germany Today," 3. That the German Christians "blew themselves up" carries two meanings. Most straightforwardly, Barth was probably meaning simply to imply a certain arrogance—that they had "puffed themselves up," would be a reasonable alternative rendering. In fact, though, Barth's somewhat awkward English phrasing was quite correct: Since the debacle of the *Sportpalast* rally in November 1933, during which Reinhold Krause—leader of the *Deutsche Christen* in Berlin—had launched an antisemitic tirade against the Old Testament, the German Christian Movement had lost significant popular and political support. While it remained in effective control of the German Protestantism, Krause's overreach led to a political shake-up of the movement's leadership, as well as to a very obvious distancing of the National Socialist government from direct involvement in church affairs. As Doris Bergen says, "Krause's speech precipitated a wave of departures from German Christian ranks." D. Bergen, *Twisted Cross: The German Christian Movement in the Third Reich* (Chapel Hill: University of North Carolina Press, 1996), 145. That is, the German Christians really had "blown themselves up!"

dire. Instead of the Nazi State trying to destroy the Confessing Church and in the process making martyrs, the Confessors were now "being strangled. Slowly, silently but efficiently" through the State's imposition of financial and bureaucratic administration. Every aspect of official church life—from the training and ordination of pastors, to the holding of synods and the handling of weekly offerings—was now controlled by state-appointed bureaucrats who were qualified not because they were members of the church, people of faith, or adequately trained for this type of work but merely because they were "old members of the Nazi Party."[78] These new tactics, said Markus, were "sly and successful, and the present state of the Confessing Church is a state of misery and helplessness." Being now "too tired and timid," the Confessing Church "does not challenge the state, as she ought to."[79] Whereas Nero's persecutions had created martyrs from whose blood the church had grown, Markus said, Hitler was more cleverly depriving the church of its breath, all the while declaring the church's freedom. As proof of Hitler's effectiveness, said Barth, even Martin Niemoeller had been forgotten.[80]

Markus concluded his talk to the League of Nations Union with a call to arms.

> Dear friends! It is easy to make such [criticisms] far from the battlefield. It is easy to advise and admonish the Confessing Church members to be brave. We can't go to Germany, to help our brothers, we can't undergo their suffering. Yet we are to think and do something in this country. . . . Should not we stand with a [vengeance] against Hitler? . . . Was it right to retreat before Hitler's claims in Munich? . . . My personal [view] is this: we would comfort our fellow believers in Germany more, we would contribute more to the struggle of the Church in this world, if we stood for another . . . policy of the western democracies [than appeasement]."[81]

[78]Barth, "The Religious Situation in Germany Today," 4.

[79]Barth, "The Religious Situation in Germany Today," 4.

[80]"Church in Germany: 'Strangling Process' of the Nazis," *The Scotsman*, February 22, 1939.

[81]Barth, "The Religious Situation in Germany Today," 7. On May 7, 1939, Markus delivered a similar speech during the evening service at John McConnachie's church in Dundee, in which he outlined four theses of Nazism's "positive Christianity—namely, that the church is national (*völkisch*); antisemitic; spiritual (and thus with nothing to say politically); and 'ordered' (that is, according to National Socialism)—and their evangelical counter-theses." Handwritten notes. MBL. Series I. Box 2.

During his stay in Scotland, Markus not only informed the Scottish church of the grave ecclesial situation that was unfolding in Germany. He also told his father what he thought of the situation in the Scottish church, at least as he could infer it from his university studies. And, to put it mildly, he was less than impressed.

> The New College lectures . . . are continuing . . . [but] the cream of the students is skimmed off now, all the more intelligent ones have got fellowships for study on the continent. . . . The remainder is a sort of good-hearted but not . . . inspiring students. The discussions . . . are shallow and the spirit is meek. . . . Baillie[82] is lecturing on eschatology . . . during this term. I meant I could set a store by this fact alone, but the lectures are so pure, so untheological and merely speculative that I can't like them at all. . . . Thomson[83] did not improve at any rate, Curtis[84] is unspeakably old and godly. . . . What I do enjoy as to theological studies is only a private . . . appointment with Porteous[85]—we discuss Jonah once a week—and my studies on English apostel [*sic*] literature. But also this hole will be digged . . . out soon. So I'm looking forward to my departure for England with eagerness.[86]

Before leaving Edinburgh, Markus sat the annual examinations in Old and New Testament and patristics. Perhaps surprisingly, given Karl's aversion to the topic, penciled ticks on the side of the exam papers show that Markus chose to write an essay on "the importance and limitations of natural theology" in the light of Thomas Aquinas' *De Deo*.[87]

By the middle of 1939, it was clear to most observers that a new European war was now almost inevitable. So, "just a few days before the outbreak of

---

[82]Professor John Baillie studied at Edinburgh, Jena, and Marburg. After teaching in both Canada (Emmanuel College, Toronto) and the US (Auburn and Union Theological Seminaries), he returned to Scotland in 1934 having been appointed professor of divinity at Edinburgh until 1959. He served as principal of New College and dean of the faculty of divinity, from 1950 to 1956.

[83]Professor G. T. Thomson—who, while in Aberdeen, had translated the first part-volume of Karl Barth's *Church Dogmatics*—was professor of Christian dogmatics at the University of Edinburgh from 1936 until his retirement in 1952.

[84]Professor W. A. Curtis, who had studied at Heidelberg and Leipzig, was professor of biblical exegesis in Edinburgh from 1915 to 1946. He was appointed dean of New College in 1928, and then from 1935 until his retirement, assumed the joint office of dean and principal.

[85]Professor Norman Porteous was appointed to the chair of Hebrew and Semitic languages at the University of Edinburgh in 1937. He served as dean and principal from 1964 until 1968.

[86]M. Barth to K. Barth, April 26, 1939.

[87]"Patristics Annual: Third Year. Selections from St Thomas Aquinas. *De Deo*," exam paper, July 1939. MBL. Series V, file 14.

the [Second World] War,"[88] Markus returned home. This, though, seems not to have been Markus's first preference. While still in Scotland, he wrote to both Hartford Theological Seminary in Connecticut and Union Theological Seminary in New York indicating his wish to undertake graduate studies in the United States. Both institutions responded positively and encouraged him to apply for scholarship funding. Was this an attempt by Markus to escape the coming conflagration in Europe? Perhaps—though if it was, the thought was fleeting. By the time Hartford and Union had responded to him, Markus had changed his mind—or at least decided to defer any such plans until, at the earliest, 1940–1941.[89]

And so it was back to Switzerland. Before returning home, however—and making good on his desire to visit England, about which he had already written to Karl—he spent some time with the Society of the Sacred Mission, an Anglican religious community based in Kelham Hall, Nottinghamshire.[90] Notorious for its spartan traditions and the rigid authoritarianism of its leadership, it is not entirely clear why Markus may have chosen to visit it. One possibility is that he had heard about Kelham from Bonhoeffer, who had stayed there briefly in late March 1935.[91] Regardless of the reason, it would seem that he made at least one lasting friendship. In 1990, just four years before his death, Markus received a letter from John Jameson, a retired Anglican priest from Northumberland in the United Kingdom. Expressing his sadness at Markus's recent ill health and wishing him a speedy recovery, Jameson recalled that he was approaching

[88]Barth, "Lebenslauf," 1.

[89]R. H. Potter to M. Barth, February 21, 1939, March 10, 1939; H. H. Tryon to M. Barth, April 13, 1939. MBL. Series V, file 6.

[90]Built between 1859–1862, Kelham Hall was purchased in 1903 by the Society of the Sacred Mission—an Anglican religious order that had been founded in 1893 by Herbert Kelly—to be the mother house of the Society and its theological college. It remained so for the next seventy years. Both Kelham and the Society "broke new ground in opening its doors to non-graduates, boys and men from all backgrounds." According to David Woodhouse, "The spartan tradition at Kelham in those days owed as much to [the legacy of] First World War economies as it did to monastic asceticism." See D. Woodhouse, "The Right Rev Eric Mercer: Conscientious Bishop of Exeter," obituary, *The Independent*, November 26, 2003.

[91]Bonhoeffer evidently learned a great deal about theological education and formation—most especially its grounding in the community's life of prayer—from his visits in 1935 to both Kelham and the Anglo-Catholic Community of the Resurrection at Mirfield, near Oxford. See the letter between D. Bonhoeffer and E. Cromwell, March 20, 1935, *DBWE* 17, 54-57; also K. Clements, *Bonhoeffer and Britain* (London: Churches Together in Britain and Ireland, 2006), 85-86.

the fiftieth anniversary of his ordination. "I think [the celebrations] will be an enjoyable event, though I don't much like all the fuss. Still, I have so many things to thank God for through all the years. It seems incredible to me that it is over 50 years since you shared my study at Kelham."[92]

On his return to Switzerland, two things were almost immediately different for Markus. In the first place, he was no longer a student. Given the prevailing political climate, his years at university had hardly been carefree. Nonetheless, Markus was now faced with the reality of turning his mind and energies away from formal study and toward its practical application in pastoral ministry. This was never a complete separation—as we will see in the following chapters, Markus retained a commitment to the necessary nexus, as he saw it, between the work of the theological academy and the service offered by the church. However, insofar as he was no longer formally a student, the focus of his energy had to shift. In the second place, Europe was on the brink of war. As it had been during the Great War of 1914–1918, Switzerland was formally neutral. This did not, though, mean that Markus was either uninvolved or unaffected. Of particular significance to him was the way in which the Nazis' genocidal persecution of the Jews—a persecution that had begun from almost the moment Hitler had assumed the German chancellorship and had now accelerated with ferocious intensity under cover of the conditions of war—formed his theology of Jewish-Christian relations. In both instances—the relationship between theology and church, and the relationship between Jews and Christians—would become characteristic markers of Markus's life and work from this time forward.

[92]J. Jameson to M. Barth, November 30, 1990. MBMC. Series II. Correspondence. Box 4 (1990s). This was not the first time that Jameson had been in contact. In 1946, and again in 1950, Jameson visited Markus and Rose Marie in Bubendorf, and they continued their correspondence—at least sporadically—while the Barths were in the US. "I am afraid our correspondence has languished during the past year or so, but I trust our friendship has not, and I very often think of you all, remembering the Summer of 1939 (so long ago) when you were at Kelham, and those wonderful times in 1946 and 1950 when you were such kind hosts to me in good old Bubendorf." J. Jameson to M. Barth, May 4, 1954, 1-2. MBL. Series I. Box 12.

3

"A PASTOR NEEDS TO BE THERE FOR ALL THE NEIGHBORS"

Politics and the Pastorate, 1940–1953

On his return from the United Kingdom, and having now completed his theological studies, Markus commenced work as an assistant pastor in Zürich under the supervision of Paul Vogt, the so-called "pastor to the refugees" (*Flüchtlingspfarrer*).[1] Vogt was almost certainly already known to Markus, as Karl had been working with him since 1937 on the Confessing Pastors' Family Aid project.[2] Markus and Vogt, perhaps in part because of their similar political views, remained close for the rest of their lives. Markus's tenure as Vogt's assistant, however, as well as his time in Zürich generally, were short-lived. In early 1940, Markus was called to the

[1]Paul Vogt (1900–1984) studied theology in Basel, Zurich, and Tübingen before entering the pastorate in 1926. His commitment to social welfare emerged early in his ministry, with the first of his relief agencies—a center for the provision of aid to unemployed men—being established in 1931. Two years later, he founded a second agency, "*Sonneblick*," which is still operational. During World War II, Vogt and Karl Barth were two of the principal—but also two of the very few—Christian leaders to publicly protest against the Nazis' genocide of the Jews.

[2]Originally intended as a support network for Confessing Church pastors and their families, the *Bekenntnis-Pfarrer-Familien-Hilfe* soon became a prominent and vital aid organization for refugees fleeing Germany. In 1938, its name was changed to more accurately reflect its new emphasis: *Schweizerisches Evangelisches Hilfswerk für die Bekennende Kirche in Deutschland* (Swiss Protestant Aid Association for the Confessing Church in Germany). See C. Tietz, *Karl Barth: A Life in Conflict* (Oxford: Oxford University Press, 2021), 283-84.

pastorate of Bubendorf, a small village of barely 1,100 inhabitants,[3] twenty kilometers to the southeast of Basel. Markus's appointment was initially as a locum pastor to replace Rolf Eberhard—a former student of Karl's, whose own pastorate in Bubendorf had commenced in 1931—who had entered active military service in 1939. When it became evident that Eberhard's military career would keep him out of pastoral work for the foreseeable future, Markus was confirmed in his role as Bubendorf's substantive pastor.[4]

Not unlike Safenwil, when Karl had first begun pastoral work there nearly thirty years earlier, Bubendorf combined rural life with small-time industrial activity. As Anneliese Häner-Frey—whose parents moved to Bubendorf in 1942—recalled, the villagers "either worked in their vegetable gardens, the fields and forests . . . or in the Lapanouse watch factory, the sawmill, or the TIBA stove and oven manufacturer."[5] That Bubendorf should be Markus's first pastoral appointment had something of a family precedent: almost exactly a century earlier, Franz Albert Barth (1816–1879)—who had studied under the great Johann Tobias Beck, and who was Markus's great-grandfather—had also been sent to Bubendorf for his first parish assignment.[6]

The first momentous event of Markus's pastorate was not, though, anything church related but rather his wedding in May to Rose Marie. They were married in a side chapel of the Basel Münster by Eduard Thurneysen, who had moved his pastoral ministry there from St. Gallen in 1927. While the two had been engaged for some time, the decision to marry in May was sudden, and caught many of their family and friends by surprise. Fearful of a German invasion of Switzerland that would disrupt any wedding plans,

---

[3]In 1941, Bubendorf had a population of 1,338. Swiss Federal Statistical Office STAT-TAB, *Bevölkerungsentwicklung nach Region, 1850–2000.*

[4]Rolf Eberhard (1909–1966) was promoted to captain in 1939, and then from 1942 served as intelligence officer for the 22nd Regiment. As the war drew to a close, he was promoted again to the rank of commander of the Fusilier Company III/54. See Manuela Nipp, "Rolf Eberhard," Personenlexicon des Kantons Basel-Landschaft, accessed May 14, 2024, https://personenlexikon.bl.ch/Rolf_Eberhard.

[5]A. Häner-Frey, "Erinnerungen," March 12, 2013. MBL. Series I. Box 5. Joseph Lapanouse began his watch-making business in 1924 in Hölstein, just outside Basel. Five years later, the company relocated to Bubendorf where, by the 1960s, it was employing five hundred workers. The TIBA stove company was founded in 1902 in the small village of Titterten, about 8 kilometers from Bubendorf. In 1947, TIBA moved its production to Bubendorf.

[6]E. Busch, *Karl Barth: His Life from Letters and Autobiographical Texts*, trans. J. Bowden (Grand Rapids, MI: Eerdmans, 1994), 2, 306.

the couple decided that sooner was better than later. One sorry consequence, though, was that Nelly Barth—who had followed official advice and taken Hans Jakob, then fifteen, to Beatenberg to be further away from the Swiss-German border—was unable to attend her eldest son's wedding. Karl, though, despite being in the middle of his first period of service in the Swiss army, was able to be there, arriving "very tired from the night watches" and wearing his auxiliary service helmet. "According to a rumor, this helmet fell to the ground during the ceremony."[7] This somewhat memorable interruption to the wedding did not, however, presage any difficulties in either the marriage or the Bubendorf pastorate. On the contrary, the next thirteen years in parish ministry "were, for the young pair, instructive, exciting, and blessed."[8]

Markus's pastoral ministry was, it would seem, more obviously successful than his father's first parish experience in Safenwil had been, and it came more naturally to him. One parishioner recalled Markus and Rose Marie living a "practical Christianity," which was "by no means [either] pious or evangelical" (*fromm oder evangelikal*). While pastoral care was not, by his own admission, Markus's strong point, he nonetheless sought ways to mix with the townsfolk, occasionally eating with them at the local pub and being a visible presence at the various village festivals.[9] To help break down barriers between the church and the wider community, Markus would also occasionally hold worship services outside the church building on, for example, the grounds of the local shooting club, gymnastics club, or music society.

---

[7]"Lebenslauf," Markus Barth funeral booklet, July 8, 1994, 22.

[8]"Lebenslauf," Markus Barth funeral booklet, 23.

[9]A. Häner-Frey, "Erinnerungen." Erich Geldbach has helpfully distinguished between *Evangelikal* and *evangelisch*. Whereas the latter term has, in German, historically been used almost synonymously with Protestantism in general, *Evangelikal* has, since the 1960s, come to denote a rather more conservative Protestantism that draws its inspiration from the North American evangelical revival that took place under the leadership of people like Billy Graham. It is precisely this latter form of conservative American Protestantism which, at least according to Anneliese Häner-Frey, was *not* modeled by the Barths. See E. Geldbach, "'Evangelisch,' 'Evangelikal,' and Pietism: Some Remarks on Early Evangelicalism and Globalization from a German Perspective," in *A Global Faith: Essays on Evangelicalism and Globalization*, ed. M. Hutchinson and O. Kalu (Sydney: Centre for the Study of Australian Christianity, 1998). Cited in J. Enns, *Saving Germany: North American Protestants and Christian Mission to West Germany, 1945–1974* (Montreal: McGill-Queen's University Press, 2017), 15.

But Barth did not work alone. Through it all, he was aided by Rose Marie, who offered her own form of pastoral care. It had been evident from at least as early as their time in Edinburgh that the two fully intended on having a shared ministry. Now in Bubendorf, they were able to put that into effect. For her part, Rose Marie was instrumental in establishing the mothers' association while, as a trained nurse, she also provided advice to younger mothers on caring for their infants. As shall be seen, this companionship in ministry was to become a hallmark of the Barths' marriage and work for the rest of their lives. Between 1943 and 1945, Markus was also assisted by Esther Pestalozzi. The daughter of Rudolf and Gerty Pestalozzi—owners of the "Bergli" summer chalet in Oberrieden, where Karl Barth did so much of his writing—Esther came to Bubendorf principally as a community worker (*Gemeindehelferin*) but also to help Markus type up the doctoral dissertation that he was writing for the University of Basel. Alongside this work, she was employed in parish duties under Markus's direction. In addition to writing up his sermons, and then distributing the copies to his parishioners, she organized the village children's nativity play, visited the sick, and led some school-based religion classes. Markus was, however, strict in his instructions to her: "Just tell the Bible stories; don't draw any morals from them!"[10]

Much of Barth's pastoral work was, unsurprisingly, taken up with his adult parishioners. He did not, however, neglect Bubendorf's teenage population. They, it seems, appreciated the clarity of Markus's catechetical instruction—quite possibly, he had learned from his own, rather more dire experiences as a confirmand in Münster—as well as his sense of fun. On at least one occasion, he and Rose Marie took the youth group dancing—a wholly unremarkable activity until one learns that, toward the end of the war, Rose Marie organized a dance party that, in order not to offend the villagers, had to be held in the vicarage's study with the shutters closed.[11] And whereas Karl's Safenwil sermons had—by his own later

[10]E. Röthlisberger to R. M. Barth, interviews, 2014–2015. MBL. Series II. Box 1. Halfway through her time with the Barths, Esther married Fred Röthlisberger—a soldier stationed in Bubendorf—whom Markus had known when they had been part of the Zofingia fraternity together a decade earlier.

[11]E. Röthlisberger to R. M. Barth, interviews.

admission—been far too academic in style, most of Markus's parishioners, though certainly not starved by him of biblical exposition, valued his emphasis on the simple truth of God's gracious nearness.[12]

ON COMMUNION

One of the best examples of the priority that the young pastor gave to God's "unspeakable" grace is an exposition of holy communion that he provided in 1945 to his congregation in Bubendorf. Grandly titled "Theses on the Interpretation of the Synoptic Reports of the Last Supper," Barth's intention was to ground his exegesis—which, in its scholarly iteration, would appear as one of his first academic publications[13]—in the pastoral realities of congregational life. Unashamedly confessing that we come to the Lord's table not as people who are "flawless or righteous" but as "lost sheep and lost children, who have acted foolishly and unfaithfully," Barth presses home the point that the very invitation to the table bears witness to "how far we have distanced ourselves from God, how deep we have fallen, and how great our guilt is."[14] "Not one of us has done good. There is nothing good in us wretched sinners."[15] Nevertheless, says Barth, our "common brother, Jesus" makes the many of us to be his brothers and sisters. Through the preaching of the Word, we are promised grace and forgiveness. But not only this—Barth continues by affirming the presence of Christ not just in the Word but in the meal itself. Having "invited us to partake in the meal of reconciliation and love," says Barth, Jesus "doesn't want to promise us his love through words alone; he wants to give us certainty and security that in the meal Jesus Christ is amongst us, that his goodness is greater than our wickedness, and that his faithfulness is not undone by our unfaithfulness."[16]

We can hear in this language the sort of gospel message that Barth wished to convey to his parishioners. That is to say, while these "theses"

---

[12]"Lebenslauf," Markus Barth funeral booklet, 23-24.

[13]M. Barth, *Das Abendmahl: Passamahl, Bundesmahl, und Messiasmahl*, Theologische Studien 18 (Zürich: Evangelischer Verlag, 1945).

[14]M. Barth, "Thesen zur Auslegung des synoptischen Abendmahlsberichtes," 2. MBL. Series V, file 6.

[15]Barth, "Thesen zur Auslegung des synoptischen Abendmahlsberichtes," 2.

[16]Barth, "Thesen zur Auslegung des synoptischen Abendmahlsberichtes," 2.

emerged from Barth's scholarly exegetical engagement, it is evident that the main audience Barth had in mind in writing it was the local church community and not primarily the theological academy. That pastoral liturgical concerns were his chief concern becomes clear by the fact that the lecture, on which the article was based, was first delivered to Barth's fellow Reformed ministers in Basel.

A similarly expansive view of the eucharistic meal was outlined in a paper penned by Markus two years later for the journal *Kirchenfreund*. There he contends that the creation of community—specifically, of a *single* community—is "the content and meaning of the Lord's Supper."[17] In this, the church—as Christ's earthly embodiment in the present age—is radically different to any other institution. "It has as its goal, content and [measure of] success . . . the creation of a [community] that is different from all clubs and societies." Why, asks Barth? Because the "sharing and participation in this meal" is a uniting into one body of the "table companions of Jesus Christ," whose unifying characteristic—and that which marks them out from members of all other societies—is that "they support and serve one another."[18] Insofar as this is the purpose of the Lord's Supper, Markus insists that there are "political, social, and economic" consequences that follow.[19] In particular, racial and political divisions are healed, for in this meal *one* community is made out of "Jews and Arabs, white and black Americans, French and Germans, Communists and Christian Democrats."[20]

Christologically, this communal unification is grounded in the solidarity of Christ with humanity, to which the Lord's Supper testifies. Jesus, insists Barth, "not only came close to humanity, but became one with humanity." In his birth, Jesus "took flesh and blood. . . . He came close, he became *the same*, he became a brother [to us] so that [we] could become brothers

---

[17]M. Barth, "Gemeindeaufbau in biblischer Sicht," *Kirchenfreund: Blätter für biblisches Bekennen in der Kirche* 81, no. 6 (March 1947): 81.

[18]Barth, "Gemeindeaufbau in biblischer Sicht," 82.

[19]Barth, "Gemeindeaufbau in biblischer Sicht," 81.

[20]Barth, "Gemeindeaufbau in biblischer Sicht," 81. This political consequence was to become of ever-increasing importance for Barth, not least through his various exegeses of Paul's letter to the Ephesians.

[to each other]." That fellowship of Christ with humanity is expressed in the dominical meal "[b]ecause here, Jesus shares what is his own."[21]

Barth does not limit himself in this article to speaking only of this unifying, or "community building," purpose of the Lord's Supper, even though that emphasis is expressly highlighted in the article's title. He also enters debates about the sacramentality of Holy Communion. On one hand, the meal cannot simply be understood as a memorial for the dead (*Totengedächtnismahl*),[22] for that would celebrate the cross without also celebrating the resurrection. Nor, however, can it be claimed that there is anything of particular import in either the elements themselves (*der . . . Substanz des Bechers und des Brotes*), or in the liturgical actions and words of the minister (*des Handelns des Liturgen und die liturgischen Worte*). To place the emphasis on these would be to ignore that which Luther recovered, that is, the reception in faith of the eucharistic gifts.[23]

Of course, Barth does not deny the presence of Christ, and therefore also of grace, in the Lord's Supper. But his physical presence, insists Markus, is to be located in the "brother and sister who join in thanksgiving," that is, in the witness to forgiveness and justification, "which is evident in the peace and unity between brethren."[24] Barth thus concludes his article on the same generously inclusive note with which he starts. Insofar as fellowship at the Lord's Supper is a reception of harmonious community, forgiveness, and therefore *life*, he warns against "overzealous exclusions" from the eucharistic table. Fearfully closing off the Lord's Supper from others, indeed any manner of contempt for others (*Menschenverachtung*), is nothing other than a contradiction of the Supper itself.[25] In a final swipe at sacramentalist readings of Holy Communion, Barth reiterates his

---

[21]Barth, "Gemeindeaufbau in biblischer Sicht," 81.

[22]Barth, "Gemeindeaufbau in biblischer Sicht," 83.

[23]"Satisfactory exegesis of 1 Corinthians 10:16-17—the text on which the whole article is based—requires neither a flight into material mysticism (*dingliche Mystik*), superstitious belief in the efficacy of a cultic ritual, nor a retreat into an omniscient skepticism (*allwissende Skepsis*)." Barth, "Gemeindeaufbau in biblischer Sicht," 83.

[24]Barth, "Gemeindeaufbau in biblischer Sicht," 83.

[25]Barth, "Gemeindeaufbau in biblischer Sicht," 84. It is likely that Barth had in mind the sort of race-based exclusion that had been implemented within German Protestant churches following the adoption of the Aryan Paragraph in September 1933.

primary contention: to focus one's attention on "aesthetic, antiquarian or imaginative" interpretations of the Lord's Supper by attending to questions of eucharistic *Substanz*, or to the way in which the Supper is a repetitive absolution of individuals, or to "incidental" (*nebensächlicher*) manual actions, is to prioritize matters that are in fact entirely secondary—an emphasis that appears altogether odd when in the Supper Christ is really expected, redemption is celebrated, and human solidarity (*die Bruderschaft der Menschen*) is attested.[26] As a liturgical expression of this last point, Barth introduced an agape-style meal for the parishioners in Bubendorf, at which communion was celebrated around the dining table of the parish house.

Both of these articles on the Eucharist, written early in Barth's pastoral ministry and only two years apart, demonstrate what would become a dominant refrain throughout his career. While theological inquiry required a keen attention to detail and a commitment to the consistent witness of Scripture, it was just as important for Barth that, for the sake of its inner integrity, theology was done in the service of the church. It was entirely fitting, then, that two of his first academic publications spoke so clearly to the needs of the local Christian community. And it was this conviction that would later lead a disenchanted Barth away from the University of Chicago and back to a confessional seminary.

THE POLITICAL PASTOR

Confessing pastors and refugees in Bubendorf. While Markus appears to have moved into parish work more seamlessly than his father, there was nevertheless at least one aspect of Karl's pastoral ministry that Markus was determined to emulate, namely, a refusal to isolate political activism from parochial duties. We have already seen how closely Markus witnessed his father's involvement with the Confessing Church, including Karl's frustration with the Confessing pastors' reluctance to act politically. Markus's pastoral supervisor in Zurich, Paul Vogt, had also modeled for him a deeply political ministry, most notably though his establishment

[26]Barth, "Gemeindeaufbau in biblischer Sicht," 84.

of *Freiplatzaktion*, an organization that provided aid and relief to refugees fleeing Nazi-controlled territories.[27] And as has just been seen, even Markus's early explorations into eucharistic theology were not without their political implications. It should not be surprising, then, that Markus's own pastoral ministry was, from the outset, both socially and politically engaged.

Throughout the war, part of this activity involved meeting with visitors from Germany, many of whom were former students of Karl's from Bonn, and most of whom brought news from the Confessing Church. One such visitor was Dietrich Bonhoeffer who, on August 31, 1941, met with both Karl and Markus at Karl's home on the Bruderholzallee. The day was auspicious for a number of reasons. It was at this meeting that Bonhoeffer outlined his and the other conspirators' desire to secure international ecumenical support for a peace treaty between the Allied forces and Germany in the event of a successful *coup d'état*.[28] But this was also the day on which Karl was to become a grandfather for the fourth time.[29] Rose Marie was heavily pregnant with her first child, Peter, but was nonetheless determined to meet Bonhoeffer herself before going to the hospital. "My mother," recalls Peter, "wanted to participate [in the meeting] so I had to wait."[30] There were other visitors from Germany, too, of course—lesser known than Bonhoeffer, perhaps, but whose needs were just as desperate. Most significant among these was a family of German Jewish refugees—the Eisenstädts—who were sheltered by and lived with the Barths in Bubendorf until the end of the war.[31] In the meantime, the Barths' own family continued to grow in size: at the end of 1942,

[27]Founded in the fall of 1942, *Freiplatzaktion* housed approximately 1,700 refugees from Nazi-occupied territories, accommodating them free of charge in apartments or with host families.

[28]See V. Barnett, "Bonhoeffer and the Conspiracy," in *The Oxford Handbook of Dietrich Bonhoeffer*, ed. P. Ziegler and M. Mawson (Oxford: Oxford University Press, 2019), 69.

[29]Karl's three older grandchildren—the two daughters and one son of Franziska and Max Zellweger—were Sonja Elisabeth Zellweger (January 16, 1936–November 2, 2012); Ursula Zellweger (March 5, 1938–); and Max-Ueli Zellweger (April 7, 1941–). The fourth child in this branch of the family, Dieter Zellweger, was born June 21, 1947.

[30]Interview with Peter Barth, January 3, 2020.

[31]Interview with Peter Barth, January 3, 2020. Having escaped the Majdanek camp in mid-1942, Robert Eisenstädt and his pregnant fiancée Eva Müller crossed the border between Germany and Switzerland on February 21, 1943. They lived in Bubendorf until May 20, 1947, when they were granted visas to the US.

Rose Marie gave birth to their first daughter, Anna, with Ruth being born just eighteen days after the end of hostilities in Europe.[32]

Figure 3.1. Grandfather and grandson: Karl and young Peter in Bubendorf, 1942

Emissary to prisoners of war. Once the war was over, Markus was occupied with a very different sort of political activity. During the winter of 1946–1947, and with his youngest son less than six months old,[33] he worked as an emissary for the Ecumenical Commission for the Pastoral Care of Prisoners of War, visiting German POWs who were being held in camps throughout England and Scotland.[34] With almost 300,000 German prisoners remaining in England at the time,[35] Barth visited twenty-one of the sites in which they were being held, including Camp 174 in Norton, Nottinghamshire. Intriguingly, one of the inmates Barth may have encountered at Norton, although there is no record of it in his biography, was a young—and at this stage, still newly Christian—Jürgen Moltmann. Moltmann had been transferred to Norton from Kilmarnock, in Scotland,

[32]Peter Barth (August 31, 1941–); Anna Barth (December 27, 1942–); Ruth Barth (May 26, 1945–).

[33]Lukas Barth (August 18, 1946–May 11, 2018).

[34]Barth notes that, with the exception of his time in Scotland, the collaboration between the Ecumenical Commission and the YMCA—the latter of which was responsible for organizing the trip—proved disastrous. As a result of both an unexpected visit to London by Bishop Dibelius, which coincided with Barth's arrival, and the loss of a letter to the YMCA in the pre-Christmas rush, Barth's appearance in London was a "complete and unpleasant surprise" (*völlige und . . . unliebsame Ueberraschung*) to the local YMCA leader. There was no itinerary, and no car available. According to Barth, he had to arrange everything. "It can be concluded from these and other facts that future visits from the Ecumenical Commission would be better if the organization was not left exclusively to the YMCA." M. Barth, "Bei den deutschen Kriegsgefangenen in England: Bericht über die Reise von Pfr. Markus Barth über Weinachten/Neujahr 1946/47," 3-4. MBMC. Box SF36, file 3.

[35]Not all of these prisoners were held in POW camps, of which there were about three hundred. Some were housed in hostels, while some thousands lived with farming families, for whom they provided free labor. See Barth, "Bei den deutschen Kriegsgefangenen," 2.

in June 1946 and so would have been there at the time of Markus's visit. Unfortunately, if the two did meet, it was evidently not momentous enough for either to have remarked upon it.[36]

Table 1. List of British internment camps visited by Barth during the winter of 1946–1947

Camp name	Camp number	Location
	Camp 16	Longniddry, East Lothian
Featherstone Park	Camp 18	Haltwhistle, Northumberland
Hostel Pellmellor	Sub-camp 18	Haltwhistle, Northumberland
	Camp 69	Darras Hill, Northumberland
	Camp 76	Calthwaite, Cumberland
Hostel Brampton	Sub-camp 76	Calthwaite, Cumberland
	Camp 103	Cockermouth, Cumberland
	Camp 104	Milnthorp, Westmorland
Hostel Silecroft	Sub-camp 104	Cumberland
Braham Castle	Camp 109	Dingwall, Ross-shire
Hostel Fearn	Sub-camp 109	Ross-shire
Hostel Kilburn	Sub-camp 122	Brondesbury Park
	Camp 123	Kirknewton, Midlothian
Hostel Sighthill	Sub-camp 123	Kirknewton, Midlothian
Hostel Woodhouse Lee	Sub-camp 123	Edinburgh
	Camp 165	Watten, Caithness
	Camp 174	Norton, Nottinghamshire
Hostel Ravensbourne	Sub-camp 237	Chiselhurst, Kent
Military and Provisional Hospital		Inverness
	Camp 300	Wilton Park, Buckinghamshire
Shotover House	Camp 687	Wheatley, Oxfordshire

Primarily charged with assessing the suitability of the prisoners' conditions, Barth was determined not only to observe the camps but "to a certain extent also to work in [them]" as something of a spiritual adviser to the inmates—and this not simply to those who intentionally sought spiritual

[36]In his autobiography, Moltmann mentions K-L Schmidt, Fritz Blanke, and Anders Nygren, but not Barth. Of course, Barth was there as a pastoral emissary and had not yet even begun his academic career, let alone made his name in it. See J. Moltmann, *A Broad Place: An Autobiography*, trans. M. Kohl (London: SCM, 2007), 32.

care but to all of them.[37] As he noted in a letter to some of the German prisoners, "If there is one thing that has dawned on me during this journey, it is that a pastor needs to be there for all the neighbors . . . and that he should try to offer something to everyone, in a form that is tolerable to everyone. The beautiful service on Sunday morning and also the Bible study is perhaps not all that can and may happen there."[38]

Barth's counsel, however, was not limited merely to the inmates' spiritual care. At least in this letter from early 1947, he crossed over into the more politically fraught question of where the German POWs should live after their repatriation to a now-divided Germany. Urging them to "learn Russian, for God's sake," and to avoid the Western sloganeering about communist threats, he advised them to "think about it and decide for yourself whether you don't want to dare to start all over again and not just look back to the old, familiar bourgeois system." Something, he surmised with particular regard to the church, "is about to break out in the Russian zone, which seems to me to be more promising than all the bishops and liturgies in West Germany."[39]

As for Barth's hopes that he might be of spiritual assistance to the inmates, perhaps he was overly optimistic. In any event, in this endeavor he found himself frustrated. For a start, he was rushed from one place to the next, sometimes having only one or two hours in any camp. As he was to complain later, "It is simply not enough to address the prisoners in a lecture. . . . It is far more beneficial when a camp sets aside at least 24 hours, so that you don't have to think about the onward journey from the moment you arrive."[40] Official regulations also hampered his efforts to do anything more than record his observations, as the visitor's permit issued to him by the War Office stipulated that he leave each camp no later than 10:00 p.m. This, he said, was detrimental to genuine companionship and conversation with the prisoners, because deep conversations and genuine friendship

---

[37]Barth, "Bei den deutschen Kriegsgefangenen," 1.

[38]M. Barth to unnamed inmate recipients, February 5, 1947, 1. MBL. Series I. Box 30.

[39]Barth to unnamed inmate recipients, February 5, 1947, 2.

[40]"Es hat sich als vorteilhaft erwiesen, wenn pro Lager mindestens ein Zeitraum von 24 Stunden zur Verfügung stand, und wenn man bei der Ankunft nicht schon an die Weiterreise denken musste." Barth, "Bei den deutschen Kriegsgefangenen," 3.

were impossible to cultivate when the visitor was able to leave the camp in the evening for a warm bed and running water.[41]

It was clear that Barth was also dissatisfied with the attitude of the YMCA staff who ran the camp activities. As far as he could observe, most were content to limit their involvement to the sale of sports equipment and playing cards, while those few who did want to provide more robust opportunities for the prisoners distrusted Barth's motives for visiting. Moreover, he was concerned to find that many of the camp commandants were similarly dissatisfied with the degree of pastoral care that the YMCA was providing. "They do nothing but sell footballs," complained one colonel to Barth. "Where is the spiritual help we want?"[42]

The commandants themselves, however, came in for far greater praise. While he was not aware of any who understood or spoke German, Barth was nonetheless convinced that the majority had been carefully selected and were well suited to their roles. "A striking number" of them were (or at least professed to be) Christians, and generally spoke well to their prisoners. Indeed, Barth could think of only one commandant who was—quite justifiably, in Barth's opinion—truly hated by his German inmates.[43]

One aspect of camp life of which Barth was especially critical was the program of denazification that was being undertaken throughout the camp network. "The task . . . is so difficult that it cannot be carried out without mistakes being made." It was no wonder, he reported, that the aspect of life in the prison camps which made "almost everyone who still remains in captivity foam with rage" (*in höchster Wut schäumen kann*) was the Political Intelligence Department that was responsible for the prisoners' re-education.[44]

Barth encountered difficulties with one PID officer in particular. After having held a discussion with some inmates at Featherstone Park Camp, he

[41]Barth, "Bei den deutschen Kriegsgefangenen," 3.

[42]Barth, "Bei den deutschen Kriegsgefangenen," 4.

[43]Barth, "Bei den deutschen Kriegsgefangenen," 4.

[44]Barth, "Bei den deutschen Kriegsgefangenen," 6. On September 18, 1944, Winston Churchill's War Cabinet decided that the denazification and re-education of captured German soldiers would be handled by the Political Warfare Executive, in close cooperation with the Political Intelligence Department (PID) of the Foreign Office. For an account of the establishment of the PID, and the difficulties with which it was faced, see R. Mayne, *In Victory, Magnanimity, in Peace, Goodwill: A History of Wilton Park* (London: Frank Cass, 2003), 1-11.

was taken to task by the local PID representative—Captain Herbert Sulzbach[45]—who had taken offense at the content of Barth's lecture. Sulzbach served Barth with a formal warning, advised the War Office that Barth's credentials should be rescinded, and demanded that he be banned in future from speaking to the prisoners. According to Sulzbach, Barth had, in the space of just one evening, destroyed half a year's worth of the PID's re-educational work in the camp.[46] In his own report of the occasion, Sulzbach described Barth's lecture as "well meant, yet dangerous." By "ridiculing our Grading system"—that is, the categories into which Germans were placed to determine the extent of denazification they were deemed to need—"sneering at our administration," and (in Sulzbach's opinion) equating the French Sureté with the Gestapo, Barth was guilty of minimizing the Nazis' crimes. Barth, complained Sulzbach, "has no idea of German mentality," and the POWs who listened to him would no doubt have "left the lecture convinced that the German people still are the best."[47]

Thankfully, Barth got on much better with the camp's commandant—Lieutenant-Colonel H. McBain, of the Durham Light Infantry—who took him "under his full protection." Quite contrary to Sulzbach's animosity, McBain urged Barth to use his ecumenical contacts and send to the camp

---

[45]Capt. Herbert Sulzbach (1894–1985) was born into a wealthy German Jewish family in Frankfurt-am-Main. At the outbreak of World War I, he volunteered for military service, and on August 8, 1914 joined the 63rd (Frankfurt) Field Artillery Regiment. He was awarded the Iron Cross (2nd Class) for his role in the Battle of the Somme, and then the Iron Cross (1st Class) following the Battle of Villers-Cotteret in 1918. At the end of the war, he was awarded the *Front-Kämpfer Ehrenkreuz*. In 1938, as the Nazis' persecution of German Jews intensified, Sulzbach fled to England with his wife, Beate, where in 1939 he was imprisoned on the Isle of Man as an "enemy alien." In 1940, Sulzbach volunteered for, and was accepted into, the Auxiliary Military Pioneer Corps, rising from the rank of private to that of captain. For much of the Second World War, Sulzbach built and guarded defenses against an expected German invasion. In 1944, with an increasing number of German soldiers being captured, he was transferred to the Interpreters' Pool and posted to the POW camp in Comrie, Scotland. He also served at the Droitwich and Featherstone Park camps, where he was responsible for the "re-education" program for German Army officers. It was during this time that he encountered Markus Barth. Sulzbach was demobbed from the British Army in 1948 and, in 1982, awarded the OBE for services to Anglo-German reconciliation. The hostility between Sulzbach and Barth seems to have been unusual. According to most accounts, Sulzbach was almost universally liked, by both the German prisoners and his English colleagues. See A. Hepburn, "Reconciliation and the Work of Herbert Sulzbach," *Kirchliche Zeitgeschichte* 25, no. 1 (2012): 180-95.

[46]Barth, "Bei den deutschen Kriegsgefangenen," 7.

[47]H. Sulzbach, "Report on a Lecture by Pfarrer Barth," December 20, 1946. MBMC. Box SF36, file 3.

"a really spiritual man" for the provision of spiritual counsel to the prisoners.[48] McBain's wish to offer pastoral care to the prisoners in his charge was evidently serious: in early 1947, he commissioned a church to be built on the grounds of the camp—a Nissen hut, with mock-Bavarian frontage—which was consecrated by the bishop of Newcastle on April 21, 1947.

THE DISSERTATION DEBATE

Once his work for the Ecumenical Commission concluded in the spring of 1947, Barth was able to concentrate on a different sort of project. After seven years of study, he was awarded his doctorate by the University of Göttingen, for a thesis titled "Der Augenzeuge: Eine Untersuchung über die Wahrnehmung des Menschensohnes durch die Apostel."[49] This academic success had not come without controversy. Initially hoping to submit his dissertation to the University of Basel in 1945, where his father was still teaching, Markus had been somewhat unceremoniously turned away. On March 26, 1945, Markus had met with the dean of the faculty of theology—the noted New Testament scholar, Karl Ludwig Schmidt, whom Markus had first met in Aarau in 1937, and who had since become his *Doktorvater*—and had come away from the meeting feeling encouraged about the prospects for his doctoral studies.[50] By June of the same year, however, Schmidt was equivocating. "Dear pastor, today it turned out that our Faculty is unable to hold oral doctoral examinations for you this semester."[51]

---

[48]Barth, "Bei den deutschen Kriegsgefangenen," 7. Barth evidently sent a copy of his report of his camps tour to McBain but, concerned that it might cause even more offense, requested that McBain not share it with Sulzbach. "[We] did not get on too well, as you may remember . . . [and] it would be a pity if my record would be a hindrance to further [pastoral] visits in the camp from abroad." M. Barth to Lt.-Col. H. McBain, April 1, 1947, document D/DLI7/426/89, Durham County Record Office.

[49]Markus's brother, Christoph, also completed his doctorate in Basel in the same year. His dissertation was supervised by the Old Testament scholar Walter Baumgartner (1887–1970) on the topic "Die Errettung vom Tode in der individuellen Klage- und Dankliedern des Altern Testaments." After being awarded his doctorate, Christoph went to Indonesia where he taught theology. There he met and married the theologian and missionary Marie-Claire Frommel (February 20, 1927–December 22, 2019).

[50]"Based on our meeting, which you kindly enabled . . . I hereby request of you that I be admitted to the doctoral examinations in the Faculty of Theology." M. Barth to K. L. Schmidt, April 3, 1945. MBMC. Subject Correspondence 4. Box 8.

[51]K. L. Schmidt to M. Barth, June 26, 1945. MBMC. Subject Correspondence 4. Box 8.

The problems were more complex than simply finding a suitable time for the exams. As Markus himself acknowledged, "I see that the Faculty of Theology cannot accept my dissertation without such methodological and material revisions as would completely change the nature and purpose of the work. . . . I hereby withdraw my application to be admitted to the doctorate."[52] He did not, though, put the thesis aside entirely. In November, Schmidt wrote to Markus advising him that he had become aware, through an advertisement from Evangelische Verlag Zollikon, that Barth was planning to publish his dissertation as a monograph in early 1946. Barth was told in no uncertain terms that if he wished his dissertation still to be considered for a doctoral degree, he would need to withdraw the publication.

But why was Markus still constrained by the university's regulations when he had already withdrawn his application for the doctorate? The answer comes from the dean of the faculty himself, who informed Markus that, despite Markus's request, his dissertation had not been formally withdrawn from consideration. "I let your dissertation continue to circulate in order to give you the chance . . . to gain admission to our faculty, that at times you have tried to force." Schmidt was clear, however, that Markus himself had now sabotaged those plans. "Your actions [in seeking publication] have now destroyed that opportunity."[53] Clearly unimpressed that Markus had "thought it right" to involve his father in the dispute, especially given that Karl had on more than one occasion been critical of Schmidt's deanship, he warned Markus that any attempt "to allow 'Die Augenzeugen' to see the light of day" would be regarded by the faculty as an act of inconsiderate recklessness [*Rücksichtslosigkeit*] that would be repaired only if Markus withdrew his thesis from publication and allowed it to be examined through the regular process.[54]

---

[52]M. Barth to K. L. Schmidt, June 29, 1945. MBMC. Subject Correspondence 4. Box 8.

[53]K. L. Schmidt to M. Barth, November 20, 1945. MBMC. Subject Correspondence 4. Box 8.

[54]K. L. Schmidt to M. Barth, November 20, 1945. Karl Barth and Schmidt had long had a tumultuous relationship. In the wake of Barth's famous Tambach lecture in 1919, Schmidt had been one of those who had compared him to the heretic Marcion, whereas during the years of the *Kirchenkampf*, the two had found themselves at least politically on the same side. In 1941, by which time they were both in Basel, Barth wrote to Schmidt noting, rightly, that "over the years our relationship has swung from one pole to another." Schmidt's deanship, and his handling of

Markus's response to the dean was to raise the possibility of legal action.[55] Schmidt, though, was not deterred, and indeed responded with his own warning. "It does not seem to me, [or] to any of the colleagues who submitted a written vote on your dissertation, that you would want to let the so-called legal situation prevail, after you have first violated it in so many different ways." If Markus was determined to take that action, then, said Schmidt, he should be aware of a number of facts.

First, the dean noted that Markus had sought to involve his father in the debate, whose own evident conflict of interest should by rights have excluded him from participation. Second, Schmidt accused Markus of repeatedly trying to intimidate him with "shocking invectives" (*ungeheuerliche Invektiven*)—by telephone, in the corridor outside the lecture theater, and even in the dean's own study. "Based on my considerable experience, I can only say that your behavior has been without parallel [*analogielos*]." Third, Markus was guilty of unwarranted academic arrogance. "You submitted a dissertation for assessment by our faculty, and now you don't know what else to do other than rant and rage when it isn't accepted as is." As Schmidt wrote to Karl on July 1: "Your eldest son seems to me like a child who has handed over his favorite doll to be fixed, and then gets angry when it is returned—repaired—but looking a bit different. 'No, I want my dear old doll!' Oh, this [behavior] has been going on for years."[56]

The conflict spilled over into the entire faculty. At one stage, Schmidt reprimanded his colleagues for their "unparliamentary behavior" (*unparlamentarischen Verhaltens*) during a meeting at which the case was discussed—an accusation at which Thurneysen, who was by then teaching practical theology at the University of Basel, took offense. At the meeting in question, he said, "The necessary objectivity and gravitas were lacking." Instead of dealing with the formal issue—that is, that the dissertation had already gone to press, which ordinarily would have happened only after its

Markus's case, was the occasion of another blip in their long-standing relationship. See K. Barth to K. L. Schmidt, February 4, 1941. Cited in Busch, *Karl Barth*, 201.

[55]M. Barth to K. L. Schmidt, November 24, 1945. MBMC. Subject Correspondence 4. Box 8.

[56]K. L. Schmidt to K. Barth, July 1, 1945. Cited in K. L. Schmidt to M. Barth, November 24, 1945. MBMC. Subject Correspondence 4. Box 8.

examination and acceptance for the doctorate—the meeting "slipped into a material discussion about the value or unworthiness of the work." Thurneysen complained that while nothing approaching an objective, factual assessment of the thesis was undertaken, there were nonetheless claims made about its alleged "horrific mistakes" (*entsetzliche Fehler*), with the result being "an overall clear and unanimous condemnation of the [dissertation]."[57]

Unsurprisingly, perhaps, Thurneysen himself had a completely different view. Reminding Schmidt that some readers of the thesis had found it to contain "brilliant insights," he argued that, at least in his opinion, the dissertation was "not entirely unworthy" of sitting alongside the exegetical work of people like Wilhelm Vischer and Karl Barth. But Thurneysen went further, surmising that Markus was being judged, as it were, guilty by his association with Vischer and Barth. His work was certainly following along similar lines as theirs, and thus, argued Thurneysen, the major flaw in Markus's thesis was that its author consistently drew out exegetical conclusions on the basis of rigorous historical-critical method that he had learned from those two older scholars. His colleagues who wished to condemn the thesis were doing so simply because they did not share Markus's (or, therefore, Wilhelm Vischer's and Karl Barth's) hermeneutical presuppositions. "I suspect that it was precisely here—in the exegetical details, and the opinions and interpretations arrived at by Pastor Barth—that [the dissertation's] readers found themselves unable to agree, and thus came to negative and unfavorable judgments about the work as a whole."[58]

Needless to say, the whole episode was painfully divisive among the faculty members themselves, as well as casting Markus, perhaps unfairly, in a very poor light. Regardless of, as Thurneysen put it, the worth or unworthiness of the dissertation, Markus's own actions and attitudes had provoked considerable antagonism toward him. It therefore represented something of a reconciliation when, in 1973, he was able to return to the same faculty as a full professor.

---

[57]E. Thurneysen to K. L. Schmidt, November 30, 1945. MBMC. Subject Correspondence 4. Box 8.
[58]E. Thurneysen to K. L. Schmidt, November 30, 1945.

Nevertheless, debates over his doctoral dissertation did not prevent Markus from engaging in wider academic scholarship. In June 1949, he wrote an article on the high priestly ministry of Jesus as portrayed in the letter to the Hebrews.[59]

PARISH TENSIONS

Meanwhile, Markus and Rose Marie's ministry in Bubendorf continued, at least for most of their parishioners, to thrive. The family home was certainly a happy and vibrant place. Frieda Handschin, a sixteen-year-old girl who began working with the Barths in 1948 as a live-in maid (*Haustochter*), recalled them as being "a very loving family [in which] the children always came first." Music, she remembered, was an ever-present joy. "The cello was often played. We also sang a lot, led by Markus . . . on the piano." It was also, and hardly surprisingly, a house full of visitors and lively conversation. There were "many visits from German theologians. . . . But things really got going when 'Dr. Babbe' professor Karl Barth came to visit. Then there was discussion for nights on end, literally about everything under the sun [*über Gott und die Welt*]. Unfortunately, his visits were always very short." Handschin would later recall her eighteen months in Bubendorf as "a beautiful and exemplary time," the credit for which went most particularly to Markus and Rose Marie.[60]

And yet, not quite everyone shared such a positive view of the Barths' work. In March 1950, Dr. Georg Stutz, a leading psychiatrist in the Basel region and one of Barth's parishioners,[61] wrote to President Hug of the church directorate complaining that Barth's sermons were driving people away. "One cannot accept the present pastor's beliefs and customs. His sermons are often incomprehensible, and over our heads [*zu hoch*]." Stutz's

---

[59]M. Barth, "Jesus Christus, der grosse Hohepriester des neuen Bundes," in *Der Kirchenfreund: Blätter für biblisches Bekennen in der Kirche* 83, no. 6 (June 1949): 145-50.

[60]F. Stalder-Handschin, "Errinerungen an meinen Aufenthalt im Pfarrhaus Bubendorf in den Jahren 1948-49," 2008. MBL. Series II. Box 1.

[61]Gustav Georg Stutz (1897–1961) studied medicine in Geneva, Basel, and Zürich. After completing his doctorate in 1924, he undertook further training in psychiatry and somatic medicine. In 1926, he was appointed senior physician (*Chefartz*) at the Psychiatric Polyclinic Friedmatt in Basel. Then, in 1932, he moved to Liestal to take up the post of chief physician and head of the Hasenbühl Psychiatric Clinic.

Figure 3.2. Karl and Markus riding in Bubendorf, 1945

Figure 3.3. Markus and Karl at the parsonage in Bubendorf, 1950

unusual suggestion was that perhaps some money could be found to finance a car club to transport parishioners to alternative church services in neighboring Liestal or Ziefen.[62]

That Markus's ministry was—and had, since Edinburgh, been intended to be—one he shared with Rose Marie was also a source of both mutual inspiration and concern. When Markus began a weekly Bible study group for the parish's men, for example, Rose Marie decided—together with her friend, Hedy Frey-Feldmann—to start a similar group for the women. Urging them to broaden their horizons beyond their own domestic circumstances, she encouraged the women of the town to get together regularly for wide-ranging discussions on church issues, theology, and political events throughout the wider world. Well-known speakers from around the country—including the feminist theologian and peace activist Marga Bürig, renowned (and controversial) travel writer René Gardi, and Carl Stemmler[63]—were occasionally invited to address the group on matters of contemporary interest. It is, perhaps, not surprising that these women's discussion evenings were met by some of the men with suspicion and even outright opposition.[64] Nor is it surprising that with at least some people openly distrustful of the Barths, Rose Marie herself felt exposed. In 1953, after having left Switzerland, she recounted to an American church group that "in the village of Bubendorf (where I [was] a minister's wife [for] 13 years) people watched my passing from behind their

[62]G. Stutz to W. Hug, March 23, 1950. MBMC. Subject Correspondence 4. Box 8.

[63]A. Häner-Frey, "Erinnerungen." Marga Bürig (1915–2002), having written her doctorate on the German dramatist, Friedrich Hebbel, converted to Protestantism but never studied theology formally. In 1947 she founded the Swiss Evangelical Women's Association and, in the 1950s, became one of the leading women's voices in world ecumenism. René Gardi (1909–2000) worked particularly in Africa and, through his books and films, helped shape twentieth century Swiss attitudes to Western African culture and architecture. In more recent years, his paternalistic—indeed, racist—views have been subjected to intense criticism, not least through Mischa Hedinger's 2019 documentary, *African Mirror*. Indeed, given how attuned the Barths were to racism, it is odd that they allowed him to speak at one of the mothers' evenings. Their decision to do so is even stranger—and, one would have to say, profoundly unwise—in light of Gardi's conviction in 1944 for the sexual abuse of students while he was a teacher in the Bernese town of Brügg. As for Carl Stemmler, it is unclear from Häner-Frey's recollections which one it was who spoke to the women's meeting in Bubendorf. It could have been either the conservationist and animal-rights activist (1882–1971), or the zoologist and politician of the same name (1904–1987).

[64]A. Häner-Frey, "Erinnerungen."

Figure 3.4. The Bubendorf parsonage

window-curtains and I always felt observed and judged by some mysterious village-law."[65]

It was not only the Barths' encouragement of their parishioners to think broadly and boldly that provoked dissent. It was, for some, the very fact that theirs was a *shared* ministry. Again, it was Georg Stutz who took particular offense. That Markus and Rose Marie worked together in ministry was, he believed, an inappropriate blurring of professional boundaries. "There is insufficient trust in the pastor's personality. . . . [He] mixes too much and too intensely in his parishioners' private lives, and then tells everything to his wife." As a result, said Stutz, the people of the Bubendorf parish were turning to him for help, rather than to the church.[66]

It is quite possible that the concerns raised by Stutz over Barth's ministry were more to do with professional territoriality than with any widespread disquiet over Markus's pastoral work. Certainly, there is little to no evidence outside Stutz's complaints that Barth's duties as a minister were received with anything other than gratitude. Nonetheless, the middle months of 1950 did witness a deepening of the conflict between

[65]R. M. Barth, "America, with the Eyes of a Greenhorn," address delivered to the Women's Association of the Presbyterian Church in Dubuque, April 30, 1953, 4.

[66]G. Stutz to W. Hug, March 23, 1950. MBMC. Subject Correspondence 4. Box 8.

Stutz and Barth. Not only did Stutz feel that Markus was "over-sharing" pastoral details with Rose Marie, he also believed that the two were actively meddling in some of his medical cases. "I think it is advisable if everyone sticks to their own professional responsibilities. . . . It is hopelessly *auf dem Strich* when untrustworthy people interfere in my business."[67] A brief holiday in France with his father in April 1950 provided Barth with a much-needed respite from the parochial tensions but did not resolve them.[68] In June, Stutz lodged a formal complaint with the church authorities, contending that Barth was not merely disrupting his work but indeed "sabotaging" [*sabotieren*] it. Both Markus and Rose Marie had, he claimed, insulted one of his employees over the telephone, sought to disguise their "indecent interference" [*unanständige Einmischung*] with "Christian phrases," and were attempting to destroy his work in a number of the institutions of which he was in charge. "I would like this pastor, who is desperate for validation [*geltungssüchtige*], and his wife to be expressly forbidden to interfere in [my] care of the mentally ill that I have built up over the past 18 years."[69]

Barth was stung by these accusations, and not surprisingly felt compelled as a consequence to reassert his authority over the parish. In November 1950, he penned a pastoral letter to "all the married men of Bubendorf and Ramlingsberg," in which his frustrations overflowed.

---

[67]G. Stutz to M. Barth, March 30, 1950. MBMC. Subject Correspondence 4. Box 8. The phrase "*auf dem Strich*" is ambiguous. It could simply mean something like "on the brink," or "close to the line"—implying that Stutz thought Markus was venturing into areas of professional service for which he was unqualified. However, the phrase can also be translated loosely as "on the game," or "on the streets," in which case Stutz may have been wishing to imply that Barth's actions were not just unprofessional, but indeed, in some sense, immoral. It is worth noting that, according to Markus's daughter Ruth—herself a psychologist—Markus had for some time a blind spot when it came to the value and efficacy of the psychological sciences. That changed in the last few months of his life, when he spoke regularly with his neighbor, the renowned Sicilian psychotherapist Gaetano Benedetti (1920–2013), with whom he shared theological conversations. Personal correspondence with the Barth children, April 12, 2023.

[68]From April 10 to 17, Karl and Markus traveled through Burgundy, the Loire, and across to the Atlantic coast, enjoying "the excellent food and wine which this country offers, eating crabs large and small, oysters and snails." K. Barth to C. Barth, May 7, 1950, in Busch, *Karl Barth*, 369. See also *Karl Barth—Rudolf Bultmann Briefwechsel 1911–1966*, ed. B. Jaspert (Zurich: TVZ, 1994), 231n504. Note that Karl and Markus were accompanied on this trip by Rose Marie, Charlotte von Kirschbaum, and Arthur Frey.

[69]G. Stutz to the Kirchendirektion des Kantons Baselland, June 1, 1950. MBMC. Subject Correspondence 4. Box 8.

Figure 3.5. Holidaying in France, 1950. Markus, Karl, Rose Marie

Lamenting that he had "been preaching to empty pews for ten years now,"[70] Barth upbraided the towns' men for neglecting their duty as the spiritual heads of their households. Preempting and rejecting the objection that the men were too busy at work to attend to religious duties, he reminded them that "ours is not the first generation to work hard. Our fathers accomplished enormous things, but also listened regularly to God's word—and neither they nor their children regretted it, nor suffered from it. Quite the contrary!" Barth's exasperation culminated in a challenge to his male parishioners to take more seriously their responsibility "not only for the physical but also for the spiritual flourishing [*Gedeihen*]" of their families, and to set for them an example not only by their words, but also by their actions [*auch mit Taten und mit dem Beispiel*]."[71]

There is no record of how well or badly Barth's letter was received by its recipients. There seems little doubt, though, that the unmistakable frustration expressed within it was in fact occasioned only in part by Bubendorf and Ramlingsberg's married men. No matter how exasperated

[70]M. Barth, circular letter, "To the Married Men of Bubendorf and Ramlingsberg," November 16, 1950. MBL. Series I. Box 35.

[71]Barth, circular letter, November 16, 1950.

Figure 3.6. Markus and Rose Marie in Bubendorf

with them Barth may have been, the letter was likely also the venting of his irritation at Stutz, with whom he had been in conflict for the entire year. Thankfully, however, 1950 ended up on a much happier note. In early December, Rose Marie and Markus welcomed their fifth child, Rose-Marie, into the family.[72]

THE "BAPTISM BOOK": UPENDING KARL

At the start of 1951, Markus published his second major monograph, *Die Taufe—Ein Sakrament?*[73] While the book went largely unnoticed by most of the academic theological world, it was not ignored by Markus's father. Indeed, the new study was to have major implications for Karl's

[72]Rose-Marie Barth (December 3, 1950–). To avoid confusion in what follows, readers are invited to note the similarity of name between mother and (youngest) daughter, with a hyphen being the only difference: Rose Marie (mother), and Rose-Marie (daughter).

[73]M. Barth, *Die Taufe—Ein Sakrament? Ein exegetischer Beitrag zum Gespräch über die kirchlicher Taufe* (Zurich: Evangelischer Verlag, 1951). Arthur Cochrane, who was soon to be a colleague of Markus's in Dubuque, was one of the few English-speaking theologians to take the book seriously. "I would hail it," he said to Markus in 1956, "not only as the first book to say anything original about baptism, but as pointing us in the true direction that the doctrine of the church should take." A. C. Cochrane to M. Barth, February 3, 1956. MBL. Series I. Box 31.

own understanding of baptism. Having already engaged with similar issues in 1943,[74] Karl was persuaded by Markus's book to completely rework his earlier, more sacramental understanding of baptism. So profound was Markus's influence on this aspect of his father's late theology that when Karl returned to the topic again toward the end of his life, his final theology of baptism "left not one stone upon another" of its earlier iteration.[75] David MacLachlan has gone so far as to say that the change in Karl's thinking on this matter—occasioned by his son's work—is comparable in magnitude, if not in broader influence, to the changes that took place in Karl's theology between the two editions of his Romans commentary.[76]

So, what of Markus's argument? Building his case on close textual analysis of every New Testament passage that deals with baptism, he contended that the Christian rite can be—and must be—understood primarily in those scriptural terms themselves. The meaning of baptism, argued Barth, is not to be found in any precursive Jewish ritual, nor in the many and various analogies from pagan mystery cults but in the unified and harmonious teaching about it that is supplied by the New Testament itself. "Nothing but conceptual confusion would be attained if one compared [baptism] to a Greek mystery or a Jewish rite."[77]

On the basis of this exegetical study, Barth proceeded to reject the legitimacy of baptismal sacramentality. In responding to the rhetorical question posed by the title of his book, he offered an unequivocal no to any suggestion that baptism is a means of grace. In doing so, Barth was arguing against the grain of his Reformed contemporaries. Lamenting the capitulation of modern Protestant scholarship to the presumed

---

[74]K. Barth, *The Teaching of the Church Regarding Baptism*, trans. E. Payne (London: SCM, 1948).

[75]*CD* IV/4, x, 46. David MacLachlan argues that one reason why Markus may have thought his father's 1943 discussion of baptism needed repair was its lack of sustained biblical exegesis. D. MacLachlan, "Like Son, Like Father: Reflections on the Influence of Markus Barth on Karl Barth's Thinking about Baptism," *Journal of Reformed Theology* 14, no. 3 (2020): 190. Curiously, in a later letter to his father, Markus apologized to Karl "for once saying that not one stone from your baptismal book is left unturned. You know," he said, "that that [comment] was more about the remnants of the Calvinist-Augustinian view of the sacraments than about yourself." M. Barth to K. Barth, April 10, 1960. MBL. Series V, file 4.

[76]MacLachlan, "Like Son, like Father," 184.

[77]Barth, *Die Taufe*, 101.

normativity of Roman Catholic baptismal doctrine,[78] Barth instead maintained that the only event that can rightly be considered a sacrament is the death and resurrection of Jesus. Rather than baptism effecting what it indicates, it instead indicates what has already been effected in the free work of God in Christ.

The second and subsequent target against which Barth took aim was the theology and practice of infant baptism. This is hardly surprising in light of his having already prosecuted the case against baptismal sacramentality. Insofar as baptism "is no arbitrary and automatic act of worship, but is voluntary and conscious," said Barth, any baptism that is administered "without awareness, faith and willingness on the part of the baptized and the baptizer . . . is as unthinkable as Jesus' baptism would have been without his will and consent, and without the obedience of John the Baptist."[79]

Barth's book, with its vehement rejection of there being any New Testament basis for the practice of infant baptism, was at odds with his Reformed tradition and, at least according to one commentator, possibly even cost him employment in a Swiss university.[80] Aside from being ecclesiastically provocative, the study received mixed reviews. The well-known American Baptist historian Norman Maring perhaps predictably described it as an "even more formidable" assault upon infant baptism than that waged by Karl.[81] McCormick Theological Seminary's Floyd Filson, on the other hand—though appreciative of its "thoroughgoing exege[sis]"—thought it "too long and heavy," and with a tendency to draw overly fine

[78]Barth, *Die Taufe*, 365. Barth cites the Catholic theologian Rudolf Schnackenburg (1914–2002) as having recognized the return of Protestant teachings on baptism to their place of nativity in Roman sacramental theology.

[79]Barth, *Die Taufe*, 315. Two years later, in response to a reader of the book who asked why, if baptism is devoid of any representative significance or sacramental efficacy, it is a necessary part of a Christian's response to Christ, Barth answered: "The baptism is 'of value' to our personal response to Christ, because Christ ordered it to belong to our response. So, it is [Christ's] institution of baptism . . . and not a significance of its own, that makes the baptism necessary. If you ask: why did Christ institute just baptism, then I think we have to answer: because he wanted to make it clear, that obedience and faith in him is not an affair of private life and invisible decision only, but is much more: of public confession—with the specific character of an act of repentance." M. Barth to E. Stuckenbruck, May 15, 1953. MBMC. Subject Correspondence 1. Box 5.

[80]N. Maring, "Is Baptism a Sacrament? Review of *Die Taufe—Ein Sakrament?*," *Foundations* (January 1960): 74.

[81]Maring, "Is Baptism a Sacrament?" 74.

distinctions.[82] Perhaps its length was one reason why it was overlooked for so long by so much of the academy. In any event, Markus's book did two things. First, insofar as it persuaded Karl to revise his earlier views, it served to secure Markus's place as a serious theologian in his own right. Second, it was likely one of the main reasons why, two years after its publication, Markus found himself appointed to a New Testament professorship in the United States.

A CHURCH CONSTITUTION?

In addition to the development of his own academic work, Markus spent the latter part of 1951 involving himself in the wider politics of the Swiss church. At issue was the question of whether the Evangelical Reformed Church in the canton of Baselland should have its own constitution and, if so, how it should be drafted and what it should contain.[83] For his part, Barth was adamant that the church had no need to fear either a constitution or a public debate about it. "The church itself is a public matter" (*eine öffentliche Angelegenheit*), he insisted, and so discussions about its proper ordering were properly held in the open.[84] He was equally adamant that the church needed a constitution as an "important and urgent" priority. "A church that has no constitution is sloppy and disorderly. Everyone does, and thinks, and says whatever suits them. The much-vaunted freedom of conscience becomes a cloak for willfulness, unbelief, tyranny, and hollowness."[85]

---

[82]F. Filson, "Review of *Die Taufe—Ein Sakrament?*" *Theology Today* 10, no. 1 (April 1953): 130-31.

[83]Since the separation of the Canton of Basel from Basel-stadt in August 1833, the Reformed Church in Baselland had had no formal constitution of its own. Rather, individual laws and regulations were approved as necessary by the civic authorities. While the church had not, by and large, been negatively impacted by that arrangement, there had since the 1930s been increasingly loud calls for the conclusion of a separate church constitution to bring the ecclesial polity of Baselland into greater alignment with the other Swiss cantons. There had been two votes—in 1943 and 1946—by which amendments to section 32 of the state constitution had been approved, and a further vote by the Baselland's district administrator (*Landrat*) on April 3, 1950, which enabled the various churches in the canton to organize their own affairs. It was at this point that a constitutional council was appointed to consult and then draft a new constitution for Baselland's Evangelical Reformed Church—and it was into these discussions that Markus Barth put forward his views.

[84]M. Barth, "Um eine Verfassung der Reformierte Kirche in Baselland," *Reformierte Kirchenzeitung* 17/18, September 1, 1951, 330.

[85]Barth, "Um eine Verfassung der Reformierte Kirche in Baselland," 330.

For a church not to have a constitution, said Barth, would suggest that its members either did not believe anything at all, could not agree on what they believed, or believed "only in themselves, in money, or in the evil world."[86] Such a church could certainly not call itself a Reformed church.

Significantly, however, the purpose of a church constitution was as much about Christian witness as ecclesial governance. By its constitution, argued Barth, a church demonstrates its witness in the world. How? Because by its constitution—its way of ordering its own life—a church demonstrates "whether and how its belief becomes action" on behalf of the world.[87] It is no surprise, then, that the first necessary element of any church's constitution should be a confession, an opening statement that articulates precisely what "these so-called Christians actually believe, know, and want." Acknowledging that such confessions are too frequently "bland and boring," Barth urged the authors of this proposed new constitution to write their confession in such a way that it had "horns and teeth." Such a confession "has to be there, if the church is to be more than just a company of shoulder-shruggers, tea-aunties, and lonely people."[88]

For Barth, what this meant in practical terms was that a church confession had to affirm the lordship of Christ over every part of life. It is simply not true, he said, that "faith and love, justice and mercy . . . [have] nothing to do with the management of capital, economic progress, wages, [or] truthfulness in journalism." Insofar as all aspects of society come equally under Christ's rule, so too a church confession had, and has, to be intentionally embedded within the challenges and crises of modern life. What is particularly noteworthy is that the first of such social crises listed by Barth was the scourge of antisemitism.

---

[86]Barth, "Um eine Verfassung der Reformierte Kirche in Baselland," 332.

[87]Barth, "Um eine Verfassung der Reformierte Kirche in Baselland," 330.

[88]Barth, "Um eine Verfassung der Reformierte Kirche in Baselland," 330. Markus had evidently learned from his father's example in the drafting of the first Barmen Declaration of January 1934, "Erklärung über das rechte Verständnis der reformatorischen Bekenntnisse in der Deutschen Evangelischen Kirche der Gegenwart." Arguably the most important document in the immediate pre-history of the more famous Barmen Declaration of May 1934, this text not only articulated the positive points of doctrine that were to be affirmed but also made clear what errors had to be decisively rejected. As Klaus Scholder has said, "For the first time since the Reformation a confession was not content with a positive statement but declared clearly and emphatically" those heresies that had to be anathematized. See Scholder, *The Churches and the Third Reich* (London: SCM Press, 1987–1988), 1:580.

> If we want to say today what we believe when we call Jesus Christ "God's Son and our Lord," we have to speak in modern language and keep our eye on modern heresies. [For example] there is the deep-seated and widespread hatred of Jews. The confession of a true church can, may, and will say that Jesus was born of the Jewish people, and that he prevents and forbids a division of humankind according to nationality, [or] skin color.[89]

Barth's singling out of antisemitism as the primary "modern heresy" against which the church had to be on guard is hardly surprising given how closely associated he had been with his father's and the broader Confessing Church's fight against Nazism less than a decade earlier. It would return to the forefront of his mind and activity from the 1960s onward. But it is worth noting that his insistence here on the praxis-oriented nature of a confession—that a confession of faith is a matter of obedient action as well as a statement of beliefs—was also a lesson that he had learned from his father. In a lecture to the general assembly of the German Reformed Alliance, on June 6, 1925, in Duisburg, Karl Barth had argued that a church's confession obliged that church not merely to speak but also to act, since a confession is a matter of faith *and obedience*, and not of faith alone.[90] It is clear that Markus had taken these words of Karl's to heart, and had recognized their timeliness for the new debate.

Barth also made it clear what he thought the priorities of the constitutional council—those who had responsibility for the document's content—should be. Certainly, the shape and function of the various regulatory and bureaucratic systems had to be clearly articulated. "But order and the demarcation of boundaries is not an end in itself." On the contrary, these should simply serve "joyful service . . . active faith . . . and the [principle] of the priesthood of all believers."[91] In this spirit, Barth went on to note that, while it would be far preferable for the greater part of church funds to be spent on acts of loving-kindness (*Liebestätigkeit*), it was regrettably the

---

[89]Barth, "Um eine Verfassung der Reformierte Kirche in Baselland," 332.

[90]See K. Barth, "Wünschbarkeit und Möglichkeit eines allgemeinen reformierten Glaubensbekenntnisses," in K. Barth, *Die Theologie und die Kirche. Gesammelte Vorträge, Bd. 3* (Munich: Christian Kaiser Verlag, 1928), 76-105.

[91]Barth, "Um eine Verfassung der Reformierte Kirche in Baselland," 330-31.

case that such funds were more usually exhausted by expenditure on stipends and building maintenance. "It is worrying," he said, "that this is the case." Nevertheless, there was no need for the constitution either to be boring or distanced from the cares of the world. What was needed was for its authors to "be courageous, and above all: to have a desire and love to obey the Bible."[92]

In many respects, Barth's advice was heeded. When the constitution was finally approved, on July 8, 1952,[93] it naturally included regulations for the church's structure and governance. It also, however, began with a statement of faith—"Wesen und Aufgabe der Kirche"—and, affirming Barth's insistence that the church exist for and within the whole of life, specified the church's role within the wider community. The Christian community, it said, "represents the validity of the Gospel in everyday life" and "is committed to fighting, through Jesus Christ, all people's physical and mental hardships, and their causes."[94] At least in these two important respects, the church's constitution borrowed heavily from Barth's suggestions, evidencing how increasingly influential his voice was within the Swiss church.

THE END OF PARISH LIFE

There were other highlights of Barth's ministry in Bubendorf. To celebrate Christmas in 1952, he arranged the staging of an Albrecht Goes nativity play that was broadcast by the iconic Radio Beromünster—at the time, the most popular radio station in the region. The play was translated into the local dialect, and its narrative actions transposed onto the inhabitants of Bubendorf, encouraging the townspeople to ask, If Christ were born in Bubendorf, how would we welcome him? For Goes himself, who had not yet ventured out into a full-time literary career, the broadcast provided him with possibly the largest single audience he had by that time ever enjoyed. For Markus, it was a creative way of seeking to tell the Christmas story

[92]Barth, "Um eine Verfassung der Reformierte Kirche in Baselland," 331.

[93]The constitution came into effect on January 1, 1953.

[94]"Verfassung der Evangelisch-reformierten Kirche des Kantons Basel-Landschaft," July 8, 1952, https://refbl.ch/refbl-wAssets/docs/Kirchliche-Gesetzessammlung/03-Kirchenverfassung-Kirchenbundesverfassung/3.1-Verfassung-der-ERK-BL.pdf.

outside the parameters of a formal church service and to people who might not otherwise hear it.[95]

The previous month, Barth had facilitated another event that, in a very different way, also sought to proclaim the Christian message to as wide an audience as possible. On November 21, the always controversial pastor Martin Niemoeller arrived in Bubendorf at Barth's invitation to deliver a public lecture. This was something for which the Barths had been hoping since 1942, and which Niemoeller himself had been promising since 1946.[96] Choosing Niemoeller as a drawcard public speaker, however, was always bound to provoke an outcry. In predominantly Anglo-Saxon countries like England and Australia, Niemoeller had been lauded as perhaps the German church's highest profile anti-Nazi. His years in the Dachau and Sachsenhausen concentration camps between 1938 and 1945 were taken as self-evident proof of his impeccable credentials.[97] In Western Europe, though, Niemoeller's reputation was significantly more tainted. He had long attracted both attention and controversy, not only because of his initially sympathetic attitude toward the Nazi Party but because in the immediate post-war years, he was a vocal critic of the denazification process, the arms race, and the continuing division of Germany. Espousing the same strident nationalism in the late 1940s that had, in the early 1930s, seen him ally with the National Socialists, Niemoeller argued passionately that he would prefer German unification to partition, even if that unification were to be under communist rule. Given that, in his youth, Barth had himself toyed with communism, his invitation

---

[95]Albrecht Goes (1908–2000) was a German pastor who was ordained into the German Evangelical Church in Württemberg in 1930. Conscripted into the German Army in 1940, he served as a military chaplain in Russia, Poland, Hungary, and Austria before returning to parish ministry after the war. In 1953, Goes left full-time parochial work to pursue a career as a poet-playwright. His most successful books were *Unruhige Nacht*, set on the Russian front, and *Das Brandopfer*—a fictional examination of the Holocaust through the eyes of a butcher—both of which were later made into films. The nativity play which Markus Barth arranged to have broadcast on Radio Beromünster was most probably *Die fröhliche Christtagslitanie*, which was first published in 1949.

[96]"Und so wurde, was wir schon seit 1942 im Stillen erhofften und seit 1946 verheissen bekommen hatten, Ereignis." M. and R. M. Barth, "Rundbrief: An unsere Freunde und Verwandten in der Nähe und in der Ferne!" December 7, 1952, 3. MBL. Series I. Box 12.

[97]In the US, Niemoeller's reputation was somewhat more complicated. Church historian Matthew Hockenos has shown that while tens of thousands of Americans flocked to hear him speak during his first visit to the United States in 1946, there was also a considerable groundswell of opposition, including from Eleanor Roosevelt. M. Hockenos, "Martin Niemoeller in America, 1946–1947: A Hero with Limitations," *Contemporary Church History Quarterly* 18, no. 2 (2012).

to Niemoeller was, at least for some people, confirmation that he had never fully left that political affiliation behind.[98]

Perhaps unsurprisingly, the local police, on instructions from the Swiss Federal Council, forbade Niemoeller's speech. Local media outlets published warnings against Niemoeller, while various right-wing groups "advocated, prophesied and hoped for" confrontation and sabotage.[99] There were also some members of the parish itself who were outspoken in their opposition to Niemoeller's visit. They "prophesied evil things about the evening, and our own future in Bubendorf" if the event should be permitted to go ahead, recalled Rose Marie.[100] Markus was forced to distribute a flyer that sought to clarify the theological, rather than political, purpose of the address. After appealing the Federal Council's decision, the ban was overturned, and Niemoeller was able to speak. In the end, the crowd waiting to hear him was so large that the lecture had to be delivered twice.[101] As for Niemoeller, whom Barth described as a "messenger of peace in [today's] peaceless world," he demonstrated himself to be "nothing other than an ambassador of Christ."[102]

---

[98]The suspicion was not entirely without foundation. In the days immediately following Niemoeller's lecture, Barth wrote to the communist journalist-politician Emil Arnold (1897–1974) to thank him for the objective fashion in which his newspaper, *Vorwarts*, had covered the event. Arnold had joined the Swiss Communist Party in 1921 and, at the time of the Niemoeller lecture, was a representative of Basel-stadt in the Swiss Federal Council. In a reply to Barth's letter, Arnold condemned an unflattering caricature of Niemoeller that had appeared in a rival paper—the Social Democratic *Arbeiter Zeitung*—and said that, while he did not share Barth's religious convictions, he hoped that Barth, as well as Niemoeller, would remain staunch friends of peace and opponents of German rearmament. Despite their differences, they "simply had to stand together" (*man muss ganz einfach zusammenstehen*) in the pursuit of global peace. E. Arnold to M. Barth, November 29, 1952.

[99]"Empfahlen, weissagen und wünschten andere Kreise Sabotage und Zwischenfälle." M. Barth, "Vorwort," in M. Niemoeller, *Der Christen Weg Zwischen Ost und West* (Riehen: Schudel, 1952).

[100]M. and R. M. Barth, "Rundbrief," December 7, 1952, 2.

[101]"Lebenslauf," Markus Barth funeral booklet, 23. The police authorities in Baselland were in favor of banning the lecture, fearing a "pilgrimage of Communists" from Basel to Bubendorf. Various members of the Federal Council were in support of Basel's position, however others were concerned at the precedent such a ban might set. Noting that the Swiss public was "very sensitive to bans on public speaking," there was also an acknowledgment that Niemoeller was "a hero in the eyes of many Christians" (*ein Held in den Augen vieler Christen*). See "Sitzung des Bundesrates vom 21. November 1952," 2-3.

[102]Barth, "Vorwort." Niemoeller, said Barth, was "a pastor with all his heart," and no matter how many people might "abuse [his] name and work, that says nothing about Pastor Niemoeller himself," but could only speak poorly of his detractors. M. Barth, "Bleiben wir bei der Wahrheit!" November 20, 1952. MBL. Series I. Box 12.

Niemoeller's visit turned out to be one of the last major events of Barth's ministry in Bubendorf and was, in some ways, emblematic of his entire pastorate. For Markus, the proclamation of the gospel was always his primary concern, be that among German prisoners of war, in debates about proper ecclesial governance, or in the creative use of radio programs. That the task came with political ramifications was unavoidable; neither good nor bad in itself, it was simply an ingredient of the primary evangelical purpose. If, therefore, anyone happened to be disturbed by those political ramifications, then, for Barth, their problem was less with him as the agitator and more with the mandates of the gospel itself. As an inevitable consequence, and as with all pastoral appointments, Markus's ministry in Bubendorf thus had its share of ups and downs. While he certainly upset some of his parishioners from time to time, Markus seems never to have bewildered them in quite the same way that Karl (at least in his own recollections) did in Safenwil.

Nevertheless, parish work was not the only vocation to which Markus felt called. From as early as 1939, he had been putting out feelers to his various contacts in Switzerland and abroad regarding possible academic appointments. He had even made it known to Princeton Theological Seminary that he would be open to a call if a vacancy were to arise. Such a call into the academy was not to come for fourteen years after Barth's first tentative explorations. And when it did come, it was not from Princeton but from Dubuque.[103] Thus in December 1952—after a thirteen-year pastorate that had been "instructive, exciting, and happy"[104]—Markus preached his final sermon in Bubendorf. Fittingly, Karl was there to support him on what was evidently an emotional occasion for all concerned. As Karl himself recalled, "I even cried a little in church, because the ending and his farewell affected me so deeply."[105]

---

[103]There were at least two other academic opportunities that presented themselves to Markus at around the same time. One was an invitation to teach in Berlin, which Markus declined because, by virtue of both Karl's reputation and his own friendships there, he could not be certain that he was being offered it "on merit." The second invitation was to a seminary in Bangalore, India (most likely, the United Theological College). This offer, too, was declined, on account of how young Markus's children were at the time, and a concern that in India it might prove difficult to provide for their various educational needs. Personal correspondence with the Barth family, February 12, 2022.

[104]"Lebenslauf," Markus Barth's funeral booklet, 32.

[105]Quoted in Busch, *Karl Barth*, 391.

4

"I TRY TO MAKE GREEK AS IMPORTANT TO THEM AS POSSIBLE"

The Iowa Years, 1953–1955

On February 25, 1953, after what a newspaper report called a "stormy Atlantic crossing [in] the Queen Mary,"[1] Markus, Rose Marie, and their five children arrived in Dubuque, Iowa. The previous December, Klaas Stratemeier, who had been professor of New Testament at the University of Dubuque's Theological Seminary since 1940, had died. Prior to his death, however, and in anticipation of his planned retirement, Stratemeier—together with his colleague Arthur C. Cochrane[2]—had already nominated Barth to be his successor.[3] This nomination, accompanied as it was by a

[1]"Dr Markus Barth Moves to Dubuque with His Family," *Dubuque Christian American* 27, no. 6, March 1953. The ship had departed from Cherbourg on February 18. M. Barth and R. M. Barth, "Rundbrief," December 7, 1952. MBMC. Subject Correspondence 1. Box 5.

[2]Cochrane was already known to the Barth family. As part of his doctoral studies at Edinburgh, he had lived in Germany from 1935–1937, studying the Reformed confessions and becoming acquainted with the activities and clergy of the *Bekennende Kirche*, not least Karl Barth. Cochrane would later publish numerous pieces on both Barth and the German *Kirchenkampf*, including *The Church and the War* (Toronto: Nelson, 1940), and *The Church's Confession Under Hitler* (Philadelphia: Westminster, 1962). In 1948, he joined the University of Dubuque Theological Seminary as professor of systematic theology and stayed there until 1971, when—in a serendipitous reversal of fortunes—he moved to Pittsburgh Theological Seminary where, by this time, Markus Barth was already teaching.

[3]See "Dr Markus Marth Moves." Barth had first received a request to consider a call to Dubuque in May 1952, with the dean, Elwyn Smith, even visiting the Barths in Bubendorf. M. and R. M. Barth, "Rundbrief," December 7, 1952, 1.

glowing endorsement from the acclaimed ecumenist Willem Visser 't Hooft, had secured Markus's invitation, which was ratified unanimously by Dubuque's board of directors on November 24, 1952. The appointment was for three years, with Barth's title to be visiting professor in New Testament. "We all look forward," wrote the seminary's president, Rollo La Porte, "with highest hopes to your coming and to the contribution your work in the classroom and your family life will make to our common vocation."[4] Having been hoping for an academic appointment for some years, Barth eagerly accepted the offer and its conditions. "My wife and I," he wrote to La Porte, "fully agree that this invitation cannot be rejected. . . . I hope that we shall be given day by day, the force, courage, and humbleness . . . without which we should be unable to contribute in any way to the instruction of the students and the community life of the seminary."[5]

Even before their arrival, Markus had expressed his enthusiasm for the adventure that lay ahead, and not least for the type of institution to which he was going. With close ties to the Presbyterian Church, the seminary in Dubuque sought to train "not scholars, but country pastors," with the curriculum consequently being devoted to matters of practical relevance to the life of a church community: "sermons, teaching, and the gathering of the congregation."[6] Clearly anticipating with some relish the opportunity ahead of him, Markus did not have to wait long before getting started. His teaching duties began less than a week after the family's arrival, on March 4.

ENTERING ACADEMIA

As indicated above, the appointment to Dubuque was for three years. Given that Barth's offer letter did not mention the prospect of a renewal of contract at the end of that period, and that he was titled only a visiting professor, it would appear that the seminary at least did not envisage a longer tenure.[7] Even before leaving Switzerland, however, the Barths

---

[4]R. La Porte to M. Barth, November 16, 1952. MBL. Series I. Box 12.

[5]"Dr Markus Barth Moves to Dubuque with His Family."

[6]M. Barth and R. M. Barth, "Rundbrief," December 7, 1952.

[7]In the offer letter, La Porte did advise the Barths to apply for "permanent immigrants' visas"—but he noted that such visas carried no expectation of remaining permanently in the United States.

themselves anticipated that their American adventure might last longer.[8] For Markus, the transition into academia presented him with an opportunity to "continue, promote, and consolidate" the research he had already begun.[9] Yet leaving parish ministry was not without sadness. Even though Markus had, in his own words, "longed for a new job for a long time," the abruptness of the departure from Bubendorf was not easy. "Suddenly, it has become evident that many people here really did like us."[10] That this seems to have surprised Barth is indicative perhaps of two things. First, it was a realistic acknowledgment that a pastor's job is not, in fact, to be liked. But second, it reflected a sober recognition that all the Barths' intentions and hopes to the contrary, not all had gone smoothly for them in Bubendorf, and that—as must inevitably happen over the course of nearly fifteen years—their manner of ministry had not always been to everyone's liking.

The Barths' arrival in Dubuque attracted not only the enthusiastic greetings of the seminary community but also extensive—and some rather odd—media attention. Less than two months after arriving, they were featured in the city's *Telegraph Herald*, under the rather predictable caption, "The Swiss Family Barth," and in which any semblance of privacy was quickly dissolved. The article began by giving out the Barths' address—1740 Grace Street, which was a short five-minute walk to the seminary—and continued to provide a detailed inventory not only of the family's furniture but even of the children's personalities, all of which served to portray the family as utterly other. Readers of the feature piece learned of the "great oval table of heavy walnut," the "elaborately hand-carved" chairs that "would be treasured by any museum in America," the "huge Empire

---

It was simply more bureaucratically expedient, insofar as all other visa types required renewal every six months. See La Porte to Barth, November 16, 1952.

[8]"Wir rechnen aber jetzt schon mit einer evtl. Verlängerung des amerikanischen Aufenthaltes." M. and R. M. Barth, "Rundbrief," December 7, 1952, 1.

[9]In later years, Markus expressed the view that there had also been another reason for accepting the job in America. As he told the Barth's Japanese exchange student in Pittsburgh, Keiko Furukawa, "[M]any American theologians and ministers misunderstand Karl Barth and so I must talk to them about the true Karl Barth in order to correct such misconceptions." K. Watanabe, "Living with the Barth Family 1963–1964," 4. MBL. Series II. Box 1.

[10]M. and R. M. Barth, "Rundbrief," December 7, 1952, 2.

cabinet," and the six-branched Breton chandelier. Rose Marie—the "bright-eyed mother"—was quoted as saying that such furniture was essential for them to bring, because "you see, we were not called to be Americans." Only their beds remained back in Switzerland, being simply "too large" for American houses.[11] As for the children, they too were depicted as objects of some wonder: Anna's "costume" and hairstyle—"she still clings to her long heavy braids"—marked her as different from the neighboring girls; and all of the Barth children were, it was reported, "always overheated" in school, "unaccustomed [as they were] to the use of electricity and daylight at the same time!"[12]

Neither was Rose Marie herself, however, shy in venturing her own perspectives on her new home. At the end of April, having been in the US for less than two months, she expressed her opinion that in the American psyche, novelty seemed to trump all other values—even beauty—and that American women, without being superficial, nevertheless appeared "far less affected by what goes on in the world" than their European counterparts. Given how hard Rose Marie had worked to encourage the women of Bubendorf to educate themselves about both local and global issues, this difference between the women of both countries must have been especially noticeable.[13]

---

[11] "The Swiss Family Barth in Dubuque," *The Telegraph Herald*, April 12, 1953, 10-11.

[12] "Swiss Family Barth," 10-11.

[13] R. M. Barth, "America, With the Eyes of a Greenhorn," address delivered to the Women's Association of the Presbyterian Church in Dubuque, April 30, 1953, 2, 6. This observation about an apparent discrepancy between the respective levels of political engagement between American and Swiss women is particularly interesting, given the different histories of women's suffrage in the two countries. The 19th Amendment to the US Constitution—which prohibits both the US and its states from denying the right to vote to any US citizen on the basis of gender, and which thus effectively enfranchised women—was passed by the US House of Representatives on May 21, 1919, and by the Senate on June 4 the same year. Tennessee's ratification of the amendment in August 1920 gave it the 36th and final state approval that was needed in order for the 19th Amendment to become law throughout the country. Iowa—the state in which the Barths first made their home, and in which Rose Marie commented upon the (from her observation) political *dis*engagement of American women—ratified the 19th Amendment on July 2, 1919, making it one of the first US states to do so. By contrast, whereas Swiss women had been extended voting rights at the cantonal level from 1959, their enfranchisement in national elections was made possible only after the passing of a referendum in February 1971. That Rose Marie was so active in encouraging women's political engagement even during Markus's Bubendorf pastorate demonstrates how far ahead of the Swiss national mood she was, and perhaps helps explain why she was so surprised at the apparent political disinterest among American women.

Figure 4.1. Markus in his library in Dubuque, 1953

Markus himself lost no time in getting to work and in making a favorable impression at the seminary. He took to his new responsibilities "with pleasure and joy," teaching courses—as he had been directed in his offer letter—on Romans and Revelation. Recognizing that many of his students were "burdened" with other jobs and duties that left them unable to devote themselves entirely to their studies, Markus was nonetheless delighted that they were, overall, "attentive and open-minded."[14] The pleasure seems to have been reciprocated; a marketing brochure printed shortly after his arrival gleefully announced that "his teaching has been most enthusiastically received by his students."[15] While Donald Gowan recalls that Barth's accent was something "we midwesterners sometimes found baffling when it was wrapped around new terms such as *Sinaiticus* . . . or *Bezae Cantabrigiensis*," the new European professor was at once "the most challenging and the most accessible member of the faculty."[16] Like his father, who had gone from pastorate to professoriate in rapid time, and with no real preparation for academia, Markus too had moved to a full-time faculty appointment directly from thirteen years in pastoral ministry. And yet he soon established himself not just as a good teacher but as "a great teacher" and "model scholar." The standards he expected of his students were dauntingly high. Gowan remembers, for example, that "he did insist on trying to

[14]R. M. Barth, "Rundbrief," May 1, 1953. MBMC. Subject Correspondence 1. Box 5. It is worth noting that in this letter, Rose Marie mentions that she also attended Markus's Romans lectures, thereby continuing her own theological education.

[15]Dubuque Seminary, untitled brochure (1952), 10. MBL. Series III—Newspapers.

[16]D. E. Gowan, "In Memory of Markus Barth: A Personal Note," *Horizons in Biblical Theology: An International Dialogue* 17, no. 2 (1995): 94.

teach us classical Greek (rather than *Koine*) in one semester, the only thing for which I need to forgive him."[17] Nonetheless, Barth's demands were tempered by gentleness, hospitality, and "the full and overflowing measure of . . . the 'good news' of Christ."[18]

Again, just as Karl had done from the earliest days of his own teaching career in Göttingen, Markus soon established in Dubuque a regular pattern of weekly "open forums" at the family home. There, students could gather to ask questions, discuss topical issues, and explore recently published books. One of the first texts that the group delved into was Karl Barth's *Romans*, with Markus astonished that the students were unable to see how "Dr. Karl's" book was relevant to their own churches' circumstances. "The students do not immediately recognize their churches in the mirror of Romans."[19] His students' difficulties in applying a key theological resource to their own contexts notwithstanding, Markus persisted with the open forums. Indeed, they became a regular part of Markus's teaching style, and he continued the pattern throughout his career—in Chicago, Pittsburgh, and then, from the 1970s, back in Basel.

During his thirteen years in Bubendorf, Barth had been a pastor whose energies had always been expended on wider ecclesial as well as local parochial matters. Similarly in Dubuque, Barth's interests did not remain limited to the classroom but extended also to the life and health of the American churches more broadly. In late September, he delivered the opening lecture to the annual School of Missions for Cedar Rapids's Westminster Presbyterian Church on the topic "The Church in Present Day Europe."[20] This invitation had come hard on the heels of some speaking engagements on the other side of the Rocky Mountains. During the July summer holidays, the entire family had traveled west, through South Dakota to Spokane and on to the Pacific, before returning home via Alberta. In Spokane's First Unitarian Church—where he renewed an old friendship with Glenn Holman, with whom he had studied in Edinburgh—Markus outlined what he perceived

[17]Gowan, "In Memory of Markus Barth," 94.

[18]C. Dickinson, "Markus Barth and Biblical Theology: A Personal Re-View," *Horizons in Biblical Theology: An International Dialogue* 17, no. 2 (1995): 97.

[19]R. M. Barth and M. Barth, "Rundbrief," March 1, 1954, 3.

[20]"First Speaker at Westminster Missions School," *The Gazette*, September 26, 1953, 3.

to be the three greatest challenges facing the church "in this time of crisis in the world." First, he argued that the church needed "to convey the message of God" instead of preaching "morals or a 'bourgeois' way of behavior." Second, the church had to find its way back to unity; a divided church, he said, "cannot hope to teach the world [anything]." And third, the church needed to remember—and then to embody in its life and proclamation—the undivided and inclusive "humanity of Christ," recognizing that "even behind the iron curtain there are human beings and not devils."[21] On the ecumenical front, Barth was also instrumental in reopening dialogue between his own Presbyterian seminary and the neighboring Lutheran Wartburg Seminary, also in Dubuque, which "had fallen asleep years ago, but is now apparently possible again."[22]

The trip westward from Dubuque was not, as it turned out, an isolated visit but became an annual holiday for the whole Barth family for the next decade. Sometimes, as they did on this first holiday in 1953, they would venture into Canada or the Teton Mountains in Wyoming.[23] More frequently, however, the family would head to Colorado, where they would spend four weeks camping, hiking, and riding. During these holidays, "Papa [Markus] tried to pass down to [the children] principles of the Swiss cavalry: how to keep a silver coin on the saddle while galloping." Evenings around the campfires would be spent singing folk songs, reading from such literary classics as the Grimm fairy tales, *1001 Nights*—all in *Hochdeutsch*—and listening to Markus share stories of his experiences in Nazi Germany. Perhaps above all, Rose Marie and the children were able to enjoy having Markus—"*unser Ferien Vater*" ("our holiday dad")—"quite carefree and relaxed [having] left all his theological books and papers back home."[24]

Barth's initial courses at the seminary, on Romans and Revelation, had been chosen for him. After having completed those, he began to choose his

---

[21]"Pastor Outlines College's Needs," *Spokesman-Review*, July 11, 1953, 11. The immediate political context made this an especially provocative comment: in June 1953, Soviet troops had crushed a workers' rebellion in East Germany.

[22]R. M. Barth and M. Barth, "Rundbrief," March 1, 1954, 5.

[23]"Swiss Climber Likes American Mountains," *Spokane Chronicle*, July 17, 1953, 5.

[24]"Driving West! The Barths in Summer in the USA," recollections from the Barth family, May 7, 2019. MBL. Series II. Box 7.

next set of classes himself. They included seminars on 1 Corinthians, the Synoptic Gospels, and in the fall semester of 1953, an introduction to the New Testament.[25] In this last course, he took some students by surprise on account of his rejection of any in principle fixity of the scriptural canon.

> What is canonical still remains open. We have not God's word distilled in a bottle. But when we hear it and when He uses it—then it is—by God's grace, not by a past miracle of inspiration—God's word. The church has to ask again and again: Is this the voice of the good shepherd? She will to her surprise hear in these books the voice of God. If further excavations produced another gospel, or letter of Paul, I see no reason why such books should not be recognized as canonical too. The Canon is still open. The church has—be it in maintaining, limiting or enlarging the Canon—always to make a new decision and to obey afresh. Christians cannot create, or make, or possess, or master their canon—they only can recognize and receive it. To this aim, interpretation will serve.[26]

As for his first cohort of students, they were an eclectic mix that included an electrician, a farmer, a teacher, a forestry worker, an English naval officer, an elderly Salvation Army officer, a lawyer, and even a former professional boxer.[27] That most of these students were entering into ministry as a second career after having already established themselves in a previous profession was just one way in which they differed from the typical European theology student with whom Markus had previously been familiar. Another difference was that most of them were married, and many already had children. Both Markus and Rose Marie were also astonished by the amount of work outside the classroom that was expected of the students.

> Some live with their families in tiny two-room huts that the university rents out. Most [of the students], however, look after one, if not two, churches. In these situations, the wife and children live in the local vicarage. The father [after spending the week at the seminary] goes home on a Friday

---

[25]MBMC. Series V. Course Materials. Box 2.

[26]R. Cerretti, lecture notes (verbatim). MBMC. Series V.

[27]R. M. Barth and M. Barth, "Rundbrief," March 1, 1954, 2. Later, Markus was to recommend the naval officer—a John Gill—for doctoral studies at Union Theological Seminary in New York. M. Barth to C. Richardson, February 22, 1956. MBL. Series I. Box 31.

> night, in a 200-500 km round-trip, does the necessary pastoral visits, and then preaches on the Sunday—usually on a text that he has studied with Markus the week before. Sundays are also busy with church meetings, or pastors' conferences.[28]

On top of this, most of the men, and many of the wives, needed to work extra jobs in the city in order to pay for their tuition. "You can imagine how this affects their study."[29] Two years later, Barth was to express in a letter to his mother Nelly much of the same concerns about the pressures that were still being placed upon his students. It has to be said that some of those pressures were imposed by Markus himself: "I try to make Greek as important to them as possible." But mostly, he knew that his students were simply overwhelmed by the demands of parish work that was additional to their formal studies. "The poor, poor, fellows. So much is placed on their shoulders . . . [that] they find it almost a luxury to sit down and read a book." When lectures were listened to only for whatever utility they might have for the Sunday sermon, and not for the sake of learning as such, Markus despaired that his students would find it impossible to preach "for a lifetime."[30] Nevertheless, despite these difficulties, Markus was able to identify a few "extremely clear minds" within the group, some of whom he encouraged to undertake further studies abroad in Europe.

In November 1953, Markus traveled to Chicago with his colleagues Arthur Cochrane and Joseph Mihelic for a meeting of the Society of Biblical Research, at which the topic of conversation was "The Messiah in the Old Testament."[31] Later that month, the Barths were pleased to renew an old friendship from their Edinburgh days with a visit from Norman Porteous.[32] Shortly after his departure, the Barths celebrated their first Christmas in Dubuque. The festivities were brightened by gifts from family and friends in Switzerland, not least amongst which were various Mozart records.

---

[28]R. M. Barth and M. Barth, "Rundbrief," March 1, 1954, 3.

[29]R. M. Barth and M. Barth, "Rundbrief," March 1, 1954, 3.

[30]M. Barth to N. Barth, May 5, 1955. MBL. Series II. Box 11.

[31]E. Wright to M. Barth, October 22, 1953; M. Barth to E. Wright, November 28, 1953. MBL. Series I. Box 12.

[32]N. Porteous to M. Barth, December 8, 1953. MBL. Series I. Box 12.

These, wrote Rose Marie, were "food for the European soul."[33] Meanwhile, the children had adapted to school well, with Anna and Ruth helping stage a Christmas performance of "The Magic Nutcracker." More disruptive, though, was the sudden departure of the family's Swiss housekeeper, Mey, in the weeks leading up to the Christmas holidays. It was, wrote Rose Marie, "a great upheaval." This left the Barths needing to adopt certain "American" habits, namely, of looking after themselves without domestic help. They chose not to follow all American customs, however; Markus was not expected to wash the dishes, or do the weekly shopping like "American dads," but was deemed to have fulfilled his obligations by helping Peter with his Latin homework and narrating the nightly Bible story.[34]

Having successfully negotiated their first year in the US, the Barths found 1954 to present a new set of challenges. Throughout the year, everyday life was itself set against the backdrop of increasing Cold War tensions, and the "saber-rattling" of the local newspapers and radio programs. Rose Marie, who was an avid reader of the *New York Times*, was especially troubled by the Army vs. McCarthy proceedings, the "political stubbornness" of the Geneva Conference, the "hypocrisy" of the CIA-backed Guatemalan coup, and the Oppenheimer security hearings. She was equally distressed by those Americans among whom the Barths lived "who were not upset by any of this."[35]

These daily stresses impressed upon the family the need to find friendship and comfort in a close and supportive church. It did not,

---

[33]R. M. Barth and M. Barth, "Rundbrief," March 1, 1954, 1.

[34]R. M. Barth and M. Barth, "Rundbrief," March 1, 1954, 1. The children themselves have indicated that they do not recall Mey's departure causing significant disruption. Rose Marie's letter, however, suggests that she and Markus were perhaps more acutely affected by it. Personal correspondence with Ruth Barth, July 2021.

[35]R. M. Barth, "Rundbrief," 1st Sunday of Advent, 1954, 1. The Army vs. McCarthy hearings (April to June 1954) were a series of televised proceedings by the US Senate's Subcommittee on Investigations regarding the alleged pressuring of the Army by Senator Joseph McCarthy. The Geneva Conference (April to July 1954) was a largely unsuccessful attempt to resolve residual problems following the Korean armistice. The Oppenheimer security hearings (April to May 1954) investigated concerns that Robert J. Oppenheimer—a key scientist in the Manhattan Project that had developed America's atomic bomb—had potentially treasonous associations with communists. The 1954 Guatemalan coup d'état was the result of a covert CIA operation code named PBSuccess. It deposed the democratically elected Guatemalan President Jacobo Árbenz, installing in his place the military dictatorship of Carlos Castillo Armas.

however, prove easy to find one. Whereas Markus's position at the seminary licensed him ex officio to a Presbyterian synod, it took Rose Marie and the children much longer to locate a home church in which they could feel supported. Not that there was a shortage of options—Rose Marie counted fourteen different denominational choices in Dubuque, from the Lutherans and Presbyterians, to Congregationalists and Methodists, yet none of which seemed suitable. The Lutheran sermons, she complained, were too dominated by popular psychology, while the Congregationalists—notwithstanding "a very enterprising pastor"—were little more than a "charming club." After toying with the idea of remaining "unchurched," Rose Marie and the children finally found a small community church at the other end of Dubuque—in a depressed and "sometimes smelly" part of the city—in which the pastor preached and prayed diligently from the Scriptures and ran children's activities that were "unreligious." That, thought Rose Marie, was especially important for Sunday school. It was not perfect—indeed, Peter and Lukas were decidedly unsatisfied (*vollkommen unbefriedigt davon*) with it—but it did provide the family with a Christian community that was independent of Markus's work in the seminary.[36]

DUTIES BEYOND DUBUQUE

The spring semester of 1954 was as busy for Markus outside the classroom as it was inside it, with his work taking him away from home for weeks at a time. At the end of March, Barth traveled to the small town of Herman, in Sheboygan County, Wisconsin, to speak at an annual theological convention in the historic Mission House district. There he delivered lectures on "The Christology of the Old Testament" and the "Unity of the New Testament."[37] A little more than a month later, he was on the road again, this time to Oregon. During the first week of May, he was the keynote speaker at the Northwest Ministers' Convocation at the Menucha Retreat and Conference Center. Then, on May 8, he spoke to the Religious Directors' Association at the University of Oregon before finishing his trip by

[36]R. M. Barth and M. Barth, "Rundbrief," March 1, 1954, 3-4.

[37]"Markus Barth Will Speak at Convention," *The Sheboygan Press*, March 26, 1954, 12.

preaching at Central Presbyterian Church in Eugene.[38] In Portland, speaking at the ministers' retreat, Markus again ventured into politically sensitive areas by cautioning his audience not to fall into the trap of dividing the world into "bad Communists, and good, liberal-minded citizens." This, he said, was a polarizing mindset that the church could not afford to entertain. Indeed, he went further; such an either-or attitude had been characteristic of National Socialism. The more intractably opposed to the enemy one became, he warned, the more like that enemy one was destined to become. While Markus's message was provocative—and one, in fact, that he would continue to express throughout his time in America—it was nevertheless received so well that he was offered a job in Portland (which he did not accept) as professor of religion.[39]

In July 1954, Markus's work took him to New York. This trip, however, was completely different from his earlier engagements in Oregon. Replacing Georges Casalis as Bible study leader for a students' summer camp, he was able to witness the social outreach programs of the famous Judson Memorial Church, in Greenwich Village, just off Washington Square.[40] Clearly delighted by the bohemian character of the neighborhood, Markus was particularly impressed by the community work that was being done by local pastors, who held "Sunday and evening services in an old butcher's shop," and who used that space during the daytime for "a kind of employment office and social counselling center."[41] The latter half of the summer, once Markus had returned from New York, was filled with a family holiday to the Timber Creek Campground in Colorado. Just two

---

[38]"Markus Barth Visits Campus," *The Eugene Guard*, May 1, 1954, 2; "Markus Barth at Central Pres. Both Sermons," *The Eugene Guard*, May 8, 1954, 3. The Menucha Center was purchased by Portland's First Presbyterian Church in 1950 from Julius Meier, who had served as governor of Oregon from 1931 to 1935. The primary residence was repurposed and converted into an ecumenical retreat center.

[39]R. M. Barth, "Rundbrief," 1st Sunday of Advent, 1954, 1-2.

[40]Founded in the late nineteenth century by the American Baptist preacher Edward Judson (1844–1914), the church had always existed within, and served, an ethnically and economically diverse group of communities and had gained a reputation for social advocacy. In the immediate aftermath of World War II, it had begun intentional ministry among veterans and Greenwich Village's increasingly large artist community. In the 1950s, at the time when Markus first visited, it was the first—and at that stage, only—institution in the neighborhood that was providing counseling to drug addicts.

[41]R. M. Barth, "Rundbrief," 1st Sunday of Advent, 1954, 2.

days after heading home to Dubuque, Rose Marie left for the Second Assembly of the World Council of Churches in Evanston, Illinois, where she was a delegate—an opportunity that was to have some unforeseen outcomes for the family as a whole.[42]

Through the following fall semester, Markus once again taught Romans—making "new discoveries—at least for . . . himself and his students," as well as courses on the Synoptic Gospels and James. During the final weeks of the year, the midweek open forums that Markus held in the family home were devoted—at the students' own request—to a consideration of the liturgy of the Roman Mass, with some Catholic priests invited in to answer some of the trickier questions.[43] That ecumenical spirit was also evident in a second round of conversations between the Presbyterians and Lutherans, held in early September. Seeking to capitalize on the presence in the United States of several key European theologians who had traveled to Illinois for the WCC Evanston Conference, Markus suggested Heinrich Vogel, Hendrikus Berkhof, and Bishop George Bell as keynote speakers for the Presbyterian-Lutheran conversations. Were they not to be available, Barth proposed Tom Torrance, Heinrich Grüber, and Josef Hromádka as suitable alternatives.[44]

In January 1955, Markus and Rose Marie traveled to the east coast, where Markus was scheduled to deliver two lectures to the editors of the Presbyterian Church's religious instruction material on Rudolf Bultmann's "demythologization."[45] His presentations were evidently impressive. In a

---

[42]R. M. Barth, "Rundbrief," 1st Sunday of Advent, 1954, 3-6. The Evanston Conference (August 15–31, 1954) took as its theme "Christ—the Hope of the World." Among the delegates were Josef Hromádka from Prague, and three former inmates of Dachau—Martin Niemoeller, Heinrich Grüber, and Ernst Wilm. Markus was not a delegate at the conference but visited Rose Marie for one day halfway through.

[43]R. M. Barth, "Rundbrief," 1st Sunday of Advent, 1954, 8-9. It made sense that the students were intrigued by Roman Catholic liturgies given Dubuque's historically large Catholic population.

[44]"Suggestions concerning an Ecumenical meeting in Dubuque for ministers of all denominations." MBL. Series I. Box 12. Both Josef Hromádka and Bishop Bell were unable to attend, while Tom Torrance promised to try his hardest to be there. "When can I get to Dubuque—which I *must* do if I possibly can? . . . But rest assured that I will do all I can [to get there]." T. Torrance to M. Barth, May 22, 1954. See also J. Hromádka to M. Barth, May 3, 1954; G. Bell to M. Barth, June 9, 1954. Vogel and Berkhof, however, agreed to attend. M. Barth to G. Bell, June 5, 1954. MBL. Series I. Box 12.

[45]The invitation had come from Norman Langford, editor and chief of curriculum for the Presbyterian Board of Christian Education. N. Langford to M. Barth, October 7, 1954. MBL.

letter of thanks to Markus after the event, Norman Langford was fulsome in his praise. "The group was positively stunned by the profundity and eloquence of what you had to say, and your presentation is one of the most brilliant that any of us has ever heard."[46] From Philadelphia, the couple traveled north to Princeton, where they were received warmly by President John Mackay. Given their earlier distress at their Iowan neighbors' disinterest in the country's escalating anti-communism, Markus and Rose Marie were delighted to hear Mackay give "a theological-sociological political lecture, in which, to great applause, he fired a few well-aimed arrows at [Joseph] McCarthy and his supporters."[47]

THE CALL TO CHICAGO

The biggest news for 1955, however, came in May when Markus was elected to the Federated Theological Faculty of the University of Chicago as associate professor of New Testament.[48] The call to Chicago had something of a convoluted history to it. During Rose Marie's participation in the previous year's Evanston Conference she had met, through the Scottish theologian Tom Torrance, an English Congregationalist minister, Oliver Jenkins, who in 1938 had briefly encountered Markus at a camp in South Wales. When Markus traveled to Evanston for one day to visit Rose Marie, he and Jenkins met again. Having thus reacquainted himself with Markus and his work, Jenkins—who was at the time studying ecumenics in Chicago—brought Markus's name to the attention of Coert Rylaarsdam, who in 1955

Series I. Box 12. Aware that Bultmann's work had garnered significant support from among some American "liberals," Langford noted that—while many of those who worked in Presbyterian Christian education had "come originally from a somewhat liberal background"—this was no longer the prevailing attitude. On the other hand, Langford was "inclined to think that Bultmann's point of view might be seized upon by some as a rather convenient way of getting around intellectual difficulties arising from Bible study." It was precisely this danger that he was hoping Barth could address. N. Langford to M. Barth, October 15, 1954. MBL. Series I. Box 12.

[46]N. Langford to M. Barth, January 7, 1955. MBL. Series I. Box 12.

[47]R. M. Barth, "Rundbrief," June 1955, 3.

[48]J. C. Brauer to M. Barth, May 16, 1955. MBL. Series I. Box 12. The Federated Theological Faculty was an ecumenical consortium of the four theological schools associated with the University of Chicago, namely, Chicago Theological Seminary (United Church of Christ); Meadville Theological School (Unitarian Universalist); Disciples Divinity House (Disciples of Christ); and the Divinity School of the University of Chicago. Inaugurated in October 1943, the FTF was discontinued in 1960.

was deputy dean of the Federated Faculty.[49] Rylaarsdam immediately began advocating for Markus to receive a call, seeing in him something of a kindred spirit; not only was Rylaarsdam also a biblical scholar but, like Markus, was increasingly committed to the pursuit of Jewish-Christian dialogue and reconciliation.[50]

The negotiations around Markus's new appointment dominated the first five months of the year. Letters flew between Dubuque and Chicago, which were followed up by personal visitations. In early April, Barth met with some of the faculty and gave a presentation on the theme "Faith in the New Testament," in which he also spoke, as he had in Philadelphia, on Bultmann's work. According to his children, Markus particularly impressed his interviewers by his knowledge and appreciation of J. D. Salinger's *The Catcher in the Rye*.[51] Then, in mid-April, Jerry Brauer—at the time dean of the Federated Theological Faculty—traveled to Dubuque to spend time not only with Markus but with the rest of the family as well.[52] There was, naturally, some haggling about the rank of Markus's appointment; a preliminary offer was made at the level of assistant professor. By mid-May, this had been

---

[49]R. M. Barth, "Rundbrief," June 1955, 1-2. John Coert Rylaarsdam (1906–1998) studied at Brunswick Theological Seminary, Princeton Theological Seminary, Cambridge University, and the University of Chicago, from where he graduated with his PhD in 1944. He was appointed to the theological faculty at Chicago in 1945 and remained there until his retirement in 1971.

[50]According to Jerald Brauer, dean of the Federated Theological Faculty in Chicago at the time of Barth's appointment, Rylaarsdam "was way ahead of his time. He was a prophetic figure [in interfaith relations] . . . [and] had a concern and sensitivity to Judaism and Roman Catholicism at a time when the Protestant public at large was either antithetical to or not that concerned with either of those groups." "In Memoriam: J. Coert Rylaarsdam," *The University of Chicago Chronicle* 17, no. 16 (May 14, 1998).

[51]P. Barth, A. Barth, R. Naveau, and R.-M. Barth-Häfeli, "Chicago Memories," November 2020, 5. MBL. Series II. Box 7. Markus's introduction to Salinger's novel had been through his youngest daughter, Rose-Marie, who had bought a copy and given it to her father to read.

[52]C. Rylaarsdam to M. Barth, March 29, 1955; J. C. Brauer to M. Barth, April 21, 1955; A. C. McGiffert to M. Barth, April 25, 1955; J. C. Brauer to M. Barth, May 16, 1955. MBL. Series I. Box 12. In a curious mistake, Bauer's formal offer of appointment was to an associate professorship in *Old* Testament! As an interesting side note, it would appear that at the same time that Markus was in discussions with Chicago, he had also put out feelers to the Harvard Divinity School. His contact there was Glenn Holman, whose friendship he had renewed two years earlier in Spokane. Holman was a Congregationalist minister whom Markus had first met in Edinburgh, and who had also studied at Chicago Theological Seminary. In a letter from April 1955, Holman wrote to Markus, saying: "They [Harvard Divinity School] did have an opening, but it was in Old Testament. . . . Thus, that possibility is eliminated, and Harvard replied that they were putting [your] information on file, but have nothing at present to offer. Therefore, Chicago is indeed a wonderful opportunity for you." G. Holman to M. Barth, April 20, 1955.

revised upward to an associate professorship, coming with a slightly higher salary but not tenure. For his part, Markus did not express particularly firm views either way. Indeed, he "personally [did] not know what the difference between assistant and associate professor at the FTF might be." His desire, he said, was not for better finances or for the promise of a longer-term appointment. Rather, his preference for an associate professorship was "simply because I should like to share fully in the responsibilities of the faculty and not to be in the position of a fifth wheel," which he feared might be the case if he took an appointment at a lower rank.[53]

Also of note is Markus's attraction to the inherently ecumenical nature of the Federated Theological Faculty. At the time a bold venture into ecumenism, Arthur McGiffert—president of the Chicago Theological Seminary from 1946 to 1958—told Markus that "more than nearly any other theological enterprise in the country, [the FTF] reflects that unique combination of the one and the many of unity and diversity which characterizes the Ecumenical Movement."[54] Markus needed no further convincing. Expecting "the best things from the ecumenical spirit which rules in the FTF," Barth commented that "long before the discussions in regard to an eventual . . . call to Chicago began I had become convinced that under the present church circumstances in America a strictly denominational theological education could not be the best possible way of training ministers." He also noted that an ecumenical environment would provide a richer ground for his research.[55] As he noted in a letter to his mother, Dubuque's "narrow spirit" had rendered "the academic, intellectual, and cultural life" of the city "oppressive."[56] The fact that the Federated Faculty was located within a multidisciplinary university was a further advantage. As Elwyn Smith—dean of Dubuque Seminary—admitted, "It may well be that your intuition with respect to the environment in which you think you can work

[53]M. Barth to J. C. Brauer, April 23, 1955. MBL. Series I. Box 12.

[54]A. C. McGiffert Jr. to M. Barth, May 12, 1955. MBL. Series I. Box 12.

[55]M. Barth to A. C. McGiffert Jr., May 14, 1955. MBL. Series I. Box 12.

[56]M. Barth to N. Barth, May 5, 1955. MBL. Series II. Box 11. It was evidently not just the city's culture that Markus found stifling. Peter Barth recalled that his father felt himself "muzzled"—that is, as though he was forced to wear a *Maulkorb*—by the Presbyterian sponsors of the seminary faculty, who sought to prevent Markus (and others) from expressing theological and political views with which they did not agree. Personal correspondence with Peter Barth, July 2021.

best is right, and that . . . in the end a University position is the place where you can do your most effective work."[57]

Of course, Markus's decision to leave Dubuque was met with considerable sadness by both his colleagues and his students. President Couchman noted that the university was profoundly grateful for "the constantly good and scholarly job" that Markus had done in the two years he had been there. "It is obvious to those of us who know something about the place that your contribution has been significant and Dubuque will be stronger as a theological seminary for having had you in the center of its academic affairs."[58] Certainly, Markus got the feeling that some of his colleagues, at least, felt spurned by his decision to leave Dubuque, and that his imminent departure made his opinions in faculty meetings both redundant and unwelcome.[59] But if indeed this resentment was felt at all, it was far from universal, with the Old Testament scholar Joe Mihelic more representative of the general attitude. As he wrote to Markus, "I was glad that you came into our midst. Your leaving [has] left a void, and personally I believe that it will be difficult to fill."[60] Even more telling, though, was the gratitude expressed by Lawrence Marshburn, a student in the Bachelor of Divinity program. Ruing his absences from a few too many of Markus's classes, Marshburn wryly acknowledged that he had squandered his "first (and probably) last, and only opportunity to benefit even a little from your having been here at Dubuque. You make Biblical study an exciting, inspiring, and rewarding study. I covet the opportunity to participate in your class."[61]

---

[57]E. Smith to M. Barth, May 24, 1955. MBL. Series I. Box 12. As Barth himself told Gaylord Couchman, president of the University of Dubuque, "The wider scope of work and the sharper criticism with its effect on my own research work calls me to follow the new call." M. Barth to G. Couchman, May 17, 1955. MBL. Series I. Box 12. In a letter to the Rev. Albert Kinzler, pastor of a German-speaking Presbyterian congregation in Lansing, Iowa, Smith repeated what Markus had already said about his reasons for leaving: "Dr Barth feels more at home in a large university center than in a denominational seminary where he questions whether he would enjoy the same intellectual freedom that is possible in the University of Chicago." While this may sound as though the parting of ways was somewhat acrimonious, Smith went on to reassure Kinzler that "they [the Barths] leave with the blessing of our school and with no friction whatsoever. . . . We hope to retain their friendship and respect, and plan to bring Dr Barth back as a part-time professor when he has established himself in his work at Chicago." E. Smith to A. Kinzler, January 5, 1956. MBL. Series I. Box 31.

[58]G. Couchman to M. Barth, August 8, 1955. MBL. Series I. Box 12.

[59]M. Barth to N. Barth, May 5, 1955. MBL. Series II. Box 11.

[60]J. Mihelic to M. Barth, January 19, 1956. MBL. Series I. Box 31.

[61]L. Marshburn to M. Barth, December 8, 1955. MBL. Series I. Box 12.

Marshburn was not the only student to feel the loss of Markus to the seminary deeply. Loren Parker, a pastor who had returned to Dubuque for further theological studies, wrote to Markus, saying that "I will be very sorry to see you go. It is a source of gratitude to me that I have been able to sit under a man of your scholarship and devotion." Markus's departure, though, was perhaps a blessing in disguise. Betraying a rather uncharitable superiority over an institution that had become known for its theological liberalism, Parker went on: "Many of us will pray earnestly for you as you go to the University of Chicago. We hope that you will be able to be used to restore to that famous institution a humbler dependence on the Word, and a deeper study and appreciation of it."[62]

As for Markus's own feelings on leaving Dubuque, they were inevitably mixed. Excited by the prospect of work in a larger and richer research environment, Markus was both grateful to the seminary for the opportunities it had afforded him as well as conscious of his own shortcomings. "I want to thank you," he wrote to President Couchman, "for all that I owe to the University of Dubuque." Chief among the things for which he was thankful were the call to a professorship in the first place, and the warm collegiality of the faculty with whom he had been able to work. "These persons and things made me much more a receiver than a giver." Nonetheless, Markus felt, too, that he had failed to ease the tensions between both the university and the seminary, and between the "modern practical and the traditional scholarly theological fields. . . . I was unable to convince the other 'camp' that even by insisting upon academic work I meant nothing else but to serve the reformation of the church." Similarly, and perhaps acknowledging why Chicago was such a promising venture for him, Markus also regretted his inability to lead the seminary away from "a traditional, denominational, pietistic evangelism" and toward a "more openminded ecumenical thinking in theological and secular matters."[63] That these bridge-building tasks had not, in fact, been expected or required of Markus by either the University or the seminary was, for him, inconsequential. Having seen the problems, Markus left Dubuque unnecessarily annoyed with himself for having failed

[62]L. Parker to M. Barth, January 7, 1956. MBL. Series I. Box 31.

[63]M. Barth to G. Couchman, January 24, 1956. MBL. Series I. Box 31.

to solve them and frustrated that that he had been prevented from speaking as freely about them as he would have wished.

The only other issue to resolve was, of course, the timing of Markus's departure from Dubuque and his commencement in Chicago. Initially uncertain whether Dubuque would release him early from his contract, Markus alerted Jerry Brauer to the possibility that he may not be able to start the new post until July 1956.[64] Indeed, in alerting Dubuque University's administration of his new appointment, Markus made it clear that he did not wish to create any difficulties by departing prematurely. "I feel bound by the kindness shown to me from the beginning by the administration of the University of Dubuque, to serve up to the end of the time of my contract—i.e. till June 1956. And I am ready and willing to do this with all energy and joy."[65] As it turned out, though, Smith from Dubuque and Brauer from Chicago negotiated a compromise that allowed Barth to start his new job in mid-January.[66] With the exception of a brief interlude preparing for and delivering guest lectures on "some new aspects of Christology" to the Wisconsin Congregational ministers' retreat in early September,[67] the remainder of the year was thus spent concluding courses and packing up the house.

In September, Rose Marie and the children left Dubuque for Chicago so that the children could begin the new school year in their new home. Markus, meanwhile, stayed in Dubuque to complete his responsibilities there, traveling to Chicago on the weekends. Finally, by December 1955, the family was together again. Their house—at 4846 South Kimbark Avenue, on Chicago's South Side—had been found by Rose Marie, who had deliberately sought out a racially integrated neighborhood.[68] Not only did it have the type of diverse demographic that the family was looking for, it also had good schools and was ideally located just two miles north of Markus's

[64]M. Barth to J. C. Brauer, May 17, 1955. MBL. Series I. Box 12.

[65]M. Barth to G. Couchman, May 17, 1955. MBL. Series I. Box 12.

[66]M. Barth to J. C. Brauer, June 1, 1955; J. C. Brauer to M. Barth, June 8, 1955. MBL. Series I. Box 12.

[67]J. G. Morgan to M. Barth, May 28, 1955; M. Barth to J. G. Morgan, May 19, 1955. MBL. Series I. Box 12.

[68]P. Barth, A. Barth, R. Naveau-Barth, and R.-M. Barth-Häfeli, "Chicago Memories," November 2020, 1. MBL. Series II. Box 7.

new office at the university. Strangely, perhaps, one of the first requests of the family on their arrival in Chicago was made neither of Markus nor Rose Marie but of the children. On December 26, Peter, Anna, Ruth, Lukas, and Rose-Marie were interviewed by WTTW-Channel 11 for a feature program about "Christmas in Switzerland." Just as had been the case three years earlier in Dubuque, the Barths were, from the moment of their arrival, the focus of much curiosity.[69]

[69]*Hyde Park Herald*, December 21, 1955.

5

"WHY DID THIS SCHOOL APPOINT DR. MARKUS BARTH?"

Chicago, 1955–1963

IT TOOK ALMOST A FULL YEAR of living in Chicago before Rose Marie found the time to write a circular letter to friends and family back in Switzerland. When she did write, though, she was quick to reassure them that despite its infamous reputation, the Barths were enjoying their new home in Chicago's South Side.[1] "We are all grateful for our new, spacious house," she reported.[2] More than just the house, though, the neighborhood itself was a refreshing change after Midwestern Iowa. Perhaps because Chicago was a much bigger, more multicultural city than Dubuque—in which, as has been seen already, the Barths were initially greeted with a degree of exotic fascination—they were free "to be who we are . . . to act as we see fit, not only as strange loners, but on the contrary as thoroughly accepted members of the whole [community]."[3]

The neighborhood was not, of course, without its problems. The Barths were surrounded by evidence of poverty, a lack of adequate resourcing of the local public schools, and a disturbingly high crime rate. Markus's

[1]"Trotz allem was an Schrecklichem oder Lächerlichem über diese Stadt bekannt ist—Es gefällt uns hier." R. M. Barth, "Rundbrief," November 1956, 1.
[2]R. M. Barth, "Rundbrief," November 1956, 2.
[3]R. M. Barth, "Rundbrief," November 1956, 1.

female students were even encouraged to carry umbrellas under their coats if they had evening classes, or if they went to the weekly open evenings at the Barths' house, to use in the event of being assaulted on their way.[4] Nevertheless, despite these various causes for concern, Rose Marie was pleased to report that the three eldest children—Peter, Anna, and Ruth—had settled in relatively well to their new routines and were "fulfilled with their school life and homework." The two youngest children, meanwhile—Lukas and Rose-Marie—roamed freely around a neighborhood that was full of children their own age, most of whom were either black or Jewish.[5]

ENCOUNTERING AMERICA'S RACIAL DIVIDE

What came as more of a shock, however, was the depth of racial discrimination and inequality, which was exacerbated by the large number of black families arriving into the area each day. Their own neighborhood of Kenwood was not alone in having a particularly high proportion of black families. While Kenwood coped with this demographic shift generally well, in many other districts this ethnic integration was far from harmonious. "Not everyone likes it," wrote Rose Marie. Despite intentional efforts on the part of the city authorities to develop integrated low-cost housing options, "from the moment the Negroes . . . moved in, 200 police officers had to be called up [from outside the neighborhood] to protect them from attacks by the whites." With black tenants being charged disproportionately high rental charges, the inevitable consequence was that multiple families had to live in houses intended only for one family—thus causing overpopulation in black areas and the "transformation in less than 10 years of a neat and tidy suburb into a sad slum."[6] Recounting these realities to friends and family back home in Switzerland evidently moved Markus's mother, Nelly,

[4]In 1951, the Kenwood area had the 6th highest crime rate of the 41 Chicagoan districts, at 40.7 offenses per 1000 residents. However, some criminologists have argued that the higher crime rate was at least as much to do with racial profiling tactics employed by the police. See D. R. Flood, *Rape in Chicago: Race, Myth, and the Courts* (Urbana-Champagne: University of Illinois Press, 2012), 92-93.

[5]R. M. Barth, "Rundbrief," November 1956, 1.

[6]R. M. Barth, "Rundbrief," November 1956, 3. Neither this nor Rose Marie's use of the word "Negro" (*Neger*) to refer to African Americans should be interpreted as meaning that either Markus or Rose Marie shared the discriminatory attitudes toward their black neighbors. What is clear, however, is

Figure 5.1. 4846 Kimbark Ave., the Barths' home in Chicago, 1955–1963

deeply. "In your letters you have explained to us in great detail how burning the question of race is, and what it means to discern a Christian position, and then live by it," she wrote to her son. "I wish you and Rose Marie much strength in your great task."[7]

Possibly the Barths were more observant about racial tensions than others. In any event, a newspaper report from late April portrayed Kenwood in a slightly more positive light than Rose Marie's letter. Tony Weitzel, from the *Chicago Daily News*, wrote of the neighborhood as a place where "wonderful Americans" have "faced up to the fact that they [live] in an interracial community . . . and are making it work. Kenwood is flourishing." Indeed, the residents seem "to pay no attention at all to each others' color."[8] As it happened, Markus and the rest of the family were featured prominently in the article. Not only was Markus "bringing luster to an already distinguished name" through his work at the university, the family as a whole had "won respect and warm friendships. Friendships, for the record,

that they were astute enough observers to identify both the causes and consequences of the systemic racism in American society of the mid-1950s.

[7]N. Barth to M. Barth, March 13, 1956. MBL. Series II. Box 11.

[8]T. Weitzel, "The Town Crier," *Chicago Daily News*, April 25, 1956, 70.

that are inter-racial." Weitzel highlighted in particular an American Indian family whose apartment had been destroyed by fire and who were housed by the Barths until they could return to their home. "Rosemarie Barth," Weitzel wrote effusively, "bedded them down somehow, made them comfortable with her own five little ones. The Barth home almost bulged with children."[9]

Many of the Barths' other neighbors were Jewish immigrants. To their right lived the Abrahams, whose father was a psychiatrist; on the left was Mrs. Lazarus, from whom the Barth children learned piano.[10] Perhaps surprisingly, these families still felt themselves to be outsiders; even more surprisingly, Jews were, at least according to Rose Marie's observations, still denied entry to some of the city's hotels. For their part, though, the Barths were delighted to be living in a neighborhood so infused with Jewish culture. There was, reported Rose Marie, "a warmth and liberal-mindedness" among their Jewish neighbors and a premium placed on the centrality of the family "that does one good." Of particular interest, though, given the accusations of both theological and social anti-Jewishness, which have so often shadowed Karl Barth's name,[11] is the esteem with which Markus was held by members of the local Jewish community, precisely on account of his father. As one of the local shop owners once said when Rose Marie was unable to show him the university ID card needed for a store discount but instead mentioned Markus's name, "O, isn't he the son of the great Karl Barth? It's alright then, it's alright."[12]

---

[9]Weitzel, "The Town Crier," 70. None of the Barth children remembers this occasion, and so it is likely that the family did not stay with the Barths for long.

[10]Peter, however, did not learn piano with his siblings. Fully intending to return to Switzerland to complete his studies, which he did in 1958, Peter and his parents were determined that he keep up with his former classmates. This he did by taking Greek in Dubuque, and Latin in Chicago's Harvard School for Boys, which left him no time for piano lessons. P. Barth, A. Barth, R. Naveau-Barth and R.-M. Barth-Häfeli, "Chicago Memories," November 2020, 1. MBL. Series II. Box 7.

[11]For some of the most egregious examples, see inter alia F.-W. Marquardt, *Die Entdeckung des Judentums für die christliche Theologie: Israel im Denken Karl Barths* (Munich: Christian Kaiser Verlag, 1967); F. E. Talmage, ed., *Disputation and Dialogue: Readings in the Christian-Jewish Encounter* (New York: Ktav, 1975), 38; D. J. Goldhagen, *Hitler's Willing Executioners: Ordinary Germans and the Holocaust* (London: Little, Brown, 1996), 113; and H. Jansen, "Antisemitism in the Amicable Guise of Philo-Semitism in Karl Barth's Theology Before and After Auschwitz," in *Remembering for the Future: Papers Presented at the International Scholars' Conference* (Oxford: Pergamon, 1988).

[12]R. M. Barth, "Rundbrief," November 1956, 4.

Figure 5.2. Markus

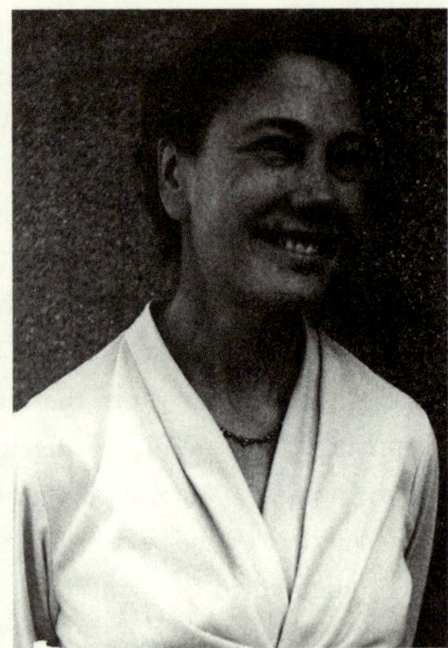

Figure 5.3. Rose Marie

TEACHING, PREACHING, AND TRAVELING

As for Markus himself, he had in the main been warmly welcomed by his new colleagues in the Federated Theological Faculty, despite some inevitable differences of pedagogical opinion. Markus's insistence that his students learn Greek for even their elective subjects in New Testament, for example, was for some an unwelcome and unnecessary innovation.[13] In some quarters, however, there was outright anger at his arrival. At the annual Student-Faculty Conference in April 1956, one "unrestrained voice" representing various anxieties among both staff and students demanded of the collected faculty, "Why did this school appoint Dr Markus Barth?"[14] Insofar as the conference's theme for that year concerned "the issue of truth and commitment" in theological education, it would seem that Barth's well-known confessional ties led some to suspect that he would eschew genuinely open theological inquiry.[15] If such was the case, then—given that

[13] R. M. Barth, "Rundbrief," November 1956, 8.

[14] B. E. Meland, "The Student-Faculty Spring Conference," *The Divinity School News* 23, no. 3 (August 1, 1956), 11.

[15] Meland, "The Student-Faculty Spring Conference," 11-12.

Barth's departure from Dubuque was, from his point of view, precisely on account of the constricting nature of its narrow confessionalism—those who held such anxieties had clearly not done their homework on him.

Markus's schedule of university lectures was quickly supplemented with requests and invitations for extramural presentations. In the first week of March, he delivered the Sprunt Lectures at Union Theological Seminary in Richmond, Virginia, on the topic of the Johannine prologue. There he won friends and admirers through "the intensity and breadth of [his] Biblical scholarship, the enthusiasm with which [he] presented [his] subject, and the winsomeness of [his] presence."[16] He also gave six nightly studies on every Wednesday of Lent at Chicago's Fourth Presbyterian Church. Questions submitted from the audience suggest that in at least some of his talks, Markus broached a few of the more controversial political questions of the day.[17] The Lenten season also saw Markus engaged as the keynote speaker for the university's Bond Chapel services, with his final sermon—on the Wednesday of Holy Week—reminding his hearers of God's transformative presence, even in the moment of death, condemnation, and despair. "In deepest misery . . . there is hope in Christ."[18] Shortly after Easter, on April 17, Markus—continuing the interest he had begun to articulate during his January 1955 visit to Philadelphia—gave another talk on Bultmann's demythologization to a fraternity gathered together by the university pastor, Donald Dawe.[19]

Markus's willingness to accept speaking invitations across the country had both familial and professional benefits. On one hand, honoraria for the additional work helped fund his children's tuition at school and, later, through their college years. On the other hand, the lectures, especially when they brought him into conversation with interested laypeople—conversations he regarded as essential for *both* sides—provided invaluable material for his publications. Similarly, these engagements

[16]J. Jones to M. Barth, March 3, 1956. MBL. Series I. Box 31.

[17]Questions based on Barth's third address were specifically concerned with the moral commands applicable to American soldiers. "Questions for Rev. Dr. Marcus Barth, School of Religion, 4th Presbyterian Church," March 7, 1956. MBL. Series I. Box 31.

[18]M. Barth, "For Criminals Only," *The Divinity School News* 23, May 1, 1956, 6.

[19]D. G. Dawe to "Fellow Friars," April 9, 1956. MBMC. Series VI. Box SF18, file 11.

helped increase his reputation as well as his public visibility. It is perhaps not surprising, then, that in March—despite having been in Chicago less than a term—Markus was approached with the offer of another job. Professor Béla Vassady,[20] "the man who introduced [Karl Barth] to Hungary in 1936," wrote to Markus in strictest confidence to ask if he would be willing to entertain a call to the Theological Seminary of the Evangelical and Reformed Church in Lancaster, Pennsylvania. The seminary's New Testament professor, Robert Moss, was due to take up the presidency of the seminary in September 1957, and so they were keen to fill the vacancy that would thereby be created. Would Markus be interested? Conscious that he had only just moved to Chicago, Vassady noted that the seminary would be willing to wait until 1958 before making the appointment if they knew that Markus was open to the call. Vassady sought to sweeten the deal by offering not only a full professorship but life tenure and a nontaxable residence on top of the annual salary.[21] The conditions of the offer were, no doubt, attractive. In the end, though, Markus decided that he had not given up a denominational college in favor of a research-intensive university, just to return immediately to the same sort of confessionalism that he had left behind in Dubuque. His declining of the offer was gracious but inevitable.

As had become his habit, Markus continued the weekly open evenings for his students. Held on Mondays and often lasting as late as midnight, up to thirty students would gather in the Barths' home to discuss a key theological text or sometimes a book of the Bible. The forums were not, however, purely academic conversations. On the contrary, they were an important way for Markus to get to know his students better and more personally than was possible in a lecture hall. Similarly, Markus made sure that he incorporated into the discussions, in a way that was not possible in his more formal lectures, some thoroughly practical applications of whatever text was being

[20]Béla Vassady (1902–1992) had been professor of systematic theology in the Reformed Divinity Faculty of the University of Debrecen. In 1946, he left Hungary for the United States where, in 1949, he was appointed professor of ecumenics at Fuller Theological Seminary. He was forced to leave two years later, as his sympathies for neoorthodoxy convinced some that his presence on the faculty was damaging Fuller's evangelical credentials.

[21]B. Vassady to M. Barth, March 26, 1956. MBL. Series I. Box 31.

discussed. This was important, he reasoned, given that the students were, in the main, preparing for various forms of ministry.[22] Just as significant as the pedagogical value of these open evenings, however, was the warmly hospitable environment that the Barth home was for so many of Markus's students. As one such student, David Maxfield, said toward the end of the Barths' time in the "windy city," "I would like to say 'thank you' . . . for extending me such a gracious hand of hospitality. . . . It is contacts such as these that help the lonely 'BD' [i.e., bachelor of divinity] student of the Divinity School to remember that he is part of a community."[23]

DEBATING TOM TORRANCE

During the summer of 1956, Rose Marie took the two eldest and the two youngest children on holiday to Colorado. Meanwhile, Markus took Ruth with him to Switzerland for two months, for most of which time he stayed in Basel with Karl and Nelly while Ruth holidayed with her godmother. They did not stay in Switzerland for the entire eight weeks, though. In July, Markus traveled with Karl to London, during which they were received by Geoffrey Fisher—at that time serving as the archbishop of Canterbury—at a reception at Lambeth Palace. From London, they continued on to Edinburgh, where Karl was to be conferred with his second honorary doctorate of laws. There, they met up with Tom Torrance and Dietrich Ritschl, the latter of whom was keen to follow up with Markus on the possibility of a teaching position in the United States.[24]

While the occasion for this visit was indeed a happy one, the meeting with Torrance was tense, bringing to a head a rather fractious disagreement between the Scottish theologian and Markus that had been simmering

---

[22]R. M. Barth, "Rundbrief," November 1956, 3.

[23]D. Maxfield to R. M. Barth, April 17, 1961. MBL. Series V, file 4.

[24]See E. Busch, *Karl Barth: His Life from Letters and Autobiographical Texts*, trans. J. Bowden (Grand Rapids, MI: Eerdmans, 1994), 422. In March, Ritschl—who was at the time serving as minister to a German-speaking congregation in Edinburgh—had written to Markus to ask if he might keep his eye out for any teaching positions that might become available in either the USA or Canada, and for which Ritschl might be suitable. D. Ritschl to M. Barth, March 9, 1956. MBL. Series I. Box 31. In June, he wrote again, expressing his delight that he would be able to see both Markus and Karl in Edinburgh, but also his hope that he and Markus might be able to discuss his prospects. "If, as I hope, I can then see you alone in the house, I would like to talk with you about my future." D. Ritschl to M. Barth, June 4, 1956. MBL. Series I. Box 31.

Figure 5.4. Karl and Markus in the garden at Bruderholzallee 26, 1956

away since the Lund Conference of 1952, and Torrance's published explication of that conference in 1954.[25] At issue was Torrance's doctrine of incorporation and its ramifications for ecclesiology and the sacraments. It was, in Markus's view, simply a more careful—but not, for that reason, any less problematic—elucidation of his former *Doktorvater* K. L. Schmidt's formula, "Ecclesiology is Christology, and vice versa." As far as Markus could discern, Torrance's consequential sacramentalism—which was, he argued, being vigorously prosecuted through the pages of the *Scottish Journal of Theology*, of which Torrance was founding editor—led him inevitably to the conclusion that it was "the institutional character of the church" rather than "the Living God and His Spirit" that was the guarantor of the church's continuity and unity.[26] Indeed, Markus read Torrance's 1954 article to be arguing that "the living God and Christ is readily and

[25]T. F. Torrance, "The Atonement and the Oneness of the Church," *Scottish Journal of Theology* 7, no. 3 (September 1954): 245-69.

[26]M. Barth to T. F. Torrance, February 26, 1956, 1. MBL. Series I. Box 31. Note that in 1959, Barth himself entered the *SJT* fray by noting that the idea of "incorporation" was one of the means by which the proper understanding and celebration of baptism had been distorted. See M. Barth, "Baptism and Evangelism," *Scottish Journal of Theology* 12, no. 1 (March 1959): 33-34.

Figure 5.5. BBC German Service radio program, 7 July, 1956. Left to right: Markus, Karl, and German-Jewish writer Alfons Rosenberg

completely substituted by the miracle of the church, even of the Sacrament."[27] That the Church of England and the (Presbyterian) Church of Scotland, in which Torrance was a minister, had recently begun a fresh round of conversations toward "unrestricted intercommunion" was further proof for Markus that Torrance's church was relinquishing its Reformed heritage under the Word of God to an arid institutional sacramentalism.[28]

For his part, Torrance retorted that while he loved him "as a brother," he was aghast that Markus had read him in precisely the opposite direction of his meaning. He suspected that Markus's perception of both his doctrine of incorporation, and the allegedly sacramentalist nature of the church union talks that were underway, was being driven by misinformation from the "American press." It is clear, argued Torrance, that "you do not have any genuine or accurate information of what is being talked about . . . you have

[27]This is Torrance's quotation of Markus's (undated) letter, which is no longer available. T. F. Torrance to M. Barth, November 30, 1954, 2. MBL. Series I. Box 31.

[28]See "Our Fellowship in the Gospel: Report of the Joint Study Group Between the Church of Scotland and the Church of England" (2010), 36-40. www.churchofscotland.org.uk/__data/assets/pdf_file/0014/3119/our_fellowship.pdf.

not studied what we have published . . . [and] you have not read any of it."[29] Nevertheless, he still hoped that the two of them might be able to talk profitably, and more amicably, during Markus's visit to Edinburgh.

By June, the tensions had been eased slightly, partly because of an exchange between Torrance and Arthur Cochrane, the latter of whom had acted as something of an intermediary on Markus's behalf. Torrance, however, was still wary: "The further our correspondence developed on the lines we had been following the more involved you seemed to get in misunderstanding what we are after."[30] One week later, he acknowledged that it was not simply a matter of misunderstandings, but that "there are real differences."[31] It would seem that their conversations in Edinburgh did nothing to resolve those differences. For Markus, at least, sharp disagreements remained between them. As he put it in a letter to Shaun Herron of *The British Weekly*, Torrance's ideas of "sacramental incorporation" were "impossible and confused." "I still disagree with [them] as much as [before]." However, he had decided to give Torrance "a chance to express himself clearer . . . before I condemn what seems to be so bad and poor." As a result, Markus told Herron that he had decided "not to write anything against Tom Torrance and his clique" in the hope that Torrance would, in the meantime, change his mind.[32]

NIEMOELLER, EISENHOWER, AND AMERICAN POLITICS

Toward the end of the year, with Markus and Ruth having returned to Chicago after the summer vacation, the Barths were visited once more by Martin Niemoeller, who had been invited to preach in the university's Rockefeller Chapel. It will be recalled that the last time Niemoeller had spoken in front of Barth had been in Bubendorf, some four years previously. On that occasion, the German pastor's address had provoked

[29]T. F. Torrance to M. Barth, February 6, 1956, 1. MBL. Series I. Box 31.

[30]T. F. Torrance to M. Barth, June 5, 1956, 1. MBL. Series I. Box 31.

[31]T. F. Torrance to M. Barth, June 13, 1956, 1. MBL. Series I. Box 31.

[32]M. Barth to S. Herron, July 10, 1956. MBL. Series I. Box 31. It should be stressed that, theological and ecclesial differences aside, Torrance and Barth remained personally on good terms, and continued a warm friendship well into their later years.

considerable controversy. This time was no different. Delivered in front of a huge crowd, Niemoeller's address was a sermon that "kept strictly to the text, but spoke directly to the situation."[33] The situation in question was, of course, the Hungarian uprising of October–November 1956, its brutal repression by Russian forces, and the Suez Crisis that unfolded contemporaneously. But Niemoeller was not alone in speaking out; Markus also voiced his opinions.

> Though I am shocked as much as anybody by [those] atrocities in Hungary and Egypt, I think the worst thing which happened in connection with these events was the reaction of the "West." The self-righteous tone in which churches and journalists, politicians and the man on the street condemned the Russian intervention, praised indiscriminately the revolutionists and relaxed in the attitude that at least *we* are better men, seemed to me as bare of culture and promise as the attack upon Budapest.[34]

As he had done in Portland back in 1954, Barth again repudiated the simplistic binarism by which Western liberalism was presumed all too easily to be the self-evident reification of good in contrast to any government or ideology that stood in opposition. In relation to the Suez Crisis, one thing that was particularly galling, to both Markus and Rose Marie, was the belligerent attitude of the Israelis and the English government, the latter as personified by Anthony Eden. "We would like to believe [they were seeking] peace, but we find it somewhat difficult."[35] This was one of Barth's first open criticisms of Israeli foreign policy since arriving in the United States. It was not, however, to be his last.

Perhaps coincidentally, Israel was on Markus's mind in the context of his academic work too. At the very time that he was shaking his head at the Israeli government's actions during the Suez Crisis, he was also beginning to consider the question of the fundamental unity of the two scriptural Testaments. This was not, for him, primarily a dogmatic question

---

[33] R. M. Barth, "Rundbrief," November 1956, 9.

[34] M. Barth to U. Campagnolo, December 29, 1956. MBL. Series I. Box 31.

[35] R. M. Barth, "Rundbrief," November 1956, 10. Showing considerable insight, Rose Marie and Markus observed that there were far too few Americans who really understood the Suez issue from a European perspective. It was regarded almost universally through the lens of English colonialism ("*unter dem Zeichen englischer Kolonial Politik*").

concerning the doctrine of revelation. Rather, it was a matter that he interpreted in a deliberately interreligious—and therefore political—sense. "Our solidarity," he noted, is "with the Jews: they are not a nation, but our brethren (our older brother . . .)."[36] That he could affirm this theologically while simultaneously critiquing the Israeli state was to become a recurring—and increasingly contentious—motif.

On January 20, 1957, Barth himself took to the pulpit of the Rockefeller Chapel, delivering a sermon on the occasion of Dwight Eisenhower's second presidential inauguration. Taking the opening verses of Psalm 72 as his text—"Give the king thy justice, O God"—Markus warned against the temptation, into which he feared the National Presbyterian Church in Washington, DC, had fallen, of glorifying the political status quo.[37] Urging the pursuit of God's righteousness, not human moral standards, Markus denounced the one-sided and myopic political favoritism that so characterized Western liberal democracy. Having taken sides "wholeheartedly with those fighting for freedom in Hungary," why, Markus asked, was India's struggle against colonial rule "bare of our support?" Having been magnanimous enough to "forgive our friends England and France for what they have done to Egyptian people" in the wake of the Suez Crisis, why was not similar forgiveness shown "to those whom we considered enemies before and who treated Budapest so barbarously? [Are] we partial in our belief in reconciliation?"[38] Acknowledging the political and racial tensions, not only globally but even in his own local neighborhood, Barth stressed that the path to peace "can only be paved by people who humiliate themselves before God. . . . Howling with the bloodthirsty wolves of competing powers did not prove helpful to Israel in its ancient history. Nor should it be the mark of Christians today."[39]

---

[36]M. Barth, notes on "The OT in the NT," November 11, 1956. MBMC. Series IV. Box SF33.

[37]M. Barth, "Give the King Thy Justice, O God," *The Pulpit* (July 1957), 6. The editors noted that while "the second inauguration of President Dwight D. Eisenhower was the occasion for the preacher's profoundly biblical reflection on the relation between the justice of God and man's political justice . . . [the] main issue . . . is so basic to our national life that *The Pulpit* offers the sermon for our Fourth of July reflection."

[38]Barth, "Give the King Thy Justice, O God," 21.

[39]Barth, "Give the King Thy Justice, O God," 22. Note that while Barth uses the word "humiliate," his meaning was probably closer to the word "humble."

This sermon was not the only time during the year to come that Barth ventured into politically sensitive territory. In a springtime address to the Christian Frontier Fellowship in Chicago, he openly criticized US foreign policy on three grounds, each of which he likened to a specific doctrinal locus. First, using the analog of sin, Barth critiqued the tendency to bifurcate the world into two distinct categories of people—the (Western democratic) good, and the (Eastern communistic) evil. "International Communism [as] the black buck; Western democracy [as] the stainless sheep" is, he argued, "one of the underlying trends of American foreign policy." While consistent with traditional Calvinist understandings of predestination, this simplistic bipartition, said Markus, was nothing other than "watered down, folklore Christianity—ancient myth and Victorian morality in perfect pious harmony." As far as Barth was concerned, not only did this bifurcation of humanity not accord with the narrative of Scripture, it also blinded the US to more complicated foreign political issues. "It is apparently not considered possible that dilemmas and problems other than the East-West controversy may exist and be of higher concern for Israel and the Arab nations, for Europe and Australia, for India and Africa."[40]

Second, Markus challenged America's sense of being entitled to "world leadership." Referencing soteriology, he agreed that the US had in fact rescued Europe from totalitarian regimes "twice within a generation. . . . Little wonder that the US is regarded as the savior and stronghold of democracy." The problem, however, was that such pretensions to global moral leadership undermine the very goal of peace that they claim to serve. "Any nation's claim to world leadership spoils the international coexistence which is a presupposition of peace" because, in the end, it is no less than "an imperialist intervention which treats other nations like animals to be dominated." Even more dangerously, insisted Barth, such a claim "interferes directly with the kingship of God." Whereas the US may indeed be "mightier, richer, more successful than any other nation has ever been," this neither necessitated, nor justified, America's idolatrous usurpation of God's own place.[41]

---

[40]M. Barth, "Reflections on US Foreign Policy," *Christianity and Crisis* 17 (October 14, 1957): 132.
[41]Barth, "Reflections on US Foreign Policy," 133-34.

Finally, with eschatology as his doctrinal referent, Barth rejected the idea—implicit, in his view, within American foreign policy—that the expansion of US democracy throughout the world was the prerequisite to the moral perfection of humankind. On the contrary, he argued, peace and righteousness would be secured, not through particular national brands of virtue, but through "the power of God through Christ to make right the affairs and life of wicked men." By repudiating any fixed "system of moral values," Barth thus insisted on the need for a constant re-evaluation of decisions, priorities, and presuppositions. "We may become open to a revision of our own political thought and action." In particular, argued Barth, this might (and should) cause the US to eschew that simplistic bifurcation of the world into good and bad; to be more cognizant of the plight of Arab nations, and those younger countries so recently liberated from colonial oppression; and to renew its commitment to the right and legitimacy of Israel to exist.[42]

ECUMENICAL WORK

Through much of 1957, Markus was heavily engaged in ecumenical conversations. In late January, he addressed the twenty-sixth annual Ministers' Week at the Chicago Theological Seminary. There his ecclesial targets were clearly the Episcopalians. Having spent the previous year locked in a battle with Tom Torrance over the latter's institutional sacramentalism, he now expressed alarm at "the increasing emphasis" being placed by some churches on "high church" liturgies, arguing that such forms of worship were hindering, not helping, the cause of ecumenism. "I'm afraid that we are trying to enclose ourselves within holy walls rather than to seek unity

[42]Barth, "Reflections on US Foreign Policy," 134. In an earlier, longer version of this article, Barth elaborated upon—and stated more pointedly—some of those themes that, in the context of the address to the Frontier Fellowship, had been referenced only in passing. For example, he left no room for doubt that his chief target was the so-called Eisenhower Doctrine—that "summary expression of the United States"—by which Russia was rendered "the wicked dragon" and the US "the blonde Siegfried." Similarly, the notion of American "world leadership"—regardless of whether the US had sought it, or had it imposed upon it by an impoverished post-war Europe—was "a dream that were better not dreamt." Insofar as it presupposed American (moral) superiority, asked Barth, rhetorically but also provocatively, "Does it not smell of the Fuehrer and his elect race?" See M. Barth, "Reflections on An Other Doctrine," *Comprendre* 17-18 (March 1957): 1-7.

in our Christian testimony to the world."[43] Curiously, perhaps, he reprised this theme in an April 1957 article for *The Reformed Review*. Writing on the Johannine prologue—which, it will be recalled, had been the focus of his Sprunt Lectures in March the previous year—he argued, among other things, that the evangelist's emphasis in John 1:11-12 is that the Christian believer becomes a child of God through miracle, juridical action, faith, and by the act of witnessing. "If only one of these characteristics were missing we [would] not [have] described a child of God."[44] But this, Barth continued, meant the rejection of any other means of Christian birth. "Absent from the prologue is any hint that the new man . . . is born out of a sacrament. . . . High Church sacramentalism . . . is not only strange but opposite to the prologue's doctrine of salvation."[45]

Much more substantial than his critique of Episcopalian sacramental theology, however, was Markus's engagement with North American Baptists, some of which came about through familial connections. When the Barths had first moved to Chicago, they had presumed that their ecclesial home would be within a Presbyterian context. An early and unhappy encounter between Rose Marie and two ladies from the nearby Presbyterian congregation, however, had forced a change of heart. In response to Rose Marie's asking if the church in question had any black congregants, the ladies reportedly answered, "Oh, no. We like Bach. Our type of church music is too cultured for them." Knowing that she could, with integrity, only belong to a church in which "there was room for Negroes," Rose Marie and the children thus began attending Chicago's First Baptist Church, which was conveniently situated less than half a mile from the family home.[46]

---

[43]"'High Church' Alarms," *Christianity Today*, February 18, 1957, 30. The Ministers' Week was held between January 21–25, with Markus's scheduled lectures for the week addressing the topic "Baptism in the New Testament and in Our Churches." While there is no necessary reason why these lectures should have lent themselves to wider questions of liturgical preference, the fact that one of the other speakers for the week—Albert Mollegen (1906–1984)—was from the Episcopal Church perhaps emboldened Barth to offer comments that may otherwise have been out of place. See *The Chicago Theological Seminary Register* 46, no. 6 (November 1956): 30.

[44]M. Barth, "A New Man Is Born," *The Reformed Review* 10, no. 3 (April 1957): 4-6.

[45]Barth, "A New Man Is Born," 7.

[46]P. Barth et al., "Chicago Memories," 2. The First Baptist Church of Chicago itself has a fascinating history. Founded in 1833, it has never been restricted to just one type of ecclesial or theological character, having had, at various times, both "pastors with a liberal theology and pastors with a conservative theology." It has been "a 'society' church and it has been a

Despite her disinclination to be rebaptized—a refusal that, though it went against their theology, was eventually honored by the congregation—Rose Marie was soon an active participant.[47] By mid-1957, both she and Peter were members, with Rose Marie taking an increasingly visible role in the life of the community.[48] But Markus, too, was involved. Though formally a member of the Presbyterian Church, Markus attended First Baptist with his family as a "friend" and "active non-member." Frequently called upon by Pastor Jitsuo Morikawa to preach[49]—including, reported

'middle-class' church." Most interesting, perhaps, has been its record on race relations. Initially an ardently pro-slavery church, that position was reversed in the years after the Civil War. By the time that the Barths began attending, First Baptist was home to a growing number of Black Americans as well as Japanese Americans, with Jitsuo Morikawa being the first *Nisei* to serve as pastor of a "white" church. Importantly, however, First Baptist's interracial character was not intentional. In a history of the church, written for its 125th anniversary in 1958, Keith Shumway noted that "the church did not become inter-racial because it had discussed the matter and decided that it was the thing to do. Any organization, especially a church, that proceeds in this manner is likely to have continued difficulties because this would mean that being inter-racial was a more important factor than the purpose of the organization." K. Shumway, "Our First 125 Years," in K. Shumway, C. Andrews and J. Bryant, *A Century and a Quarter with the First Baptist Church of Chicago* (Chicago: Chicago First Baptist Church, 1958), 12.

[47]In lieu of being rebaptized, Rose Marie penned a "Personal Confession of Jesus Christ," which she delivered in front of the congregation during a ceremony of welcome in March 1956. The only one of the children who was baptized in America was Ruth. Peter and Anna had been baptized as infants by Karl in Bubendorf, prior to leaving Switzerland. In Chicago, Ruth became active in the choir at First Baptist, after having read both Dostoyevsky and the *New English Bible*, and was baptized on April 5, 1964, when she was nineteen. That she chose to be baptized in this particular church, even after the family had moved away from Chicago to Pittsburgh, suggests something of how formative the congregation had been for her. See P. Barth et al., "Chicago Memories," 4-5; K. Watanabe, "Living with the Barth Family 1963–64," 2, MBL, series II, box 1.

[48]Rose Marie, for example, helped lead the "Explorers' Class" for those new to, or interested in, the Christian faith, as did Peter and Anna later on. Moreover, her work was warmly appreciated. As one of the senior members of the congregation wrote, "[Your] participation [is] so much just a natural expression of your continuous interest in and giving of yourself for the church." R. Nelson to R. M. Barth, October 14, 1957. Similarly, the new senior pastor, Charles R. Andrews—who joined First Baptist in 1957 from Oak Lawn Community Baptist Church, Rhode Island—said that "it is indeed a pleasure to work with you and to watch the enthusiasm you have for your teaching and the various activities in which you participate." C. R. Andrews to R. M. Barth, November 13, 1957. MBL. Series V, file 4. Andrews, in turn, was greatly appreciated by the Barths. In 1960, Markus wrote to his mother, telling her that "Our Pastor Andrews was here for an hour yesterday. He is a good man, with whom I get on well, and whose heart is in the right place. It is good for us to be cared for by him." M. Barth to N. Barth, September 4, 1960. MBL. Series II. Box 11.

[49]The website of First Baptist Church says that Pastor Morikawa left the congregation in 1955 to serve as director of evangelism for the American Baptist Convention. However, letters from Morikawa to Barth through 1956 suggest that he was still the senior pastor of First Baptist until at least the end of September of that year. This dating is confirmed by the appendix, "Some Former Pastors," in First Baptist's 125th anniversary brochure. See Shumway et al., *A Century and*

Rose Marie, on Palm Sunday—Markus was also involved in leading a small study group within the church on the question of baptism, the purpose of which was to investigate the growing phenomenon of young adolescent baptism. While the practice was not quite the same as infant baptism, the age of the candidates—mostly between ten and twelve years old—nonetheless raised the issue of confirmation, "with all its questionable side effects."[50]

At the same time as leading these studies, Markus had contact with some of the national Baptist structures. Having declined an invitation from Morikawa to be the keynote speaker at the Baptist Home Mission Society's "Evangelism and Bible" conference in July, Markus was asked if he would nevertheless provide biblical resources on evangelism, as well as some general theological guidance, to the American Baptist Convention in its preparation for the Baptist Jubilee Advance.[51] On this too, however, he disappointed Morikawa—not because he did not greatly admire the Baptists' missional "zeal" but because he was suspicious of the evangelistic methods proposed.

> I distrust utterly the confidence in method and the neglect of content. . . . If "the effectiveness of our work in Evangelism will be qualified by the methods we employ" (Workbook, p. 1), we might as well say Good Night to the Spirit and the pretension to be Christ's church. For it seems to me as if the church from the beginning had rather lived despite than from its method.[52]

---

a Quarter, 29. Certainly, by November 1956, Morikawa's letters were being sent on American Baptist Home Mission Society letterhead.

[50]R. M. Barth, "Rundbrief," November 1957, 5. Markus's Palm Sunday sermon was in an "all-age" service, with adults and children together. Afterward, the Sunday School superintendent, Annabelle Spencer, wrote to thank him for his words. It was "an excellent sermon you preached for the children this morning. I'm sure the adults enjoyed it and benefited from it also, but I was especially pleased that it was so interesting to the children. . . . You did an excellent job of making the occasion meaningful for them." A. Spencer to M. Barth, April 14, 1957. MBL. Series V, file 4. Markus's resistance to confirmation classes was likely, in part, a consequence of his own experience in 1930. But more generally, it was out of a desire to spare impressionable children from enthusiastic but ill-trained pastors. As Peter Barth notes, "Mandatory courses on dogma for 10-12 year-olds by pastors who are not necessarily gifted teachers can engender rejection and a lasting negative impression of the church." P. Barth, personal correspondence. February 12, 2022.

[51]J. Morikawa to M. Barth, November 14, 1956, November 19, 1956, and November 23, 1956. MBL. Series I. Box 31. The Baptist Jubilee Advance was a joint evangelistic movement of the various Baptist conventions of North America that lasted from 1959 to 1964 in celebration of the 150th anniversary of the beginnings of Baptist missions in North America.

[52]M. Barth to J. Morikawa, December 1, 1956. MBL. Series I. Box 31.

What he did accept, though, was an invitation to spend June at the Southern Baptist Theological Seminary in Louisville, Kentucky. The initial plan was that he grasp "the bull by the horns by speaking with Baptists about baptism."[53] Yet neither the invitation nor its acceptance proceeded smoothly. Having responded to the seminary's request for "a statement on [his] beliefs conc[erning] immersion," Markus's reply "evidently disturbed . . . the peace." What followed was something of a stand-off, with Markus refusing to go if the seminary administration had "more fear of their constituency than respect for the Bible's claims."[54] In the end, and following "a contrite letter, asking my pardon for [its] intolerant, denominational[ism]," Barth agreed to spend June in Louisville, accepting the seminary's suggestion that he choose "a less controversial topic for [his] lectures than the sacrament."[55] One result of these conversations was a concerted effort to encourage Markus to rewrite his book on baptism, *Die Taufe*, for an American audience. He was, said Rose Marie, "being assaulted from all quarters" to do so. In the end, however, the plan stalled, not least because Markus wished to undertake the revisions himself and wanted in the process to avoid theological jargon, but felt insufficiently familiar with American idioms.[56]

The second half of 1957 was more than usually frenetic for Barth, so much so that his mother, Nelly, worried for his health. "Just cancel something. . . . The world won't collapse. . . . Don't let yourself be overrun—you are not that strong."[57] Markus, however, seems not to have taken his mother's concerns too seriously. "Don't worry about me," he told her. The worst thing that could happen, he said, would be that "I'll just get a little flu," which gives me the opportunity to sleep in as long as I want to."[58] Thus, Markus continued with

---

[53]R. M. Barth, "Rundbrief," November 1957, 5.

[54]M. Barth to J. Morikawa, December 1, 1956.

[55]M. Barth to J. Morikawa, December 13, 1956. Rose Marie's circular letter at the end of the year suggests, however, that Markus did not entirely shy away from the subject. She writes that he explored the question of baptism "in front of astonished students" but "learnt nothing new" other than finding "all kinds of commentaries on the 'Baptist position' which no one has dared to touch for a hundred years." R. M. Barth, "Rundbrief," November 1957, 5.

[56]R. M. Barth, "Rundbrief," November 1957, 5.

[57]N. Barth to M. Barth, September 29, 1957. MBL. Series II. Box 11.

[58]M. Barth to N. Barth, December 21, 1957. MBL. Series II. Box 11.

his hectic pace. The major part of his teaching duties for the fall semester was focused on a "Christology in the Synoptic Gospels" seminar, as well as in preparation for a winter course on "Parables of the Kingdom," the latter of which he would teach once more in Chicago in 1960. He was also busy with preachments and other speaking engagements. In August, he continued his involvement with Baptist churches by preaching at Evanston's First Baptist Church as part of its centenary celebrations.[59] Then, on October 27, and at the invitation of the Bloomington-Normal Ministerial Association, he was the guest preacher at Bloomington's First Baptist for its Union Reformation Sunday service.[60] Earlier that month, on October 13, he preached at Christ Presbyterian Church in Madison, Wisconsin, afterward speaking at a dinner at the Presbyterian Student Center.[61]

ACADEMIC WORK: ON BULTMANN AND WIEMAN

Of course, while they did take up an inordinate amount of time given that he had no formal pastoral placement, Barth was not solely occupied with ecclesial concerns. Alongside his teaching responsibilities, he continued to pursue his research interests. In July, and bringing to fruition a project on which he had been working for the previous two years, he published a major review of Bultmann's theology of demythologization.[62] In it, he sought to identify the very respectable ground of form criticism as the basic presupposition of demythologizing, acknowledging in the process that both methods take the church, not individual religious geniuses, as the primary theological author of the earliest Christian message. Indeed, he went so far as to say that "the ecumenical movement . . . is unthinkable without this achievement."[63] While sharply critical of Bultmann's methodological approach, by which a material distinction is drawn between the forms of the kerygma and the kerygma itself, he was also appreciative of Bultmann's intent. The purpose of demythologizing, Barth averred, is to enable "modern man" to encounter "the true scandalon of the Cross"

[59]"Guest Ministers Will Preach in Evanston," *Chicago Tribune*, August 4, 1957, 146.
[60]*The Pantagraph*, October 23, 1957, 6.
[61]"Dr Barth to Talk," *Wisconsin State Journal*, October 11, 1957, 19.
[62]M. Barth, "Introduction to Demythologizing," *Journal of Religion* 37, no. 3 (July 1957): 145-55.
[63]Barth, "Introduction to Demythologizing," 145-46.

without being sidetracked by the "pseudo-scandala" of mythological language, "which lie in stories about a virgin birth, an exorcism, or the functioning of a cloud as an elevator to heaven."[64] Despite being unable finally to side with Bultmann's agenda, Barth nevertheless insisted that he had to be read "as a real theologian"—moreover, "as a Christian scholar and as a teacher of the church."[65]

Two months after the publication of this article, Markus became embroiled in a much more acrimonious debate, this time with the philosophical theologian Henry Nelson Wieman.[66] He was critical of Wieman's essay "Evaluation of the Absolute and Transcendence" and, in particular, of Wieman's concept of the freedom of God, and Wieman responded irately. Barth, he complained, "misunderstand[s] almost every point discussed," attributing to Wieman views and ideas which were the exact opposite of what he in fact "has always said and taught." For Wieman, though, the difference was not simply theological, but deeply cultural. "Even when I agree

---

[64]Barth, "Introduction to Demythologizing," 151.

[65]Barth, "Introduction to Demythologizing," 155. Less than a year later, Barth was describing Bultmann in far less charitable ways. In a review of Bultmann's *The Presence of Eternity, History and Eschatology*, he wrote that this book "reveals the inner core of Bultmann's thought. Not elements of biblical theology, but a strand of thought that started when Augustine dug into the folds of his ear, are the focus, criterion and perspective of this so-called philosophy of history. This reviewer holds that Augustine's *Confessions*—despite their moving and stimulating character—were one of the great catastrophes of Western theological thought. . . . Bultmann's little book shows the fruits of this catastrophe." M. Barth, typescript of a review of R. Bultmann, *The Presence of Eternity, History and Eschatology*, May 27, 1958, 3. MBMC. Series III. Publications. Box P11, file 17. The final review was published in *Journal of Religion* 39, no. 1 (1959): 61-62. In the same month that Barth drafted this review, he also wrote a review of Oscar Cullmann's *Christology in the New Testament*, in which Bultmann again loomed large. "Rudolf Bultmann's Theology of the New Testament rules the day [throughout this book]. It makes clear the distinction between the historic Jesus (of whom we know practically nothing and no more 2 Cor. 5:16) and the kerygma into which Christ has risen and by which he alone meets us; between the early church and the Hellenist church; between the early Christian nincompoops and the real theologians (i.e. anthropologists): Paul and John." M. Barth, typescript of a review of O. Cullmann, *Die Christologie des Neuen Testaments*, May 6, 1958, 1. MBMC. Series III. Publications. Box P11, file 4. The final review was published in *The Christian Century* (December 23, 1959).

[66]After graduating from San Francisco Theological Seminary in 1910, H. N. Wieman (1884–1975) went to Germany, where he studied under Ernst Troeltsch and Adolf von Harnack. On returning to the US, he did his doctoral work at Harvard, where he became influenced by the process thought of Alfred North Whitehead. In 1927, he was appointed professor of Christian theology at the University of Chicago Divinity School, where he stayed until his retirement in 1949. His influence on the school remained strong long after his departure, however, which is probably why Barth came to engage with his thought in the first instance.

with him verbally I suspect that the words convey meanings for him which are different from what I take them to mean. We have been reared in families, traditions and cultures so different from the other that understanding is difficult, perhaps at points impossible."[67]

Evidently, therefore, Markus's academic activities were not entirely church related. Nevertheless, the ecclesial sphere remained his focus and passion. As he later insisted on having said of him in his "contributor's notes" for an article in the Baptist journal *Foundations*, he "still considers himself a preacher [even] in his present position as associate professor of New Testament."[68]

The following year saw Barth continue his teaching and preaching duties, alongside further significant ecumenical endeavors. At the start of the year, while busy with his "Parables of the Kingdom" course, he addressed the Bryn Mawr Community Church as part of its Lenten studies on the topic of "Christ's Sacrifice."[69] At the other end of the year, in November, he once again preached at a Reformation Sunday service—this time, one that had been organized by eight churches in the Albany Park–North Park area of Chicago.[70] The very next week, from November 3–7, he traveled to Atlanta, Georgia, where Columbia Theological Seminary had invited him to be that year's Smythe Foundation lecturer. His theme for his lecture series was "The Authority of the Bible."[71] Then, on December 7, Markus was the preacher at an ordination service held in the Rollo Congregational Church in De Kalb County, Illinois.[72]

THE BROKEN WALL

By far Markus's most influential ecumenical work, however, was again done in conversation with the Baptists. On December 20, 1958, taking up the

---

[67]H. N. Wieman, response to Markus Barth (July 1958), 1. MBMC. Series III. Publications. Box P4, file 9. Barth's fullest criticism of Wieman was not formally published for another six years. See M. Barth, "The Freedom of God," in *The Empirical Theology of H. N. Wieman*, ed. R. W. Bretall (New York: Macmillan, 1963).

[68]M. Barth, "The Preacher and the Authority of the Bible," in *Foundations: A Baptist Journal of History and Theology* 2 (July 1959): 230.

[69]"'Christ's Sacrifice' Topic for Church Lenten Group," *Chicago Tribune*, February 20, 1958, 2.

[70]"Notes on News in Religion," *Chicago Tribune*, October 25, 1958, 12.

[71]"Scottish Pastor Among Religious Leaders Visiting Here," *The Atlanta Constitution*, November 1, 1958, 6.

[72]"Ordination Service at Rollo Church," *Daily Chronicle*, December 11, 1958, 19.

invitation from Jitsuo Morikawa, first offered in late 1956, to assist in the denomination's Jubilee program of evangelism, he met with sixty leaders of the American Baptist Convention at New York's George Washington Hotel. This was the first of a series of similar consultations undertaken by Barth with other Baptist groups around the country.[73]

Despite having earlier refused Morikawa's request to help the American Baptists develop their evangelistic programs, Barth now agreed to do so. He did not, of course, do so by contributing to a missional method—he remain implacably opposed to any such thing—but by providing a commentary on St. Paul's letter to the Ephesians that would be published in January 1959 under the title *The Broken Wall*.[74] Markus himself only hinted at this genesis of the book in its preface. The commentary, he said, "has been written with the intention of offering to Bible readers guidance in understanding some of the main themes" of the epistle. "May it encourage [such readers] to become faithful and brave ambassadors for Christ!"[75] Only that passing reference to the ambassadorial vocation of the Christian disciple hinted at the evangelistic program within which the book had its origin. In his foreword, however, Morikawa was less reserved. Acknowledging that the book "deal[t] little with techniques and methods," he nevertheless praised it as "a study book for evangelism." Commissioned by the American Baptist Convention for its own specific purposes, it was a book that had been written by "an evangelist at heart." Most tellingly, however—and in this, he hinted at the reasons why Barth had initially refused to be involved—Morikawa noted that Markus's most scathing criticisms were directed against churches that, precisely because of their emphasis on techniques and methods, were in fact "the greatest obstacle to evangelism!"[76]

Ironically, perhaps, the book's emphasis on evangelism and the reach of the gospel was precisely what made it theologically and ecclesially

[73]"Baptists Confer with Theologian," *Chattanooga Daily Times*, December 22, 1958, 12.

[74]M. Barth, *The Broken Wall: A Study of the Epistle to the Ephesians* (Valley Forge, PA: Judson, 1959).

[75]Barth, *Broken Wall*, 9. In a letter to Nelly, Markus expressed even more limited expectations that betrayed his own feelings of academic mediocrity. "Yesterday, at last, the Ephesians book appeared. I can only hope that it will be read, and that it will be less useless [*weniger unbrauchbar*] than *Augenzeuge* and the [1951] baptism book." M. Barth to N. Barth, January 10, 1959. MBL. Series II. Box 11.

[76]J. Morikawa, "Foreword," in Barth, *Broken Wall*, 7-8.

controversial in a number of different quarters. The Dutch socialist Mennonite theologian Frits Kuiper[77] asked whether, in light of his exegesis of Ephesians, Markus would agree that "a Jew who recognises Jesus as the Messiah, should retain his Jewish identity as a positive quality . . . [but that], on the contrary, a son of the Gentiles who recognises the Messiah Jesus . . . should repudiate any special national or cultural qualification . . . [and that] in the Messianic covenant the whole of humanity should become God's partner."[78] Kuiper's question may not have been rhetorical, but it demonstrated that he had indeed clearly understood Barth's views. Those views were expressed again by Barth in June 1959, just six months after the publication of *The Broken Wall*, in a short "meditation" he penned on the relationship between Israel and the church as it is presented in Ephesians. Using language with which Kuiper would have resonated, Barth wrote that "the fellow human whom God loves and who is to be loved is first and foremost [*zunächst und vornehmlich*] the Jew." Certainly, he continued, other relationships—fathers and mothers, masters and slaves, husbands and wives—are also included by Paul as "neighbors," "whether they are Christians or not." But the basis of all Pauline ethical admonitions, insisted Barth, is the "new relationship created by Christ between the formerly Gentile Ephesians, and the Jews"—whether Christian or not.[79]

Whereas Kuiper represented those readers who both understood and agreed with Barth's exegesis, others were far less sympathetic. Some of the strongest criticism came from within certain Baptist circles—precisely those groups that had been *The Broken Wall*'s principal intended audience. Nelson B. Baker, professor of English Bible at the Eastern Baptist Theological Seminary, wrote to express his "emphatic disagreement" with Markus's primary contention. It was not walls as such that had been broken down by

[77]Frits Kuiper (1898–1974) was born into a family of Dutch Mennonite pastors. He studied at the University of Amsterdam and the Amsterdam Mennonite Theological Seminary, after which he worked in pastoral ministry until 1963 before being called to a professorship in the Mennonite seminary in Montevideo, Uruguay. A committed socialist, he was deeply influenced by the work of Karl Barth, Franz Rosenzweig, and Vladimir Lenin. From at least the early 1940s, Kuiper was also an ardent Zionist.

[78]F. Kuiper to M. Barth, November 23, 1962. MBMC. Series II. Correspondence. Box 9, file 304.

[79]M. Barth, "Meditation über Israel und die Kirche im Epheserbrief," June 11, 1959, MBMC, Series III. Publications. Box P15, file 1.

Christ, but only a very particular wall. Paul's letter, he insisted, was about the reconciliation of believers with each other, and thus it was only the wall between believing Jews and believing Gentiles that had been destroyed.[80] For Markus, this was exegetically intolerable. "I must confess," he replied, "that it seems to me that I am a bit stubborn when against so much and so united an opposition I still hold that the attempt of my exegesis is closer to the text and meaning." Faith, argued Markus, was certainly vital—but only as the basis on which anyone could acknowledge that they were already included in Christ's community and not as the presupposition for that inclusion.[81]

In the same month that *The Broken Wall* was published, Markus was also able to spend time in conversation with Paul Tillich, who was visiting Chicago for a month from Harvard. While in so many ways the two men differed greatly, with Tillich's theology becoming "more and more strange to me" (*wird er mir immer fremder*), Markus's recollections were nevertheless full of fond admiration. Tillich was, Markus wrote to his mother, "as always, personally delightful!" After a night-time conversation that ranged across the doctrine of the Trinity, the "suffering servant" of God, and the relationship between God's freedom and human will, Markus enthused that "I can't talk with anyone as I can with him [Tillich]." Moreover, Tillich's engagement with Karl's work was, in Markus's opinion, second to none. "No one reads Papa's Dogmatics so openly, excitedly, really questioning and pondering, as [Tillich] does." In a sign of his own openness to new ideas, and fresh ways of thinking, Markus even admitted that "I look forward to him more than to many who are meant to be, or really are, like-minded."[82]

Nearly four years later, in late 1962, there was a fascinating sequel to this meeting that once again highlighted surprising points of connection

---

[80]N. Baker to M. Barth, February 26, 1963. MBMC. Series II. Correspondence. Box 9, file 308. Note that Baker's letter was in response not to *The Broken Wall* itself but to a shorter summary article on Ephesians that Barth had published in *Interpretation*. See M. Barth, "Conversion and Conversation: Israel and the Church in Paul's Letter to the Ephesians," *Interpretation: A Journal of Bible and Theology* 17, no. 1 (January 1963): 3-24.

[81]M. Barth to N. Baker, March 21, 1963. MBMC. Series II. Correspondence. Box 9, file 308.

[82]M. Barth to N. Barth, January 10, 1959. Note that the first two part-volumes of Karl Barth's *Church Dogmatics* IV on the doctrine of reconciliation, in which the motif of Jesus Christ as the obedient—but suffering—servant had been of central importance, had been published between 1953 and 1955. This idea appears to have figured prominently in Markus's conversation with Tillich.

between Barth and Tillich. While delivering some lectures at Chicago's Fourth Presbyterian Church, Markus was given some excerpts from Tillich's speech, "Die theologische Spannung in den politischen Konflikten," which he had delivered in September 1962.[83] After reading them, Rose Marie wrote to Tillich expressing her delight that, on the East-West issue at least, "we are in the same boat." Acknowledging that Tillich always spoke on theological and political matters with a slightly different emphasis and flavor to what one might hear from Karl Barth, and that some people would therefore always think them to be "miles apart from one another" (*meilenweit von einander*), Rose Marie affirmed that "you are not that, to me. It was a pleasure for me to discover this."[84]

TROUBLE IN SUNDAY SCHOOL

During these early months of 1959, Barth became unwittingly embroiled in an oddly furious debate about Sunday schools. Having been invited to address the Department of Christian Education—a division of the National Council of Churches—in Omaha, Nebraska, Barth sought to challenge some of the underlying assumptions of the accredited Sunday school teaching materials. In his view, the sociological trend toward child-centeredness and conformity that had made its way into the Sunday school curriculum "spoiled children," because it presented an expurgated view of life and of the Scriptures. In comments that were reported across the Associated Press outlets—from the *Los Angeles Times* to the *Washington Post*—Barth lamented that all that children heard in Sunday School was that "Mama loves me, papa loves me, teacher loves me, God loves me. Come age 12 or 14, they discover other people in the world and all hell

---

[83]See P. Tillich, *Berliner Vorlesungen III (1961—1958)*, ed. E. Sturm (Berlin: De Gruyter, 2009), lxiv.

[84]R. M. Barth to P. Tillich, October 18, 1962. MBL. Series V, file 4. Demonstrating her own theological insight, Rose Marie nevertheless followed up this happy affirmation of the proximity between Barth's and Tillich's ideas with a more critical note. "It isn't that I don't see any differences, or even contradictions, between KB's teaching and yours, or that I would wish to brush them under the table. I am saddened by what I have read in your Christology. Is Jesus Christ really no more to you than that? . . . Perhaps it is because of your starting-point (*Ausgangspunkt*), which is the same as Nicodemus': 'We know that . . . ,' to which Jesus' first response seems to be: 'You know nothing.' In his reply to Rose Marie's letter, Tillich appears to have taken her seriously. "I would like to have a Christological conversation with you." P. Tillich to R. M. Barth, October 30, 1962. MBL. Series V, file 4.

breaks loose." For Barth, much of the problem lay in the determination to sanitize the Scriptures in order to make them—and life generally—more palatable. "The Egyptians never drowned, John the Baptist was never beheaded. . . . [But] real life, that shows people as they are, is cut away."[85]

The response was loud and indignant. While there were some, such as the chair of Christian education for the Sunday School Union of Washington, DC, who applauded Barth's statements—"I fully agree with you in every respect"[86]—many others were outraged. "A theologian is supposed to be truthful," wrote one lady to Barth, "a person who can be depended upon to deal in facts rather than fiction. . . . May I suggest you get the facts from J. Edgar Hoover."[87] Another correspondent wrote to say that she "felt very sorry" for Barth. "My 2 year old son knows more about love, apparently, than you do." Grateful "that this world isn't depending completely on your philosophy of life in which to raise their children," she assured Barth that her whole Sunday school class was "praying for you and the rest of the lost souls in this great nation."[88] For yet another, Barth's remarks about the Sunday school curriculum were "uncalled for, untrue, vicious, un-Christian, and unworthy of one who bears the title 'theologian.'"[89]

As it happened, Barth was unable to respond himself to the furor that his comments had caused, as he had left for a speaking tour in Germany and Switzerland shortly after the Omaha meeting. It was left to Rose Marie to field the complaints and to respond to Gerald Knopf—at the time, executive secretary of the National Council of Churches' Division of Christian Education—who, having not been in Omaha at the time, had written to Barth seeking clarification about his remarks.[90] Rose Marie assured Knopf

[85]"OMAHA, NEB., Feb 12—Sunday School Spoils Children, a Noted Theologian Said Here Today," press release, Division of Christian Education, National Council of Churches, C-14.

[86]L. C. Battle to M. Barth, February 13, 1959. Also J. D Murch, managing editor of *Christianity Today*, wrote, "I am in thorough agreement with the published statements you made in Omaha. We have long needed this plain talk from one of such academic respectability." J. D. Murch to M. Barth, February 24, 1959. Both letters in MBL. Series I. Box 36.

[87]F. Lyler [?] to M. Barth, February 19, 1959. MBL. Series I. Box 36.

[88]M. B. Thornton to M. Barth, February 12, 1959. MBL. Series I. Box 36.

[89]E. H. Hood to M. Barth, February 12, 1959. MBL. Series I. Box 36.

[90]"I have three initial questions. . . . Does the release accurately represent what you said . . . and does it convey fairly what you intended to convey? Were you aware that you were in a press conference and that this release would be made or were your remarks made informally . . . ? Was

that, while the press release had "represent[ed] fairly what . . . Barth said," the interview from which the release had arisen had taken place at midnight, just after Barth had arrived in town, and that the interviewer had effectively ambushed him. "Had he written himself these statements he would have done so in a more differentiating manner."[91] Certainly, Knopf was relieved that Barth's attitude toward children's Christian education was more nuanced than had been reported and was sorry that he "ha[d] been represented in a less than complete light."[92] Barth's reputation among Sunday school teachers, however, probably took longer to recover.

DISPUTING WITH STUDENTS, COLLEAGUES, AND PASTORS

As has been noted earlier, in February through March 1959 Markus traveled briefly back to Europe, having been invited to deliver a lecture in the German city of Frankfurt on "Israel and the Church"—a theme for which, not least as a result of the Ephesians book, he was becoming well known.[93] He returned in time to mark the "mountains of exam papers" awaiting him, and to prepare the next quarter's lectures. "Up to [his] neck" in outstanding tasks, it felt, Markus wrote to his mother, like "a pressure cooker."[94]

Contributing to this pressured situation was the often combative nature of many of Markus's students, who had come to Chicago to study religion rather than theology. For such students, he recounted, the Old and New Testaments contained "nothing other than very, very out-dated books." Consequently, Markus's lectures, in which he spoke not only about matters such as authorial identity and the (real and perceived) contradictions between the various Gospel narratives, but also about "the message of John

---

this an interview which you solicited or did our own department take the initiative in interviewing you?" G. E. Knopf to M. Barth, February 24, 1959. MBL. Series I. Box 36.

[91]R. M. Barth to G. E. Knopf, February 25, 1959. MBL. Series I. Box 36.

[92]G. E. Knopf to R. M. Barth, March 2, 1959. MBL. Series I. Box 36.

[93]In 1959 alone, Barth published no fewer than three articles on this theme in addition to *The Broken Wall*. They were: "The Church and Israel in Paul's Epistle to the Ephesians (A Summary)," *The Student World* 52 (1959): 68-80; "Israel un die Kirche im Epheserbrief," *Stimme der Gemeinde* 11 (1959): 561-66; "Israel und die Kirche im Brief des Paulus an die Epheser," *Theologische Existenz heute* 75 (Münich: Chr. Kaiser, 1959): 1-47.

[94]M. Barth to N. Barth, March 6, 1959. MBL. Series II. Box 11.

and Paul, and the decision of faith they put before us," were disliked and only barely tolerated.[95] Eventually, Markus was able to win over many of these students—"I finally seem to have taken most of the skeptical or cynical students with me a little"—but their open animosity to both his beliefs and his pedagogy was clearly a source of consternation. In such times, the more strictly confessional nature of a place like Dubuque—by which Barth had come to feel constricted—was once more appealing.

It was not, however, only the students with whom Markus clashed. Another, equally protracted concern that did nothing to ease Markus's stress was the increasingly bitter conflict between himself and his dean, Jerry Brauer. Brauer, who had been dean since 1955, had long held a different vision for the Divinity School as a whole, which included a dissolution of the Federated Theological Faculty. His leadership style and determination to dramatically change the theological direction of the Divinity School put a number of faculty colleagues offside. By no later than March 1960, he and Barth were in open conflict and were still at loggerheads ten months later. So corrosive was the hostility between them that in early 1961, Paul Tillich himself offered to mediate. The offer was welcomed by Markus, who recognized that, at age seventy-four, Tillich had "experience that both my Dean and I lack completely."[96]

In early June 1959, Markus was on the road again, this time to Dallas, where he was a guest lecturer at Southern Methodist University's Perkins School of Theology. Impressed by the quality of students, who were "very bright, sharp, [and] grateful," and who—unlike those in Chicago—were driven primarily by questions concerning baptism and the resurrection of Christ, Markus's schedule was nevertheless exhausting. Each day, he lectured for two hours, with a further ninety minutes of wide-ranging conversation. As he told his mother, "I have to talk, talk, talk—which, as James tells us, is rather dangerous behavior." By the end of the month, Markus was looking forward to returning home briefly to Chicago, before heading

[95]M. Barth to N. Barth, December 22, 1960. MBL. Series II. Box 11.

[96]M. Barth to N. Barth, January 22, 1961. MBL. Series II. Box 11. An excellent overview of the changes initiated at Chicago under Brauer's deanship can be found in Garry Dorrien's *The Making of American Liberal Theology: Crisis, Irony, and Postmodernity 1950–2005* (Louisville: Westminster John Knox, 2006), 123-26.

off on a much-needed holiday with the family in the Bow Lake mountains of Alberta. "And after the holidays, a two-month reading period begins!"[97]

The holiday itself, however, also coincided with a series of presentations Markus had agreed to give—as a favor to Jitsuo Morikawa—to a Baptist conference on evangelism in Green Lake, Wisconsin. On this occasion, at least, he did not have to prepare anything new. Speaking on Matthew 5:1-20, on the theme of "Jesus the Evangelist"—"hardly very different from [the material] regarding the prophetic office of Jesus Christ in [*Church Dogmatics*] IV/3.1, but in exegetical form"—Markus was able to pull "the five lectures out of a drawer—I had already given them in the fall of 1958." What was new this time, though, was the audience. Instead of eager students, to whom he had delivered the lectures a year previously, this time he was speaking to five hundred pastors "from all over America." Rather critical of them in general as "theologically uneducated" (*theologisch ungebildeten*), Markus himself was received with a mixture of "astonishment, joy, and mild enthusiasm." A few delegates, however, noticeably "stiffened" at what he said, with Markus being suspected of "destroy[ing] the basis of the Baptist position, that is: personal acceptance of Christ, belief in hell for the unconverted, and so on."[98] One pastor, in particular, was banned from speaking or asking Markus questions on account of his belligerent hostility to Markus's allegedly heterodox views. One bright spot to emerge from the Green Lake conference, however, was Anna Barth's enthusiastic participation in the discussions and debates. Indeed, it was Anna who persuaded her father to seek a private, conciliatory meeting with the aggrieved pastor. "He doesn't understand you. That's why he is always against you," Markus later reported Anna to have said to him. In the end, on the final day of the conference, Markus had an opportunity to heed Anna's advice and was able to have "as good a conversation as it was possible to have under the circumstances" with the man in question.[99]

The year 1961 was typically busy for Markus. His teaching load remained full, with a course on Mark's Gospel over the winter, followed up by two

[97]M. Barth to N. Barth, June 10, 1959. MBL. Series II. Box 11.
[98]M. Barth to N. Barth, August 2, 1959. MBL. Series II. Box 11.
[99]M. Barth to N. Barth, August 2, 1959.

new courses the following fall. The pressure of preparing new classes was intense, and, at least as Markus reported it, was reminiscent of the early days of Karl's academic career. As Markus told his father, "I am once again on materials that are new to me. From day to day, and week to week, I don't know in advance what is actually going to happen."[100] Markus was perhaps, however, being slightly too hard on himself, as in fact even the new courses were on subjects that were not unfamiliar to him. "Worship in the New Testament" enabled him to lecture on liturgical debates, including those to do with baptism and the Lord's Supper, with which he had been increasingly engaged, while "Resurrection Accounts in the Gospels" allowed him to return to material he had first explored in his doctoral dissertation, *Die Augenzeuge*.[101] Then, in the winter of that year, he returned to John's Gospel, with a seminar course on the Johannine prologue, reprising again material from both the 1956 Sprunt Lectures and his 1957 article for *The Reformed Review*. Given Markus's developing involvement in Jewish-Christian dialogue, it is of particular interest that one of his students in these years was a young David Novak, whose own work in Jewish-Christian relations was to become of seminal importance in later decades, and who was to credit both Markus and Karl with fostering a Christian theological reverence for Judaism.[102]

THE BLAKE-PIKE PROPOSAL

One of the characteristic features of Barth's tenure in Chicago was his deep engagement in ecumenical work, particularly among the Baptists. There was, though, one other major ecumenical endeavor with which Barth was busy during this time, and that had nothing to do with any Baptist association. On December 4, 1960, at the invitation of James Clark, the Episcopal Bishop of California, the stated clerk of the United Presbyterian Church of the US, Eugene Blake, preached a sermon at San Francisco's Grace Cathedral. In it he boldly proposed a union not only of the United

[100]M. Barth to K. Barth, May 7, 1961. MBL. Series II. Box 11.

[101]MBMC. Series V.

[102]D. Novak, "Hunsinger's *Karl Barth: Post-Holocaust Theologian?*" *Studies in Christian-Jewish Relations* 14, no. 1 (2019): 1-3.

Presbyterians and Episcopalians but a merger that would include also the Methodists and the United Church of Christ. While his suggestion was nothing if not audacious, Blake was convinced that there was a gospel imperative: "To break through the barriers of nearly 500 years of history, to attempt under God to transcend the separate traditions of our churches, and to find a way together to unite them so that manifesting the unity given us by our Lord Jesus Christ, His church may be renewed for its mission to our nation and to the world 'that the world may believe.'"[103]

Bold it may have been, but Blake's proposal received both significant and serious attention. By 1962, the Consultation on Church Union had been established, with delegates from all four denominations meeting to decide on the path forward. They were encouraged in their deliberations by renowned ecumenical advocate Lesslie Newbigin, who had been in San Francisco on the day of Blake's sermon.[104]

Not surprisingly, given how involved he had been in questions of ecclesial governance during the *Kirchenverfassung* debate of 1952, and then again—peripherally—in the 1956 union discussions between the Churches of Scotland and England, this proposal also received Barth's attention. He was, however, considerably less enthusiastic about it than someone like Newbigin. Certainly, he affirmed the fundamental quest for ecclesial unity. "Every decent man, be he a Christian or not, must wish and hope that the scandalous, ridiculous, incriminating and incapacitating separation of the denominations be overcome."[105] Nevertheless, Barth was far from convinced that the Blake-Pike proposal had any merit beyond its stated goal. As he saw it, the proposal's most basic problem was that it treated the merger as though it were a mercantile agreement between business interests. "Passionate love for the one true church cannot fail to see that the means suggested in this document for achieving union are far from being

[103]E. C. Blake, "A Proposal Toward the Reunion of Christ's Church," in K. Watkins, *The American Church that Might Have Been: A History of the Consultation on Church Union* (Eugene, OR: Pickwick, 2014), 205.

[104]Newbigin had been present in the city as part of the triennial general assembly of the National Council of Churches that was being held in San Francisco in early December 1960.

[105]M. Barth, typescript of "Pool of the Rich or Pilgrimage of Servants," January 19, 1962, 4. MBL. Series V, file 8. The final version of the article was published as "The Blake Proposal: Pool of the Rich or Pilgrimage of Servants?," *McCormick Quarterly* 15, no. 3 (1962): 3-8.

spiritual means." More than that, said Barth, he missed "in the present proposal the slightest attempt to seek union in better obedience to the triune God."[106]

There were three specific problems with the proposal that Markus wished to highlight. First, it "thrive[d] on the distinction of clergy and laity," whereas the New Testament made no such differentiation.[107] Second, it enshrined the pre-eminence of the episcopacy by suggesting that "Christians should kow-tow before the majesty of bishopric and eldership." Again, argued Barth, this contradicted the apostolic witness of the New Testament, according to which "in succession to the apostles, the ministry of being a witness to Christ is given to the whole church and fulfilled by the cooperation and witness of each and all members of the body."[108] Third, and not surprisingly, Barth repudiated the proposal's sacramentalism. Being neither sacraments nor means of grace, he insisted, baptism and the Lord's Supper are instead "constitutive expressions of the mode of life given to God's children by the Holy Spirit." Whereas the Bible treats them as acts of prayer and obedience, the Blake-Pike proposal made them "the untouchable center around which the church can or should gather to feed and please herself."[109]

Despite his criticisms of this specific proposal, Barth was not, of course, opposed to church union in principle. The type of union he envisaged, however, had less to do with the bringing together of separated ecclesial traditions and much more to do with the uniting of otherwise segregated

---

[106]Barth, "Pool of the Rich or Pilgrimage of Servants," 4-5. There was perhaps an unintentional irony in Barth's trinitarian language here. During the summer of 1964, Bishop Pike—one of the "sponsors" of the proposal—while preaching at Trinity Church, Wall Street, "for the first time publicly characterized the doctrine [of the Trinity] as 'excess baggage.'" See W. Stringfellow and A. Towne, *The Bishop Pike Affair: Scandals of Conscience and Heresy, Relevance and Solemnity in the Contemporary Church* (Eugene, OR: Wipf & Stock, 2007), 25. A heresy trial against Pike had already been seriously considered three years in earlier in 1961, on account of, among other things, various views he had expressed in an article titled "The Three-Pronged Synthesis," *The Christian Century*, December 21, 1960. Pike's denial of the Trinity had not, however, been made explicit in that publication and so, by September 1961, the House of Bishops decided not to proceed against him. Three years later, Pike was more open in his advocacy of a heterodox position.

[107]Barth, "Pool of the Rich or Pilgrimage of Servants," 5.

[108]Barth, "Pool of the Rich or Pilgrimage of Servants," 5-6.

[109]Barth, "Pool of the Rich or Pilgrimage of Servants," 6.

demographics. Clearly speaking out of his experiences of racial tensions in Chicago, he outlined the manner of union for which he longed. Rather than a "cartel of rich churches," he expressed his desire for

> the common prayer and praise of beggar churches from the right and from the left, from the suburbs and from the slums, from segregated and desegregated environments. Such a new proposal would require more theological thought and work; and it would be built upon the church's secular task, i.e. upon the privilege and duty to serve God by words and actions of peace, righteousness, liberation. Every man, the whole world, ought to profit from a church union . . . not in some distant future, but right through the making of the union. . . . But church unity will be found when, unlike a business enterprise, we learn to forget our own profit and lose our life in service to others.

And this, he suggested, would not be contrary to genuine reform of governance and polity, but would in fact serve it. "If the denominations were willing to learn from the Bible first to seek and take up the commission and task given to the church in the face of slums, of segregation, of threatening total war, of glorified cynicism, then they would experience that reforms of all things structural would fall into their laps, too."[110]

TEACHING, TRAVELING, AND POLITICS

By the early 1960s, Barth had become a well-known and highly sought-after speaker throughout the States. As a consequence, his teaching commitments were routinely interrupted by invitations to speak across the country and even overseas. In the first six months of 1962 alone, he traveled to New Mexico, New York, and Oregon, followed by lecture series at pastors' conferences and synods.[111] In June, Markus even participated in a five-day conference on the "Historical Jesus."[112] Then, after five weeks of summer vacation in Switzerland, from the end of August through September, more

---

[110]Barth, "Pool of the Rich or Pilgrimage of Servants," 7.

[111]M. Barth to N. Barth, May 23, 1961. In Oregon, Markus worked for a week with other Presbyterian theologians and pastors on a "Contemporary Brief Statement of Faith," and then spoke to the Synod about evangelism, working largely off material in *The Broken Wall*. M. Barth to N. Barth, June 24, 1961. MBL. Series II. Box 11.

[112]M. Barth to N. Barth, June 24, 1961.

conferences followed at Harvard and in Toronto.[113] One of the more interesting opportunities, however, came at the very start of the year. In February, as guest speaker at the thirty-fourth meeting of the National Council of Churches' Division of Education, held at the Hotel Sheraton-Jefferson in St. Louis, Missouri, Markus again entered the political fray. That he would do so could hardly have come as a surprise to the organizers of the meeting. In fact, given his billing as "a theologian known for his outspoken views," it is likely that he was invited precisely because he would speak plainly.[114] In any event, so it turned out to be the case. In his address, which he titled "Can We Teach Sacrifice and Resurrection?," Markus began by seeking to correct some common misconceptions. Far from being "a gift to God which is either required by a blood-thirsty God or by priests who want to stay in business," the biblical concept of sacrifice denotes, he said, "a gift of God to man," offered primarily in the person of Jesus. Similarly, resurrection should not be thought of as "the continuation of individual existence in some sort of eternal Sun Valley paradise" but as "the acceptance and glorification of Christ's obedience, and the beginning of a new age." When taken together and taught correctly, insisted Barth, these two concepts define the peace that is given by God to humanity, and compel Christians "to demonstrate [in their lives] what they owe to God and to their fellowman."[115]

---

[113]M. Barth to N. Barth, November 5, 1961. MBL. Series II. Box 11. It is worth noting that Markus's extensive traveling took a toll not only on him but also on Rose Marie. In this letter to Nelly, in early November, he noted, with evident concern, that "when I got home [from Switzerland], I found Rose Marie very tense. . . . Her sleep has been anything but good for four to six weeks. It was high time that I came home." Nelly herself was worried about Rose Marie's health, and the stresses under which she was living. In early 1962, she wrote to her daughter-in-law with concern and advice: "When the heart is suffering, probably only the closest—more so than the dearest person—yes, Jesus Christ himself—is one's only consolation. . . . If you can with joy look after your husband and children [*die Deinen*] with all your dedication, as well as your new-found responsibilities for the Sunday School, [and] if you can gladly be aware of one's limits, that too much is too much . . . then from Basel, I breathe a sigh of relief." N. Barth to R. M. Barth, January 3, 1962. Rose Marie's health remained poor, in fact, for much of the year. According to Markus, her doctor was as puzzled (*rätselt*) by her symptoms as anyone else, and by March she was struggling with an illness that "sap[ped] her strength" and filled many days with "a lot of agony" (*sehr viel qualvollen Tagen*). M. Barth to N. Barth, January 14 and March 11, 1962. It was not until September that Peter could report that his mother was finally able to sleep better, and only in early 1963 that Markus felt confident enough to say that "Rose Marie is completely well again." N. Barth to M. Barth, September 8, 1962; M. Barth to N. Barth, January 25, 1963. All these letters are found in MBL. Series II. Box 11.

[114]National Council of Churches, Division of Christian Education, Press Release, February 16, 1961, 1.

[115]Press Release, 2.

Figure 5.6. Holidays, 1960. Rose Marie, Karl, and Ruth Barth

It was on the basis of this biblical-theological corrective that Markus went on to address some of the most sensitive political topics of the day. Christians must object to the "barbaric custom" of capital punishment, should refuse to participate in any preparations for nuclear war, and must also eschew the legitimacy of any talk of iron or bamboo curtains.[116] Each of these, he argued, stands in opposition to the peace of God, which is given as a gift to humankind *by* God through the sacrifice and resurrection of Christ.

Insofar as Barth's biblical exegesis and theological convictions compelled him, precisely *as a Christian*, to speak into political matters, it is hardly surprising that he also sought at this time to encourage religious publishers to do the same. In January 1962, he wrote to Arthur Cohen, head of the religion department at Holt, Rinehart & Winston, urging him to commission "a series of . . . books or booklets" that could bring theological disciplines into conversation with the political and ethical questions of modern life. This, he said, should not be "a monologue of professors and would-be professors amongst themselves" because "it is awfully stuffy when theological science is done just for science's sake and had nothing to contribute to solving questions of general concern."

> If you as the new religious editor . . . would be willing to try and do something new and urgent, angels would applaud and demons shudder. If they would not,

[116]"Desire for Peace Held Bedrock of a Christian," *St. Louis Globe-Democrat*, February 17, 1961, 6.

> you might still render a great service to Christian and non-Christian readers who still care for the possible or actual relevance of faith. Actually I mean that you might try to help churches and synagogues to recover from the bankruptcy of Christian ethics, which R. Niebuhr has declared and is exploiting when he assumes that the political and social answers have to be given by experts in politics rather than be determined through revelation and faith.[117]

Just two weeks after writing this letter, on February 2, 1962, Barth found himself personally involved in a very public political cause of significant national interest. Frank Wilkinson—civil liberties activist, executive director of the National Committee Against Repressive Legislation, and member of the Communist Party—had just been released from prison, having served nine months for contempt of Congress, and Barth had been invited to speak at a political rally in his honor.[118] His speech was remarkable, both for its critique of Christianly justified repression and its empathy toward communism as a "natural child" of Christianity.

Barth began by echoing Bonhoeffer's injunction from 1937 that, as a Christian, he had a duty to "help fighters for righteousness and freedom wherever they may be found."[119] He also, however, regretfully acknowledged that his hearers at the rally would be justified in regarding him as unrepresentative of Protestant Christianity, insofar as "the majority of both Swiss and American Christians have not been conspicuous in the front ranks of fighters and martyrs for peace without atomic weapons, for integrated schools and apartment housing, for tolerance and decency toward minorities."[120]

While such remarks might have been irksome to both ecclesiastical officialdom and Christian elites, his next set of comments must surely have sounded even more explosive. In contrast to his father—who had

---

[117]M. Barth to A. A. Cohen, January 14, 1962. MBMC. Subject Correspondence 4. Box 8.

[118]Wilkinson (1914–2006), and his co-accused Carl Braden (1914–1975), had refused to answer questions about their political affiliations that had been put to them by the House Un-American Activities Committee (HUAC).

[119]M. Barth, "Barth—Wilkinson Speech," 1. Speech for the Chicago Committee for the Defense of the Bill of Rights, February 2, 1962. In MBL. Series II. In his 1937 book *Discipleship*, Bonhoeffer had similarly insisted that blessedness accrues not simply to those who are persecuted for their confession of Christ but to those who defend and suffer for *any* just cause. See D. Bonhoeffer, *DBWE* 4, 109.

[120]Barth, "Barth—Wilkinson Speech," 1.

famously rebuffed Emil Brunner by claiming that, unlike Nazism, Russian communism was "not anti-Christian . . . [but] coldly non-Christian"[121]—Markus argued instead that communism could only be "understood and taken seriously" if it was perceived as a child of Christianity. "The hate with which the child repudiates its father, and the vehemence with which the father may declare the child's illegitimacy is a hate-love that cannot belie the actual natural bonds between both."[122] If that were not enough, he proceeded to blame the failures of Christianity for the advent of communism. "If the father of this misbehav[ing] child had not misbehaved in flagrant neglection of his privilege and duty, the child would never have been born." To put it otherwise, had the churches taken seriously their own vocation to uphold the rights of the poor and the marginalized, communism would have been rendered superfluous. Thus, Barth posits these two relations—father and child—with both sharing the same ends, and the child being made necessary by virtue of the failures of the father.

Barth was not, in fact, seeking either to excuse or valorize communism. Indeed, he spoke of his wish that it be overcome by "a better cause and a higher spirit."[123] He was, however, hoping to rebuke the churches for their moral failure in adequately addressing precisely the social ills that, in his view, communism was trying to remediate. Secondly—and in view of Wilkinson's imprisonment and the "panicking fear" of "reactionary Republican elements" and the House Un-American Activities Committee, of which Wilkinson had fallen foul—he was urging a more productive response to communism than the "panic and hysteria" that so often typified both the Christian and the Western approach. If Christians had been able to coexist with Caligula and Nero, knowing that even the Roman Empire in all its brutality was subject to "the Lord above," why should anyone—Christians included—fear communism? "A good Christian," insisted Barth, "cannot be a frantic anti-Communist."[124] Regrettably, there is no extant

[121]K. Barth, "The Church Between East and West," in *Against the Steam: Shorter Post-war Writings, 1946–52* (London: SCM, 1954), 140.

[122]Barth, "Barth—Wilkinson Speech," 2.

[123]Barth, "Barth—Wilkinson Speech," 2.

[124]Barth, "Barth—Wilkinson Speech," 2-3.

evidence of how Barth's speech was received. But, in the febrile atmosphere of early-1960s' Cold War tensions—the erection of the Berlin Wall had been completed just five months previously—any concession to communist justification would almost certainly have provoked suspicion.

Quite clearly, then, Markus's years in Chicago were extremely busy. Alongside a full teaching load in the Federated Theological Faculty, he was a frequent preacher in churches throughout the city and around the country, consulted widely on ecumenical matters, delivered guest lectures for seminaries, universities, church agencies, and student groups, and spoke often—and often critically—on public political issues. The fact of systemically entrenched racial inequality was particularly disturbing to him, with the question of interracial marriage being especially controversial. In 1960, Markus contributed to a symposium on the issue hosted by the *Social Progress* magazine of the United Presbyterian Church. There, in response to the deliberately provocative question, "Would you want your daughter to marry a Negro?," Barth responded that the question was "wrong from bottom to top," presupposing "a patriarchal, tribe-oriented, narrow attitude in him who asks and in him who is asked." More particularly, he argued that the emphasis on a specific trait—in this case, skin color—presumed that the potential groom (or bride) was not in fact a unique individual but simply the sum of a variety of traits. Such a view was a dehumanization of the person in question. Leaning into arguments he had consistently prosecuted before in his various exegeses of Ephesians, Barth concluded by insisting that "the question concerning racially mixed marriages is to be confronted, tackled, and solved day by day by such a life of the community and of each of its members that bears testimony to that love which breaks down the walls of all divisions between races, sexes, and generations."[125]

In all this, just as had been the case in their shared ministry in Bubendorf, Rose Marie was far more than simply a support for her husband's work. On the contrary, it was she who frequently took the initiative in long-term

[125]M. Barth, "Marriage Is Not the Chief End of Man," *Social Progress*, February 1960, 6-7. Note that it was not until 1967, with the *Loving vs. Virginia* ruling from the US Supreme Court, that marriage across racial lines was finally legalized across the entire country.

antiracist action, encouraging her husband to follow her lead.[126] None of this was lost on their children. In 1965, Anna joined Martin Luther King Jr., along with thousands of other demonstrators, in the now-famous march from Selma to Montgomery.

KARL BARTH IN AMERICA

Perhaps the single event by which Markus's final two years in Chicago were dominated—and, regrettably, given how much else he did, the contribution to American church life with which Markus is most usually associated—was the visit to the United States in 1962 by his father, Karl. The trip had been long in the planning, and even longer in the anticipation. Indeed, Eberhard Busch notes that Karl had been receiving invitations to North America since the late 1920s, which he had always steadfastly refused.[127] In the years after the war, however, Karl seems to have entertained such invitations more amenably. During a meeting in Basel in 1953, Karl had apparently promised the principal of Toronto's Knox College, New Testament scholar Stanley Glen, that he would be willing to deliver a lecture at Knox College in 1954 after his hoped-for participation at the Evanston WCC Conference.[128] When that visit did not eventuate, a second possible date was proposed in the fall of 1956.[129]

---

[126]Rose Marie often provided Markus with books and articles on the race issue, highlighting critical sections of them for him when he did not have time to do so himself. Personal correspondence with Anna Barth, October 2020.

[127]Busch, *Karl Barth*, 458.

[128]While Karl Barth had participated in the preparatory meetings for the second assembly of the World Council of Churches, his experience of them was not always happy. In particular, he believed that the conference should have been held in New Delhi rather than in Evanston, that the place and theological significance of Israel should be given more attention, and that the theme of the Conference—"Jesus Christ, Hope for the World"—should be understood in an apocalyptic eschatological sense, rather than the prevailing "realistic biblicist eschatology." See Busch, *Karl Barth*, 395-96; H. A. Drewes, "Intellectual and Personal Biography III: Barth the Elder (1935–1968)," in *The Oxford Handbook of Karl Barth*, ed. P. D. Jones and P. T. Nimmo (Oxford: Oxford University Press, 2020), 59-60. Curiously, Barth's promise to Glen was given in the same year that he told Visser 't Hooft that "I can't allow myself to forsake the work on the *Dogmatics* for so long in favor of such an American journey, with all its presuppositions and complications as would be necessary." K. Barth to W. Visser 't Hooft, October 18, 1953. See *GA* V.43, 278. One wonders whether Barth had had a genuine change of mind, or whether he had made a somewhat rash promise to Glen that he did not seriously entertain.

[129]J. S. Glen to M. Barth, October 1, 1956. MBL. Series I. Box 31. In this letter, Glen asked Markus whether he might be able to secure six seats in the audience for Knox College faculty, who would travel from Toronto to Chicago, if Karl's visit and lecture eventuated.

However, that visit, too, proved impossible; having traveled to England and Scotland during the summer, another long overseas trip in the same year was, by this time, too much for the now seventy-year-old. Then, in December 1956, Markus informed Charles Kegley—a Lutheran minister, and professor of philosophy at New York's Wagner College—that the University of Chicago was hoping to entice Karl across to the United States "just for a few days sometime next year. It is certain that [he] would not be able to stand a lecture tour. . . . But some hope exists that family reasons might eventually be strong enough to bring him here for a short time." If such a visit was to occur, said Markus, "the earliest date of my father's trip might be fall 1957." Even such a short visit, however, was uncertain, and so Markus implored Kegley not to mention the possibility to anyone "since everything is still so vague that no planning can be suspended [*sic*] on it in a tentative or final way."[130]

In the end, Karl was unable to get to America until 1962, with part of the delay being the longer-than-anticipated time it took the University of Basel to appoint a successor.[131] Whereas Karl was keen for Helmut Gollwitzer to succeed him—the two sharing, at the very least, similar political opinions—the university chose instead Heinrich Ott (1929–2013), a decision that left Barth feeling "bitterly disappointed."[132] When he did eventually arrive in the US, it was little short of a tour de force, with Markus himself key to its planning and success. Karl spoke of the American trip in glowing terms. It was, he said, "simply . . . wonderful: magnificent vistas of land and sea, moving encounters with all kinds of people, the full satisfaction of my curiosity about the sites of the Civil War, lively discussions with theologians

---

[130]M. Barth to C. W. Kegley, December 14, 1956. MBL. Series V, file 2.

[131]Barth had hoped to retire in 1961, but the delay in finding a replacement for him meant that he had to continue delivering lectures through the winter of 1961–1962. See Drewes, "Intellectual and Personal Biography III: Barth the Elder (1935–1968)," 65-66.

[132]C. Anderson, "Introduction," in *Karl Barth and the Making of Evangelical Theology: A Fifty-Year Perspective*, ed. C. Anderson and B. L. McCormack (Grand Rapids, MI: Eerdmans, 2015), 4. According to Nelly Barth, the decision in favor of Ott caused Karl "deep grief" (*tiefgehender Kummer*), and was occasioned because the faculty not only did not trust Gollwitzer but also "did not ultimately trust Papa [Karl] enough." N. Barth to M. Barth, April 2, 1962. MBL. Series II. Box 11. Karl Barth himself wrote to Gollwitzer, telling him that "the University of Basel is now for me deeply ruined." K. Barth to H. Gollwitzer, July 31, 1962, in T. K. Kuhn, "'McCarthy-Schwierigkeiten.' Der Streit um Helmut Gollwitzer als Nachfolger Karl Barths 1961/62," *Basler Zeitschrift für Geschichte und Altertumskunde* 109 (2009): 99.

as well as secular people of every type, astonishing attendance at my lectures."[133]

Notwithstanding Markus's earlier caution to Charles Kegley about Karl's inability to cope with a lengthy and arduous lecture tour, the program that was eventually agreed upon was by any measure punishing. Arriving in Chicago on April 7, Karl (who had traveled from Europe with his son, Christoph, and Charlotte von Kirschbaum), spent the first three weeks in and around Chicago, punctuated by short trips to Dubuque and neighboring Indiana.[134] Along with attending church services and hearing lectures from his two sons, Karl himself delivered five lectures within four days and held conversations with church leaders, theological and non-theological scholars, students, and with the *Newsweek* reporter, Mr. Lemon.[135] Over the following four weeks, from April 28 to May 26, Karl traveled with Christoph, Charlotte, Markus, and Rose Marie to Princeton, New York, Richmond, San Francisco, and various Civil War battlefields as well as taking day trips to Phoenix and Washington, DC. Karl was kept busy throughout these weeks with six more lectures, more press conferences, and numerous other meetings with students. As for Markus, as well as accompanying his father to his many appointments, he also—during one of the side trips to a ranch, south of San Francisco—took the opportunity to go horse riding with his brother, Christoph.[136]

Naturally, the lecture tour allowed Karl the opportunity to speak with people—not all of whom were either scholars or Christians—who had been, in many cases, hoping to meet him for years, and for whom, without the tour, such an opportunity would otherwise have been impossible. In addition to his well-known meetings with Billy Graham, Martin Luther

---

[133]K. Barth, *Letters: 1961-1968*, ed. J. Fangmeier and H. Stoevesandt (Edinburgh: T&T Clark, 1981), 57.

[134]The possibility that Nelly might also join the trip was evidently considered, at least by her. As she wrote to Rose Marie when thinking it through, "I can only trust that it will be given to me at the right time to know what to do, or not to do." N. Barth to R. M. Barth, January 3, 1962. MBL. Series II. Box 11.

[135]During these meetings, Anna—who was studying art—was allowed to sit in the room with the other guests, where she worked on a life-size bust of her grandfather. P. Barth et al., "Chicago Memories," 7.

[136]See J. DeCou, "The First Community: Barth's American Prison Tours," in Anderson and McCormack, *Karl Barth and the Making of Evangelical Theology*, 82.

King Jr., and William Stringfellow, Karl also visited three American prisons—Chicago's House of Correction, San Quentin in California, and New York's Rikers Island—and, at least in the latter two, spoke to some of the inmates. Markus, of course, accompanied him on these visits.[137] But Karl's American journey also proved fruitful for Markus himself. Indeed, a significant number of people with whom Markus came into contact as a result of their interest in meeting Karl remained closely connected to Markus's own work in the years that followed. Not least among them were senior members of America's Jewish communities, including Jacob Taubes[138] and Michael Wyschogrod.[139]

JEWISH-CHRISTIAN DIALOGUES

After such a busy schedule, and once Karl was safely back in Basel, Markus and the family were in need of a holiday. On July 7, they left Chicago for a

---

[137]See DeCou, "First Community," 67-69, 78-79, 83. While DeCou notes that there are no extant records of Karl Barth's visit to the House of Correction—probably because his public comments on the prison afterwards were so damning that any records were subsequently destroyed—it would seem inconceivable that Markus did not accompany him there, given that Chicago was, at the time, Markus's home city. See also Busch, *Karl Barth*, 459. Karl later expressed his regret that his "relationship with the courageous Negro Pastor Martin Luther King was confined to being photographed together in front of a church door." K. Barth, "Foreword to the American Edition," *Evangelical Theology: An Introduction* (Grand Rapids, MI: Eerdmans, 1963), 5. As for the others with whom he held meetings, Barth had, in fact, already met Billy Graham in Switzerland two years previously. While his first impressions had been positive—"He's a 'jolly good fellow,' with whom one can talk easily and openly"—Barth's next meeting was less favorable. Having witnessed Graham in action at an evangelistic crusade, he remarked that "I was quite horrified. He acted like a madman and what he presented was certainly not the gospel. . . . It was the gospel at gun-point." See Busch, *Karl Barth*, 446. Barth's reaction to meeting Graham again in America was similarly critical. "Christian faith," he said during a press conference, "begins with joy and not with fear. Mr. Graham begins by making people afraid." See Karl Barth press conference in San Francisco, May 15, 1962, *GA* 25, 525. Barth's impressions of William Stringfellow—with whom he shared a panel at the University of Chicago—were far better. "This is the man America should be listening to!" he is reported to have said in response to Stringfellow's insistence that Christianity be a religion of dissent. See R. Williams, *Christianity in Poetry and Polity: Some Anglican Voices from Temple to Herbert* (Oxford: SGL, 2004), 5. Note that Barth also met with the Romanian-born historian of religion Mircea Eliade, who had been on the faculty at Chicago since 1957 and was, consequently, a colleague of sorts of Markus. Little is known of their meeting.

[138]Jacob Taubes (1923–1987) was professor of history and philosophy of religion at Columbia University and the son of Zürich's former *Oberrabiner* (Chief Rabbi) Zwi Taubes, with whom Karl Barth had worked in July 1944 in an ultimately unsuccessful attempt to rescue nearly 500,000 Hungarian Jews from deportation to Auschwitz. Jacob Taubes had been one of those invited to meet Karl at Markus's home in Chicago during Karl's 1962 trip to the US.

[139]J. Taubes to M. Barth, April 10, 1962; M. Wyschogrod to M. Barth, June 12, 1962. MBMC. Series II. Correspondence. Box 8, file 300.

Figure 5.7. Markus and Gogo the horse, on John Wray's ranch, Colorado

Figure 5.8. Markus and Gogo

Figure 5.9. Markus climbing in the Rocky Mountains

Figure 5.10. Markus skiing in Wisconsin

four-week vacation that took them into western Canada and Colorado. It was, it would seem, just the tonic they needed. As Markus wrote to a friend on their return, they spent their time relaxing "on a lonely camping place somewhere high up in Colorado, exposed to wind, rain and heat and mosquitos, usually in rapid change from one to another. . . . Be assured, I had together with my family an excellent vacation, distinguished especially by the riding of rather rough horses."[140]

Much of the rest of 1962, and well into the following year, saw Markus step up his correspondence with Jewish leaders and enter more fully into conversations concerning Jewish-Christian dialogue. Some of this was a direct result of acquaintances he had made during Karl's visit. Some of it was a (probably inevitable) consequence of his earlier Ephesians commentary, which was still making waves within American Protestant circles. And some of it, regardless of its cause, was quite openly political. Through the middle months of the year, for example, Markus was in contact with Rabbi Stephen Schwarzschild, who had asked if Markus might address the Massachusetts Board of Rabbis on the question of Jewish-Christian relations—an invitation to which Markus happily acquiesced.[141] In September, Markus corresponded with Stephen's brother, Henry Schwarzschild—at the time, the director of publications for the Anti-Defamation League—who was hoping to nominate Stephen for the directorship of a proposed Institute of Jewish Studies at the University of Chicago.[142] Around the same time, Markus was also in communication with Marc Tanenbaum of the American Jewish Committee. Tanenbaum's group was proposing to publish in the *New York Times* a full-page statement about, and denunciation of, Nikita Krushchev's persecution of Russian Jews. Confident that Barth would be an ally, Tanenbaum invited him to be a signatory.[143] Tanenbaum's instinct was correct—Barth was sympathetic to the cause and gratified to have been

---

[140]M. Barth to V. Fletcher, June 7, 1962, August 19, 1962. MBMC. Subject Correspondence 4. Box 8.

[141]M. Barth to S. Schwarzschild; S. Schwarzschild to M. Barth. MBMC. Series II. Correspondence. Box 8, file 310.

[142]H. Schwarzschild to M. Barth, September 12, 1962. MBMC. Series II. Correspondence. Box 8, file 310.

[143]M. Tanenbaum to M. Barth, August 24, 1962. MBMC. Series II. Correspondence. Box 8, file 301.

asked to contribute. Nonetheless, he refused. Despite sharing Tanenbaum's concerns, the proposal struck him as being misdirected—why not write directly to the Russian Premier?—and, in his view, smacked of rather tasteless bravado.

> I feel honored by being called upon to join an effort in favor of freedom and dignity of the Jewish congregation's life and I am grieved with you over each news that comes of suppression and slander. But I am not willing to help sign the declaration. . . . I would support and gladly sign a similar effort made for the same purpose *if the letter were addressed and sent to Mr Kruschev*. . . . But I do not like to join the tone and the way chosen by the declaration. . . . Sheer anti-communism thus displayed is today too cheap to be valuable, to[o] negative to effect anything constructive, too much dictated by showmanship to look honest.[144]

Given Barth's discomfort with simplistic binaries that uncritically pitted East against West, there was a pro-Western, anti-communist, ideological polemic in Tanenbaum's approach that bothered him. Moreover, his open repudiations of American triumphalism, such as had characterized some of his public statements as far back as 1957, made it effectively impossible for him to put his name to Tanenbaum's open letter, no matter how much he sympathized with the cause itself.

In November 1962, the question of the church's relationship to Israel again occupied Markus's mind, this time in a lecture delivered in Ithaca, New York. Harking back to the arguments he had proposed in *The Broken Wall*, he insisted that the reconciliation of Jews and Gentiles in Christ was not only for Paul "but probably always" the "basic, essential and typical act of reconciliation from which alone can and must be derived reconciliation in all other facts and aspects of social life."[145] The theological—but also sociopolitical—consequence of this was therefore that "to be a Christian means to be a brother of the Jew." This, he said, ought not be restricted—as the Confessing Church had too often done during the *Kirchenkampf* of the 1930s, and as Nelson Baker also wished to insist in retort to Barth—to

[144]M. Barth to M. Tanenbaum, September 2, 1962. MBMC. Series II. Correspondence. Box 8, file 301.

[145]M. Barth, "The Church According to the Epistle to the Ephesians," lecture delivered in Ithaca, NY, November 12, 1962, 36-37. MBMC. Series III. Publications. Box P1, file 10.

"converted, or baptized Jews only—[but] rather . . . includes probably the Jews in every one of the possible religious, ethnic, political, cultural meanings of this name."[146] Gentile Christians, concluded Markus, can thus be the "communion of the saints of which the Apostles' Creed speaks, [only] when they do not deny but confess and live according to the brotherhood with Israel."[147] That he could say this little more than two months after having refused Tanenbaum's request illustrates perfectly what would become one of the major tensions of Markus's work and the source of considerable friction between him and his Jewish friends. How was it possible for Barth, on one hand, to affirm unreservedly Christian solidarity with the Jewish people, while at the same time retaining the right to critique, and even distance himself from, aggressive and oppressive Israeli actions?

While Jewish-Christian dialogue had thus begun to take on central significance for Markus, it was not the only theological-political matter with which he was involved. In January 1963 he was in New York for a meeting of the Presbyterian Church's Special Committee on a Brief Contemporary Statement of Faith.[148] The objective set for the committee was simple: to craft

> a short Statement of Faith written in these times, dealing with the great verities of the Word of God and facing today's burning issues. . . . [This] should be of interest and value to church officers and church school-teachers, to new members of our churches, and to any among us who wish to give plain answers about the faith we hold. It should bring to all members of our Church some sense of participation in the thrilling revival of theology.[149]

It was not a happy meeting. Arthur Come, one of the commissioners of the PC(USA)'s 1958 General Assembly, has admitted that "the major

---

[146]Barth, "Church According to the Epistle to the Ephesians," 37.

[147]Barth, "Church According to the Epistle to the Ephesians," 38.

[148]The origins of the committee's work are to be found in 1956, in the request by the Presbytery of Amarillo to the Presbyterian Church's General Assembly that the *Westminster Shorter Catechism*—long part of the Presbyterian confessional standards—be rewritten in modern language. The General Assembly appointed a committee, chaired by Arthur Adams and thus routinely known as "the Adams Committee," to undertake the task. See J. B. Rogers, "Biblical Authority and Confessional Change," *Journal of Presbyterian History (1962–1985)* 59, no. 2 (1981): 136.

[149]*Report of the Special Committee on a Brief Contemporary Statement of Faith to the 177th General Assembly, the United Presbyterian Church in the United States of America, May 1965* (Philadelphia: Office of the General Assembly, 1965), 11. Cited in Rogers, "Biblical Authority and Confessional Change," 137.

socio-cultural forces" of the day—including the ever-present threat of atomic warfare and the movement for racial justice in the US—were not discussed as such by the Special Committee, yet were "operative in its members as persons shaped by them."[150] Markus, however, was less sanguine. "In spite of my best efforts, I cannot persuade the Committee, of which I am a member, to take a considered position in matters of race, atomic war, and the East-West tensions. . . . My brothers do not want to make a decision."[151] No less frustrating for him was the complete failure of a social ethics conference that had been held in Chicago the week previously, and at which a number of significant theologians and Christian ethicists had been present. Despite the good work of people like Georges Casalis and the Orthodox theologian Nikos Nissiotis, "nothing came of it. . . . It is very disappointing."[152]

TO STAY OR TO LEAVE?

In early 1963, the Barths were faced with a significant decision arising from an unexpected opportunity. The Presbyterian-run Pittsburgh Theological Seminary, under the leadership of Donald Miller,[153] was undergoing an expansion of both its physical facilities and its faculty. Barth was on a list of highly desired appointments. In February, after having just visited the seminary in the middle of a snowstorm, Markus wrote to his father to tell him that "the Pittsburgh people really want me there" (*Die Pittsburgher wollen mich unbedingt dort haben*).[154] For their part, both Karl and Nelly encouraged

[150]A. B. Come, "The Occasion and Contribution of the Confession of 1967," *The Journal of Presbyterian History* 79, no. 1 (2001): 62.

[151]M. Barth to N. Barth, January 25, 1963. MBL. Series II. Box 11. By the end of the year, he was even more frustrated. "I cannot possibly describe to you how laborious this work is, how frequently a sluggish majority, a tedious conservatism . . . gains the upper hand." M. Barth to K. Barth, November 20, 1963.

[152]M. Barth to N. Barth, January 25, 1963. Nikos Nissiotis (1924–1986) was professor of philosophy and psychology of religion at Athens University and, through the 1960s–70s, was director of the World Council of Churches' Ecumenical Institute at Bossey.

[153]Donald G. Miller (1909–1997), a New Testament scholar, was president of Pittsburgh Theological Seminary from 1962 until 1970. Prior to his presidency, he spent twenty years as professor of New Testament at Union Theological Seminary in Richmond, Virginia. Under his tenure at Pittsburgh, endowments, student numbers, and the number and quality of faculty increased markedly. See "Dr Miller Retires as Head of Seminary," *The Evening Standard* (Uniontown), May 26, 1969, 34.

[154]M. Barth to K. Barth, February 3, 1963, 3. MBL. Series V, file 5.

the move. Evidently concerned about the toll on Markus's health that the Chicago job had increasingly taken, Nelly wrote to her son saying that "really, if at all possible you should be relieved of the risks, and the great exertions, of the many lecture tours."[155]

Figure 5.11. Rose Marie on holiday in the Rocky Mountains, 1960

But why was Markus even interested in the possibility? His family—not least Rose Marie—was happily settled in Chicago, including at First Baptist. As one of their co-congregants put it, "I cannot express to you how deeply grievous it is to me to think about the Church's loss when you [Rose Marie] will be leaving us."[156] Markus himself had intentionally turned his back on Dubuque's confessionalism in favor of the breadth and freedom of academic inquiry that Chicago represented. Would Pittsburgh not be a return to exactly the type of context he had so deliberately left? Acknowledging that his friends were likely to ask about precisely these matters, Markus preempted their questions by providing his reasons as fulsomely as he could. Noting that there were, in fact, "plenty of reasons" for wishing to leave the University of Chicago, he confirmed that "decisive" among them was the theology faculty's increasingly obvious commitment "to a type of theology that renders it a School for Religion and the Philosophy of Religion." Markus still recognized that there were pedagogical benefits to the teaching of sociology, psychology, and modern literature alongside the Bible. However, he was equally adamant that "it [is] problematic when theology

[155]N. Barth to M. Barth, February 24, 1963. MBL. Series II. Box 11.
[156]S. M. Carr to R. M. Barth, April 22, 1963. MBL. Series V, file 5.

Figure 5.12. Chicago. Anna, Markus, and a friend

becomes merely apologetics." Moreover, he went on, "It is catastrophic when hardly any students come to Chicago who simply want to become pastors." The faculty, Markus reported sadly, was really only seeking to attract doctoral students; those who still wished to study for the pastorate were "forced into a course that [leaves] far too little time for biblical studies."[157] Nor was there any opportunity for students to undertake field education prior to graduation. Keen to address what he saw as a fundamental deficiency in the curriculum, Markus had therefore proposed the introduction of a pastoral internship into the third year of study. However, while a majority of the Congregationalists in the faculty supported the idea, the other denominations refused, as did—critically—the dean, with whom Barth continued to have a strained relationship.[158] Acknowledging that he was not entirely alone in still understanding theology to be a

[157]M. Barth, "Rundbrief," February 29, 1964, 7-8.

[158]One of the professors who voted against Barth's idea was Joseph Sittler (1904–1987). A Lutheran theologian who taught at the University of Chicago Divinity School from 1957 to 1973, Sittler was one of the first proponents of Christian ecotheology and happened to live opposite the Barths on South Kimbark Avenue. P. Barth et al., "Chicago Memories," 6.

properly ecclesial discipline rather than "speculation oriented toward cultural Protestantism," Markus was forced to realize that he was simply tired of fighting a largely fruitless battle against the pedagogical trend.[159]

And so, clearly disenchanted with the theological path that Chicago's faculty of theology was treading, Markus allowed himself to give serious consideration to a return to a more explicitly confessional environment, and thus commenced negotiations with Pittsburgh Seminary's administration about a potential move from Chicago. Those discussions—which did not deal solely with conditions of employment but also with vexed questions around divergent sacramental theologies—were not always easy: "We had a long, good conversation in which they asked me, and I asked them, pointed questions regarding the right and responsibility to teach what the Bible says about baptism (and not what the Westminster Confession says)." Nevertheless, Markus noted that he would be warmly welcomed in Pittsburgh if he chose to accept an offer. Moreover, there were certain advantages to the position. Pittsburgh, he said, had a congenial receptivity to it. While nowhere near as illustrious a seminary as its counterpart in Princeton, it had the distinct advantage of not suffering from Princeton's characteristic narrowness. Also, the seminary had solid plans to become "a sort of theological faculty of the Pittsburgh University."[160] Given that Markus's move from Dubuque to Chicago had been largely driven by his desire to engage academically within the breadth of free scholastic inquiry, it is unsurprising that this was an important drawcard for him. At the conclusion of the negotiations, Markus was offered one of three new academic posts. The position—a full professorship of New Testament, as opposed to the associate professorship he held in Chicago—was too good to turn down. In March 1963, the seminary's board of directors announced that Barth would be joining the expanded team from the start of the fall semester, alongside the two other appointees—Edward Farley was named associate professor in systematic theology, while Lynn

[159]M. Barth, "Rundbrief," February 29, 1964, 7-8.

[160]M. Barth to K. Barth, February 3, 1963, 3. This was not the first time Markus had discussed the possibility of a move to Pittsburgh with his father. There is an earlier reference to an anticipated "going to Pittsburgh" from the previous month. M. Barth to K. Barth, January 23, 1963, 1. MBL. Series V, file 5. While there is little detail in this earlier letter, it does seem likely that Markus's conversations with the seminary had been progressing for some time.

Hinds, a graduate of Temple University in dramatic arts, was appointed as a speech instructor.[161]

And so the Barths' nearly eight years in Chicago drew to a close. One of the last major tasks that both Markus and Rose Marie undertook together before leaving was a lecture tour through Macon, Georgia, in the spring. There, Markus asked to meet with a group of twenty pastors, all of whom were known to be segregationists, in order to hear their side of the increasingly fractious debates over race relations. He was, he told them, from Chicago, and so had a very one-sided understanding of the issues. In response, the pastors uniformly indicated their support for the improvement of social conditions for black Americans but also insisted that they would never be accepted into the pastors' own church communities. As Rose Marie observed, the ministers were prepared privately to support the abolition of segregation but were unwilling to say so from their pulpits.[162] For his part, Markus implored them to ground their theological and pastoral responsibilities upon a renewed recognition of Jesus' lordship over *this* world and not merely to proclaim that "things will get better in heaven."[163] This final act of Barth's tenure in Chicago was thus consistent with the form of theological political engagement that had so characterized his time there. His relocation from Chicago to Pittsburgh did not, however, bring to an end his (or his family's) involvement with issues of racial discrimination. Indeed, during the final decade of the Barths' time in the United States, questions of race, and racial justice, occupied their time and energies with increasing urgency.

---

[161]"Theologian's Son Joins Seminary Here," *The Pittsburgh Press*, March 24, 1963, 72; "Three Faculty Appointments at Seminary," *The Daily Notes*, March 2, 1963, 3.

[162]R. M. Barth, "Rundbrief," October 1963, 5.

[163]R. M. Barth, "Rundbrief," October 1963, 5.

6

"MAYBE IT'S NOT ENTIRELY FOR NOTHING"

Pittsburgh, 1963–1972

THE BARTHS LEFT CHICAGO ON JUNE 25, 1963, to start the next chapter of their lives in Pittsburgh. With a busy summer ahead of them, however, they did not head immediately to their new home. Earlier in the month, Markus had been a delegate at a conference in Miami on "Crime and Delinquency: What Can the Church Do in Corrections?" before heading north into upstate New York for meetings of the Presbyterian Statement of Faith Committee.[1] Meanwhile, Rose Marie traveled back to Europe for a short holiday. A much-needed vacation in the Colorado mountains followed that was largely spent riding horses, hiking, and reading.[2] "To my chagrin," Markus wrote to his father, "I read Bishop Robinson's rather foolish book; to my delight, Rose Marie brought me [from Europe] Gollwitzer's book."[3] After teaching a short course in Princeton on the epistle of James, during which he sought to ease the

---

[1]M. Barth to K. Barth, June 12, 1963. MBL. Series V, file 5.

[2]As Markus put in a letter to his mother, "I am no longer the best rider in the family, no longer the invincible mountaineer. Lukas climbs much better . . . [while] Rose Marieli can jump very elegantly, and knows how to handle horses very well." M. Barth to N. Barth, July 19, 1963. MBL. Series II. Box 11.

[3]M. Barth to K. Barth, July 16, 1963. MBL. Series V, file 5. The first book to which Markus refers is J. A. T. Robinson's *Honest to God* (London: SCM, 1963). It is not clear, however, which of Gollwitzer's books he means.

students' concerns regarding Bonhoeffer's later theology,[4] and a further three-week introductory course on the New Testament and the Sermon on the Mount at Union Theological Seminary in New York, Markus finally arrived in Pittsburgh with the rest of the family. They got there at the end of August in time for the start of the fall semester.

MOVING ON AND SETTLING IN

For Markus, the move had come not a moment too soon. A letter to his father shows how, despite Tillich's efforts, his conflict with Jerry Brauer remained a sore point, and that he had no confidence in the direction that Chicago's Divinity School was going. "I am very happy that I do not have to return [to Chicago] under Brauer's management; the man has already appointed new professors (though as yet, no successor to me)—all of them extremely unpleasant people, whose only success so far has been a certain amount of publicity, but who offer little hope for anything more substantial. My time in Chicago really was over."[5]

The move was also, of course, a return to a deeply confessional learning and teaching environment. As he explained it to his friends, Pittsburgh was "to American Presbyterians what Zurich is to a Zwinglian, or Fribourg to a Marian Catholic."[6] Always in the background of the city, he said, "was Calvin's theology and the Westminster Confession. . . . Here, if anywhere, the church lives as an institution." What the Presbyterian community in Pittsburgh says, he noted, "has always mattered . . . [not least] because the

---

[4]"The local pastors ask me with worried expressions whether Bonhoeffer's talk of a 'world come of age' [*der mündigen Welt*] and 'religionless faith' [*Religionslosen Glauben*] . . . are now the most important things in theology. I assure them boldly and coolly that this is all just gossip, and that they should stick to the more important, if less loudly advertised, scholarship." M. Barth to K. Barth, July 16, 1963.

[5]M. Barth to K. Barth, July 16, 1963.

[6]M. Barth, "Rundbrief," February 29, 1964, 7. Markus's reference to Marian Catholicism is interesting. In 1670, the Congregation of Marians of the Immaculate Conception was founded in Poland by John Papczyński (1631–1701), receiving papal approval from Innocent XII in 1699. After a century of international expansion, the Order was all but destroyed through the various European wars of the nineteenth century and was particularly brutally crushed by Russian Czarists. In 1904, the last Marian monastery was closed, with only one Marian priest—Fr. Vincent Sekowski (1840–1911)—remaining alive. In 1909, Sekowski received two young men into the Order in secret, and—in order to rescue the Order from Czarist persecution—sent them to Fribourg to renew the Order from there in safety.

four richest families of the region are all Presbyterian."[7] That it was by the Presbyterian seminary of this thoroughly Presbyterian town that Markus was now employed gave him a degree of social and economic security, and indeed privilege.

Regardless of the benefits the move had for Markus's work, it was nevertheless a sudden dislocation for the family. In Rose Marie's words, the relocation represented for her "the breaking-off of many friendly threads of connection, that had been spun during eight years [in Chicago], and the inevitable, sudden distancing from an environment in which [she] had been so absorbed."[8] As she wrote to her friends back at Chicago's First Baptist, "I realize how numb . . . I have been all the time since I left you . . . [with] my roots withering on account of that mighty pull which severed our family from the community in Chicago and dumped us on a hill in Pittsburgh."[9] Markus himself acknowledged that, even six months after their move, his wife was still not entirely happy about their new city, nor had she found any church community to replace what she had had in Chicago.[10]

On arriving in the city, they moved straight into their house on Beechwood Boulevard, six miles from the city's center, but just a short walk from nearby Frick Park. Located in the predominantly Jewish Squirrel Hill neighborhood, the house was close to the very well-regarded Taylor Allderdice High School, which both Lukas and Rose-Marie attended.[11] Barth's full professorship had enabled them to purchase a house

[7]M. Barth, "Rundbrief," February 29, 1964, 8. Markus was not necessarily enamored of what he regarded as the institutionalization of the church in Pittsburgh. He recognized that, in response, one could always "give it up as hopeless and flee into some academic 'ivory tower' [*Höhe*], or social desert. . . . Or one could rush headlong into . . . the proud, self-assured, but not very interesting institution, and hope that God will prevent you from becoming either haughty, or assimilated [*gleichgeschaltet*] or desperate."

[8]R. M. Barth, "Rundbrief," October 1963, 1.

[9]R. M. Barth to Chicago First Baptist, November 15, 1963, 1. MBL. Series I. Box 34.

[10]"[S]ie selbst einstweilen nicht gerade glücklich über diesen Ort ist und noch keine sie unmittelbar rufende (kirchliche?) Arbeit gefunden hat." M. Barth, "Rundbrief," February 29, 1964, 7.

[11]Taylor Allderdice High School was founded in 1927 and has been recognized three times as a National Blue Ribbon School for academic excellence. Graduating from the school in the same year that Lukas and Rose-Marie commenced there was Harvey Fineberg (1945–), later to be appointed provost of Harvard University. Note that it was precisely the school's excellent reputation that led Markus and Rose Marie to look for a home in Squirrel Hill.

that was "as expected . . . very nice." On the other hand, Barth was conflicted by the relative prosperity. Is it not, he asked his mother, "located in a neighborhood that is too affluent on the outside . . . [and is it not] too noble on the inside for us to have any contact with the poor and oppressed people in other parts of the city?"[12] Whether he remained so conflicted is not clear. In any case, the Beechwood Boulevard property was to be the family home until they moved back to Switzerland nine years later. For some of that time, however, it was home to more than just the Barths. Keiko Furukawa (later, Watanabe), a Japanese pen-pal of Anna's, lived with the family between 1963 and 1965 while studying English at the university.[13] A recollection from her of those days paints a delightful picture of the family's morning routine:

> Every morning Lukas put on a record in the living room—mainly Mozart—which was heard throughout the house over a loud-speaker in the stairway. Lukas also prepared . . . breakfast and made coffee. After that he called us, "*Zumorge asse!*" Papa Markus . . . humming that morning music happily, came down from the second floor. At the table he read every day from the German prayer book and . . . said Grace: "*Segne, Vater, diese Speise, uns zur Kraft und dir zum Preise*" ("Bless, Father, this food, for our strength and for your glory").[14]

In view of how disruptive the relocation from Chicago had been, these daily patterns likely provided a much-needed sense of comforting familiarity.

The seminary itself was a vastly different environment to what Markus had been used to in Chicago. Once again, as had been the case in Dubuque,

---

[12]M. Barth to N. Barth, September 8, 1963. MBL. Series II. Box 11.

[13]Keiko was not the first Japanese student taken under the Barth's protective wing. Kyoko Motomochi Nakamura (1932–), another friend of Anna's, was cared for by the Barths in Chicago during a two-year stay in Chicago between 1960–1962, where she worked with, among others, Mircea Eliade. In later letters, she also expressed her very great appreciation for the help they had given. "I thank you very much for your constant encouragement and guidance, without which I should have been completely lost." K. Motomochi to R. M. and M. Barth, April 13, 1962; also, "I am very grateful for all that you have done for me during my stay in Chicago. Without your encouragement I could not have got the degree from the Divinity School. . . . I will write to you from time to time, and I hope I will be able to see you next time in my country." K. Motomochi to R. M. and M. Barth, August 26, 1962. Both in MBL. Series V, file 4. In 1973, partly as a result of her studies in Chicago, Motomochi published *Miraculous Stories from the Japanese Buddhist Tradition: The nihon ryōiki of the Monk Kyōkai* (Cambridge, MA: Harvard University Press, 1973).

[14]K. Watanabe, "Living with the Barth Family 1963–1964," 2. MBL. Series II. Box 1.

he was in an institution in which theology was done "in the context of church life and preaching." Rather than his lecture rooms being filled with "a majority of more or less atheistic theology students," he was now faced, once more, with "eager, almost too open-hearted students, who want to hear about the real meaning of the Trinity, of Adam, of Jesus, [and of] justification."[15] As he mentioned in a letter to Karl, the thirty-five or so students who attended the open evenings at the Barth home—where, in the second-half of 1963, they worked their way through Karl's *Römerbrief*—were, "in contrast to the Chicago students, less sceptical, haughty, 'modern': they want simply to know what Paul might have meant, and how one might live by it."[16] Such an open disposition of his students did not, of course, persuade Markus to tone down the academic rigor of his lectures. On the contrary, he pushed his students beyond what many young conservative Presbyterians would have felt comfortable with. According to one observer, Markus urged his pupils to pursue their questions and doubts relentlessly, even if that was sometimes at the expense of their evangelistic zeal. "Truth cannot be found easily. If we cannot find [it], we had better not cheaply witness to it." He also warned them not to understand the New Testament as though it were only a fulfillment of the Old, or the Old only as promissory of the New, but rather to understand the Old Testament as having its own revelatory integrity.[17]

Naturally, there were also some disadvantages to Markus's new role. His work in Pittsburgh, at least in the classroom, became far more constricted in scope than it had been. "I can no longer, [for example], give a joint seminar with a lawyer on the theme of 'Righteousness and Justice.'" In his own vivid description of the difference in pedagogical and intellectual attitudes between the two cities, "The sharp wind of foreign teachings in

---

[15]M. Barth, "Rundbrief," February 29, 1964, 8. That Markus relished this renewed ecclesial orientation to his teaching that he had so missed in Chicago and which was so central to his scholarship provided an obvious point of connection with his new colleagues. No wonder, then, that they had anticipated his arrival "with a joy and expectation [that was] touching." M. Barth to K. Barth, July 16, 1963.

[16]M. Barth to K. Barth, October 20, 1963. MBL. Series V, file 5. It is worth noting that among the regular attendees at these open evenings were some "Catholics from the nearby Duchesne [*sic*] University."

[17]K. Watanabe, "Living with the Barth Family 1963–1964," 3.

Chicago has given way to a warm breeze of goodwill."[18] There was, in addition, a somewhat ironic expectation that was being placed upon Markus by the seminary's administration. Markus's increasing frustration at the University of Chicago's insistence on prioritizing doctoral students over seminarians has already been commented upon. Now, Don Miller, in conjunction with the local university, was hoping to make the seminary a suitable environment for PhD candidates and wanted Markus to lead the way. That, said Markus "was why there [had been] particular pressure on me to come here." Thankfully, however, there remained an equally strong commitment to the formation of pastors—a commitment that evidently alleviated any concerns that Markus may have harbored that Pittsburgh Theological Seminary might be heading in the same direction as Chicago.

Six months into his new job, Markus was able to reflect with satisfaction on his decision to move with the family to Pittsburgh. As part of Chicago's Federated Theological Faculty he had felt, at least in retrospect, something of a "curiosity"—perhaps because he had always striven and called for "responsible *ecclesial* theology."[19] In the seminary, on the other hand, this attitude was not in the least curious. What was surprising, however, was the greater freedom Pittsburgh promised for the development of Markus's own research. It will be recalled that his decision for Chicago in 1955 had been motivated largely by the quite reasonable assumption that a university would provide Markus with a richer and more conducive environment than a theological college in which to pursue his writing. In the end, that had not turned out to be the case. "I was asked to deliver so many lectures, discussions, and sermons here and there throughout America that the kind of collected and peaceful work at my desk, with the aid of both old and new commentaries, and about which I really care, became less and less possible."[20] While, as will be seen, the number of requests for guest lectures and sermons did not dissipate over the next decade, it seems that Pittsburgh did allow Markus the writing space for which he yearned. It was, at least, in Pittsburgh that he began work on what was to be arguably the

---

[18]M. Barth, "Rundbrief," February 29, 1964, 8.

[19]M. Barth, "Rundbrief," February 29, 1964, 8. Emphasis added.

[20]M. Barth, "Rundbrief," February 29, 1964, 8.

most significant academic contribution of his life—the *Ephesians* commentary for the Anchor Bible series.[21]

RACISM AND THE CIVIL RIGHTS MOVEMENT

The Barths' relocation to Pittsburgh coincided with a dramatic increase in racial tensions throughout the country in the spring and summer of 1963. Martin Luther King Jr.'s arrest in Birmingham and the bombing of the Gaston Motel in the same city in May were just the start of "a rising tide of discontent"[22] that saw hundreds of cities, in both northern and southern states, paralyzed by chaotic and often violent protests.

Rose Marie, having previously chosen to attend Chicago's First Baptist Church precisely because it was a mixed-race congregation led by a Japanese American pastor, was especially sensitive to America's Christian response to the racial tensions. She was less than impressed. "Where," she asked, "is the church's response to the fight for the human and civil rights of [our] black brothers?" She was forced to conclude that "on that, the church has once again missed an opportunity." Recognizing that there were occasionally—but *only* occasionally—individual pastors who spoke and acted bravely, Rose Marie lamented the ineffectiveness of the National Council of Churches. Despite its preparedness to speak out against racism, it could influence neither the country's largest denomination—the Southern Baptist Convention—nor local church communities. Just as vexing to her were the attitudes of Christian individuals, whose views were shaped by impoverished homiletics. "The fundamentalist sermon—typical in the south, but also present in many places here in Pittsburgh—wants nothing to do with politics or society, indulges in paraphrases, spouts forth timeless 'divine truth,' holds up 'Christian principles,' but in fact, with its face averted, passes by the ethical issues of the day."[23]

Interestingly, Rose Marie was strongly defensive of President Kennedy's response to the summer's racial conflicts, in particular his "beautiful June

---

[21]Barth was contracted by Noel Freedman of Doubleday Books in May 1964.

[22]J. F. Kennedy, "Radio and Television Report on Civil Rights to the American People," June 11, 1963, John F. Kennedy Presidential Library and Museum, doi: JFKWHA-194-001.

[23]R. M. Barth, "Rundbrief," October 1963, 5.

speech on the matter."[24] Acknowledging that he had not visited in person the key flashpoint places of Birmingham, or the University of Alabama—in what had been construed by some as an apparently deliberate snub to the requests of both Martin Luther King Jr. and the novelist James Baldwin—Rose Marie remarked that she did not think this was due to a lack of courage or conviction on the president's part, or out of a desire to minimize an electoral backlash. Rather, she surmised far more charitably, Kennedy did not wish to be some sort of "deus ex machina," presuming to be able to impose a solution from the outside. Far from helping the cause of black civil rights, this would merely provide "new nourishment to the separatism of the south." Unless the southern states themselves accepted the legitimacy of the civil rights movement, without external pressure or interference, they would "forever scream 'rape by the north,' and the smouldering embers of the Civil War . . . will never be snuffed out 'at the grass roots.'"[25] Her appreciation for Kennedy's handling of this issue was most likely one of the main reasons for her shock at his assassination in November. With Kennedy's death, wrote Rose Marie, "we have lost a man who cannot simply be replaced."[26]

But what of Markus's response to the racial tensions, and to the attitude of the churches? An ecumenical conference in early February 1964—at which Markus was a delegate, and for which the "race question" (*die Rassenfrage*) was the sole theme—was an eye-opener. Attending to the civil rights struggle as "an example of the failure of the church," the conference heard from campaigners from Mississippi, who were "asked simply to share

[24]R. M. Barth, "Rundbrief," October 1963, 1.

[25]R. M. Barth, "Rundbrief," October 1963, 3. While Rose Marie did not think that political pragmatism was the reason for Kennedy's absence from Birmingham and the University of Alabama, she did appreciate the political realities of the situation. The president's actions in response to the deteriorating racial situation had already jeopardized his chances of retaining "six of the seven southern states that had voted for him in 1960." Rose Marie, at least, was deeply worried about what would happen if Kennedy lost; "if you consider the names that the [Republicans] have proposed as possible election candidates, you would get the creeps [*so könnte einem das Gruseln ankommen*]."

[26]R. M. Barth, "Rundbrief," October 1963, 2. In a curious aside, Rose Marie suspected that, in the months after Kennedy's assassination, she was being observed by the FBI. She reported hearing a "clicking" sound whenever she answered the telephone, and—in light of the identity of Kennedy's assassin—was acutely conscious of her maiden name, Oswald. Personal correspondence with the Barth family, January 17, 2022.

Figure 6.1. The Barths' chalet in Villa

their work and tell us what they thought of the church. Their report was rather splendid, but their judgment on the church was devastating."[27] Noting that there were very few Christians among the movement's leadership, Markus was nevertheless deeply impressed by the group's organizational maturity, the campaigners' singleness of purpose, and the strength of their relationships. They "embarrass," he said, "pastors, theologians and Christians" by their fervent belief in the rightness of their cause. Even more than that, however, Markus perceived in the civil rights movement a community of righteous action that put the church itself to shame. "Isn't it true that in the freedom movement the *notae ecclesiae* are much more visible than in the most beautiful church service? There is Word and Sacrament, and Martyrdom and Inspiration, and 'today is the day of salvation'; and almost all moralism, ceremonialism and particularism seem, in the spirit of the Apostle Paul, to have been completely overcome."[28]

In the summer of 1964, as they had in 1960, the family holidayed together in Switzerland. For the first time, they were able to stay in the village of Villa in a chalet that Markus and Rose Marie had had built on a parcel

[27]M. Barth, "Rundbrief," February 29, 1964, 6.
[28]M. Barth, "Rundbrief," February 29, 1964, 7.

of land they had bought back in 1960. For much of the next thirty years, at least until he was too frail to travel, the Villa chalet was Markus's sanctuary, to which he and the family would flee on every possible occasion. It was also a place of hospitality, to which children, grandchildren, and friends from around the world were regularly and warmly welcomed.[29] On this occasion in 1964, Anna's friend Keiko stayed behind in Pittsburgh to look after the house and the family dog, Olaf. There was a poignancy to this trip because, by the time that it was over, three of the children—with the exception of Rose-Marie, who still had four more years of high-schooling to complete, and Lukas, who continued to live at home while at Carnegie Tech—had left home. Peter was planning to spend a year in Göttingen as part of his theological studies; Anna was on exchange at the Munich Art Academy before commencing her final year at Oberlin College, in Ohio; and Ruth had completed her first year at Bryn Mawr College.[30]

As for Markus's work, despite his hope that Pittsburgh would give him more opportunity to focus on his writing, he found himself as much in demand for speaking engagements at universities and churches throughout the country as he had in Chicago. In 1963, Barth and Verne Fletcher[31] had published a biblical-ethical response to the pressing social issues of the day, titled *Acquittal by Resurrection*.[32] Seeking to ground Christian ethical action in the historic reality of the resurrection, the book generated significant press coverage, controversy, and a fresh round of lecture invitations. The book's appeal in media circles was due in no small part to the authors,' and particularly Barth's, insistence on the (by this time) largely

[29]Correspondence with the Barth family, March 10, 2023.

[30]R. M. Barth, "Rundbrief," March 12, 1964, 9. With the exception of Anna, who had remained in Germany, the family had reunited briefly before this trip to Switzerland during the Easter of 1964. Keiko Watanabe recalls that it was during this time that Ruth became increasingly inspired by Dostoyevsky's concept of freedom, which, as we have seen, was instrumental in her decision to be baptized. Watanabe, "Living with the Barth Family 1963–1964," 2.

[31]Verne H. Fletcher (1922–2009) was a theological ethicist and missionary. After studying at Wheaton, Princeton Theological Seminary, the Faculté Reformée in Montpellier, and the University of Chicago's Divinity School, where he completed his doctorate in 1961, Fletcher worked briefly in the Église Reformée de France before a longer stint as a missionary with the United Church Board of World Ministries in Indonesia. This was followed by fourteen years as professor of theology and ethics, and later dean, at the Near East School of Theology in Beirut, and then a further five years in Indonesia before his retirement in 1990.

[32]M. Barth and V. H. Fletcher, *Acquittal by Resurrection* (New York: Holt, Rinehart & Winston, 1963).

unfashionable idea of the historicity of the resurrection. That the book was controversial partly because by insisting on the historic reality of the resurrection, Barth and Fletcher were seen to be openly repudiating the far more popular "neo-liberal[ism]" of Paul Tillich and Rudolf Bultmann.[33]

VATICAN II, *NOSTRA AETATE*, AND CHRISTIAN ANTISEMITISM

In addition to his political activism—primarily, but not only, in relation to the civil rights movement—Barth was also engaged as a biblical scholar in more intradisciplinary debates. In February 1964, he and Jacob Taubes lobbied Geoffrey Bromiley—one of the lead translators of Karl Barth's *Kirchliche Dogmatik*—in an effort to stop the English translation of Gerhard Kittel's *Theologisches Wörterbuch des Neuen Testamentum*. Taubes, with whom Barth had first connected in Chicago during Karl's visit, had spoken to Barth of Kittel's "venom" and the presence within the dictionary of "the most obscene anti-Judaic overtones." As a result, Barth wrote to its English translator, Geoffrey Bromiley: "Please understand me right: I am all for the publication of Kittel in this country. But I consider it most urgent that we do not perpetuate that sort of mean and subtle antisemitism which permitted Germany and led them to gas 5-6 million Jews. Kittel as it stands is not innocent of that blood."[34] Bromiley's response was terse. Accusing Barth and Taubes of seeing antisemitism where it wasn't, he complained that Barth was "mak[ing] this unnecessarily difficult," and treating Bromiley's attempts to find a compromise "with mere contempt." Barth, he said, and Taubes even more so, were using "the type of vocabulary that we had hoped had vanished from the English theological scene."[35]

---

[33]L. Cassels, "Author Calls Resurrection 'Reality,'" *The Shreveport Journal*, March 28, 1964, 5. The book was also criticized for its academic flaws. Charles West, for example, thought that Barth's account of the resurrection was too thin by itself to adequately ground the ethical conclusions that Barth wished to draw from it. Fletcher's contributions were even more problematic—his moral arguments were oversimplistic, "[did] not pack the biblical punch the reader was led to expect," and did not "shine with an especially Christian originality." C. West, "Review of M. Barth and V. H. Fletcher, *Acquittal by Resurrection*," *Theology Today* 22, no. 1 (April 1965): 148-49.

[34]M. Barth to G. Bromiley, February 2, 1964. MBMC. Subject Correspondence 4. Box 8.

[35]G. Bromiley to M. Barth, March 1, 1964. MBMC. Subject Correspondence 4. Box 8.

The debate was interrupted briefly by Markus's participation in a colloquium, held at the Cathedral Church of St. John the Divine in New York, to honor the work of his former Chicago colleague, Paul Tillich.[36] Three months later, however, the controversy flared up again when Barth and Taubes co-wrote a letter to the book review section of the *New York Times*, again prosecuting the case against publishing the English edition of the *Wörterbuch*. Gerhard Kittel, they argued, had "compromised himself hopelessly during the Nazi period." His latent antisemitism was "reflected in the structure of the Theological Dictionary [as well as] in his choice of contributors." It was hardly surprising, therefore, "that some of the description of the inter-testamental period and the evaluation of apocalyptic, Hellenistic and rabbinic Judaism is often less than fair in this work." Indeed, Barth and Taubes went so far as to claim that "the spirit of the Hitler times is reflected in . . . the pages of Kittel's work and must make biblical scholars blush with shame and repentance." Their conclusion? That they—and, it was implied, a great many of their colleagues—"would consider it extremely unfortunate were the re-appearance of this work in English to become a new source of higher anti-semitism in American New Testament scholarship."[37] In a curious addendum to the episode, Barth was visited by Richard Rubenstein—to whom Barth referred as "the queer Pittsburgh rabbi," and later, even more pointedly, as "the Baal of Pittsburgh"[38]—who wished to offer his support in the fight against the Kittel book. Rubenstein's aid, however, was unwelcome. "I am dubious," Barth said to Taubes, "whether from Rubenstein anything good is to be expected."[39]

Barth's opposition to both real and perceived antisemitism took a new, ecclesio-political turn in June. Back in October 1962, Pope John XXIII had convened the Second Vatican Council.[40] Twenty months in, only one major

[36]March 6, 1964. MBMC. Series VI. Box SF34, file 47.

[37]M. Barth and J. Taubes, Letters to the Editor, *New York Times*, "Book Reviews," April 12, 1964, 34. Among the contributors to whom Barth and Taubes objected were Walter Grundmann (1906–1976), who founded and directed the infamous Institut zur Erforschung und Beseitigung des jüdischen Einflusses auf das deutsche kirchliche Leben; and New Testament scholar Georg Bertram (1896–1979), who took over from Grundmann as the Institute's director from 1943 until its dissolution in 1945.

[38]M. Barth to R. Fackenheim, March 2, 1967. MBMC. Series II. Correspondence. Box 13, file 382.

[39]M. Barth to J. Taubes, March 27, 1964. MBMC. Subject Correspondence 4. Box 8.

[40]The Council was held over four sessions, from October 11, 1962 to December 8, 1965.

Figure 6.2. Karl and Markus talking to the press, Mulheim, Germany, April 1964

document had been published, *Sacrosanctum Concilium*, the Constitution on the Sacred Liturgy.[41] It was, however, widely known that the Secretariat for Promoting Christian Unity, under the leadership of Cardinal Augustin Bea, was drafting a statement on the relationship between Christians and Jews. Markus's father, Karl, had already been approached for his input. Through Markus's mediation, Abraham Heschel had requested the elder Barth to intervene in light of growing Jewish concerns that a preliminary iteration of the document—which had apparently contained not only an unequivocal condemnation of antisemitism but also (and vitally) a rejection of the centuries-old accusation of deicide—was in the process of being significantly weakened by conservative forces within the Curia.[42]

[41]Vatican Council II, *Sacrosanctum Concilium*, Constitution on the Sacred Liturgy, December 4, 1963, www.vatican.va/archive/hist_councils/ii_vatican_council/documents/vat-ii_const_19631204_sacrosanctum-concilium_en.html. The other three Constitutions of the Council were: *Lumen Gentium*, Dogmatic Constitution on the Church (November 21, 1964); *Dei Verbum*, Dogmatic Constitution on Divine Revelation (November 18, 1965); and *Gaudium et spes*, Pastoral Constitution on the Church in the Modern World (December 7, 1965).

[42]For a detailed account of Karl Barth's engagement with the drafting of *Nostra Aetate*, see D. Herskowitz, "Karl Barth and *Nostra Aetate*: New Evidence from the Second Vatican Council," *Journal of Theological Studies* 72, no. 2 (2021): 843-74. Markus was well aware of his father's involvement in other aspects of Vatican II also. As he said in a letter from mid-1963, "Much more important and gratifying [than Basel's choice of Heinrich Ott as Karl's replacement in the

Karl (somewhat reluctantly) agreed—but Markus, too, remained personally involved.

In the first instance, Markus expressed his dismay that in resisting ecclesial attempts to whitewash the church's antisemitic history, Christian theological defenders of Jewish interests were acting only after having been prompted from without and not on their own initiative. "What is bad about the whole thing" he said to his father, "is that time and again Jews have to make us Christians aware that we should do something clear and courageous in word and deed, but clearly we are not affected and disturbed by it in such a way that we do something without a stimulus."[43]

In June, he allowed himself to be even more outspoken about the failures of Vatican II on this matter in the newly launched *Journal of Ecumenical Studies*. In an editorial titled "Salvation from the Jews?," Barth declared, "Once again those gathered around St. Peter's Chair . . . are about to betray Jesus Christ." The form of their treachery? The betrayal and sacrifice of the Jews "to our selfish interests."[44] Noting what Heschel and Tanenbaum had already observed—that a preliminary draft statement from Bea's secretariat had condemned antisemitism and sought to "silenc[e] the traditional charge of deicide"—Barth lashed the Vatican Council for refusing to endorse Bea's proposals. Not only had the anticipated "statement on the Jews" been absorbed into a more generalized "schema on Ecumenism"—with the prospect that even this would be revised, and the church's relationship to the Jewish people be understood in terms of interreligious dialogue—but the stumbling block issue of deicide was dropped entirely. This, said Barth, "opened the door to new and unspeakable harm." More than that, he said, such a blatant disregard of Jewish interests, and of the church's culpability for often violent antisemitism, had the gravest of consequences. "By excluding them . . . we shut out the Messiah."[45]

---

theology faculty] are the great changes taking place in Catholicism, which have not happened entirely without your involvement." M. Barth to K. Barth, July 16, 1963.

[43]M. Barth to K. Barth, in Karl Barth Archiv, file 9364.882. Cited in Herskowitz, "Karl Barth and *Nostra Aetate*," 852.

[44]M. Barth, "Salvation from the Jews?," *Journal of Ecumenical Studies* 1 (1964): 323.

[45]Barth, "Salvation from the Jews?" 324-26. Barth's concern about the location of the statement was prescient. In the end, of course, the Second Vatican Council's declaration on Catholic-Jewish relations was not treated in a statement of its own but was folded in to the broader interreligious

COUNTING THE COST

The second half of the year was typically busy with guest lectures around the country. In early October, Barth presented four lectures on the theme "The Apostle Paul's Message for Today" for the Presbyterian Minister-DCE Conference for the Synod of Louisiana at University Presbyterian Church in Baton Rouge between October 5–7, 1964.[46] Later in the same month, he traveled north to Massachusetts, where he delivered a series of lectures on "The Authority of the Scriptures" at Trinity Episcopal Church in Boston's Copley Square for the church's student organization, "Canterbury."[47] He rounded out the year with a presentation on December 2 to the student body of Washington and Jefferson College on the subject "Christ's Resurrection—A Challenge to Reason."[48]

The new year began, as the previous year had ended, with a fresh round of speaking engagements. In late March 1965, Markus spoke on "St. Paul and the Law" at the University of Wisconsin.[49] Seven days later, he shared the stage with Fr. George Tavard for a joint presentation on "Scripture and Tradition" at the St. Philip Catholic Church in Crafton, Pennsylvania.[50] In April, Markus again found a receptive audience among American Catholics. Invited to address the spring meeting of the Society of Teachers of Christian

---

Nostra Aetate. Barth's theological preference was that any such statement on the Jewish people should be framed ecclesiologically, not missiologically. In this, he sided with Archbishop Franjo Šeper (1905–1981), and his own father, Karl, who already in 1959 had stated that "auch die ökumenische Bewegung von heute leidet schwerer unter der Abwesenheit Israels, als unter der Roms und Moskaus! Die Kirche muß mit der Synagoge leben." ET: "The modern ecumenical movement suffers more seriously from the absence of Israel than of Rome or Moscow! The church *must* live with the Synagogue" (emphasis added). See *CD* IV/3.2, 878. Or, as Karl put it in 1966 to Cardinal Bea: "There is finally only one really great ecumenical question: our relations with the Jewish people." See R. Harries, *After the Evil: Christianity and Judaism in the Shadow of the Holocaust* (Oxford: Oxford University Press, 2003), 99.

[46]"Guest Speaker at Conference," *The Crowley Post-Signal*, October 3, 1964, 2.

[47]"Dr Barth at Trinity," *The Boston Globe*, October 23, 1964, 28.

[48]"Dr Markus Barth to Address W&J Student Body," *The Daily Notes*, November 25, 1964, 1, 8.

[49]"UW Schedules New Testament Scholar Barth," *Wisconsin State Journal*, March 20, 1965, 24.

[50]"Inter-Faith Dialogue Set at Crafton," *The Pittsburgh Press*, March 13, 1965, 4. George Tavard (1922–2007) was born in France and ordained in 1947 as a member of the Augustinians of the Assumption. Graduating with his doctorate from Lyons, he taught in England and then briefly at Princeton Theological Seminary. Pope John XXIII named him a *peritus conciliaris* at Vatican II. A noted ecumenist, Tavard gained a certain notoriety for advocating, among other things, the ordination of women to the Catholic priesthood and the freedom for priests to marry. He was also an outspoken critic of the Vietnam War. On many of these issues, he found a strong ally in Markus Barth.

Figure 6.3. Markus talking with a student during an "open evening," Pittsburgh, 1966

Doctrine, Markus spoke on "Freedom and Responsibility in Relation to the Pauline Concepts Contained in Galatians 2."[51]

It was perhaps his work on this lecture that encouraged him to pursue further work on Galatians. In May, Markus contacted Eugene Eoyang—then, the commissioning editor for Anchor Books at Doubleday—offering to write the Galatians commentary for the Anchor Bible series. His offer, though, was grounded not in a generalized interest in Paul's letter but in a subject with which Markus was now publicly and professionally associated. "If you should run into any snags with a Gal. Commentary for the Anchor Bible," he wrote to Eoyang, "I gladly offer my services. . . . My commentary might fit into that series because I try to do whatever I can to take the hidden or plain antisemitism out of the Christian interpretation of Galatians which for so many centuries has sullied it."[52] That is to say, hard on the heels of his engagement with the Kittel and *Nostra Aetate* issues of the previous year, Markus was now seeking to expand his

[51]"Protestant Theologian to Speak," *The Pittsburgh Press*, April 10, 1965, 4.

[52]M. Barth to E. Eoyang, May 8, 1965. MBMC. Subject Correspondence 2. Box 6. Eugene Eoyang (1939–) studied at Harvard University, and started as an editorial assistant at Doubleday in 1960, where he worked until 1966. In 1966, Eoyang commenced PhD studies at Indiana University, where he has worked since 1978 as professor of comparative literature. From 1961–1966, Eoyang was editor of the Anchor Books division of Doubleday.

repudiation of Christian antisemitism into a full-length exegetical monograph. Markus informed Eoyang that, were he to be deemed unsuitable for any reason to write the commentary, then Krister Stendahl—at the time, professor of New Testament at Harvard Divinity School—should be approached. As it transpired, though, neither Barth nor Stendahl wrote the Galatians commentary. Instead, it was authored by J. Louis Martyn and published in 1977.[53]

Markus's commitment to strengthening relationships between Jews and Christians was not limited to strictly academic pursuits. In a clear sign that he was fast becoming one of the country's most significant spokespeople on the topic, on July 25, Markus appeared on Canadian television as one of the experts for CBC's "Compass" program in an episode titled "Judaism—A Tradition in Transition." There he was featured alongside senior members of the various North American Jewish communities, with whom he had already established close working (and, in some cases, personal) relationships, such as Emil Fackenheim, Eugene Borowitz, Zalman Schachter, and Milton Himmelfarb.[54] Then in October, he participated in (and helped organize) what he had hoped would be "a strictly theological conference of Jews and Christians" at Harvard. In part, the aim of the conference was to address and help heal the "miserable situation" created by the Vatican's promulgation of *Nostra Aetate*. The delegate list at Harvard was certainly impressive and included Emil Fackenheim, Eugene Borowitz, and—from the Protestant side—Wolfhart Pannenberg. Abraham Heschel, Michael Wyschogrod, and Elie Wiesel were invited but could not attend. Its results, however, were the very opposite of what Barth had hoped for. Instead of engendering greater unity, the conference was characterized by a Christian rush to surrender all dogma, especially Christology, and by what Barth termed a Jewish "triumphalism" that sought to justify any and all Jewish

[53]J. Louis Martyn (1925–2015), was the Edward Robinson Professor of Biblical Theology at Union Theological Seminary in New York. In fact, Doubleday did initially award the contract for Galatians to Barth, and so his approach to Eoyang must, at first, have been received warmly. By the middle of 1974, however, the contract had been canceled, due to Markus falling behind in his work for both the Colossians and Philemon volumes. N. Freedman to M. Barth, June 3, 1974. MBMC. Subject Correspondence 2. Box 6.

[54]"Compass Takes Look at Judaism," *The Ottawa Citizen*, July 17, 1965, 58; "Judaism: Traditional Modern Role Examined, Sunday Channels 2, 6," *Times Colonist*, July 24, 1965, 15.

experience at the expense of any religious (or political) counterpoint.[55] Barth's critical response to this Jewish posturing, which he saw most completely embodied in Fackenheim's prioritization of Auschwitz above all else, was to lead to the souring—and in some cases complete rupture—of many of his friendships with Jewish colleagues. That Barth returned from Harvard dismayed and angry may not, however, have been entirely due to the conference itself. In the back of his mind there was lurking almost certainly a concern for his son, Lukas. Just nineteen years of age, Lukas had been "threatened" with conscription into the US Army for service in Vietnam—a conflict against which Barth had been a vociferous opponent. In a letter to Thurneysen, Markus said that Lukas intended to "fight it to the bitter end [*zum bitterenden Ende*], as a Conscientious Objector."[56]

Meanwhile, Markus's teaching at the seminary continued to be supplemented by his acceptance of numerous invitations to speak at conferences and symposia throughout the country and overseas. In June, he was one of the keynote presenters at the centennial celebrations for Lexington's College of the Bible.[57] Seven months later, on February 13, 1966, he was off to Oakland, Pennsylvania, to preach on "The Right of Man and the Right of God" at the Heinz Memorial Chapel Oakland.[58] This was followed the next month with a lecture on "Catholic and Lutheran Ecumenism" at the Catholic University of America, Washington, DC, on March 10.[59] Two months further on, he traveled to East Germany for a "shortened guest semester" at the University of Greifswald during the summer of 1966.[60]

This last trip proved utterly exhausting for him. A condition of his accepting the invitation was that he complete a full semester's worth of

[55]See M. Barth to Z. Schachter, October 22, 1966. MBMC. Series II. Correspondence. Box 12, file 366. See also my "Jewish-Christian Dialogue from the Underside: Markus Barth's Correspondence with Michael Wyschogrod (1962–84) and Emil Fackenheim (1965–80)," *Journal of Ecumenical Studies* 53, no. 3 (2018): 332-33.

[56]M. Barth to E. Thurneysen, October 16, 1965. MBMC. Subject Correspondence 3. Box 7. Lukas had been born on August 18, 1946, and so while Markus spoke of him in this letter as "*mein 20 jähriger Sohn*," Lukas had in fact only just turned nineteen.

[57]"Bible College Sets 100th Graduation," *The Courier-Journal*, May 3, 1965, 39.

[58]"Religious News in Brief," *Pittsburgh Post-Gazette*, February 12, 1966, 7.

[59]"Ecumenism Lecture," *Pittsburgh Post-Gazette*, March 8, 1966, 4.

[60]In early 1965, Barth wrote to his mother Nelly that he had accepted an invitation to spend the months of May and June—a *verkürztes Gastsemester* ("shortened semester")—as a visiting professor in Greifswald. M. Barth to N. Barth, February 22, 1965. MBL. Series II. Box 11.

teaching in Pittsburgh before departing for Europe. This meant that his "poor students . . . suffer[ed] from the pressure of an overabundance of material" that Markus had to teach them in nine weeks instead of the usual fourteen.[61] Once in Greifswald, the pace of work was at least as intense. "I'm really hard at work, and after Pentecost, the volume will increase like a snowball turning into an avalanche."[62] Afterward, the family likened it to cramming three semesters into a single year. Indeed, so tired was he at the end that, when he and Rose Marie traveled to Basel for Karl's eightieth birthday, Markus tried to avoid as many people as possible. Instead, he and Rose Marie headed straight to their holiday house—what Markus called his "sanctuary" (*Refugium*)—for two months to recover strength and prepare for the next term in Pittsburgh.[63] Despite the pressure that Markus's guest professorship in Greifswald had placed upon him, there were at least two bright notes at its end. The first was his discovery that the family's chalet in the mountains was a place where he could concentrate on his writing and "do solid work." The second, following his brief stay in Basel, was his delight in seeing that "finally, finally, after so many years, so much light and joy and cooperation" had been able to develop between Nelly and Karl. They could now, he thought, look forward to "an everyday life that is somehow peaceful, orderly, without bitterness and disappointments."[64]

---

[61]M. Barth to N. Barth, February 5, 1966. MBL. Series II. Box 11. Markus did take some consolation from the fact that his students were apparently very proud that their professor would soon be teaching communists!

[62]M. Barth to N. Barth, May 27, 1966. MBL. Series II. Box 11. The irony, perhaps, is that the intensity of Markus's work in Greifswald was not matched at all by his students. On the contrary, as Markus wrote to Nelly, they were "not exactly passionate about theological problems" but rather prepared for their pastoral careers in a "rather leisurely and comfortable" fashion. These students were, he said, reflective of the town as a whole. "Greifswald is just a big village with a university in it—not exactly a center in which a heartbeat of a new, or even great age, is beating."

[63]R. M. Barth to A. Barth, July 11, 1966. See also M. Barth to N. Barth, August 25, 1966. MBL. Series II. Box 11.

[64]M. Barth to N. Barth, August 25, 1966. In early 1966 Charlotte von Kirschbaum had, as a consequence of advancing Alzheimer's, been transferred from the Barth family home where she had lived for thirty-five years, into a nursing home. That Karl and Nelly were no longer sharing their marriage with a third partner likely lay behind the improved relations between them that Markus had noticed. In a poignant postscript to this, Nelly herself was able to confirm the restoration of a tender and loving relationship with Karl in these final years of their marriage. Writing to Gerty Pestalozzi just eight months after Karl's death, Nelly noted that "Karl left me with a deep peace, and did everything he could for my sake in these last years. Above all, we were able to understand [and thank] each other . . . day by day." N. Barth to G. Pestalozzi, August 27, 1969. Cited in E. Röthlisberger, *Gerty Pestalozzi-Eidenbenz: Ein Leben 1893–1978. Tagebücher und Briefe* (Brugg: Keller Druck, 1993), 395.

Markus's writing projects also continued to generate activity and enthusiasm. In early October 1966, he was able to report to Noel Freedman that he had, at last, commenced work on his Ephesians commentary for the Anchor Bible series, for which he had been contracted in May 1964. Delighted to finally be working on the project, he expressed his amazement to Freedman at how varied the series was in quality. "Bo Reicke seems to stand at one extreme, RE Brown at the other. Brown's Comm on John is a phantastically thorough and good piece of work—the highest possible scholarly level. But certainly not a commentary for the uninformed layman. . . . Reicke, on the other hand"—who wrote volume 37, *The Epistles of James, Peter, and Jude*—"flows mildly, irrelevantly, piously—just the stuff for such grandmas as would hail edifying talk."[65]

Nevertheless, in spite of being buoyed by the progress on Ephesians, Barth finished the year less than enthused about his teaching duties. "I sometimes experience terrible disappointments with the students," he complained to his mother, Nelly. "But, just when the barometer is really low, there is sometimes excellent work, and then I regain courage. Maybe it's not entirely for nothing," he reflected, "that I'm here."[66]

Markus's efforts toward systemic reconciliation between Christians and Jews took another turn at the start of the new year. Committed to scholarly engagement with the Hebrew Bible not only as part of the *church's* canonical Scriptures but in the first instance as a text of and for the *Jewish* faith, Barth lobbied the Pittsburgh seminary to employ a Jewish scholar to bolster the ranks of the Old Testament faculty. Having tried unsuccessfully to lure his friend, the Rabbi Zalman Schachter, from Winnipeg to Pittsburgh, Barth sought help from the seminary's dean, Gordon Jackson. There were, however, two obstacles in the way of Barth's objective. The first was that Jewish academics were paid only a fraction of the salaries payable to non-Jewish scholars, and so there was no financial incentive for them to join the seminary. "Still," said Barth, "if we could have the Jewish prof. financed by money from Jewish sources, even this hurdle might be taken away." To this end, Barth suggested that Jackson might approach the Pittsburgh Rabbi

---

[65]M. Barth to N. Freedman, October 1, 1966. MBMC. Subject Correspondence 2. Box 6.

[66]M. Barth to N. Barth, December 18, 1966. MBL. Series II. Box 11.

Richard Rubenstein. Barth was not, in general, friendly with Rubenstein. Indeed, as was noted in relation to the Kittel controversy, he "disagree[d] heartily and deeply with this rabbi's theology." Nevertheless, said Barth, "he knows all the Jewish sources and foundations that might well be tapped."

The second obstacle, though, was even more galling—there was almost no institutional support for his plan, with the seminary's president himself seeking to prevent it. "I regret deeply that Don [Miller] is apparently building up real bitterness against the bare consideration" of employing a Jewish Hebrew Bible scholar.[67] This was a devastating blow to Markus's hopes for the interreligious—indeed, given his commitment to the covenantal unity of Jews and Christians, *ecumenical*—revitalization of the seminary's biblical scholarship. Over the course of the next fifteen months, Markus was able to soften, though not eliminate, Miller's resistance, with the latter agreeing to allow the seminary to host a series of lectures on Jewish theological matters. In April 1968, Markus informed President Miller that the arrangements for those lectures pleased him "very much indeed." Money remained an issue, though. "Of course, it is a little bit of a pity that always the Jews have to pay for such things. . . . But be it then, something is better than nothing, and it may be that our trustees will get this way interested in the existing want and opportunity."[68] This minor victory, however, proved to be one of the few battles with the seminary administration that Markus would win. Over the next few years, his disagreements, and disenchantments, were to escalate.[69]

---

[67]M. Barth to G. Jackson, January 30, 1967. MBMC. Series II. Correspondence. Box 13, file 383.

[68]M. Barth to D. Miller, April 22, 1968. MBMC. Series II. Correspondence. Box 14, file 410. It would seem that someone—perhaps Miller himself—had suggested that the speaker for this series should be Rabbi Joseph Soloveitchik (1903–1993) of Boston. Despite Soloveitchek's formidable reputation, Markus was not keen for him to be invited to the seminary, primarily because the rabbi's antipathy to interfaith dialogue placed him squarely at odds with what Barth himself was trying to achieve. "He is explicitly opposed to all matters of interfaith (Jewish-Christian) discussions and wants to limit the realm of encounters to humanitarian matters. I, however, feel that the exchange of ideas in the latter realm and the possible cooperation in matters of civil rights and hospitals etc. makes sense only if supported by a deeper level of exchange also." M. Barth to D. Miller, April 22, 1968.

[69]While Markus was ultimately unsuccessful in securing a lectureship in Jewish Studies for the seminary, he nevertheless had a profound impact on the local rabbi, Jack Schechter, who enrolled at PTS as a direct result of Markus's work there. In the preface to his PhD, with which he graduated in 1981, Schechter wrote: "While serving my congregation in Pittsburgh as its rabbi, I knew I had to continue to study. The Pittsburgh Theological Seminary was nearby. I enrolled in its

THE 1967 CONFESSION

The first few months of 1967 saw Markus embroiled in denominational politics. In January, he became caught up in debate concerning the Presbyterian Church's new confession, of which he had been one of the drafters. While a matter of contention for the national church, the controversy was—in the opinion, at least, of one journalist—"in large part a Pittsburgh drama."[70] On one side of the argument was the Presbyterian Lay Committee, which included in its membership two prominent Pittsburgh citizens—a surgeon and a businessman[71]—and which was intractably opposed to the alleged liberalism of the confessional statement.

Their opposition was wide-ranging but included exegetical, theological, and socio-political concerns. According to the Lay Committee, a historical-critical approach to the Scriptures—according to which their divine inspiration must be seen alongside their use of human, contextually formed language—"weakens the concept of the Bible as the Word of God and is in close parallel with the positions of atheists and extreme liberals."[72] Cornelius Van Til was one of the high-profile theologians to take umbrage at the confession's articulation of Scripture, arguing that it "radically changed" what Presbyterians believed about the Bible.[73] Just as disturbingly for its

doctoral program in conjunction with the University of Pittsburgh. . . . At the Seminary I met another special man: Dr. Markus Barth, then Professor of New Testament. . . . Professor Barth was particularly interested in the biblical perspectives on the land and their pertinence to the contemporary situation. His personal passion for this subject combined with a penetrating intelligence and an incredibly luminous demeanor stimulated me considerably in doing this research. Ours was a long and friendly and intense personal and 'dialogical' association in Pittsburgh and during a memorable visit in Switzerland. I owe him more than he realizes." MBMC. Series II. Correspondence. Box 3 (1980s).

[70]R. J. Gaitens, "Pros and Cons of the Confession," *Pittsburgh Post-Gazette*, January 7, 1967, 1. The decision to draft a new confessional statement had been taken in 1958, when the United Presbyterian Church of the USA (UPCUSA) had been formed out of a merger of the Presbyterian Church in the USA (PCUSA) and the United Presbyterian Church of North America (UPCNA).

[71]These were the redoubtable Carlton Ketchum (1892–1984), president of Ketchum Inc.—at the time, the largest fundraising counseling firm in the US—and Dr. William B. Kiesewetter (1915–1981), professor of pediatric surgery at the University of Pittsburgh and chief surgeon at the Children's Hospital.

[72]Gaitens, "Pros and Cons of the Confession," 1.

[73]C. van Til, *The Confession of 1967: Its Theological Background and Ecumenical Significance* (Philippsburg, NJ: P&R, 1967), 1-5. Given Markus's involvement in the drafting of the document, it is perhaps no coincidence that van Til (1895–1987)—whose hostility toward Karl Barth had by this time already become legendary (Karl understood that van Til had even labelled him "the greatest heretic of all time")—was so resolutely opposed to it. That is, as far as van Til seems to

critics, the draft confession enjoined the Presbyterian Church to publicly oppose political and economic injustices, including all forms of racial discrimination, and to advocate for nuclear disarmament. The conservatively minded Lay Committee insisted, on the contrary, that the national church ought to stay away from political commentary. It was particularly concerned that advocacy for racial and economic justice would lead, inexorably, to interracial marriage on one hand and socialism on the other.[74] There seems also to have been a generational aspect to the Lay Committee's opposition. As Carlton Ketchum put it, the proposed confession "makes us old timers feel as though the padres are marching down the road without looking behind to see if the troops are following them."[75]

Markus, for his part, was scathing of the conservatives' arguments. Responding to the criticisms of the Lay Committee representatives—and perhaps especially his fellow Pittsburghers—he countered that "they would have us believe there is no relation between faith and integration, or between faith and international affairs." Rather, "they wish to keep salvation as an individual thing." "This," he said, "is egotistical, to say the least."[76]

The Lay Committee's campaign against the confession was prosecuted not only within Presbyterian circles but also through the national media. With the massive wealth of Ketchum's public relations company behind it, the committee was able to finance full-page adverts opposing the confession in such major outlets as the *New York Times*, the *Washington Post*, and even the *Wall Street Journal*. Even the Department of Defense conducted an inquiry as to whether, on account of the confession's purported

have been concerned, "Like father, like son!" See K. Barth to G. Bromiley, June 1, 1961, in K. Barth, *Letters 1961–1968*, ed. J. Fangmeier, H. Stoevsandt and G. W. Bromiley (Grand Rapids, MI: Eerdmans, 1981), 13.

[74]Gaitens, "Pros and Cons of the Confession," 1. As noted above, the landmark civil rights decision in the *Loving vs Virginia* case, which overturned all legal restrictions on interracial marriages in the United States, was handed down by the Supreme Court on June 12, 1967. The conservative Lay Committee's referencing of interracial marriage in its opposition to the draft confession, therefore, was no random choice but likely a strategic move designed to gain leverage from a current hot-button topic.

[75]C. Ketchum, in Gaitens, "Pros and Cons of the Confession," 4. That Ketchum used a military analogy is not entirely surprising. He served in the US Army during World War I and then returned to service as a colonel in the US Army Air Forces in World War II, with postings to England, Europe, and Africa.

[76]Gaitens, "Pros and Cons of the Confession," 4.

"disarmament mentality," Presbyterians might need to be classed as national security risks. (It decided that they weren't!)[77]

In any event, these various accusations against both the theological and political propriety of the confession eventually came to nothing. After months of debate, more than 90 percent of the presbyteries of the United Presbyterian Church in the USA voted for the confession's approval. Its final adoption was ratified at the 179th General Assembly, held in Portland, Oregon, in May 1967.

As well as his involvement in these denominational politics, Markus was also busy through the first half of 1967 with a series of guest lectures and sermons throughout the east coast of the country. Suggestive of where Markus's theological and political commitments had landed, there was a noticeable emphasis in these lectures on two particular concerns that lay close to his heart: Jewish-Christian dialogue and the futility of Cold War tensions. In the last of four Memorial Bible Lectures he gave for the Laurinburg Presbyterian Church in North Carolina on January 15–17, Markus spoke on the issue of "Dialogue Between Christians and Marxists."[78] He reprised a version of the same lecture the following month at the University of Rochester, when he spoke to the question, "Christians and Marxists: Is Dialogue Possible?"[79] Then, on March 12 and back in Pittsburgh, he again addressed the issue of Christianity and communism in a lecture for Woodland United Presbyterian on the topic "The Church in East Germany."[80] Four days later, Markus had the chance to speak to that other pressing matter—Jewish-Christian relations—when he delivered the Samuel Hyman lecture for the Hebrew Institute of Pittsburgh. His presentation was titled "The Messiah: One Idea, Two Concepts."[81] Through the second half of April, Markus was traveling again. His first stop was to

---

[77]See R. E. Mumma, "The Presbyterian Confession of 1967," *The Harvard Crimson*, July 14, 1967.

[78]"Series of Bible Lectures to Be in Laurinburg," *The Robesonian*, January 13, 1967, 3. The other lectures included "Justification and the Neighbor—A New Look at Galatians" (Sunday, January 15); and "Reconciliation of the World—Ephesians" (Monday, January 16).

[79]"Theologian Plans Talks at University," *Democrat and Chronicle*, February 12, 1967.

[80]"Religious Notes," *Pittsburgh Post-Gazette*, March 11, 1967, 6.

[81]"Biblical Scholar to Lecture Thursday," *The Pittsburgh Press*, March 13, 1967, 11. The lecture was funded by the Hyman Family Foundation, which was formed in 1957 by Pittsburgh businessman and philanthropist Samuel Hyman (d. 1977).

Gettysburg College, Pennsylvania, where he preached at Christ Chapel on April 16.[82] From there, he traveled west to Indiana. Drawing on his exegetical studies of Romans, Galatians, and Ephesians, he presented four lectures on the topic of "Reconciliation" April 25-28 to an enthusiastic audience at the Mennonite-affiliated Goshen College.[83]

From the latter half of 1967 through mid-1968, Barth was on sabbatical. Together with Rose Marie, he spent the year in Switzerland, dividing his time between the family's chalet in the Swiss Alps and Dietrich Ritschl's home in Reigoldswil. Nelly, for one, hoped that it would prove a refreshing break for her son and daughter-in-law.

> A difficult year lies behind you—and yet you can now concentrate on your work, which would hardly be possible given the external and internal unrest in Pittsburgh. You know that God's faithfulness and love prevails over those who endure and hope! One day it will get light—beyond all expectations! How often you have written to me in a comforting and uplifting way! Now I can [do the same]—may I address you like this—out of quiet happiness! God bless you [and] your Rose Marie and your talented and dear big children![84]

Their youngest daughter, Rose-Marie, traveled to Switzerland with them so that she could complete her high-schooling as a boarder at Geneva's International School.

THE FALSE LOGIC OF THE EAST-WEST BINARY

Markus's commitment to the cause of Jewish-Christian reconciliation has already been explored, alongside his theological repudiation of all forms of Christian and political antisemitism. But it is also possible to reconstruct the logic of his opposition to the ideological binarism of the Cold War, so much of which was predicated—in the US, at least—on a widely assumed synchronicity between Christianity and liberal democracy.

Barth had already signaled the need to critique this overly simplistic dichotomy on at least two occasions previously. As far back as 1953, he had written an article for *The Christian Century* in which he was scathingly

---

[82]"Speaks Here Next Sunday," *The Gettysburg Times*, April 12, 1967, 1.
[83]"Dr Barth Gives First Bible Talk," *The South Bend Tribune*, April 25, 1967, 6.
[84]N. Barth to M. Barth, October 4, 1967. MBL. Series II. Box 11.

critical of the tendency "to label every enemy a crypto-Communist" and to assume that "fear of communism . . . [is] identical with a true witness to Christ." Such a mindset—too frequently "standing on or seated below European pulpits"—was little more than a baptized McCarthyism. On the contrary, Markus wrote, faithful Christian discipleship in the Soviet Union pointed an accusing finger at Western Christianity, "tell[ing] us that our Western liberty, morality and way of living [are] poisoned by a materialism, a hypocrisy and a callous acceptance of war that are worse than the theories and some of the deeds of the Eastern potentates."[85]

Fourteen years later, he had written again for the same magazine and offered another critique of Western democracy's arrogant self-identification with Christian righteousness. In an article published in November 1966, he reflected on the lessons learned during his eleven-week term as guest professor at the Ernst Moritz Arndt University in the Baltic city of Greifswald in the German Democratic Republic. In his opinion, neither East Germans generally, nor even East German Christians specifically, yearned any longer for deliverance from communism. Indeed, "the behavior of 'Christian' parties in control in some western countries," the widespread prevalence of racial injustice, and "above all" America's involvement in the Vietnam War had shaken any trust that East German Christians might once have had in Western democracies. Any presumption that Western liberal capitalism might offer a more hopeful, or indeed more Christian, future than Soviet-style communism was no longer tenable—if, indeed, it ever had been.[86] Perhaps, he mused, that was why some East German Christians were prepared to voluntarily participate in the Communist Party's elections and parades, and in so doing prove "their solidarity [as Christians] with the highest goals of Communistic humanism."[87] Noting, in fact, that in the context of Cold War East Germany, it was the church that was proving more belligerent than the state, he

[85]M. Barth, "The Mission and Misery of Europe's Churches," *The Christian Century*, November 11, 1953, 1291.

[86]"East Germans Now Accept Communism," *Dayton Daily News*, November 25, 1966, 10. The material for this article was initially delivered in October 1966 as a lecture in Greifswald, titled "Kirche und Kommunismus in Ost-Deutschland." MBMC. Series III. Publications. Box P16, file 3.

[87]M. Barth, "Kirche und Kommunismus in Ost-Deutschland," 3.

advised that it was time for Christians "to be realists and accept the challenge to stand within (and not against) the Socialist revolution."[88]

Evidently, Markus was no less adamant in his rejection of any necessary ideological polarity between East and West now than he had been years before. But he did not just repudiate the binary separation; he sought ways to build bridges between the two. In late 1967, emerging as the product of material he had been delivering as lectures through the first half of the year, Markus published an article titled "Developing Dialogue Between Marxists and Christians."[89] Decrying the shared complicity of both West and East in perpetuating mutual animosity, Markus noted with dismay that "neither listens to the other—except to increase the ammunition with which he will shoot back." This, though, was not merely political belligerence but was in fact predicated on pseudo-religious grounds. The moral rightness of one side and the consequent depravity of the other was justified by recourse to an apocalyptic dualism. "Unless you believe in the enemy's devilish nature," Markus wrote, "the heavenly character of your own words, deeds, way of life becomes dubious."[90] In such a situation, what was needed, argued Markus, was a form of dialogue that he termed "mutual confessional." Refusing to champion one's own cause and demonize the cause of the other,

> [t]he presupposition of this dialogue is the will of both partners to be . . . "absolutely honest"—honest not only to God or to the conscience in the secret moments of prayer or self-criticism, but also publicly, before one's fellowman, including the opponent. This honesty will make both partners see and admit that they alike have dirty feet, blood on their hands, and nebulous thoughts in their minds.[91]

Typically, Markus did not propose this "mutual confessional" model as though it were either self-evident or independently applicable, but as a dialogical form possible only when grounded in Scripture. In particular, he once again had in mind Paul's letter to the Ephesians and all the theological

---

[88]Barth, "Kirche und Kommunismus," 5.

[89]M. Barth, "Developing Dialogue Between Marxists and Christians," *Journal of Ecumenical Studies* 4, no. 3 (1967): 385-405.

[90]Typescript of Barth, "Developing Dialogue Between Marxists and Christians," 4. MBMC. Series III. Publications. Box P4, file 2.

[91]Typescript of Barth, "Developing Dialogue Between Marxists and Christians," 8.

lessons he had learned from that epistle, going back to *The Broken Wall* fourteen years previous. Refusing the assumption that Romans and Galatians represent the heart of Pauline theology and thus the sum of the gospel, Markus instead argued that Ephesians—despite its authorial ambiguity—is "probably the latest and certainly the most political, socially minded and peaceful" of Paul's letters, and without doubt the more significant. The prioritization of Romans and Galatians—with their emphases on salvation from sin—had caused Christians, Barth lamented, to reduce the "cosmic act of God" to a "psychic drama within the human self." Ephesians, however, speaks of Christ's death and resurrection as the event that "unites Jews and Gentiles, near and far, pious and godless people."[92] This, wrote Markus, was the basic fact on which it was possible to conceive of dialogue—even reconciliation—between even such intractably opposed enemies as the democratic West and the communist East. Such dialogue between Marxists and Christians, he acknowledged, "may not save us. But it is among the best things we can do."[93]

THE SEMINARY AND THE SEE OF PETER

Back at the seminary, meanwhile, Markus was becoming increasingly disenchanted with the direction in which it was heading. As far back as 1966, he had been complaining to his parents that Pittsburgh was intellectually stultifying. Acknowledging that perhaps it was "not entirely for nothing" that he was there, Barth was nonetheless frustrated by the typical caliber of student he was teaching and expressed a yearning for "the critical and stimulating winds of a real university" (*den kritischen und anregenden Winden einer wirklichen Universität*).[94] By 1969, his frustration was less with the students and more with the seminary's administration. The curriculum committee in particular, under the leadership of Ed Farley, was seeking to implement what he believed to be radical and poorly

---

[92]Typescript of Barth, "Developing Dialogue Between Marxists and Christians," 10.

[93]Typescript of Barth, "Developing Dialogue Between Marxists and Christians," 15.

[94]M. Barth to N. Barth, November 5, December 18, 1966. MBL. Series II. Box 11. Barth expressly excluded places like Yale, Harvard, and Union Theological seminary from his considerations. Rather, he was hoping for a move to "a younger institution, with less tradition, and more open-minded."

conceived changes to the syllabi. These included a reduction in class hours and a lowering of expectations in Greek and Hebrew. Barth pulled no punches in his condemnation of the changes. As he wrote to Farley,

> Despite my attempts to cooperate at all levels, in the Bibl[ical] Division and in the curr[iculum] committee at the implementation of the curric[ulum] majority proposal adopted by the faculty, I remain passionately and thoroughly opposed to that proposal. I consider it detrimental to our school, pernicious to serious education, a catastrophe in the service we are pledged to render the UPUSA,[95] and a plain nonsense in academical regard. Since you and the Dean did the decisive work in the subcommittee that drafted this proposal, since your personal vote made it the curr[iculum] committee's majority proposal, and since your speech . . . persuaded the faculty to endorse it, I cannot help but consider you personally responsible for the situation we now have before us.[96]

Such criticisms notwithstanding, by the fall term of that year, not only had the curricular changes been formally approved but Barth had been appointed chair of the curriculum committee. He was thus in the invidious situation of having "to implement that which I consider foolish."[97] Barth, however, was not the only one voicing criticism of the seminary's administration. Indeed, the divisions among the faculty had become so deeply entrenched that both the president, Don Miller, and the dean, Gordon Jackson, were forced to resign their posts. For Barth, too, it was increasingly clear that his time in Pittsburgh, with its "disagreeable academical climate," was coming to an end.[98]

There were, though, moments of joy during the year. In early October, Barth's daughter Ruth married a Belgian economics student, Bernard

---

[95]Presumably, Barth here means the UPCUSA—the United Presbyterian Church of the USA—which had been formed in 1958. See n70 above.

[96]M. Barth to E. Farley, March 30, 1969. MBMC. Subject Correspondence 4. Box 8. William Edward Farley (1929–2014) studied at Louisville Theological Seminary and Union Theological Seminary before earning his PhD in philosophical theology at Columbia University in 1957. After teaching at DePauw University from 1959, he was appointed to Pittsburgh Theological Seminary in 1963, where he stayed until his final appointment to Vanderbilt University in 1969. Ironically, given what Barth thought was his disastrous leadership of curricular change at Pittsburgh, one of Farley's most acclaimed achievements was his redesign of the curriculum of Vanderbilt's Divinity School in the 1980s.

[97]M. Barth to N. Freedman, September 7, 1969. MBMC. Subject Correspondence. Box 2.

[98]This was how Barth later described the seminary's culture once he had returned to Switzerland. M. Barth to R. Hardie, June 23, 1973. MBMC. Series II. Correspondence. Box 18, file 480.

Naveau, in the Roman Catholic Diocese of Sion. The ceremony was held in a small Catholic chapel in La Sage, just down the road from Villa, with Ruth's brother, Peter, officiating. Described by Barth as a "great and joyful festival," he was most impressed by the wedding liturgy. It used "the best marriage questions I have ever seen," leading him to hope that it would come to be used even in Protestant churches. "The weather . . . was absolutely splendid, the wedding party was small, the behavior of all, including the dress, unofficial and relaxed."[99] The ecumenicity of the service was both appropriate and deliberate, insofar as Barth traveled to the wedding directly from a meeting with Pope Paul VI in Rome. Indeed, the timing of the wedding, said Barth, had been determined "so as to coincide as much as possible with a [New Testament] conference in Rome, and a private audience with the pope."[100] His time there was "exhausting but productive," with "a sermon in the basilica . . . , a visit with the Waldensian faculty,"[101] as well as his meeting with Paul VI, during which he broached the "Israeli-Arab question"[102] alongside the broader issue of Jewish-Christian relations. The audience evidently went better than even Barth could have anticipated—the Pope's final words to Barth were, "You have a friend in Rome."[103] Unlike his first trip to Rome as a teenager in 1934, this time Barth stayed in a Benedictine monastery, where he was able to enjoy "the silence, the beautiful architecture, and the open-mindedness [*den offenen Geist*]."[104] Shortly after his return from Rome, Barth traveled to New York in early November to participate in a colloquium between Catholic, Protestant, and Jewish scholars on "The Covenant and the Land of Israel." Then, on November 29, just as his disaffection with the seminary was peaking, Barth was announced as first holder of the newly established Errett M. Grable Chair of New Testament at Pittsburgh.[105]

---

[99]M. Barth to J. Gribomont, October 18, 1969, 1-2. MBL. Series I. Box 22.

[100]M. Barth to N. Freedman, September 7, 1969. MBMC. Subject Correspondence. Box 2.

[101]M. Barth to N. Barth, October 1, 1969. MBL. Series II. Box 11.

[102]M. Barth to N. Freedman, September 7, 1969.

[103]M. Barth to J. Gribomont, October 18, 1969, 2.

[104]M. Barth to N. Barth, October 1, 1969.

[105]"Grable Chair Established at Seminary," *Pittsburgh Post-Gazette*, November 29, 1969, 12. Errett Grable (1889–1959) was a Pittsburgh business leader who founded Rubbermaid, Inc., an international housewares company. The best-known appointee to the Errett M. Grable

OPPOSING VIETNAM, OPPOSING ISRAEL

During the Barths' final two years in the United States, Markus devoted himself even more assiduously to the various political causes in which he had become involved. These were, in particular, his fierce opposition to the Vietnam War and to the complex dynamic—felt especially acutely in the US—inherent in Jewish-Christian relations. Indeed, the two issues were not unrelated. Barth had been an outspoken critic of America's military involvement in Vietnam since the mid-1960s, holding Presidents Johnson and Nixon particularly culpable for unleashing misery and bloodshed. "Shame and horror" surrounded any attempt to speak of what Nixon had come to represent,[106] while the "criminal warmaking" of both the Johnson and Nixon administrations was, in Barth's opinion, analogous to the "measure of horrors committed in Auschwitz and Hiroshima."[107] His stance lost him close friends, not least among various North American Jewish communities. Michael Wyschogrod and Emil Fackenheim, for example, became increasingly incensed by Barth's equation of America's war crimes against the Vietnamese with the actions of the Israeli military against the Palestinians. As Fackenheim put it, "[Your] comparison between mighty America fighting in Viet Nam, and Israel, encircled by Arab nations is a first rate example of 'false consciousness.'"[108] Barth's interest in southeast Asia was not exclusively focused on Vietnam—in May 1970, he signed an open letter opposing the war in Cambodia and insisting on the return of US servicemen and women.[109] That month saw Barth animated on another front as well, joining with Raymond E. Brown and Krister Stendahl, among others, in condemning the annual Oberammergau Passion Play for its persistent antisemitism.[110]

Chair since Barth left Pittsburgh has been Dale C. Allison, who held it from 2001–2013 before moving to Princeton Theological Seminary. Between Barth and Allison, the chair was held by Ulrich W. Mauser (1926–2008) between 1977–1990. The chair has been vacant since Allison left Pittsburgh.

[106]M. Barth to V. Fletcher, February 8, 1970. MBMC. Series II. Correspondence. Box 16, file 433.

[107]M. Barth to R. Hardie, July 28, 1973.

[108]E. Fackenheim to M. Barth, September 25, 1972. MBMC. Series II. Correspondence. Box 19, file 500. For a more detailed exploration of the tensions caused by Barth's stance on Vietnam and the Israeli-Palestinian conflict, see my "Jewish-Christian Dialogue from the Underside."

[109]"Silent No More," *The Pittsburgh Press*, May 14, 1970, 26.

[110]G. W. Cornell, "Religious Play Said Still Anti-Semitic," *The Berkshire Eagle*, May 16, 1970, 3. In their statement, the authors lamented the fact that the play "still contains features which perpetuate a false

Nonetheless, it was the Vietnam conflict that most particularly aroused his ire, with his stance equally arousing the hostility of others toward him.

Yet Barth was even more outspoken in his engagement with the Israel-Palestine question. In early February, he shared a platform with Eugene Borowitz and Edward Flannery at the twentieth annual Maurice Gusman Institute for the Clergy at Miami's Temple Israel. There he again denounced antisemitism and affirmed his conviction that Jews belong to—and are already in—the household of God, "whether [they] confess Jesus or not."[111] At the same event, Barth also foreshadowed a likely National Council of Churches' statement on Israel's right to exist. However, Barth's own position was nuanced, and short of the unequivocal affirmation of Israel, for which many of his Jewish friends and colleagues wished. His commentary on the NCC deliberations hinted at his own outrage at Israel's oppression of the Palestinian people. In response to the argument that Israel's conflict with the Arab world was one of Jewish survival, he retorted somewhat heatedly, "That is what I heard Hitler say in the 1930s when he tried to justify killing Jews and Communists." There was no doubt, Barth said, that Israel had a legitimate claim to the land on which it was situated. Nevertheless, its tenure should be as "steward" not "possessor," with a responsibility of care and protection for *all* who lived there, and not only Jews.[112] Eugene Borowitz, for one, was appalled at Barth's suggestion. "If it wasn't you talking, Dr. Barth," he is reported to have said, "I would walk off this stage right now."[113]

Barth elaborated on his views further in a letter to Verne Fletcher the following week, in which he justified his thoughts by reference to Martin Buber's idea of *Yihud*.

> I have the idea that regarding the State of Israel you are as unable as I am to become a "Christian Zionist." Neither can we simply be all-out supporters of

---

understanding of the relationship between Jesus and the Jewish people," and that "in its pejorative portrayal" of Jews "the text of the Gospel is violated and other historical information is neglected."

[111]B. Wilcox, "Jews Belong to House of God, Prof Says," *The Miami News*, February 3, 1970, 6; A. Taft, "Theologian: Christians Hate Christ," *The Miami Herald*, February 4, 1970, 48.

[112]B. Wilcox, "Church Council Might Back Israelis' Rights in Mideast," *The Miami News*, February 4, 1970, 8.

[113]B. Wilcox, "Inter-communication Critical, Says Rabbi," *Miami News*, February 5, 1970, 32.

> the unhappy Nasser. Last Monday I spoke to a Jewish-Christian gathering and tried to explain to them why and how I thought we ought to seek and find a way toward a third alternative. Among the homework to be done for it would be research in matters of a theology of the land. It is obvious that so far neither the Israelis nor Christians have cared too much about what the Bible may have to say regarding stewardship rather than possession, equal rights for the strangers rather than monopolies of the invaders. I am still looking around for a collection of documents containing all that since . . . Buber's days has been said about a *Yihud*, i.e. a common state, or a federation of states, of Arabs and Jews.[114]

Nor was this the first time Barth had spoken in this way. During his earlier audience with the pope in October 1969, Barth had raised the idea of a "federal Arab-Israeli state of Palestine" under Israeli administration, which he credited to Buber, and about which he seems first to have heard from, among others, Ernst Simon in Jerusalem.[115] At the end of 1971, he participated in two symposia at Pittsburgh's B'nai Israel Synagogue, together with Dr. Ailon Shiloh, in which he prosecuted his views further. In the first, Barth gave a presentation on "A Christian Perspective on Israel," to which Shiloh responded. In the second, Shiloh spoke to the question "Jerusalem: To Whom?," with a response from Barth.[116] As we will see in more detail in a later chapter, the Israel-Palestine question continued to dominate much of Barth's more public presentations over the next few years.

SECURING KARL BARTH'S LEGACY

Quite aside from Markus's own academic, ecumenical, and political activities, much of his remaining time in the US was spent negotiating the

---

[114]M. Barth to V. Fletcher, February 8, 1970. MBMC. Series II. Correspondence. Box 16, file 433.

[115]M. Barth to A. Lacoque, January 11, 1970. MBMC. Series II. Correspondence. Box 16, file 440. See also M. Barth to C. Barth, July 25, 1969. MBMC. Series II. Correspondence. Box 15, file 418. In this letter, Barth asked his brother Christoph whether the idea should be discussed with the pope. A letter from the end of October, to a pastor in Amsterdam, suggests that indeed he did. "On October 3rd of this year I had a private audience with the Pope [in which] I gave him the same vision. . . . Of course, the Muslims must recognize the State of Israel. [The whole situation] must be rethought if there is ever to be any peace between Ishmael and Isaac." M. Barth to A. A. Spijkerboer, October 26, 1969. MBMC. Series II. Correspondence. Box 16, file 434.

[116]"Editors Slate Talks: Synagogue to Offer Adult Study Classes," *Pittsburgh Post-Gazette*, October 16, 1971, 20.

administration of his father's estate in the wake of Karl's death late the previous year. One of the first and most pressing matters was to decide who should be appointed to write Karl Barth's biography. This was not an easy decision, and it generated considerable disagreement among Karl's children. The obvious contender was Eberhard Busch, who had served as Karl's secretary since 1965 after Charlotte von Kirschbaum had become too ill to continue the work. Busch, indeed, had already sought not only to position himself as the author but also to identify the type of biography he wished to write. "It seems to me sensible and appropriate," Busch told Christoph Barth, "that there should be only a single, large, so to speak 'official,' biography written about Karl Barth—much like Bethge's official Bonhoeffer book."[117] Markus, however, was unconvinced, writing in the margins of Busch's letter a vociferous "*Nein! Nein!*" While acknowledging Busch's expertise—he was, Barth agreed, "obviously competent in many things"—Markus's concerns were twofold. First, he was unwilling to grant any familial imprimatur to a project for which the methodological approach was unclear. "We don't yet know how he wants to go about the task. If it fails, it can hardly be considered 'official.'" Second, Markus was equally reticent to accede to Busch's request that his be the only biographical project. Such exclusivity would deny the opportunity for alternative scholarly investigations. "We are not a papal office," Barth wrote to his siblings. "The exclusive right to access the [Karl Barth] archives, which Busch is requesting, would mean not only that others, but even the four of us, would be shut out."[118] One month later, Markus advised his youngest brother Hans Jakob to inform Busch that while the biography might go ahead under his name, he should not think of it as *the* official account of Karl Barth's life—such an idea was "problematic."[119]

---

[117]E. Busch to C. Barth, M. Barth, H.-J. Barth, and H. Zellweger, February 3, 1969. MBMC. Series II. Correspondence (1920–1969). Box 1, file 16. Eberhard Bethge's *Dietrich Bonhoeffer: Eine Biographie*, had been published in German just two years previously, in 1967. It proved so popular that a second edition was published in the same year.

[118]M. Barth to C. Barth, H.-J. Barth, and M. Zellweger, February 10, 1969. MBMC. Series II. Correspondence (1920–1969). Box 1, file 16.

[119]M. Barth to H.-J. Barth, March 2, 1969. MBMC. Series II. Correspondence (1920–1969). Box 1, file 16. In this letter, Markus also expressed some rather more scathing views of Busch that evidently

Figure 6.4. Charlotte von Kirschbaum and Karl, 1967

Figure 6.5. Rose Marie and Karl, 1967

It was not only the biography that needed to be sorted out. Just days after Karl's death, Markus, together with other members of the family, began working on the establishment of the Karl Barth Archives and the *Nachlasskommission* ("Legacy Commission"), with their intentions chiefly toward devising a structure for the publication of Barth's literary corpus. The *Nachlasskommission*, the provisions for which had been stipulated in Karl's will, first met on December 14, 1968. In its initial form, it consisted of Markus, his brothers Christoph and Hans Jakob, Max Zellweger, and Eberhard Busch. In June 1970, Franziska was coopted into the commission. The second part of securing Karl's legacy was the creation of the Karl Barth Foundation (*Stiftung*) as a charitable organization through which the activities of the commission could be funded. This took slightly longer to put into place, with Markus noting in mid-1971 that it was still "in process of formation."[120] Its founding members were Markus Barth, his brother-in-law Max Zellweger, Frank Vischer, Georges Casalis, and Eberhard Jüngel. In July 1971, they were joined by Max Geiger, Alexander Bronkhorst, and Ernst Wolf, with the foundation being endowed with an initial capital of 20,000 francs. Through the middle months of 1971, Markus sought to secure the World Council of Churches in New York as the recipient of tax-deductible donations to the *Stiftung*. Despite lengthy negotiations with both New York and Pittsburgh law firms, it did not in the end prove possible.[121]

THE LAST YEARS IN PITTSBURGH

Barth's final two years in Pittsburgh were spent in much the same way that he had spent the previous seven—combining his teaching for the seminary with guest lectures at other universities and pastors' conferences, and with forays into the political arena. Toward the end of October 1970, Barth traveled to Bethel College in North Newton, Kansas, to deliver the Menno Simons Lectures. Returning to a theme that had served as a key theological

---

prejudiced him against Busch taking on the project. In Markus's perhaps uncharitable opinion, Busch found it hard to finish things he started, and thought rather too much of his own importance. "Dass er eine angefangene Sache nicht abschliessen kann, [und] er sich selbst enorm wichtig."

[120] M. Barth to E. Smith, May 6, 1971. MBMC. Series VI. Box SF27, file 12.

[121] M. Barth to E. Smith, May 6, 1971; E. Smith to M. Barth May 11, 1971. MBMC. Series VI. Box SF27, file 12.

Figure 6.6. Markus and Rose Marie in Villa, 1970

motif for Barth for thirty years, his four presentations were billed as "Baptism as a Pledge of Humility," "Baptism as a Burial," "Baptism for Revelation," and "Baptism as a Prayer." Such matters were certainly dear to his heart, but as he wrote to Bethel's famous Mennonite historian Cornelius Krahn, they were also "old manna warmed up and re-hashed." For that reason, he had offered instead to present lectures on the topic "Marry: Why, How, Whom—and Whether? (Paul on Freedom in Love and Sex, Eph. 5:21-33)." Perhaps unsurprisingly, Krahn and the rest of the Bethel College administration requested Barth to stick to his original lectures on baptism![122]

At the seminary, in the winter semesters of both 1971 and 1972, he taught his "Introduction to the New Testament: The Epistles." A review of Brevard Childs' *Biblical Theology in Crisis?*, written in January 1971 while Barth was on holiday in Villa, suggests a theme that likely featured heavily in this course. "It will be a great day," Barth writes, "when Childs' call is heard for the uniting of Old and New Testament interpretation, for an open-minded dialogue between Jews and Christians, and for an ethical Biblical interpretation that encourages the church to fulfill its mission to the whole human

[122]M. Barth to C. Krahn, March 29, 1970. MBMC. Series II. Correspondence. Box 2 (1970s).

community."[123] A month after penning this review, in early February 1971 Markus and the Republican-turned-Democrat Senator Harold Hughes together spoke at the United Methodists' annual Iowa Pastors' School at Simpson College in Indianola. Barth's lectures were, perhaps predictably by now, on Paul's letter to the Ephesians.[124] Later in the year, Barth's scholarly interest in Ephesians was given a different kind of voice through his involvement in the "Thesis Theological Cassettes" project. Toward the end of the year, he was invited by Rabbi Jack Schechter to give two addresses on the general topic of "Israel" to Pittsburgh's Congregation B'nai Israel. While the lectures themselves provoked "intensive, sharp dialogue,"[125] the opportunity also gave Barth confidence that his stance of critical solidarity with Israel was welcomed at least by some in America's Jewish communities. As he wrote to Schechter afterward, "The meetings in your synagogue . . . proved that we are *collegial workers* in the LORD's vineyard rather than strangers meeting on a far-out road."[126]

Six months later, in mid-1972, Barth—together with his brother Christoph and sister-in-law Renate—spent two months in Israel, including in the occupied territories. There he met with sympathetic Israeli colleagues and Palestinian leaders—including the mayor of Hebron, a former governor of the Old City of Jerusalem, "and several kinds of sheiks"—as well as "poorer Palestinians" within the general population. The trip was informative and moving, giving Barth a much better understanding of "the great misery of the Palestinians."[127] On his return to America in June, Barth was invited to participate in a further conference on the Arab-Israeli conflict, hosted by the Near-East Ecumenical Bureau for Information-Interpretation in London. Key among the issues to be discussed were the (dis)continuities between the Old and New Testaments, the significance of "Land, People, and Promise" in

---

[123]M. Barth, typescript of a review of B. Childs, *Biblical Theology in Crisis? Interpretation* 25 (1971): 6. Note that the published version of this review omitted the words printed here.

[124]"Hughes, 5 Others, to Address Pastors," *Des Moines Tribune*, January 30, 1971, 3. Harold Hughes (1922–1996) served as governor of Iowa from 1963 to 1969, and was then elected to the US Senate until 1975. A devout Christian, Hughes shared with Barth an admiration for the Kennedys and an increasing disenchantment with the Vietnam War and Johnson's presidency.

[125]J. Schechter to M. Barth, November 28, 1971. MBMC. Series II. Correspondence. Box 18, file 482.

[126]M. Barth to J. Schechter, November 31, 1971. MBMC. Series II. Correspondence. Box 18, file 482.

[127]M. Barth to G. Habib, August 25, 1972. MBMC. Series II. Correspondence. Box 18, file 494.

God's economy, and the theological meaning of Jerusalem.[128] Barth was keen to participate and expressed the hope that he could follow up the recent "intensive discussions with Palestinian leaders" that he had had in May and June, with whom he had "reached a very good mutual understanding." In August, however, less than a month before the conference was due to take place, he withdrew. Ongoing tensions at the seminary, he said, made it impossible for him to attend.[129] Such problems, exacerbated if not entirely caused by the seminary's "new and incompetent leadership ([of] Bill Kadel)," forced Barth to withdraw from a similar conference planned for September.[130]

Meanwhile, other opportunities were opening up. In October 1971, Barth had received the offer of a professorship at the United Theological College in Bangalore, India. This was the second time that UTC had invited him to join the faculty, the first call coming when Barth was still in Bubendorf. Neither Markus nor Rose Marie were entirely opposed to the idea. As Markus wrote to Nelly, "[We] want to seriously think about whether we shouldn't reconsider the earlier invitation."[131] In the end, however, there was no need to pursue the possibility, as a far more favorable option emerged. Through the course of 1972, Barth was in steady contact with Basel, with the hope that he

---

[128]F. Bahnan to M. Barth, June 24, 1972. MBMC. Series II. Correspondence. Box 18, file 494.

[129]M. Barth to F. Bahnan, July 17 and August 24, 1972. MBMC. Series II. Correspondence. Box 18, file 494. A letter from Barth to his publisher, Noel Freedman, suggests a slightly different reason for his withdrawal, namely, his fear that he would be a lone moderating voice in an otherwise hostile anti-Israel environment. "Originally, I had planned to go. . . . But then I copped out—some people from Geneva on whose presence I had counted could not participate and I became afraid that I might be so insulated and helpless in London that I could not prevent, in the worst case, disaster from happening, and in the best: my name being misused for an openly or secretly anti/Semitic declaration." M. Barth to N. Freedman, November 9, 1972. MBMC. Subject Correspondence 2. Box 6.

[130]This conference, due to be held in Canterbury, was being organized by the World Conference of Christians for Palestine. The aim was "to discuss the oppression of the Palestinians and the Zionist movement as a political distortion of Judaism." G. Habib to M. Barth, August 17, 1972. Barth again responded that difficulties at the seminary made it impossible for him to accept the invitation. He added, however, that if the conference intended to produce a public statement, its authors would need to ensure that it was "based much more solidly on a good theol[ogical] foundation, and that its rhetorics are much, much farther removed from propaganda talk" than previous statements had been. "The true statements we have to make, have also to be wise—and just not only to the Palestinians but also to the Jews, whether they be chauvinistic Zionists or moderates or in open opposition to Golda Meir and Gen[eral] Dajan." M. Barth to G. Habib, August 25, 1972. This response is significant insofar as it demonstrates Barth's concern that advocacy for the Palestinian cause not be, or be identified with, a blanket hostility toward Israel.

[131]M. Barth to N. Barth, October 31, 1971. MBL. Series II. Box 11.

might succeed Oscar Cullmann on the latter's retirement. Barth was not the only candidate for the role, though. According to Hermann Wichers, chief archivist at the Basel-Stadt State Archives, there were four other candidates for the position—three from Germany and another from Basel.[132] At least as far as Barth himself was led to believe, a certain "Herr Klein" was one of them. Barth wrote to his mother that Klein was "in his own way, a competent and honest man." He did, however, interpret Paul "in exactly the opposite way" to what Barth thought was right, thus making him—at least in Barth's own mind—unsuitable for the role.[133] Waiting for the university to make its decision was deeply frustrating for Barth. Indeed, the job was offered to one of the German candidates first, who then withdrew his candidacy on the grounds of insufficient remuneration.[134] Finally, in September 1972, Barth received the call inviting him to be Cullmann's successor as professor of New Testament in Basel. After twenty years in the United States, it was now possible for Barth to plan a return to Switzerland.

The timing of the call could not have been better. Barth's growing discontent with the seminary in Pittsburgh—its fortunes had not markedly changed with the replacement of Don Miller as president by Bill Kadel in 1971—made such a move back to Switzerland immensely attractive. In typically candid fashion, Barth complained that the seminary's leadership was "uneducated" and that the students were now forced to endure "a stupid and academically unworthy course of study."[135] Nevertheless, Barth was concerned that he not leave things in any way undone. He was particularly disturbed by President Nixon's disastrous handling of the war in Vietnam. Thus, before making a final decision, he sought Kadel's advice as to whether he had a duty as a theologian to stay and defend social progress and civil rights. Whatever misgivings he may have had, however, seem soon to have been allayed. In a letter to Pope Paul VI in mid-September, Barth wrote

[132]Personal correspondence with H. Wichers, March 13, 2023.

[133]M. Barth to N. Barth, February 27, 1972. MBL. Series I. Box 33. While he does not directly identify him, the Klein to which Barth refers in this letter was most likely Günther Klein (1928–2015), a New Testament scholar whose *Habilitation* dissertation from 1961 explored the unity of the church in Paul's letters. At the time of Cullmann's retirement, when Basel was seeking to find a suitable replacement, Klein was serving as professor of New Testament in Münster.

[134]Personal correspondence with H. Wichers, March 13, 2023.

[135]M. Barth to N. Barth, February 27, 1972.

that "I have just been chosen to become the successor to Prof. Oscar Cullmann in Basel," giving no indication that he was considering turning it down.[136] In any event, it is clear that by mid-October at the latest, the issue had been decisively settled in favor of Barth's return. Herman Halperin, a rabbi in Pittsburgh, wrote to the Basel-based legal historian Guido Kisch informing him about Barth's imminent relocation back to Switzerland, and encouraging them to make contact with one another. "I can say, without qualifications, that Professor Barth is one of the genuine *chaside omit ha-olam* of our time, and of all times."[137]

One of his last public engagements outside the seminary was on October 16, 1972, when he presented the keynote address at an interdisciplinary conference on "Human Images and the Idea of Man" held at Indiana University of Pennsylvania. Barth spoke on the topic of "The Idea of Man in Paul."[138] Probably the last mention of Barth in the American press before his departure for Switzerland was on December 3, 1972. Rabbi Marc Tanenbaum, with whom Barth had been in contact for ten years, publicly listed Barth as an ally in a scathing critique of the Christian evangelization of Jews.[139] The Barths left the US on the last day of 1972. They did not return to Switzerland immediately, however. Markus and Rose Marie fulfilled "a long dormant wish"[140] by spending two months on holiday in Mexico, while their new house outside Basel was renovated in preparation for their arrival.

---

[136]M. Barth to Pope Paul VI, September 14, 1972. MBMC. Series II. Correspondence. Box 19, file 500. In a circular letter from March 1973, Rose Marie wrote to friends saying that the invitation to succeed Cullmann had been "immediately accepted," and that her and Markus's plan had always been to retire to Basel. R. M. Barth, circular letter, March 1973. It is quite likely, then, that Markus's conversations with Kadel may have been more for the sake of due diligence, and not out of any serious thought that the Basel invitation would be declined.

[137]H. Halperin to G. Kisch, October 16, 1972. MBMC. Series II. Correspondence. Box 19, file 502. The term used by Halperin to describe Barth is normally translated as "righteous among the nations." While there was no official sanction to Halperin's use of it, the gesture was an extraordinary honor to bestow upon Barth.

[138]"Barth to Speak: 'Human Images' Theme of Meet," *The Indiana Gazette*, October 12, 1972, 13.

[139]A. Taft, "Jews Meet to Face Threat of Increased Christian Evangelism," *The Miami Herald*, December 3, 1972, 28. Throughout 1971, Barth and Tanenbaum had worked closely on a project to identify and eliminate the antisemitic elements of the Oberammergau Passion Play.

[140]R. M. Barth, circular letter, March 1973.

7

"THERE IS STILL COLOSSIANS AND PHILEMON TO BE DONE"

Return to Basel, 1973–1994

On their return to Switzerland, Markus and Rose Marie set about re-establishing themselves in a city, and a country, in which they had not lived for twenty years. Their new house at Inzlingerstrasse 275, in Riehen, was barely a kilometer from the German border. From there, it was a half-hour commute for Markus into his work at the university. Initially, he would drive; in later years he rode a Moped before finally preferring to travel by tram. This was to remain the Barths' home for the next twenty years, until both Markus and Rose Marie died.

Less than six months after the Barths had returned to Switzerland, Markus was back in North America, this time in Toronto. He had been invited to attend the inaugural meeting of the Karl Barth Society of North America, which was established under the auspices of the Toronto School of Theology. The ad hoc committee by which the society was first run included two of Karl's former students, David Demson and Martin Rumscheidt, along with the Canadian Christian educator and writer James Smart. The minutes of that first meeting recorded Barth's thanks for the invitation to be present and that he "admired the committee 'spirit.'"[1]

[1]Minutes of a meeting of the Karl Barth Society of North America, May 1, 1972, Knox College. MBMC. Series VI. Box SF25, file 2.

AGAIN, ON ISRAEL

It will be recalled that one of Markus's concerns at leaving the States—a concern that he had shared with Bill Kadel prior to his departure—was a fear that he might be reneging on his commitment to various political concerns that were dear to his heart. He need not have worried. His return to Switzerland did nothing to dampen either his commitment or his engagement. In particular, he remained acutely exercised by the need for a sustainable political settlement in the Middle East. Since 1969, he had been part of a "Study Group on Christian-Jewish Relations," which, from its inception, had been co-sponsored by both the National Council of Churches' Commission on Faith and Order and the Secretariat for Catholic-Jewish Relations of the National Conference of Catholic Bishops. The group had agreed to tackle as its first priority the broad topic "Israel: People, Land, and State." By August 1973, barely six months after Barth's return to Basel, the group was ready to publish the first fruits of its endeavors. A fourteen-point "Statement to our Fellow Christians"—written by (among others) Barth, John Oesterreicher, Roy Eckhardt, Edward Flannery, Franklin Littell, and John Pawlikowski—was touted as the first ever Catholic-Protestant-Orthodox declaration on Jewish-Christian relations generally, and the state of Israel particularly.[2] While primarily intended as a theological document and not a political manifesto, the statement nevertheless not only affirmed the Jews' ongoing place in God's covenantal promises but also insisted on a rightful Jewish claim to land. Noting that there was no Christian consensus on this matter, the statement's authors ventured the view that "modern Israel is the homeland of a people whose political identity is sustained by the faith that God has blessed them with a covenant."[3] And, in a nod to the Palestinian conflict, there was also a plea for Israel not be judged by a "double standard [that is] not applied to any other nation on earth."[4] It is possible

[2]See B. L. Kaufman, "Israel Is Entitled to Land, Christian Theologians Agree," *The Cincinnati Enquirer*, August 19, 1973, 26; C. Cox, "Churches Work to Excise Anti-Semitism," *News-Pilot*, August 26, 1973, 19; C. Cox, "Churches Fighting Anti-Semitism," *The Danville News*, September 15, 1973, 11. For the text of the statement, see Study Group on Christian-Jewish Relations, "Statement to Our Fellow Christians," www.bc.edu/content/dam/files/research_sites/cjl/sites/partners/csg/csg1973.htm.

[3]"Statement to Our Fellow Christians," paragraph 7.

[4]"Statement to Our Fellow Christians," paragraph 9.

in this last clause, however, to detect Barth's ameliorating influence. The statement included an acknowledgment that Israel's actions have at times appeared "belligerently expansionistic" and a recognition that Christians need not "endorse every policy decision [of] the Israeli government." Given Barth's frequent and vocal criticisms of Israel's actions against the Palestinians, it is likely that these sentences were added, if not at Barth's insistence, then at least with his approval.

Slightly more than a year after the statement's publication, Barth had occasion to venture again into the politically sensitive discussions around the Israel-Palestine conflict. He did not do so unilaterally but at the invitation of the Bern chapter of the Christlich-Jüdische Arbeitsgemeinschaft der Schweiz. On June 25, 1974, at the group's request, Barth delivered a public lecture in a packed Calvinhaus on the topic "Israel and Its Arab Fellow-Citizens."[5] In his opening remarks, Barth noted both the miracle and the needfulness of Israel's existence, affirming that Israel had been born out of necessity and had ever since lived in that same state of necessity. Even following their victory during the so-called Six Day War of 1967, Barth insisted Jews have remained "unsafe strangers" (*unsichere Fremde*) in the land of their forefathers, living in a state of permanent emergency (*permanenter Notstand*). "It is a miracle that [this] country was not only able to emerge, but that it has lasted as long as it has."[6]

In turning his remarks toward the Palestinian issue, however, Barth ventured into more sensitive territory. Questioning whether the Palestinians' sense of identity had developed sufficiently even to speak of them yet as a people or a nation, he noted that their plight was nevertheless more desperate than Israel's, simply because Israel had achieved global recognition (*da Israel ein weltweit anerkannter Staat sei*). While insisting that nothing in the Palestinian desperation justified terrorism, Barth inadvertently undercut his assertion by implicitly criticizing Israel's own political stance. Terrorism, he said, was "the last resort to communicate total frustration, when rational communication was no longer possible." If this critique of

[5]CJA der Schweiz, "Einladung—Vortrag von Professor Dr Markus Barth über 'Israel und Seine arabischen Mitbürger.'" MBMC. Box SF21, file 3.

[6]M. Barth, cited in "Jüdische Zuhörer verliessen den Saal," *Der Bund*, June 27, 1974, 17.

Israeli state policy was confronting enough, Barth's next remarks turned the audience against him completely. Controversially and provocatively, he sought to argue that the anti-Jewish terrorist attacks in Munich (1972) and Ma'alot (1974) were outweighed in gravity by the Israeli massacre of 107 Palestinians in Deir Yassin in 1948.[7] Barth's attempt to qualify this by saying that from a Christian perspective, true reconciliation was possible only when both sides gave up their dreams of a victorious peace (*Sieg-Frieden*)—that is, a peace founded on the victory of one over against the other—proved futile.[8]

Perhaps predictably, the lecture provoked a storm of controversy. Many in the audience left the lecture hall in loud protest, while the Bernese Rabbi Dr. Roland Gradwohl described Barth as "an advocate and henchman of the murderous scoundrels" (*Anwalt und Handlanger der Mordbuben*) and who had by his remarks "forfeited his legitimacy as a theological expert" (*Legitimation als theologischer Sachverständiger verwirkte*).[9] The day after the address, one attendee sent Barth a short—but abundantly clear—message: "Shame, shame on you, you little, unworthy son of a great father."[10]

---

[7]"Jüdische Zuhörer verliessen den Saal," *Der Bund*, June 27, 1974, 17. In April 1948, 130 members of the Zionist paramilitary groups Irgun and Lehi attacked the village of Deir Yassin outside Jerusalem. Some of the victims were summarily executed after being paraded through the streets of West Jerusalem, while others were shot trying to escape. The Munich crisis to which Barth referred was the capturing of nine members of Israel's Olympic team at the 1972 Munich Olympics by the Palestinian militant organization Black September. All nine hostages were killed, along with two other members of the Olympic team who had been shot prior to the kidnapping. The Ma'alot massacre took place in May 1974, when members of the Democratic Front for the Liberation of Palestine took 115 Israelis hostage—105 of them children—in the Netiv Meir Elementary School. When Israeli special forces stormed the school two days later, twenty-five of the hostages were killed.

[8]"Jüdische Zuhörer verliessen den Saal," In his closing remarks, Barth expressed his regret at his use of the word "outweigh" (*aufwiegen*)—a word that one commentator described as "outrageous" (*ungeheurlichen*)—noting that it had not been in his prepared manuscript. See "Ein Mann—ein Satz—ein Vortrag," in *Jüdische Rundschau*, July 11, 1974, 10.

[9]"Jüdische Zuhörer verliessen den Saal," Roland Gradwohl (1931–1998) graduated from Leo Baeck College in 1966. In addition to being the editor for many years of the *Israelitisches Wochenblatt* in Switzerland, Gradwohl was involved in various Jewish-Christian dialogues, including the Warsaw consultations (1998) for the Leuenberg Documents. See Mario Fischer and Martin Friedrich, eds., *Church and Israel: A Contribution from the Reformation Churches in Europe to the Relationship Between Christians and Jews* (Leipzig: Evangelischer Verlagsanwalt, 2021), 6.

[10]"Pfui über Sie, schämen Sie sich, kleiner, unwürdiger Sohn eines grossen Vaters." M. Kunz to M. Barth, June 26, 1974. MBMC. Box SF21, file 3.

While Barth's remarks caused offense to many in the audience, they were not without independent support. Johan Snoek, with whom Barth had met a fortnight before the Bern lecture, wrote to him in early July:

> I am not astonished that your lecture evoked criticisms and dissension. However . . . every sensible human being should—even if not perhaps agreeing with all your points of view—refrain from getting angry with your analysis. In my opinion, we ought, as good friends of the people of Israel, to explain certain basic facts of the political situation to our Jewish brethren, whether they like it or not. This sometimes creates some misunderstanding. Yet, I am sure that even within a year the official Israeli position will have moved toward many points you developed in your lectures.[11]

Snoek was, perhaps, overly optimistic. Years later, Barth told one of his sons-in-law that as a consequence of his 1974 Bern lecture, he was—apart from one lecture in Ascona in the 1980s—never again invited to address Switzerland's Jewish communities.[12]

Barth's continuing engagement with the Israel-Palestine conflict proved extremely time-consuming. Indeed, the extent of his endeavors in this field led to at least one unfortunate consequence in his academic work. In mid-1974, Doubleday's Noel Freedman wrote to Barth, advising him that his contract to write the Galatians commentary for the Anchor Bible series had been canceled. This, said Freedman, was "in view of the fact that there is still Colossians and Philemon to be done. In other words, they insisted that a contract be signed with some other scholar for the volume on Galatians."[13]

---

[11]J. Snoek to M. Barth, July 16, 1974. MBMC. Box SF21, file 3. Johan Snoek (b. 1920) was a Dutch Reformed pastor who lived and worked for ten years in Israel and served for five years as section head for the Church and the Jewish People with the World Council of Churches. In a later piece of correspondence, Snoek cautioned Barth—who was redrafting his Bern lecture into an article—that any parallels that he might draw between Israeli actions against Palestinian terrorism and "Hitler-Germany will make it more difficult—if not impossible—for many Jewish and pro-Israel readers to hear you." J. Snoek to M. Barth, September 10, 1974. MBMC. Box SF21, file 3. That Barth was prepared to draw such comparisons at all might seem extraordinary—however, he had already clashed heatedly with Emil Fackenheim over precisely this point. See my "Jewish-Christian Dialogue in Review: Markus Barth's Correspondence with Emil Fackenheim (1965–1980)," *Journal of Reformed Theology* 14 (2020): 246-62.

[12]Correspondence with the Barth family, March 14, 2023. Because of how widely he had been shunned by most of Switzerland's Jewish communities, Markus's invitation to address the Ascona chapter of the CJA was particularly touching.

[13]N. Freedman to M. Barth, June 3, 1974. MBMC. Subject Correspondence 2. Box 6.

Barth was less than impressed, not least because Doubleday's decision was communicated to him only weeks ahead of their release of his long awaited two-volume Ephesians commentary. Unable to respond for a month due to "a dramatic clash with hyper-Zionists of the Jewish and Christian type during and after a lecture I gave in Bern on Israel and the Palestinians," Barth decried what he described as the "one-sided" "cancellation of what we [had] arranged." Having had no indication that such a decision was imminent, Barth told Freedman that he had, in the meantime, turned down two other publication contracts on the understanding that the Doubleday work was going ahead. "Now," he lamented, "I have neither sparrow nor dove."[14]

SACRAMENTAL AND ECUMENICAL WORK

Barth was not, however, solely occupied with Jewish-Christian dialogue, nor with contractual disputes. On the contrary, he retained a lively interest in a subject that had long been both academically and pastorally decisive for him: the question of sacramentality. Over the winter of 1974–1975—during the first of two terms as dean of the faculty—he devoted himself to reading a new book by his former colleague at Pittsburgh, Arthur Cochrane, titled *Eating and Drinking with Jesus*.[15] In that work, Cochrane had argued against a sacramental understanding of the Lord's Supper and had insisted instead that the eucharistic meal ought to be seen as a symbol of God's grace that encompasses every aspect of human life. He urged also a restoration of *agapē* meals as a better means of mission and evangelism than the joyless affair that in most churches, in Cochrane's view, the Eucharist had become. Barth was unsurprisingly appreciative. "Many thanks for the gift [of the book], the contents of which I had somehow anticipated after reading your essay in *Junge Kirche* about a year ago. It is indeed necessary," wrote Barth to Cochrane, "to tear away the myth 'sacrament' from the Lord's Supper as much as from baptism; this job can only be done on the ground of solid biblical argumentation."[16]

---

[14]M. Barth to N. Freedman, July 9, 1974. MBMC. Subject Correspondence 2. Box 6.

[15]A. C. Cochrane, *Eating and Drinking with Jesus: An Ethical and Biblical Enquiry* (Louisville: Westminster, 1974).

[16]M. Barth to A. Cochrane, February 18, 1975. MBMC. Series II. Correspondence. Box 2 (1970s).

Figure 7.1. Markus Barth as dean of the theological faculty of the University of Basel during the Dies academicus festivities, November 1977

This attention to sacramental theology was timely. In early March 1975, Barth participated in the fifth session of the World Alliance of Reformed Churches—Roman Catholic Church Dialogue in Rome. He had previously been a participant at the WARC-RCC dialogue in Woudschoten in February 1974.[17] For the Rome talks, Barth was allocated to Group IV, which was given responsibility for the theme "The Eucharist and the Church," with the final draft statement being composed largely by Barth and the Scottish Jesuit theologian James Quinn.[18] Set out in four parts, the statement contained an affirmation that the Eucharist is the "constitution of the church as a community of love" but also that it is a necessary "source and criterion" for the church's needed renewal in view of the "division of the churches at the precise point where the church should be [most manifestly] one." Strikingly, for a document jointly authored by a Catholic theologian, while there is reference to the Eucharist as a "sacrificial meal," there is no mention of it being a sacrament—perhaps it was here that Barth, having so recently appreciated Cochrane's work, stuck to his theological

[17]R. Smith to M. Barth, February 12, 1974. MBMC. Series VI. Box SF18, file 25.

[18]James Quinn SJ (1919–2010) studied at the University of Glasgow and Heythrop College before his ordination in 1950. Heavily involved in the Secretariat for Promoting Christian Unity, he was the Vatican's observer at the General Assembly of the World Alliance of Reformed Churches in 1964 and participated in the formal dialogues between Rome and WARC from 1973.

guns.[19] Of course, this draft text was significantly reworked before its final inclusion in the 1977 agreed statement, "The Presence of Christ in Church and World." There, the word *sacrament* does appear in the same section on which Barth and Quinn had worked two years previously and from which it had in that earlier iteration been absent. But other, more "Barthian" elements remained, not least an insistence on the need—as Barth had noted to Cochrane—for a thoroughgoing *biblical* basis of eucharistic theology as well as a recognition of the "urgent need" for a mature consideration of "certain forms of Christian fellowship, [namely] 'agape-celebrations.'"[20] Thus, while Barth may not have been entirely happy with the eventual document, its ultimate form was not without his telltale fingerprints upon it.

One particularly notable event that shook not only Barth but the rest of the family as well was the death in July 1975 of Charlotte von Kirschbaum. An integral part of the family's daily life since formally joining the household in 1929, Charlotte had been diagnosed in 1965 with a form of dementia that, in early 1966, required her admission to a nursing home in Riehen. Notwithstanding the particular difficulties that Charlotte's presence in the Barth home had caused over so many decades for Karl and Nelly, it is equally clear that she had become a beloved part of the extended household, and her illness and death impacted them all. Shortly after her passing, Nelly, together with Markus and his siblings, penned some reflections on her life, to be shared at her funeral. They spoke fondly of Charlotte as their "Aunt Lollo," who in death was their "dear departed" (*liebe Verstorbene*). Her death, they said, was for her "a salvation"—but for the Barth children, it was the loss of someone "close to the family . . . whose nature and work will never be forgotten."[21] Thus, in spite of what might be inferred from some of the more recent commentary surrounding what Karl himself referred to as their "*Notgemeinschaft*," it would be wrong to understand Charlotte's death as a final, welcome release for the Barths

---

[19]M. Barth and J. Quinn, "The Eucharist and the Church." MBMC. Series VI. Box SF18, file 26.

[20]Dialogue Between the World Alliance of Reformed Churches and the Secretariat for Promoting Christian Unity: 1970–77, "The Presence of Christ in Church and World," §§71, 92. See www.christianunity.va/content/unitacristiani/en/dialoghi/sezione-occidentale/alleanza-mondiale-delle-chiese-riformate/dialogo-internazionale-cattolico-riformato/documenti-di-dialogo/testo-in-inglese1.html.

[21]N. Barth, F. Zellweger-Barth, M. Barth, C. Barth, and H. J. Barth, "Charlotte von Kirschbaum: Einige Angaben aus ihrem Leben," July 28, 1975, *GA* V.45, xxxiv.

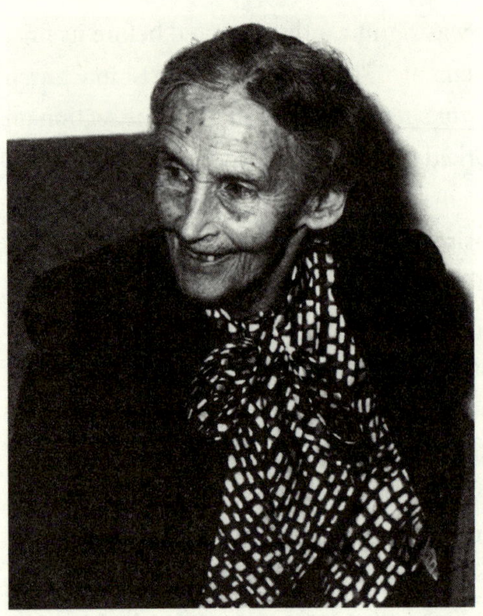

Figure 7.2. Nelly Barth, Christmas 1975

from years of domestic turmoil and pain. Rather, it was a genuinely sad occasion for all concerned—including for Nelly, under whose name the eulogy was written[22]—with Charlotte remembered as an indispensable and honored part of all their lives. Markus's wife, Rose Marie, was particularly affected, having forged a close friendship with Charlotte from as early as her own student days in the late 1930s.[23]

It was noted earlier that one of Barth's regrets from his time in the US was that he had been unable to persuade the leadership of Pittsburgh Seminary to fund a lectureship in Jewish studies. It was an ambition he was unwilling to relinquish. In January 1976, he submitted a formal proposal to Basel's faculty of theology for a similar position. His submission envisaged the expansion and deepening of the faculty's research and teaching programs by the appointment of a Jewish scholar, who would initially be paid by nongovernment sources.[24] To his great chagrin, he was to remain as thwarted in Basel as he had been in Pittsburgh. "You should have seen how all but three of my colleagues collected fishy counterarguments," he wrote to his old friend Jack Schachter. "The old

[22]Nelly's own tenderness toward Charlotte is evident in letters she wrote to Gerty Pestalozzi in the final years of Charlotte's life. Less than a year after Karl's death, Nelly wrote that "if only now our dear Lollo can go home soon" (*Wann jetzt nur unsere liebe Lollo bald heimgehen darf*). N. Barth to G. Pestalozzi, August 27, 1969. Almost exactly a year later, Nelly confirmed, "Yes, Lollo is still alive, [but] as if in a shadow. Sometimes she opens her eyes. What is the good Lord waiting for? But she is peaceful, and she will go to our grave[site]." N. Barth to G. Pestalozzi, August 31, 1970. Cited in Röthlisberger, *Gerty Pestalozzi-Eidenbenz: Ein Leben*, 395, 401.

[23]The affection was clearly reciprocal. In her will, which she had drawn up in 1965, von Kirschbaum designated Karl as her sole heir, with the proviso that, should she outlive him, "his descendants" were to take his place as her heirs. MBMC. Series II. Correspondence. Box 22, file 564.

[24]M. Barth, "Memorandum betr. Lehrauftrag für Judaica," January 1, 1976.

anti-Judaism is, to my grave regret and great surprise, not yet dead."[25] Finally, in 1998, two decades after Barth had first proposed it and four years after his death, the Institute for Jewish Studies was founded as a department within the theology faculty.[26]

THE POLITICS OF PUBLISHING

Through 1978, Markus was busy with various publication projects. The start of the year saw him finalizing the manuscript for his short book *Jesus the Jew*. Consisting of the revised text of two lectures that had initially been delivered in 1973–1974, the book was intentionally aimed at a wider audience than just pastors and theologians. Indeed, Markus's hope was that it would speak also to laypeople—in fact, to "everyone who is looking for a new or deepened understanding of Israel and of the church."[27] That Barth hoped for a wide and non-expert readership did not, however, mean that he was prepared to make every concession asked of him. An exchange with his editor at John Knox Press is instructive for understanding a key theological point on which, in this text, he insisted. While agreeing to remove gender-specific language, Barth nevertheless declared himself "[o]bstinate . . . in one issue: the Jews have to be called our brothers, not our neighbors. But perhaps you will forgive me this hardness of heart. . . . *One* father, ergo one family here and there, not just neighborliness!"[28] Barth's insistence on retaining the term *brother* was, at least in part, a response to those critics who believed that his love for Israel was compromised by his support for Palestinian rights. As he expressed it in the book's foreword, "The brotherhood between Jews and Christians proves true only when both sides do not dodge the pain of *critical* solidarity."[29]

---

[25]M. Barth to J. Schachter, July 20, 1976. MBMC. Series II. Correspondence. Box 23, file 572. Schachter, for whom Barth had unsuccessfully sought a faculty position in Pittsburgh, had in the meantime been appointed to a professorship of Judaica in Los Angeles.

[26]Two decades later, in 2017, Markus's daughter-in-law, Shabnam Edith Barth, founded the *Jüdisch-Christliche Akademie* in Basel, which offers in-person and online short courses on Jewish and Christian literature, history, and culture.

[27]M. Barth, *Jesus the Jew*, trans. F. Prussner (Atlanta: John Knox, 1978), back cover.

[28]M. Barth to J. Crawford, January 23, 1978. MBMC. Subject Correspondence 2. Box 6.

[29]Barth, *Jesus the Jew*, 6.

Through the summer semester, he traveled to Canada as visiting professor at the Vancouver School of Theology, a task he would joyfully undertake on a number of future occasions. There he spoke on Israel and the prospects for peace in the Middle East, arguing for the creation of a "mini-state"—governed jointly by the PLO and local Arab leaders—including Gaza and the West Bank. This, he said, was consistent not only with Arafat's plan, with whom Barth had met in December 1973, but also with Martin Buber's vision.[30]

On his return to Basel, and during the latter half of 1978, Barth had a more difficult set of conversations with another of his publishers, this time around the delay in the production of his commentaries on Colossians and Philemon for Doubleday's Anchor Bible series. Between August and September, Barth corresponded with Eve Roshevsky about his progress, advising that his deteriorating eyesight—which had necessitated surgery—rendered the work harder and slower than he wished. While sympathetic to his situation, Roshevsky noted that Doubleday would be prepared to extend some leniency but "cannot accept an infinite delay."[31] That Doubleday was pressing him to produce more work despite his health troubles must have been particularly infuriating given the earlier cancellation in 1974 of his contract to write the Galatians commentary. But it was not only Doubleday that wished to see the two commentaries published as quickly as possible. Toward the end of summer 1979, one of Markus's former students wrote to him expressing how keen he was to get his hands on Markus's next contributions to the Anchor Bible series.

> Dear Markus,
> What a thoroughly delightful surprise! My most appreciated instructor writing his oldest and smallest pupil. . . . How warmly I recall those unforgettable

[30]"Theologian 'At Bat' for Peace in Mideast," *The Province*, July 22, 1978, 14.

[31]E. Roshevsky to M. Barth, September 19, 1978. See also M. Barth to N. Freedman, December 28, 1978, in which Barth apologized that eye surgery had significantly hampered his capacity to write. MBMC. Subject Correspondence 2. Box 6. Eventually, the Colossians commentary was not published until 1994, the year of Barth's death. Barth's declining health had required Astrid Beck to take over the lion's share of the translation work from 1985, and for Barth to be the proofreader and contact person for any questions of material substance. From 1991, however, Barth's health was such that even this role was largely beyond him. See M. Barth, H. Blanke and A. Beck, *Colossians*, Anchor Bible 34B (New York: Doubleday, 1994), x. According to Helmut Blanke, Barth was not well enough even to read the full text of the final prepublication draft. Personal correspondence with H. Blanke, October 4, 2023.

> Seminary experiences: at your home, in class & elsewhere . . . such newness of insight & direction you kindled for me . . . inexpressible & utterly priceless. . . . How I would enjoy attending your Basel seminar. . . . Incidentally a great many sermons I preached on Eph[esians] were probably not so bad because of your Commentary and I shall look forward with a great deal of gusto to Col & Philemon.[32]

Such a letter is illustrative of a number of key points. First, it demonstrates that Barth remained in contact with former students even years after his teaching had finished. Second, it shows how important Barth's long-standing tradition of home hospitality and the *offene Abende*—learned from both Karl and his grandfather, Fritz—was, not only as a pedagogical device but also as a way of building communities with his students. And third, the letter highlights Barth's great utility as a pastorally oriented scholar whose writings were (and were intended to be) helpful to the preacher in the pulpit. This last point—the necessity of doing theology in the service of preaching—was underscored three years later in a short exchange between Barth and the American Baptist scholar Bernard Ramm. Favorably contrasting Ramm's *After Fundamentalism* with von Balthasar's much earlier book on Karl Barth,[33] Markus not only acknowledged that Ramm "possess[ed] an excellent knowledge of my father's writings" but also that he had identified an aspect of Karl's work that von Balthasar had ignored. "What is missing in Balthasar's book . . . is gloriously present in your own new work: the recognition of what central role preaching played."[34] This was not simply an identification of something that had been important to Karl. Much more than that, it was an affirmation by Markus that the homiletical orientation of Karl's theological work was something that Markus himself had learned to value and absorb into his own approach.

---

[32]A. Showalter to M. Barth, August 27, 1979. MBMC. Series II. Correspondence. Box 3 (1980s).

[33]See B. Ramm, *After Fundamentalism: The Future of Evangelical Theology* (San Francisco: Harper & Row, 1983); also H. U. von Balthasar, *Karl Barth: Darstellung und Deutung Seiner Theologie* (Koln: Verlag Jakob Hegner, 1965). Von Balthasar's book had been translated into English in 1971; ten years later, it was continuing to impact the English-speaking theological world—hence Markus's comparison between Ramm's book and von Balthasar's. Curiously, however, given this comparison, Ramm mentions von Balthasar only twice in his book.

[34]M. Barth to B. Ramm, July 5, 1983. MBMC. Series II. Correspondence. Box 3 (1980s).

While conversations with Doubleday continued, other publishing possibilities also beckoned. One of Markus's former students from Pittsburgh, Daniel Griggs, contacted him in late 1979, proposing that he prepare for publication an English translation of Barth's 1951 monograph, *Die Taufe*.[35] It will be recalled that Barth himself had been urged to undertake the work in 1957, but that he had at the time declined, feeling that his own command of American English was insufficient. Now, more than two decades later, someone was offering to do the work for him. Again, though, Barth demurred, though not this time for linguistic reasons. Rather, he felt that the task was wholly unnecessary. As he wrote to Griggs in reply:

> One thing, however, has to be considered and mulled over . . . before you begin: In my father's *Church Dogmatics* vol IV 4, the results of my book are taken up, sieved and tested, reshaped, improved and enriched—and in *that* form, the results of my exegetical labors are already accessible to a wider public, in print. Read the foreword of said *Dogmatics* volume to see what the relation between Barth father and son is in that quarter, and compare, if you wish, the detail[ed] treatment of any of the important texts? Of course, my procedure is more technically exegetical and his more dogmatical. But he also avoids exaggerations or unprotected overstatements of which I as a young hun [*sic*] may have been guilty. And the better is the enemy of the good—if my book be good at all.[36]

Markus's reticence to see the book translated won the day. Griggs abandoned the project, with a new translation effort being delayed another forty years, when another of Markus's doctoral students—David MacLachlan—recommenced the work.

The following year, Barth was engaged in a further series of rather strained negotiations with Doubleday, again over the commentaries project. By then, however, the obstacle was not Barth's eyesight but his involvement in another international controversy, namely the plight of black South Africans under P. W. Botha's apartheid regime. A month-long visit to black townships in mid-1980, together with Rose Marie, had resulted in yet further delays to the Colossians and Philemon commentaries. He wrote to Freedman in late October, explaining the circumstances:

---

[35]D. Griggs to M. Barth, December 4, 1979. MBMC. Series II. Correspondence. Box 2 (1970s).
[36]M. Barth to D. Griggs, December 15, 1979. MBMC. Series II. Correspondence. Box 2 (1970s).

> This summer I was urgently invited by black ministers in South Africa to teach them and their congregations in their miserable situation. Pupils have been shot by the hundreds this summer, babies are starving to death in the homelands, a proud white (reformed!) church claims that all forms and consequences of Apartheid correspond to the will of God and that Rom 13 prescribes the black Christians how to behave vis-à-vis the state.

Accepting that this ministry came at the expense of his publishing responsibilities, Barth nonetheless insisted that his "responsibility for living and suffering people has taken priority over my literary duty and aspiration."[37]

A SWISS VOICE INTO SOUTH AFRICAN STRUGGLES

Close engagement with the South African situation continued into the following year. In September 1981, just before the start of his second term as faculty dean, Barth prepared a theological response to the question of reconciliation in the context of apartheid.[38] Leaning heavily into his earlier work on Ephesians, Barth began by insisting on the universality of God's reconciling work. "Reconciliation," he said, "is granted with God and between brothers, Israel and the Gentiles, married people, *all things*."[39] There was, he claimed, no legitimate theological reason for believing that interracial reconciliation was somehow excluded from God's purposes. Then, taking up a form of critique that prefigured later postcolonialist discourse, he noted that in order for reconciliation to be spoken of meaningfully "in the present situation of the black, coloured, Indian population of South Africa and their confrontation with a domineering white minority, a [new] terminology is required," which would be more reflective of those non-White experiences. Barth was suggesting nothing less than the utilization of a more properly indigenous term—a word that "should be equally wholistic as the Hebrew 'shalom'"—and that did not therefore simply reimpose "white man's problems . . . upon a majority

---

[37]M. Barth to N. Freedman, October 28, 1980. MBMC. Subject Correspondence 2. Box 6.

[38]M. Barth, "Reconciliation: An Outline of Theological Reflections, Prepared at the Request of South African Churchmen in Response to the Proposed Formula 'Confrontation and Reconciliation,'" September 16, 1981. MBMC. Box SF36, file 9.

[39]M. Barth, "Reconciliation," 1. Emphasis added.

population" through the too-easy incorporation of "Latin-rooted English" words.[40]

Barth warned, however, that any genuine reconciliation was difficult, hard-won, and required humility on both sides. "It is characteristic of the reconciliation brought by God and sought by people that no one of the human hostile parties can declare itself the winner."[41] Unsurprisingly, his paper concluded with two theses, both of which were necessarily provocative. First, there can be "[n]o reconciliation without truth and courageous admission of differences"; second, "the churches are more than co-responsible for Apartheid . . . [and so] white Christians [must be] listeners and learners rather than teachers."[42]

In July of the following year, Barth traveled to Leuenberg for the annual *Karl Barth-Tagung*. These conferences, which had begun the year following Karl's death, had become the preeminent occasions for systematic exploration of the elder Barth's theological legacy, drawing attendees—theologians, historians, pastors, students, journalists, even lawyers—from around Europe and even further afield. By 1982, Markus—who had made a point of traveling to Leuenberg each year while still in America—was now part of the preparatory group whose task was to determine the conference's annual themes and programs. Naturally regarded as an "elder statesman" among the Leuenbergers, he was, in 1982, also one of the conference speakers. His presentation on sacramental theology allowed him to speak to a subject that was, according to Christian Link, "his real specialty."[43] Link's recollection of that lecture reveals something of Barth's passion for his subject and his capacity to hold an audience enthralled. In a four-hour lecture during which Barth hardly paused for rest, he "poured out from [his] cornucopia . . . so much that was new, never heard of, seriously worth considering."[44] Barth's own memory of the presentation was somewhat more self-critical. It had been four times too long and had taken him (he feared) too far from his Reformed tradition, and even from his father's

[40]M. Barth, "Reconciliation," 2.

[41]M. Barth, "Reconciliation," 7.

[42]M. Barth, "Reconciliation," 9.

[43]Personal correspondence with C. Link, March 8, 2023.

[44]C. Link to M. Barth, August 1982. Cited in personal correspondence with Link, March 8, 2023.

teachings. He was also somewhat embarrassed that, with nerves on edge, he feared that he had been "unspeakably rude" to a number of other delegates. For Link, though, even this deprecation was commendable, demonstrating Barth's total commitment to his vocation and to the interests of his community rather than to his own.[45]

During this time, Markus and Rose Marie's concern for the increasingly desperate situation in South Africa remained at the forefront of their minds. In 1983, Rose Marie joined a protest group that encouraged economic boycotts. Its rallying cry was "*Kauft keine Früchte aus Südafrika*" ("Don't buy fruit from South Africa"), with Rose Marie and others picketing for hours the largest grocery store in Riehen.[46] The next year, both she and Markus traveled for a second time to South Africa to provide support and counsel for those who were struggling against Apartheid. Barth's assistance was particularly significant for the lawyer Richard Rosenthal, who had commenced secret negotiations between the Botha regime and the exiled African National Congress, and for whom Barth acted as a personal mentor.[47] In the end, however, Barth recalled these efforts to assist in the South African struggle with frustration, and for much the same reasons as he had encountered in his involvement with Israel-Palestine. "I have once tried," he wrote to Rosenthal,

> to make a little bit of a contribution to the struggle in which Allan Boesak and other friends are engaged. . . . I wanted to help them spiritually. But then I gave

---

[45]Personal correspondence with Link, March 8, 2023. Two other attendees also recall both the quality of the lecture and its length. Rolf Erler—later, the editor of volume one of the *Barth-Charlotte von Kirschbaum Briefwechsel*—recalled that the general feeling in the room was one of "'Karl Barth redivivus.' [Markus] seemed to the young crowd to be the living [image] of Karl Barth, which is probably the main reason why most people were prepared to patiently endure the four hour [lecture]." R. Erler to D. Zellweger, March 19, 2023. Eberhard Busch had similar memories. "I tried to sneak away during a break, exhausted just from listening." In the end, though, he stayed for the second half, and was glad to have done so. "[While] the second part was just as long as the first . . . it was indeed important to hear it. It went like the wedding of Cana. 'You have kept the best wine until now.'" E. Busch, April 2022.

[46]See "Kauf Keine Früchte aus Südafrika," April 30–May 8, 1983, https://museum.evang.at/wp-content/uploads/2015/04/3_Informationsmaterial-Fruechteboykott.pdf.

[47]Rosenthal had something of a standing invitation to stay at the Barths' chalet in Villa whenever he was in need of rest and recuperation. As Rosenthal put it after one such stay, "'Villa' never disappoints. In some way, it heals and nurtures each person." R. Rosenthal to M. Barth, July 3, 1988. MBMC. Series II. Correspondence. Box 32, file 743. For his own perspective, see R. Rosenthal, *Mission Improbable: A Piece of the South African Story* (Athlone: David Philip, 1998). Personal correspondence, February 4, 2019.

> up because from the distance in Europe in which I am living, I am hardly entitled to tell my friends in SA that here and there in their theological argument they may go overboard or astray. They ask only for applause . . . and consider even the slightest suggestion of a change . . . an indication of treason against their cause.[48]

While geographical distance clearly hindered Barth from engaging in South Africa as closely as he might have wished—and in this, as his reasoning to Rosenthal makes evident, there was an admirable refusal to speak as the "wise white European"—there was evidently also another reason behind his withdrawal from the struggle. Rightly or wrongly, Barth seems to have sensed the same sort of uncritical self-righteousness on the part of the anti-Apartheid movement that he had encountered among those staunchly pro-Israel Jews who refused to see any justification for the Palestinians' cause. Having been burnt before, he was reluctant to be so again. "About ten or fifteen years ago . . . I had traveled several times to the state of Israel, and had written not just about the Jews but also the Palestinians. Already then because I could not simply subscribe to the radical claims of Israeli friends, I had run into trouble."[49]

AN INVITATION FROM JAPAN

In the middle of the decade, Markus received an unexpected invitation that came largely as the result of his children's friendships from the Pittsburgh years. Anna had become pen pals with an English literature student from Japan, Keiko Furukawa, who had then stayed with the Barths for two years while on exchange in Pittsburgh. Afterward, they had remained in contact, with Markus and Rose Marie often providing counsel on matters of faith. Now, twenty years later, Keiko sought to arrange a visit by Markus to Japan as something of a reciprocation for their earlier hospitality to her. In early June 1985, Barth began negotiations with Hideo Ohki[50]—who was at the time teaching systematic theology at the Tokyo Union Theological Seminary—for a possible fellowship and lecture tour under the auspices of the Japanese Society for the

[48]M. Barth to R. Rosenthal, July 27, 1987. MBMC. Series II. Correspondence. Box 28, file 728.

[49]M. Barth to R. Rosenthal, July 27, 1987.

[50]Hideo Ohki (1928–2022) received his ThD from Union Theological Seminary in New York in 1960. Later, he served as president of the Tokyo Union Theological Seminary.

Promotion of Science (JSPS). Perhaps aware that Ohki had already published various works on Karl Barth's theology, Markus sought to ensure that in any tour of Japan he might undertake—and which did not, in the end, take place for another two years—he would be able to speak to his own work and not simply his father's. As a passionate appeal to be considered on his own merits, his words to Ohki are worth repeating in detail.

> I am not a specialist for recent Karl Barth studies in Europe. The piles or mountains of articles and monographs on issues treated by my father, the results or tendencies of conferences and congresses devoted to the study of this or that aspect of his work, also many or most of the ongoing discussions about him are not at all or certainly not enough known to me. And I do not wish to pretend that—with the little I know or understand e.g. of Balthasar's, Küng's, Torrance's, Jüngel's, Pannenberg's, Moltmann's, Marquard's use of elements of my father's thought and theological intentions—I am competent to speak in lectures before an austere and most wise public. You yourself, dear Mr Okhi, have certainly much deeper knowledge and insight and experience in such tasks. . . .
>
> Therefor[e], when Karl Barth is the topic of a meeting, I would certainly like to listen and partake in discussion and to answer questions—all within the limits posed by my lack of reading, understanding and competence. *If however, also lectures are expected of me, their topic(s) ought to stem from the New Testament fields on which I have been working. . . .* Fields of my choice have been, for instance, fundamental aspects of Pauline theology (including the political implications of his work), the Epistle to the Hebrews and its relevance for biblical hermeneutics, Israel and the church, or Baptism and the Lord's Supper (the latter in critical distance from, and opposition to practically all that the Lima Papers propose as points of convergence). *Certainly, in all my work my dependence upon my father will be visible, and, so I hope, a testimony to his life's work will be given. But on the whole, I have never attempted simply to represent or promote his work, but rather within the narrow frame of my competence in exegetical matters, to contribute to it.* The Foreword to *Church Dogmatics* IV/4 shows in a rather exuberant way that my father once saw reason to enjoy what I had done—even in criticising him partially. . . . *Doing work as a real or a seeming Barthian has so far never been my calling or my intention.*[51]

[51]M. Barth to H. Okhi, June 4, 1985. MBMC. Subject Correspondence 3. Box 7. Emphasis added. There may have been another, slightly more humorous reason why Markus did not wish to be identified as a Barthian. Immediately prior to Markus's departure for Dubuque, Karl had taken

Somewhat ironically, despite Markus's insistence that he be seen and understood apart from his father's work, it was precisely at this time that he commenced work on what was to become arguably his most significant contribution to the work of the Karl Barth *Nachlasskommission*. In 1985, the commission began debating whether to permit the publication of the full correspondence between Karl and Charlotte von Kirschbaum. Despite being aware of how explosive the release of these letters would be, it was the children—Markus, Christoph, and Franziska—who, in 1985, were the ones to insist upon their publication. This decision was not taken lightly. On the contrary,

> [a]s the only living children of Karl Barth we decided, *after a long time of reflection* and because many who were close and not close at all urged us to do so, to publish this partially very intimate correspondence. In face of the tittle-tattle which has been circulating since the middle of the 1920s, we thought the time has come to bring the bright and the bleak aspects of that very special and unique love in which our father was bound to our "aunt Lollo," out into the open.[52]

The ramifications of that decision on later Barthian scholarship is a story in itself.[53] The point here is that at the very same time as he was urging Hideo Ohki to respect him as a theologian in his own right, Markus was at the forefront of decisions about his father's legacy that would have a momentous impact on the scholarly memory and reception of Karl Barth.

THE END OF TEACHING AND WRITING

In 1985, Barth formally retired from his post as professor of New Testament at the University of Basel, a little earlier than his mandated retirement date

---

him aside and warned him about what a "Barthian" was: "Someone who understands Karl Barth up to a point, and then gives up independent thinking." Anecdote recounted by Markus Barth to Helmut Blanke. See H. Blanke, "Markus Barth Biografie," unpub. April 2022, 3. MBL. Series II. Box 1. It is somewhat ironic, then, that Charles Dickinson—who was a student of Markus's in Chicago, Greifswald, and Pittsburgh, and who lived with the Barths for two years in their Pittsburgh home—referred to Markus as Karl's "living breathing" "representative in America." C. Dickinson, "Markus Barth and Biblical Theology: A Personal Re-View," *Horizons in Biblical Theology* 17, no. 2 (1995): 96.

[52]See C. Tietz, "Karl Barth and Charlotte von Kirschbaum," *Theology Today* 74, no. 2 (2017): 88. Emphasis added.

[53]See in particular Tietz, "Karl Barth and Charlotte von Kirschbaum," 86-111; S. Plant, "When Karl Met Lollo: The Origins and Consequences of Karl Barth's Relationship with Charlotte von Kirschbaum," *Scottish Journal of Theology* 72, no. 2 (2019): 127-45.

of March 31, 1986. His final lecture, which was delivered on February 21, and which took Romans 11:33-36 as its text, explored the idea of prayer as the proper form of theology.[54] This slightly premature retirement was not unexpected. His health had not been good for some years, with his heart and eyesight—he had suffered since childhood with myopia and more recently with glaucoma—deteriorating noticeably. During the summer semester of 1983, he had been forced to take medical leave due to very high blood pressure, even spending six weeks in a hospital as a result. Nevertheless, he resisted bringing his teaching to an end for as long as possible. As he said to one of his doctoral students, David MacLachlan, he "need[ed] the presence of and dialogue with the students in order spiritually to stay alive."[55] As a consequence, he continued to teach one course a year—usually an introductory class to the New Testament—for the rest of the decade.

He also returned briefly to Pittsburgh in April 1986, where he delivered the Schaff Lectures, in which he combined his interests in both Jewish-Christian dialogue and sacramental theology. Under the general theme of "The Lord's Supper," Barth delivered four addresses on "Communion with the Crucified and Returning Lord," "Communion Among the Guests," "The One and Only Sacrament," and "Communion with Israel."[56] This theme had been on his mind earlier in the year, too, when revising his entry on Ephesians for the *Oxford Companion to the Bible*. In the typescript for that entry, which he had written in January, Barth spoke of Jews and Gentiles as "mutual brothers and sisters," and he expressed his longing for that day when "the perfect bridegroom, Christ, [will] come to meet them at the last day, [and] the present imperfection of the Christians will vanish. Since Christ already is the head over [Jews and Gentiles] and fills and directs them, the diversity of the members of his body, far from disturbing the oneness and unity of the body, supports and expresses its harmony."[57]

---

[54]M. Barth, "Theologie—ein Gebet (Rom 11, 33-36)," *Theologische Zeitschrift* 41, no. 3 (1985): 330-48.

[55]M. Barth to D. MacLachlan, September 20, 1984. MBMC. Subject Correspondence 1. Box 5.

[56]*Pittsburgh Post-Gazette*, April 7, 1986, 10.

[57]M. Barth, typescript for "Ephesians," *Oxford Companion to the Bible*, January 2, 1986. MBMC. Series III. Publications. Box P4, file 6, 2. The phrase "Jews and Gentiles" was added in pen. Curiously, this particular phraseology of Jewish-Gentile mutuality did not find its way into the

Figure 7.3. Rose Marie's 70th birthday dinner, 1983. Left to right: Rose Marie, Rose-Marie, Markus, Anna

For two months of the following year, through mid-March to mid-May 1987, Barth was finally able to visit Japan, happily timing his trip to coincide with the spring blooming of Japan's cherry blossoms.[58] His itinerary was typically crammed full—engagements were planned in Tokyo, Nagasaki, Osaka, Hiroshima, Kyoto, and Fukuoka—and included a sermon at the Nagasaki Peace Memorial Church, where he learned about the "hidden Christians" of the Tokugawa shogunate, visits to two house churches, and a speech to the annual meeting of the *Nihon Singaku Gakkai* Congress (The Japanese Theological Society Congress). In all, he delivered a series of seven lectures and sermons, being accompanied throughout by his wife and youngest daughter. Also traveling with them was Keiko Watanabe, who had not only been instrumental in arranging the tour in the first place but who also translated the lectures as they were given.

As he traveled and taught, he was as good as his commitment to Hideo Ohki, given two years previously, in which he had promised to speak to his own scholarship and not simply speak about his father. He also refused to

published version of the article. See M. Barth, "Ephesians," in *The Oxford Companion to the Bible*, ed. B. Metzger and M. D. Coogan (Oxford: Oxford University Press, 1993).

[58]He and Rose Marie, along with their youngest daughter Rose-Marie, were there for two months, between March 13 and May 15. Barth's JSPS fellowship was hosted by the International Christian University (Tokyo).

Figure 7.4. At Osaka Castle in Japan, May 1987. Left to right: Markus, Keiko Watanabe, Rose Marie, and Rose-Marie

discuss the current state of European New Testament scholarship, given that he was "not all too happy" about it. There was, he said, too much emphasis on the "personality cults" that surrounded various individual scholars such as Rudolf Bultmann, Ernst Käsemann, and Joachim Jeremias. As for what Barth himself thought to be vital, and about which he wished to speak to his Japanese audience, he states,

> Only a small minority of scholars is kept busy by the questions and fields which I deem really important, that is all that has to do with Jesus, the Jew; Paul as a good Jew, even *in* his utterances against misuse of the law; a new relation between Christians and Jews which might prevent further Auschwitzs and Maidaneks; movements toward a rediscovery of the original meaning or meanings of baptism and the Lord's Supper.[59]

It was his baptismal theology in particular on which he wished to speak—that subject which, since his pastorate in Bubendorf, had been so close to his heart. "Matthew 3:13-17 (the baptism of Jesus) *rather than* Matthew 28:19 . . . is the biblical institution of baptism," he told his

[59]M. Barth to M. Yamauchi, December 1, 1986. MBMC. Subject Correspondence 3. Box 7.

audience at Tokyo's International Christian University. This, Barth insisted, could only mean a thoroughgoing refutation of infant baptism. Moreover, "in following Jesus' example," the baptized person "takes the first step on the way to be followed, in Jesus' case: the way to the cross, in our case, the way of following him in carrying the cross." Thus, Barth concluded, baptism—while never appropriately for infants, was nonetheless always "a 'beginning.'" Of what? Of "fulfill[ing] the obligations of a witness in word and deed to Jesus Christ and God's grace."[60]

The following year, and despite failing health, Barth managed in July 1988 to visit the Vancouver School of Theology, offering a course titled "A Walk Through the New Testament." Student appraisals of his course were glowing, but one student's expression of gratitude was particularly gratifying to Barth. "Do you realize," he wrote in response, "that nothing pleases me more among possible effects of my teaching activities than to hear that preaching is encourage[d] and helped?"[61]

FINAL TRAVELS, FRAILTIES, AND CONTROVERSIES

While in Vancouver, Barth renewed his friendship with Tom Torrance's brother, James, himself a theologian of some note. "It was such a pleasure to be with you for those few weeks in July in VST . . . [and] to renew old friendships. . . . As we said, it would be great fun to have a shared course sometime. Perhaps it would not be quite so strenuous for you if we both did it together!"[62] In the same northern summer, Barth also revived another old friendship, this time with his former student, the American rabbi David Novak. Having written to Novak in early June, Barth received a return letter later in the month in which Novak expressed both his gratitude that he was still remembered by his former teacher and his interest in "discuss[ing] with [Barth] Jewish-Christian dialogue, which seems to be theologically dominant at present."[63] On his return to Switzerland, Barth

[60]Notes of Markus Barth's lecture to the ICU, penned by Rose Marie Barth. Emphasis added.

[61]M. Barth to J. M. Wilson, October 27, 1988. MBMC. Series II. Correspondence. Box 32, file 740.

[62]J. Torrance to M. Barth, February 11, 1989. MBMC. Series II. Correspondence. Box 3 (1980s).

[63]D. Novak to M. Barth, June 20, 1988. MBMC. Series II. Correspondence. Box 3 (1980s). Novak also sent as a gift to Barth a copy of his "The Quest for the Jewish Jesus" (*Modern Judaism* 8, no. 2 [1988]), with the following dedication: "To my teacher, Prof. Markus Barth, with warm regards."

did not offer any courses at Basel during the second half of the year but, in lieu of formal teaching, once again held seminar evenings at his home in Riehen for a few of his more advanced students. This, it would seem, was at *their* request, and not at his instigation.[64]

In late 1988 Barth suffered a heart attack,[65] which put him out of action for some time. Having seen him so recently in Canada, it was not surprising that James Torrance made contact.

> Dear Markus, it was so good to hear your voice today. I was distressed to hear from a friend in Vancouver that you had had a heart attack, so phoned you, and was relieved to know that you are feeling much better. I trust that the improvement continues and that you are soon restored to full health and strength. You have so much to contribute. May you have many long years of good health to continue the great work you are doing . . . God bless you, my good friend. With all good wishes, Yours, James.[66]

While the long-term damage to his heart did not initially appear to be too serious—he "got away with a blue eye,"[67] as his doctor put it—Barth did have to forego a series of lectures on Romans in Ann Arbor. He was also forced to cancel two courses that he had been hoping to teach during January 1989 at New College for Advanced Christian Studies Berkeley, on Ephesians and Pauline ethics. He did, however, manage to travel to Prague in April for a series of lectures, and also to return to VST in July for its annual summer school. But the stresses of

---

Novak, of course, was soon after to become a key figure in American Jewish-Christian relations, coauthoring (among other pieces) *Dabru Emet: A Jewish Statement on Christians and Christianity*, in September 2000.

[64]R. M. Barth, circular letter, December 19, 1988. MBL. Series I. Box 32. Letters 1980s–90s.

[65]It seems, in fact, that there were two heart attacks. In a letter to Petr Macek of Prague in February 1989, Barth spoke of his slow recovery from an "*infarctus*" the previous October. Toward the end of the year, he noted in a letter to Ulrich Mauser, then the vice president for academic affairs at Pittsburgh Theological Seminary, that he was still recovering from a heart attack on November 29, 1988. See M. Barth to P. Macek, February 8, March 9, 1989; M. Barth to U. Mauser, December 28, 1989. MBMC. Series II. Correspondence. Box 32, files 737, 739.

[66]J. Torrance to M. Barth, February 11, 1989. Torrance was not the only theologian of note to make contact and wish Markus a speedy recovery. "Lieber Markus, mit den herzlichen Wünschen zu Deiner baldigen Genesung." H. Prolingheur to M. Barth, December 9, 1988. MBMC. Series II. Correspondence. Box 3 (1980s).

[67]R. M. Barth, circular letter, December 19, 1988. To "get away with a blue eye" (*mit einem blauen Auge davonkommen*) has the idiomatic meaning of getting off lightly with something.

these tours took their toll. Shortly after arriving home from Prague, Barth's "heart and lungs . . . began to act up."[68] By August, he was unwell enough that he had to cancel plans to co-teach a course with Joel Green on "Paul: The Man and His Message" that had been slated for New College during the winter of 1990. A further heart attack had rendered Barth's participation impossible. In his apologetic letter of withdrawal, Barth nonetheless managed to indicate to Green where the two men would have differed had they been able to teach alongside each other. Here again, Barth's commitment to a cruciform basis of Jewish-Christian solidarity was evident.

> Dear Joel, Many thanks . . . for the excellent syllabus which you have prepared for our common course in the winter of next year. Though I would have given Paul's theology of the cross (and the resurrection) and of the community (which ought to include Israel, the one people of God to which the gentiles are admitted) a somewhat earlier and more basic position.[69]

Barth was not the only one to be disappointed that his health made him unable to return to Berkeley. The Brethren theologian Vernard Eller wrote to Barth from the University of La Verne: "Though I well understand the *necessity* of your missing the New College appointment, I can't say how sorry I am that it had to happen. I very much looked forward to meeting you and learning from you."[70]

Despite his decreasing capacity for teaching and lecturing tours, Barth remained remarkably active in and outspoken on various church-political concerns. Between 1989 and 1990, Barth became strangely embroiled in the controversy surrounding the United Church of Canada's decision on gay rights that had been taken two years previously. Following the release in 1988 of a task force report titled *Gift, Dilemma, and Promise: A Report and Affirmations of Human Sexuality*, the UCC's General Council had decreed that "all persons, regardless of sexual orientation, who profess their faith in Jesus Christ are welcome to be or become members of The United Church of Canada," and moreover that "all members of the United Church are

[68]M. Barth to P. Macek, April 27, 1989. MBMC. Series II. Correspondence 2. Box 32, file 737.
[69]M. Barth to J. Green, August 22, 1989. MBMC. Subject Correspondence 2. Box 6.
[70]V. Eller to M. Barth, undated. MBMC. Box SF34, file 7.

eligible to be considered for ordered ministry."[71] In the inevitable entrenchment of factions within the UCC that followed on from that decision, rhetoric became charged, with a perhaps equally inevitable set of comparisons made by the opposing sides to the *Kirchenkampf* of the 1930s and the necessity of a new Confessing Church. As one irate correspondent wrote to Barth, "We are not that fortunate in Canada to have the likes of [General] George Patton get rid of the heretics for us."[72]

That Barth should have gotten involved was neither necessary nor inescapable. But, once again, he was dragged in by virtue of his father. The conservative evangelical lobby group Community of Concern, in its self-identification as the *Bekennende Kirche* of the day, issued an invitation to Barth to speak at its Faithfulness Today conference in March 1990, an invitation that Barth, somewhat rashly, initially accepted. On being alerted as to the CoC's agenda, however, Barth withdrew his acceptance to the group's fury. His reasons for pulling out were twofold. In the first instance, and with "German Christian," "Barmen Declaration," and "Confessing Church" labels being deployed by both sides, he refused to allow either side to "capture the name Barth for a party concern."[73] But second, and more intriguingly, Barth was not in principle opposed to the UCC's decision. While unwilling to be held to a fixed position—he was, he repeatedly said, an "outsider"—he nevertheless felt that the UCC's decision, while "far from . . . excellent," was better than the conservative response, which "looks to me even worse." "As much as I know at the present about the situation," he said, "I might rather support the report on sexuality than side with those on the opposite side who argue in a legalistic, moralistic, judgmental way."[74]

Certainly, it would be imprudent to argue from this alone that Barth was a (surprising and early) theological affirmer of gay rights. His reasons for pushing back against the conservative Community of Concern were as much about his discomfort with its dogmatic and unpastoral moralism as

[71] C. J. Summers, "United Church of Canada," glbtq, 2008, http://glbtqarchive.com/ssh/united_church_canada_S.pdf, 4.

[72] H. Wipprecht to M. Barth, September 1, 1989. MBMC. Series II. Correspondence. Box 33, file 757.

[73] M. Barth to V. Hart, August 15, 1990. MBMC. Series II. Correspondence. Box 33, file 747.

[74] M. Barth to Mrs. Morrison, August 23, 1989. MBMC. Series II. Correspondence. Box 33, file 747.

they were about any considered sexual progressivism. Nevertheless, his preparedness to give an in-principle endorsement of the UCC decision—at least until better arguments to the contrary might be put forward—is suggestive of a greater ethical liberalism than might have been expected.

In the midst of these and other controversies, Barth continued—albeit far more slowly, and now with coworkers Helmut Blanke and Astrid Beck—to work on his various publications, not least for the Anchor Bible series.[75] In September 1991, Noel Freedman wrote to thank Barth for sending through the latest installment of his Philemon commentary. "Now that you have made a good start to the Commentary proper, I hope that you can continue to write and in that way come to a conclusion in a reasonable time. Everyone from the publisher to the potential readers is eager to see the end of this work." Freedman's gratitude was not-too-subtly tinged with a perhaps understandable anxiety that the various delays by which Barth's work on these commentaries had been hampered over the preceding fifteen years would continue. Nevertheless, he was also keen to encourage Barth, noting that work on the Colossians commentary was "continu[ing] apace," and that the eventual publication of this volume would make Barth "one of our chiefest contributors to the series."[76] Sadly, Freedman's attempts to spur Barth on in his efforts ignored the fact that, by now, Markus's own involvement in the commentary projects was almost nonexistent. His health, which had been flagging for some time, was by 1991 so seriously compromised that he was unable "to correspond or work on the text."[77] A short letter to Vincent Flack on Boxing Day 1991 suggests that Barth's intent was still to write. "I am still pushing ahead with my Philemon studies . . . more than half of the whole book is now finished in typed

[75]Helmut Blanke had begun working with Barth in 1983 as a young doctoral student. Barth had suggested that while he focused on the Philemon book, Blanke might begin with a dissertation on Col 1–2, which could then be expanded into the Anchor Bible commentary, for which Barth had already drafted the introduction. By 1987, Blanke had completed his doctorate and had also finished his exposition of Col 3–4. According to Blanke, the plan was that Barth would translate his student's completed work into English for inclusion in the commentary. With ill health preventing him from doing so, however, Astrid Beck was assigned the task of translating the Colossians commentary, with Barth acting as proofreader. Personal correspondence with H. Blanke, October 4, 2023.

[76]N. Freedman to M. Barth, September 15, 1991. MBMC. Series II. Correspondence. Box 4 (1990s).

[77]A. Beck, "Preface," in Barth, Blanke and Beck, *Colossians*, x.

Figure 7.5. Rose Marie and Markus at the chalet in Villa, 1992

form."[78] But in spite of this hope, and as a consequence of four heart attacks and "a slight brain stroke" in June 1990[79] that had rendered him too weak to work, it was in the end Blanke and Beck whose work made the publication of the two commentaries possible.[80]

As Barth's health continued its rapid decline, he remained buoyed in spirit by the consideration of former students and friends. In the spring of 1993, the ethicist and missionary Verne Fletcher, with whom Barth had

[78]M. Barth to V. Flack, December 26, 1991. MBMC. Series II. Correspondence. Box 4 (1990s).

[79]M. Barth to R. Rosenthal, August 23, 1990. MBMC. Series II. Correspondence. Box 32, file 747.

[80]Blanke notes that until May 1992, Barth was "the main player" (*der Hauptakteur*) in the Philemon project. After that time, Blanke worked on vv. 17-25, using the notes that Barth himself had made. Personal correspondence with H. Blanke, October 4, 2023. The Colossians commentary was published in 1994, just prior to Markus's death. His Philemon commentary, on the other hand, despite having been under commission with Doubleday as part of the Anchor Bible series since the early 1970s, was ultimately published by Eerdmans in 2000 as part of its Eerdmans Critical Commentary series. There is, however, an editorial link that helps explain the change. In 2000, Noel Freedman ceased his work for Anchor Bible, with which he had been busy since 1956, and began production of the ECC series, on which he worked until his death in 2008. His coeditor of that series was Astrid Beck, who had worked with Barth on translating both the Colossians and Philemon commentaries. The Anchor Bible's commentary on Philemon was published in the same year as Barth's ECC version, having been written by the American Jesuit Joseph A. Fitzmyer. His commentary is 160 pages compared to Barth's 561 pages.

coauthored a book in 1963, wrote of his "unpleasant surprise" at finding Barth "confined to a horizontal position." Nevertheless, he was pleased to note that his friend's "swan song—so far as scholarship is concerned—is in sympathetic hands for completion and final polishing. We hope that your days are bearable. You are fortunate to have Rose-Marie and Peter at your side."[81] Friends and colleagues were clearly concerned, and not without reason, that Barth's death might be imminent.

It was in the end, however, Barth's wife of fifty-three years, Rose Marie, who died first, succumbing to pleural cancer in September 1993. She had continued to care for her husband even in her own failing health and was in turn accompanied through her last illness by her son, Peter. Keiko Watanabe, Rose Marie's "Japanese daughter," flew from Japan to be with her in her final days. With Rose Marie's death, Peter Barth took over primary responsibility for caring for his father in his own final illnesses.[82]

Since mid-summer 1992, Barth had been largely bedridden. On the weekends, his daughters—who would take turns traveling from their respective homes in Belgium, Bavaria, and southern Switzerland—would read to him (the Psalms and Isaiah were among his favorite texts) and take him on "imaginary walks." Among his other visitors was his neighbor, Gateano Benedetti, who would come each Sunday morning with a raft of theological questions he wanted to discuss. Despite his immobility, however, Barth's vision of the world remained broad, with a final trip to Japan being among his last but unfulfilled wishes.[83]

Markus died on July 1, 1994, just ten months after Rose Marie's death. His funeral service was held one week later on July 8 in the *Theodorskirche* in Basel. In his eulogy, Ekkehard Stegemann spoke on behalf of the rector of the University of Basel and the dean of its theological faculty expressing their collective thanks "for all that Prof. Markus Barth [had done] for our Alma Mater." Noting that he had been "a kind man, and a committed

---

[81] V. Fletcher to M. Barth, March 14, 1993. MBMC. Series II. Correspondence. Box 4 (1990s). Note that while Fletcher spoke of "Rose-Marie," he meant Markus's wife, Rose Marie.

[82] In the family's written eulogy, penned for their father's funeral, the children gave special thanks to Peter, "who faithfully and lovingly cared for [Markus] until the end [*der ihn bis zuletzt treu und liebevoll pflegte*]." From Markus Barth's funeral booklet, 27, 32. MBL. Series V. File 13.

[83] R. Naveau-Barth to K. Watanabe, March 21, 1994. MBL. Series I. Box 32. Letters 1980s–90s.

Figure 7.6. The Barths together on the day of Rose Marie's funeral, 7 September, 1993. Left to right: Peter, Ruth, Rose-Marie, Markus, Anna with Rose-Marie's daughter Martina, Patricia Naveau (Ruth's daughter) and Bernard Naveau (Ruth's husband)

Figure 7.7. Lighting a pipe in Villa, 1992

teacher and researcher," Stegemann added that Barth's work had "increased the reputation of our university beyond Basel, Switzerland, and Europe." And with perhaps a hint of poignant regret that, so frequently in Karl's shadow, this younger Barth had not always been given his due, Stegemann apologized "for what we missed" (*Für das, was wir an ihm versäumt haben, bitten wir um Verzeihung*).[84] Even in death, it would seem, Markus could not quite escape the towering legacy of his father.

[84]E. W. Stegemann, "Gedenkensprache," Markus Barth's funeral booklet, 9. Ekkehard W. Stegemann (1945–2021) was professor of New Testament and theology at the University of Basel from 1985 until his retirement in 2013. He shared with Barth a passion for Jewish-Christian dialogue and managed—where Barth had been unsuccessful—to establish at the university a regular lectureship and foundation for Jewish Studies.

8

"I ALWAYS FELT HE WAS A KINDRED SPIRIT"

Markus Barth's Legacy

ALMOST THREE YEARS after Markus Barth's death, a young, recently graduated New Testament scholar, Peter Wick, wrote a testimonial in honor of Barth's teaching excellence. In his remarks, he spoke of Barth as "one of the few really great exegetes of this century" (*den wenigen ganz grossen Exegeten dieses Jahrhunderts zu zählen ist*).[1] Not only could Barth fill large auditoriums with students across all faculties and disciplines, his research "gave important impetus to exegesis and theology" by virtue of his willingness to depart from existing patterns of interpretation and to confront the texts "in completely new ways."[2] Donald Gowan, who studied under Barth at Dubuque, seconded Wick's glowing endorsement of Barth's pedagogical skill. "I have had many good teachers in the past," wrote Gowan in a memorial piece, "but [Markus Barth] was the only one I would call a great teacher."[3] This opinion has been affirmed once again more

[1]P. Wick, testimonial, June 19, 1997. MBMC. Series II. Correspondence. Box 4 (1990s). This fond recollection was reiterated by Wick to the author in personal correspondence, October 22, 2022. Peter Wick (1965–) studied at the Universities of Basel and Fribourg, and then at the Hebrew University of Jerusalem. His D.Theol thesis, which he completed at Basel in 1993, was on the rhetorical structure of Paul's Letter to the Philippians.

[2]Wick, testimonial.

[3]D. Gowan, "In Memory of Markus Barth: A Personal Note," *Horizons in Biblical Theology: An International Dialogue* 17, no. 2 (1995): 93.

recently by Joseph Small, who was a student of Barth's at Pittsburgh between 1963 and 1966. "He was exceedingly busy . . . and yet he gave so much of himself to me and to other students. He didn't have to do it, he did it because he was more than a scholar, more than a professor—he was a teacher."[4]

Given that for so long, Barth remained under the shadow of his father's work, this attestation from his students of his own extraordinary contribution to the teaching of biblical studies is indeed worth noting. And in an age in which research has taken the place of greater honor in university education than teaching, Markus's commitment not simply to the education but indeed the formation of his students is an increasingly rare gift. That his collection of personal correspondence is full of letters from past students with whom Barth remained in close contact, and for whom he remained a mentor and confidant, is a testament to the impact he had on them. But Markus's significance extends far beyond the New Testament academy, and arguably impacted a greater number of cognate disciplines than his father's. This final chapter, then, having now narrated the major themes and events of his life, is an attempt to summarize—and to briefly engage with—the key legacies of Markus Barth's life's work under three headings: his biblical (especially New Testament) scholarship; his contributions to a theology of the sacraments;[5] and his pioneering, though not uncontroversial, work in Jewish-Christian relations.[6]

As has been the case with the rest of this book, the aim of this closing chapter is not so much to offer an overall assessment of Barth's influence—though certainly, some degree of evaluation will be, and has been,

---

[4]J. D. Small, "The World of the Bible—Always Strange, Always New: Markus Barth as a Teacher," *Journal of Reformed Theology* 14, no. 3 (2020): 180.

[5]I use this term advisedly, instead of the simpler term "sacramental theology," for the chief reason that I think Barth would have recoiled at any suggestion that he had a "sacramental theology," insofar as that term inherently legitimizes the concept of sacraments as such. As we will see, and as has already been noted in previous chapters, Barth was determined to refuse sacramental legitimacy.

[6]These three sections correspond to the obituary written for a local newspaper by Barth's colleague at the University of Basel, Rudolf Brändle. In it, Brändle noted that there were three areas in particular in which Barth was especially interested, namely: the New Testament witness to baptism and the Lord's Supper, Pauline texts and themes, and a criticism of theological anti-Judaism. See R. Brändle, "Markus Barth gestorben," *Basellandschaftliche Zeitung*, July 5, 1994, 21.

impossible to avoid entirely—but to identify clearly what that influence in fact was. While some readers might find the absence of explicitly evaluative commentary frustrating, there is a simple reason for omitting it from this study. Insofar as Markus Barth's various works and activities ranged across multiple fields of theological inquiry and political-ecclesial concern, each with its own methodological integrity, his contributions deserve to be properly assessed by scholars with particular expertise in those various fields. So, while hopefully identifying the key elements of Barth's contributions, the purpose of this chapter is in fact to encourage others to take up the evaluative task themselves from within their own disciplinary perspectives.

Figure 8.1. Portrait in Basel

NEW TESTAMENT SCHOLARSHIP

One week after Barth's death, his son Peter received a letter of condolence from the British New Testament scholar Charles Cranfield. Born in the same year as Barth and, curiously, also a chaplain to German prisoners of war in the late 1940s, Cranfield recognized in Barth a theological ally. "My wife and I," he wrote to Peter, "were very sorry to learn of your father's death, and want to express our sincere sympathy with you and all the family at your great loss."

> I first met your father in 1939, when I was newly come to Basel, hoping to spend a year there as a student. . . . In later years I have valued his work as a New Testament scholar, and his friendship—though we met only a few times—has

meant much to me. I always felt he was a kindred spirit. I have always been encouraged by his faithful witness to the gospel, and thank God for it.[7]

Cranfield's memories are illuminating for, despite Barth's preparedness to range widely across disciplinary boundaries, Cranfield situates him squarely within New Testament scholarship. And this is where Barth was most properly at home. While he was never shy of drawing theological conclusions from his biblical studies, Markus Barth was—first and foremost—a New Testament scholar. Indeed, it was perhaps in this disciplinary expertise that he differed most from his father, who was quick to note that Markus was "by far my superior in New Testament studies."[8] If Karl was primarily a theologian who nevertheless sought always to ground his dogmatic work in Scripture, Markus was primarily a scholar of the Bible, who nevertheless sought to extrapolate his exegesis theologically. Philip Ziegler has articulated well how closely Markus tried always to keep this nexus between these two disciplines. Through his "signal and lasting contributions to Pauline scholarship," Barth became "particularly well known for bringing his biblical scholarship to bear upon contemporary theological debates."[9] As Barth himself put it, in his description for a 1990 course on "The Authority and Interpretation of the Bible," "What are the intention and limits of the talk of inspiration and authority, of the methods of biblicistic and historical-critical interpretations, [and] the use of sociological and psychological approaches and straight-jackets?" And how, Barth wished his students to ask, ought the Bible be read "whenever its message is to be taken to heart under ever changing conditions?"[10]

Barth's venture into the New Testament academy did not, however, begin with unreserved acclamation. We have seen in an earlier chapter how his doctoral thesis, under the supervision of K. L. Schmidt, was the

---

[7]C. E. B. Cranfield to P. Barth, July 7, 1944. MBMC. Subject Correspondence 3. Box 7.

[8]K. Barth, *CD* IV/4 (fragment), x.

[9]P. Ziegler, "Remembering Markus Barth: A Biblical-Theological Existence. An Introduction," *Journal of Reformed Theology* 14, no. 3 (2020): 167.

[10]Course description, "Authority and Interpretation of the Bible," January 26, 1990. Barth hoped to offer the course for the Vancouver School of Theology July 16–28, 1990. This would have been his third time at VST as a visiting scholar, following his previous trips in 1978 and 1988. In the end, ill-health prevented him from going, and so this course was never taught. MBL. Series V. File 7.

subject of intense controversy even before its formal examination. In its published form, *Der Augenzeuge* also received mixed reviews.[11] The Bavarian Jesuit, Florian Schlagenhaufen, commented that there were "quite a few objections" that could be made against the book. Not least among those objections were that Barth had, in Schlagenhaufen's opinion, made claims that could not be supported by Scripture, and had conversely ignored accounts about the apostles that Scripture does narrate. Above all, he complained that "too little attention has been paid to the genuinely early Christian conception of the Messiah."[12] Ernst Käsemann was even more scathing. Polite enough to pay tribute to Barth's energy and erudition, and to the richness of his theological ideas, Käsemann employed those compliments rather churlishly to hope that the young pastor might be able to "outgrow his present results" (*er selber über seine heutigen Ergebnisse hinauswächst*). While Käsemann thus retained faith in Barth's own scholarly future, his first book was a different story. It could never work, proclaimed Käsemann, not only because of the "serious problems" of content it contained, but more so because of the "unscientific methodology" on which it was based.[13]

Barth's final work, his posthumously published commentary on Philemon, bookended his career with similarly equivocal responses to those he had received for *Augenzeuge*. John Byron commended the work for its scale, and for its detailed historical and sociological analyses. But he also lamented an insufficient critical engagement with contemporary scholarship, which, he complained, "leav[es] the reader wondering how Barth has arrived at his conclusions and with whom he is agreeing or disagreeing."[14] Some of the book's problems were, he conceded, "not Barth's but the result of other circumstances"—by which, of course, he meant Barth's death prior to the work's completion. However, perhaps Byron's major criticism was intended directly for Barth. It was a shame,

[11]M. Barth, *Der Augenzeuge: Eine Untersuchung über die Wahrnehmung des Menschensohnes durch die Apostel* (Zollinkon-Zurich: Evangelischer Verlag, 1946).

[12]F. Schlagenhaufen, review of *Der Augenzeuge*, in *Zeitschrift für katholisches Theologie* 69, no. 2 (1947): 236.

[13]E. Käsemann, "Review of *Der Augenzeuge*," *Theologische Literaturzeitung* 73, no. 11 (1948): 670.

[14]J. Byron, "Review of *Philemon*," *Journal of Biblical Literature* 121, no. 2 (2002): 385.

argued Byron, that Barth "interacts almost exclusively with those interpretations that represent liberation theology. In some ways, Barth provides a mini-treatise on [it], in which he attempts to show that it is not based on Marxist ideology but on the tenets of the gospel."[15] "Charlie" Moule was scarcely more political. In his view, Barth's *Philemon* was a "gargantuan feast," characterized as much by its "choking mass of words" as by its exegetical care. While it did indeed contain "a great store of genuinely learned and valuable material," the commentary as a whole lacked the sparse elegance of Fitzmyer's contemporaneous commentary on the same epistle and was hindered by "unidiomatic English throughout, sometimes to the degree of unintelligibility."[16] Other reviewers, however, were much more positive. Carolyn Osiek lauded the book for its "full attention . . . to the history of scholarship on the letter" and, despite acknowledging some minor shortcomings, commended the commentary as "a major contribution to [Philemon] studies that will take its place among the most significant efforts [in the field]."[17]

Osiek's appreciation for Barth's focus on the scriptural text was evident also in Floyd Filson's generally positive reception of Barth's second book, *Die Taufe*. Certainly, Filson complained that the book was overly long—brevity seemingly as elusive for Barth at the start of his career as it was at its end!—but it was nonetheless "a thoroughgoing exegetical study," which was, in fact, where "much of [its] value" resided.[18] And clearly, this close textual concentration was where Barth's passion and skill lay. As Fred Sanders has noted, "Markus Barth was a profound exegete and a powerful expositor."[19] David MacLachlan recalls an incident that illustrates perfectly this devotion to the text—for one of Barth's seminars in Basel, in which MacLachlan was a student, the class spent an entire semester considering just the six verses of Galatians 2:15-21.[20]

---

[15]Byron, "Review of *Philemon*," 384.

[16]C. F. D. Moule, "Review of *Philemon*," *The Journal of Theological Studies* 52, no. 2 (2001): 823.

[17]C. Osiek, "Review of *Philemon*," *Biblica* 83, no. 2 (2002): 295-96.

[18]Filson, "Review of *Die Taufe*," 131.

[19]F. Sanders, "The Other Barth," August 24, 2017, https://scriptoriumdaily.com/the-other-barth/.

[20]D. MacLachlan, "Like Son, like Father: Reflections on the Influence of Markus Barth on Karl Barth's Thinking About Baptism," *Reformed Theological Journal* 14 (2020): 188n15.

Key to Barth's exegetical work was a commitment to keep all questions on the table. As he told his one-time student, and later coauthor Helmut Blanke, "Asking questions is not the problem—it's a problem when there is no self-criticism."[21] Such openness to what Barth called "scientific exegesis" (*wissenschaftlichen Exegese*) led him not only to ask controversial questions but also to adopt controversial opinions. For example, it was Barth's view not only that Ephesians was a genuinely Pauline epistle but that it—rather than Romans—was Paul's real "testament."[22]

Barth's approach to exegesis situated him in what Charles Dickinson has described as a sort of second order "biblical theology," somewhere on a continuum between his father in the 1920s and Brevard Childs in the 1970s. According to Dickinson, Markus's hermeneutical principles were best articulated in his short 1962 paper "Vom Geheimnis der Bibel" and a longer version of that paper two years later that was published as *Conversation with the Bible.*[23] The Bible, says Barth, is both a "charter of liberty" granted by God to humankind as well as a "dialogue of lovers" between the same. These characteristics set both the content and the authorization: as to content, the Hebrew and Christian Scriptures testify to God's free decision to invite humanity into a free relationship; as to authorization, the Bible is as such "'The Authority of a Charter of Liberty' by which the Holy Spirit of God in fact authorizes, inspires, and liberates not things but persons."[24] Perhaps he was overstating the case, but this hermeneutical approach of Barth's explains why Dickinson could later lament that while

> we had heard and received in full and overflowing measure from Markus—in and out of class—about the greatness of God, the "good news" of Christ, and many other priceless theological treasures, we had never heard from him about form criticism, redaction criticism, or the history of traditions. "Demythologizing" was a sacrilege, for there neither was nor could be any

---

[21]H. Blanke, "Markus Barth Biografie," 2. MBL. Series II. Box 1.

[22]Blanke, "Markus Barth Biografie," 3. The epistle to the Romans represented, because of its emphasis on justification, a "foreshortening" (*Verkürzung*) of Paul's theology.

[23]C. Dickinson, "Markus Barth and Biblical Theology: A Personal Re-View," *Horizons in Biblical Theology* 17, no. 2 (1995): 104. See also M. Barth, "Vom Geheimnis der Bibel," *Theologische Existenz heute* 100 (1962): 1-46; and M. Barth, *Conversations with the Bible* (New York: Holt, Rinehart and Winston, 1964).

[24]Dickinson, "Markus Barth and Biblical Theology," 104.

"myth" in the Bible. The "quest for the historical Jesus" was errant nonsense: Albert Schweitzer had shown that; and the "new quest" of E. Käsemann, G. Bornkamm, and J. M. Robinson was nonsense on stilts.[25]

A more positive interpretation of Barth's hermeneutics is provided by Joseph Small. Having experienced the same teacher as Dickinson in some of the very same classes, he recalls that "what struck [him] at the outset . . . was Markus's conviction that these writings [the Bible] were, in a profound sense, true."[26] While committed, as we have seen, to "scientific exegesis"—of a sort that might produce five hundred pages of commentary on just twenty-five verses of Scripture!—Barth's truest passion, as both theologian and pastor, was for "the unique power of the Bible that flows from the fact that the biblical words are words of love between God and man." To read the Bible properly, therefore, was to read it as one might read "love letters, rather than the study of a law book."[27]

Of course, central to Barth's New Testament scholarship was his determination to employ it in the service of that other great passion of his, Jewish-Christian dialogue. Not that the scriptural word should be interpreted in light of a nonscriptural precommitment to a Jewish-Christian a priori. On the contrary, for Barth—as indeed had been the case for his father, Karl—the message of the Bible explicitly mandates a critical yet indissoluble solidarity of the church with both the biblical and postbiblical Jewish people. That is, the Bible *precedes* socio-theological commitments, not the other way around. For Karl Barth, "The people of Israel with whom the Yahweh of the Old Testament entered into covenant, and the community of the New Testament which has Jesus Christ as its Head . . . are no chance conglomeration of individuals, but whole, and indeed in the strictest sense a single whole . . . with a common justification and sanctification."[28]

---

[25]Dickinson, "Markus Barth and Biblical Theology," 97. Dickinson laid the same charge directly to Barth, in a letter from 1976. "I remember no mention of such methods [in your classes at Pittsburgh] either. Indeed you said you 'presupposed' such critical methods in your own theological exegesis; but you never discussed [them], to my recollection, except to put them down." C. Dickinson to M. Barth, January 7, 1976. MBMC. Series II. Correspondence. Box 23, file 567.

[26]Small, "The World of the Bible," 173.

[27]Barth, *Conversations with the Bible*, 9.

[28]K. Barth, *CD* III/3, 190.

Writing at the very time of the Sho'ah, Karl was compelled by the insistent and unrelenting witness of Scripture and not by any secularized notion of a "common humanity" requiring an unbreakable solidarity of the church with the Jews. The particular community of the elect, as the community of Israel and the church, is what one must encounter if one is to "keep to Holy Scripture."[29]

Markus put the matter somewhat more directly. Writing in 1984 of the message of Ephesians—which, as we have seen, he understood to be the determinative summary of Paul's teaching—he insisted that "the presumption and basis of [the apostle's] thinking and writing are . . . the reconciliation and unification of Jews and Gentiles through Jesus Christ. . . . In this letter, Christ is not without the church, the church not without Jews and Gentiles." Indeed, the "unification of Jews and Gentiles is the first, fundamental and paradigmatic event upon which depend and follow the overcoming of sexual, historical, economical divisions."[30] Far from being a primary commitment before and outside of Scripture, Barth thus exegetes Scripture—in this case, the letter to the Ephesians—as providing the hermeneutical ground for the church's solidarity with the Jews.

His reasoning was spelled out in greater detail in both *The Broken Wall* and his Anchor Bible commentary on Ephesians. In the former, which he wrote as "a study book for evangelism"[31] that was based on Ephesians, Barth says that "the church lives in a special relationship with Israel. . . . By 'Israel' we understand not only ancient Israel . . . [nor] do today's Jews in their dispersion over the world (or in the young state of Israel) exhaust what is meant."[32] Clearly implying a generously comprehensive definition of the "Israel" that is in solidarity with the church, Barth goes on to insist that, while Paul elsewhere (such as Gal 3:28; Col 3:11; and 1 Cor 12:13) includes Jews and Gentiles "as but one among many of the inimical pairs that

---

[29]K. Barth, *CD* II/2, 195-96. Note that the term *Sho'ah* has become, for many Jews, the preferable word to refer to the Nazis' genocidal persecution of European Jewry and so will be used interchangeably with the more common—but these days less preferred—*Holocaust*.

[30]M. Barth, "Traditions in Ephesians," *New Testament Studies* 30 (1984): 18-19, 22-23.

[31]J. Morikawa, "Foreword," in M. Barth, *The Broken Wall: A Study of the Epistle to the Ephesians* (Valley Forge, PA: Judson, 1959), 7.

[32]Barth, *Broken Wall*, 123.

have been reconciled,"[33] in Ephesians it is primarily and fundamentally the reconciliation between Jews and Gentiles that is the foundation of all other social healings. "According to Ephesians, social peace in any realm and in any form is a consequence of the peace which was made between Jews and Gentiles."[34]

Similarly in his two-volume commentary on the same letter, Barth argues that "the members of the church are not so equalized, leveled down, or straitjacketed in a uniform as to form a *genus tertium* that would be different from both Jews and Gentiles. Rather the church consists of Jews and Gentiles reconciled to one another by the Messiah who has come and died for both."[35] The resulting "'one new man' is . . . an organic body consisting of distinct members . . . a continuous mutual encounter, exchange, bewildering or joyful surprise of free persons. . . . Above all, the joining of 'the two' into 'one new' whole reveals that neither of the two can possess salvation, peace, life without the other. Jews need Gentiles, Gentiles need Jews . . . [in order to be] saved at all."[36] As Randi Rashkover has rightly observed, "Barth's moral claims concerning Jewish-Christian relations derived from his *scripturally based* understanding of the theological significance of the Jews."[37]

Later in the chapter, we will explore Barth's singular contribution to Jewish-Christian dialogue in more detail. The point here is simply to highlight the direction of his methodology. Whether the matter at hand was the relationship between Christians and Jews, questions of ecclesial polity, or sociopolitical controversies in 1960s America, Barth began from his expertise as a New Testament exegete, and only then proceeded to the presenting issue.[38] Paul Nimmo, in a slightly different context, rightly

---

[33]Barth, *Broken Wall*, 125.

[34]Barth, *Broken Wall*, 125.

[35]M. Barth, *Ephesians: Introduction, Translation, and Commentary on Chapters 1–3*, Anchor Bible 34 (New York: Doubleday, 1974), 310.

[36]Barth, *Ephesians*, 311.

[37]R. Rashkover, "Markus Barth: The Jews Are Our Brothers," *Journal of Reformed Theology* 14 (2020): 264. Emphasis added.

[38]One might recall in this context his insistence in 1951 that the authors of any church constitution must, above all, "have a desire to love and obey the Bible"; and the grounding of his critique of Eisenhower's foreign policy in Ps 72.

Figure 8.2. Portrait in Basel

identifies Barth's trajectory: there is "a clear sense of the ordering of the theological disciplines—*from* exegesis *to* theology and practice."[39] To put it slightly differently, the contemporary context was the environment into which the Bible *must be allowed* to speak, not the arbiter of how the Bible *must be made* to speak. It was perhaps this prioritization of listening to the scriptural text that endeared Barth to his colleagues, even when they did not always see eye-to-eye. As Barth's Swiss contemporary Eduard Schweizer recalled, despite differing on some basic theological presuppositions, "there was an inner attitude . . . in which we were completely one."[40]

A THEOLOGY OF THE SACRAMENTS

In correspondence with the Baptist theologian Bernard Ramm in 1983, Markus noted that in Karl's own opinion, Markus's best books were those "that went beyond [Karl's] thinking." At the time, and despite his "unkind health," Markus was endeavoring to "finish a book on the Lord's Supper for which my father had asked me and which agrees and differs as much from his previous teaching as my book on baptism did."[41] These remarks lead us into the second major area in which Markus Barth's legacy can and must

[39]P. Nimmo, "Markus Barth on the Lord's Supper," *Journal of Reformed Theology* 14 (2020): 202.

[40]E. Schweizer to P. Barth et al., 1994. MBL. Series II. Box 1.

[41]M. Barth to B. L. Ramm, July 5, 1983. MBMC. Series II. Correspondence. Box 3 (1980s). Bernard L. Ramm (1916–1992), primarily a Christian apologist, had spent the academic year 1957–1958 with Karl Barth in Basel. His 1983 book *After Fundamentalism*—the publication of which was the reason

be appreciated. We have already noted Karl Barth's comment that Markus was his superior in biblical scholarship. Significantly, Karl made that remark in his final, fragmentary writings on baptism, for it is here—in the field that would ordinarily, but with Markus cannot properly, be called "sacramental theology"—that Markus's development of and divergence from his father's theology is perhaps best demonstrated. Before considering Markus's understanding of such matters, then, and the ways in which he agreed with and differed from his father, it is helpful to review the changing nature of Karl's theology of the sacraments.

George Hunsinger helpfully and rightly notes that there is "no systematic account of 'sacrament' or 'sacraments' in Karl Barth's mature theology. His discussion of these concepts is always occasional, ad hoc, and secondary to other concerns."[42] Nevertheless, it would be incorrect to conclude that Barth is uninterested in the sacraments or consistently negative toward them. Despite Jüngel's claim that Barth's antisacramentalist theology of baptism as presented in the final fragments of *CD* IV/4 is the hermeneutical key to the entire *Dogmatics*,[43] in fact his sacramental theology is nuanced and changeable. To refer again to Hunsinger, "Barth changed his mind significantly [on this question] while writing *Church Dogmatics*."[44] So, for example, we see throughout the 1920s–1930s Barth employing sacramental terminology, at least with respect to baptism, seemingly with little difficulty. This is not to say that he ever granted to sacraments any effective power to mediate grace. Thus, in his lectures on the Reformed confessions, he says: "It must be emphasized that the sacraments effect nothing through their own power. . . . Grace cannot be bound to the sacraments in such a way that whoever receives the signs receives *eo ipso* the matter."[45]

for the correspondence with Markus—was highly regarded by Markus as a "glorious" illustration of the central role played by preaching in the early development of dialectical theology.

[42]G. Hunsinger, "Sacraments," in *The Oxford Handbook of Karl Barth*, ed. P. D. Jones and P. T. Nimmo (Oxford: Oxford University Press, 2019), 451. See also my "The Abandonment of Inauthentic Humanity: Barth's Theology of Baptism as the Ground and Goal of Mission," *Pacifica* 26, no. 3 (2013): 229-45.

[43]See E. Jüngel, *Barth-Studien* (Zurich: Benziger 1982), 285-87.

[44]Hunsinger, "Sacraments," 451.

[45]K. Barth, *The Theology of the Reformed Confessions*, trans. D. L. Guder and J. J. Guder (Louisville: Westminster John Knox, 2002), 177.

Nonetheless, the elder Barth was able to grant to the sacraments the character of necessary witness, with baptism being described by him as the *sacramentum initiationis*, the attestation of "my re-birth by the Spirit."[46] It is true that by the 1950s, Karl was very much less enamored of the whole idea. He would, he said to an English-speaking seminar class in Basel, "prefer to abrogate the word 'sacraments' entirely, or alternatively 'use [it] for all ecclesiastical actions.'" "Sacraments," he is recorded as saying, "do not play such a great role in the New Testament as they do in the brains of many theologians."[47] However, as we have seen, this more critical assessment of the place and role of sacraments was not in fact representative of Karl's longer history of sacramental engagement.

In contrast, Markus is generally assumed to have been more consistently opposed to any sacramentalism within his own theology and pastoral practice. To what extent this was in fact the case is the question to which we now turn. It is worth noting at the outset that, as Paul Nimmo has put it, there has been a "lamentable neglect" of scholarship on this aspect of Barth's theology.[48] Nonetheless, there are some things that can and should be said.

Baptism. As discussed in earlier chapters, Barth's 1951 book *Die Taufe* had put "a sacramental understanding of baptism . . . on the defensive."[49] Indeed, Barth's insistence on retaining the question mark in the book's title was purposeful—without it, the sacramentality of baptism might have been presumed, thus implying the opposite of Barth's entire argument.[50] In the book, he stated unequivocally, "In the New Testament neither the word 'sacrament,' nor the word '(necessary) sign' . . . is ever used as a term for baptism. . . . There is no talk about, magical or mythical, causative or rational, real or kerygmatic, a realization or a making present in connection with the carrying out of baptism."[51]

---

[46]K. Barth, *The Heidelberg Catechism for Today*, trans. S. C. Guthrie (London: Epworth, 1964), 96, 100.

[47]K. Barth, *Karl Barth's Table Talk*, ed. J. Godsey, SJOT Occasional Papers 10 (Edinburgh: Oliver & Boyd, 1963), 86.

[48]Nimmo, "Markus Barth," 201.

[49]MacLachlan, "Like Son, like Father," 185.

[50]MacLachlan, "Like Son, like Father," 188-89.

[51]M. Barth, *Die Taufe—Ein Sakrament? Ein exegetischer Beitrag zum Gespräch über die kirchlicher Taufe* (Zurich: Evangelischer Verlag, 1951), 11.

By being baptized, Barth wished to stress, one makes a confession that has the character of repentance but does not thereby enact anything that is, as such, *effective*. As the Anglican liturgist Bryan Spinks says, Barth's primary theological point was that "baptism is not an unfailing tool which effects what it portrays, but is to be understood as confession, obedience, hope and prayer. It is not a sacrament, but a rite which indicates what has already been effected by the free work of God."[52]

Nonetheless, the book left a number of questions unanswered, at least to some readers. Earl Stuckenbruck, for example, who at the time was working with the European Evangelistic Society in Tübingen, queried the utility of baptism in Barth's theology, if it was "devoid of any representative or efficacious significance."[53] Barth's response was that baptismal value was to be found in the obedience of response to Christ's command, and not in the rite as such. He was prepared to accept that it remained unclear whether this act of obedience was a work "performed by God on man, or a work offered by man to God." Nevertheless, he was adamant that clarity on this point could be found only in a better doctrine of the Holy Spirit, and not in "the traditional doctrine of sacraments."[54]

Eight years after *Die Taufe*, Barth returned to a consideration of baptism in an article for the *Scottish Journal of Theology*. The choice of journal is intriguing, in that he was deliberately taking issue in the article with Tom Torrance who, as editor of *SJT* had, according to Barth, been prosecuting a form of high church sacramentalism within the journal's pages. While Barth did not mention Torrance by name, the Scotsman's views were clearly in Barth's sights.

In his opening claim, Barth lamented that the church's understanding of baptism had deteriorated to it being simply "an event or act of *pious* individual or collective, *egotism*." This interpretation of the rite was, said Barth, driven by the quest for certainty of salvation. In this context, "High Church scholars and liberal Baptist orators" were alike in their teaching of baptism

[52]B. Spinks, *Reformation and Modern Rituals and Theologies of Baptism: From Luther to Contemporary Practices* (Aldershot: Ashgate, 2006), 140.

[53]E. Stuckenbruck to M. Barth, April 2, 1953. MBMC. Subject Correspondence 1. Box 5.

[54]M. Barth to E. Stuckenbruck, May 15, 1953. MBMC. Subject Correspondence 1. Box 5.

as "an event between God and the baptizand, a means of God's grace for the sinner."[55] Logically consequent upon this misunderstanding was a presumption, he argued, that baptism—insofar as it adds to the membership of the church—constitutes "the victory of the Church over the world." Baptism becomes nothing other than "an orderly . . . act of expansion and increase of what is sometimes called the mystical body of Christ. It not only indicates, but is, progress of the Kingdom, of the Church."[56]

There was also a clericalism that accrued to this interpretation, to which Barth was especially allergic. Once baptism is understood as being a "re-presentation and *actualisation* . . . of God's work," the inevitable consequence is that "God's, Christ's, the Spirit's sphere of activity is co-extensive with the Church's, that redemption becomes actual only if handled by the ordained minister or priest, that the sacramental. . . . Church is somehow medium or channel of grace between God and the world."[57]

Rather than pointing people to Christ, the church, said Barth, became by this conception of baptism a means in itself. "The Church [has become] busy with herself when she teaches and administers baptism." Baptism was thus rendered "a magical act . . . or like a sort of kabbala," with the end result being a doctrine and practice of baptism that was separated from its New Testament origins, and in particular from its association with evangelism.[58]

In place of this ecclesiocentric doctrine of baptism, Barth proposed instead a return to the pattern of John the Baptist. Far from being "a super-ritual, a really effective ritual," John's baptism was "a form of prophetic protest against misused, misunderstood . . . temple service [and] priesthood."[59] Startlingly, Barth then suggested that, in conformity with this pattern, baptism is properly understood only as an ethical rite, "not a 'liturgical rite.'" Thus, stripped of all liturgical content—"if liturgy is (falsely) understood to mean a holy interaction or effective mutual 'remembrance' between God and the worshipping community"—baptism becomes

---

[55]M. Barth, "Baptism and Evangelism," *Scottish Journal of Theology* 12, no. 1 (March 1959): 32.
[56]Barth, "Baptism and Evangelism," 34.
[57]Barth, "Baptism and Evangelism," 34.
[58]Barth, "Baptism and Evangelism," 35.
[59]Barth, "Baptism and Evangelism," 36.

proclamatory only: "a public attestation and proclamation . . . of what has been and will be 'completed' in Christ."[60] Once again, this time in the more positive connection of how baptism *should* be understood, Barth associated it with evangelism—that is, with the church's external gaze to those who are strangers rather than with the church's internal preoccupation with mediatorial liturgies.

Surprisingly, perhaps, Barth employed the word *sacrament* only six times throughout the entire article—once positively in relation to Augustine, and five other times in relation to doctrines and practices that Barth believed to be wrong. Nonetheless, it is clear that in this piece Barth was developing further his critique of baptismal sacramentality that he began with his earlier book, *Die Taufe*. His scathing repudiation of "High Churchmanship," with its (alleged) emphasis on the church as the site of liturgical mediation between sinners and God, and his reprioritization of the ethical and (purely) proclamatory character of baptism, were none-too-subtle swipes at the journal's editor, Tom Torrance. They were also, however, his now categorical responses to the questions that had been left unanswered by the 1951 book. If *Die Taufe* had retained a question mark in the title—*Ein Sakrament?*—the *SJT* article decisively and forever removed it. After 1959, it was simply impossible to read Barth as keeping baptismal sacramentality on the table.

This antisacramentalist conviction, built as it was on "formidable exegetical study,"[61] had ramifications beyond Barth's own academic work. As was shown earlier, it was central to his falling out with the Scottish theologian Tom Torrance in the early 1950s, with the latter being accused by Barth of theologically illegitimate high-church sacramentalism. Ten years later, the same convictions led to Barth's highly critical response to the Blake-Pike Proposal for church union. Whereas the proposal "treat[ed] the sacraments as the untouchable center" of church life, Barth insisted that they were vital but not grace-giving "expressions of the mode of life" that is proper to the children of God.[62]

[60] Barth, "Baptism and Evangelism," 38.
[61] MacLachlan, "Like Son, like Father," 184.
[62] M. Barth, "The Blake Proposal: Pool of the Rich or Pilgrimage of Servants," *McCormick Quarterly* 15, no. 3 (1962): 6.

Thus, as he said in correspondence with Frits Kuiper in 1962, "Baptism is not an act of *making* them covenant partners. It is rather an act by which, upon the work of the Spirit and the Word, God makes them acknowledge that they do belong to it—and that they have done so ever since the crucifixion and resurrection of Jesus Christ."[63]

Barth remained steadfastly convinced of this throughout the rest of his life. Indeed, by 1970 he seemed certain that he would not be altering his views. When invited to deliver the Menno Simons Lectures at Bethel College in October of that year on the topic of baptism, he balked—he could do so, he advised Cornelius Krahn, but the content would be "old manna warmed up and rehashed," suggesting that Barth's opinions had not significantly changed over the preceding twenty years and were unlikely to change into the future.[64] As he penned in a letter during his visit to Japan in 1987, "Your accounts of how and why and when you became Christian confirmed my view that baptism is an act of confession (and not of quasi-mechanical addition of church members)."[65]

The Lord's Supper. Barth's interest in theologies of the sacraments is evident also in his published works on eucharistic theology, consisting primarily of three main (and relatively short) works, namely: "Das Abendmahl" (1945), the more concise "Gemeindeaufbau in biblischer Sicht" (1947), and *Das Mahl des Herrn* (1986), the last of which represents his final and most considered word on the subject. As we will see, there is an increasingly antisacramentalist posture adopted by Barth as he develops his thoughts across these texts. Certainly, his rejection of eucharistic sacramentality was

[63]M. Barth to F. Kuiper, December 2, 1962. In MBMC. Series II. Correspondence. Box 9, file 304. Note that the "them" to whom Barth is referring is "the whole of mankind, all Jews and all Gentiles."

[64]M. Barth to C. Krahn, March 29, 1970. MBMC. Series II. Correspondence. Box 2 (1970s).

[65]M. Barth to unknown, April 1987. MBL. Series II. Box 13. The letter is curious for a number of reasons. First, it is written in Rose Marie's handwriting, not Markus's, and yet—insofar as it refers to the author "hav[ing] held a 3-hour seminar on baptism" at the International Christian University in Tokyo—almost certainly conveys Markus's thoughts. Quite possibly, it was dictated by Markus to his wife. Second, the heading at the top of the letter says "For Rose-Marie." However, she has confirmed that, on the basis of various other details in the letter, she was not, and could not have been, the intended recipient. Whoever the recipient was, the ideas about baptism conveyed within it confirm and correspond precisely with Markus's previously articulated theology of baptism.

largely fixed by the time of the 1947 article, but the principal rationale for its rejection had changed by the mid-1980s.

In the first of these works, originally delivered as a lecture to fellow Reformed pastors in October 1945, Barth chose to focus on the Synoptic accounts of the Lord's Supper as his primary biblical source material, with a slight preference for the Markan narrative over against the Matthean and Lukan versions. As for the John 6 and the 1 Corinthian passages—those texts that have typically been the ground of doctrinal determinations regarding the Lord's Supper—Barth certainly understood them to be "no less important." Nevertheless, he advised that they be employed only where necessary, and as commentaries on the more central synoptic texts (*nur wo nötig als Kommentare*).[66] His thinking seems to have been that they were evidence of later ecclesial developments and not themselves reflective of what we might call Jesus' own *Urabsicht* ("original intent"). Such an exegetical choice was necessary, he believed, in order to rehabilitate the church's very earliest conception of the Lord's Supper not merely as a Passover meal, but indeed as the Passover's crowning (*Krönung*) and telos.[67]

When read in this light, the meal can—indeed, Barth would say, must—be understood as a celebratory covenant meal that serves as "a corporate act of memory in which the congregation recalls with joy and gratitude the reconciliation effected in Jesus Christ."[68] What it does not do is in any way *effect* that reconciliation itself. It is entirely consistent with this, then, that Jesus' own words "do not contain any statement concerning the substance of bread and wine." What is important is the use to which the elements are put, not the substance that they contain.[69]

For Barth, however, this did not mean that the meal was *merely* memorial. There is, in the sharing of the meal, an "event of a divine deed in human occurrence," which consists in the impartation of the benefits of Jesus' death to those who gather to eat.[70] Barth's language at this point is

[66]M. Barth, *Das Abendmahl: Passamahl, Bundesmahl, und Messiasmahl*, Theologische Studien 18 (Zürich: Evangelischer Verlag, 1945), 5. See also Nimmo, "Markus Barth," 204.

[67]Barth, *Das Abendmahl*, 7; Nimmo, "Markus Barth," 210.

[68]Nimmo, "Markus Barth," 210.

[69]Barth, *Das Abendmahl*, 17, 20. See also Nimmo, "Markus Barth," 205-6.

[70]Barth, *Das Abendmahl*, 24, 31.

careful and nuanced. On one hand, the divine activity at the heart of the meal is not to be considered in the manner of an *opus operatum*. In a sense, Jesus' presence in the meal becomes true insofar as the Lord's Supper is the epitome (*Inbegriff*) of his promise to be, by the Spirit, where two or three are gathered in his name.[71] Nonetheless, Jesus' words over the bread and wine—"This is my body," and "This is my blood"—"state what actually takes place or is effected in the physical action." The event of the meal becomes "the physical form of the spoken Word."[72] While not in any traditional sense a sacramental reading of the Lord's Supper, Barth here offers something that is clearly more than memorialist.

Paul Nimmo has rightly noted that this first contribution from Barth to eucharistic theology was ambitious, responsive to contemporary church concerns, and driven by a determination to ground the debate in the witness of Scripture. While his exegetical decisions and hermeneutical methods were at times "cavalier," this short book nevertheless set the ground for much of his later work on the Lord's Supper.

Two years later, Barth published his second study on the Eucharist, "Gemeinde Aufbau in biblischer Sicht." Three features of this article differentiate it from the earlier publication. First, Barth's exegetical focus is 1 Corinthians. Elevated from its status in "Das Abendmahl" as only a "commentary" on the Synoptic texts, Barth here prioritizes the Pauline material over the Gospel accounts. Second, and the reason for this exegetical reprioritization, is Barth's focus on the Lord's Supper as a community-building event. The emphasis in this work is less on the character of the Lord's Supper as a messianic Passover and much more on its purpose as a meal that creates community out of hitherto-alienated people. "The aim, content, and success of the Lord's Supper is the creation and representation of a community that is different from all other associations and communities."[73] And third, whereas Barth's language in "Das Abendmahl" allowed for a lightly sacramentalist reading, that possibility has largely disappeared from

---

[71]Barth, *Das Abendmahl*, 49.

[72]Barth, *Das Abendmahl*, 23.

[73]M. Barth, "Gemeindeaufbau in biblischer Sicht," *Kirchenfreund: Blätter für biblisches Bekennen in der Kirche* 81, no. 6 (March 1947): 82.

the 1947 work. There, the presence of Christ can be found not in the substance of bread and wine, nor in the liturgical actions over the bread and wine at their consecration. Barth insists that Paul's theology allows us "neither an escape into material mysticism, nor into a superstitious belief in the efficacy of a cultic act." On the contrary, Christ is present in the fellowship that is established at his own table; he is present in the forgiveness and justification that are not given but only witnessed to in that table fellowship. And, if he is in any sense bodily present, it is only in the sister and brother who join in the thanksgiving, and who share the cup and the bread.[74]

That this antisacramentalist posture was where Barth was heading is confirmed by a letter he wrote to George Mendenhall toward the end of his time in Dubuque. Speaking of the "theological exploitation of the Eucharist," Barth noted that his own research had demonstrated "the great differences between the respective NT teaching and the Churches' (prot[estantism] included) sacramentalism," and thanked Mendenhall for his "general attack on sacramental institutionalism"—an attack that had to be launched "as soon as possible."[75]

In the late-1980s, fully four decades after his first published work on eucharistic theology, Barth returned to the subject in what would prove to be one of the last pieces of writing he would live to see published. In 1986, he had delivered a series of lectures in Pittsburgh, Dubuque, and Ann Arbor. The lectures were subsequently published in German and in abbreviated form in English.[76] Just as in 1945 he had appealed for a new understanding (*Neubesinnung*) of the Lord's Supper, in these latter lectures he noted again the urgent need for doctrinal and exegetical reappraisal. "A language," he said, "has been fabricated for describing the mystery" of this

---

[74]Barth, "Gemeindeaufbau in biblischer Sicht," 83.

[75]M. Barth to G. Mendenhall, April 23, 1955. George Mendenhall (1916–2016) was a Lutheran minister and Old Testament scholar who, having earned a PhD in Semitic languages from Johns Hopkins University in 1947, taught at the University of Michigan from 1952 to 1986.

[76]The lectures were delivered at Pittsburgh as the Schaff Lectures, as the Donnell Lectures at the theological seminary of the University of Dubuque, and at the University of Michigan. In the published versions, they appeared as *Das Mahl des Herrn* (Neukirch-Vluyn: Neukirchener Verlag, 1987); and *Rediscovering the Lord's Supper: Communion with Israel, with Christ, and Among the Guests* (Atlanta: John Knox, 1988). The English translation was, according to Nimmo, a "concise paraphrase" of the original German text. See Nimmo, "Markus Barth," 202.

meal—a language "that is certainly learned, deep [and] mysterious, but hardly very clear and persuasive. . . . The Supper," Barth lamented, "has been wrapped in a smokescreen."[77]

Barth's response to this so-called fabrication was once again to turn to Scripture. This time, however, and in marked contrast to the earlier two publications, he deliberately engaged with all four Gospels as well as the Pauline epistles. Where he was consistent with his 1945 work was his opening insistence that the Lord's Supper, in its first iteration in the Gospels, was a "carefully prepared and properly conducted Passover meal."[78] Precisely here, though, is the reason for Barth's now-adamant denial of the eucharistic meal's sacramentality. Just as the Passover itself was instituted as "a memorial to a unique, complete, and perfect act of God"[79]—a remembrance that excludes, for Barth, any sense of repetition, validation, actualization, or even application of God's basic action—so too the Lord's Supper is to be understood as a memorial that excludes any "presentation or re-presentation of the death of Jesus . . . [either] symbolically or otherwise."[80] As Nimmo notes, both events are characterized as events of remembrance of liberation, not events of liberation per se.[81] Going much further than he did in 1945, Barth repudiated the "widespread, high sacramental understanding of the Lord's Supper," according to which Jesus is both "giver *and* the gift."[82] "The Gospels," he said, "never speak of *real presence*."[83] Moreover, "the term sacrament" is itself "nonbiblical."[84] Arguing that the Lord's Supper cannot be seen to have "the causative, effective, creative—in short, sacramental—power of pagan cultic actions" of which St. Paul, in his letter to the Corinthians, showed an awareness, Barth insisted instead that the eucharistic meal belongs to the discursive world of the Jewish Passover, which is "significative and proclamatory."[85]

---

[77]Barth, *Rediscovering the Lord's Supper*, 2.
[78]Barth, *Das Mahl des Herrn*, 21.
[79]Barth, *Rediscovering the Lord's Supper*, 12
[80]Nimmo, "Markus Barth," 213.
[81]Nimmo, "Markus Barth," 223.
[82]Barth, *Rediscovering the Lord's Supper*, 18.
[83]Barth, *Rediscovering the Lord's Supper*, 51.
[84]Barth, *Rediscovering the Lord's Supper*, 101.
[85]Barth, *Rediscovering the Lord's Supper*, 36-37.

That Barth was concerned to keep the eucharistic meal totally distinct from any hint of association with pagan ritual processes might be thought of as sufficient cause for his rejection of its sacramentality. However, as has been hinted, there was an even more decisive reason. A sacramentalist hermeneutic, in Barth's opinion, severed the covenantal unity of Christians and Jews. We have noted already that Barth had deemed Jewish-Christian dialogue to be a theological matter of first importance since at least the 1960s. Much of that work had focused on questions of covenant, Israel's political legitimacy, and the elimination of supersessionary hermeneutics. Now, in the last decade of his life, Barth brought this commitment to Jewish-Christian unity to bear on his theology of the sacraments. Sacramentalism, he said, "makes obsolete all elements of remembrance and celebration that may tie the church to Israel."[86] To put it otherwise, if the primary gathering meal of the church, by which the church is itself constituted as a community of hitherto-alienated peoples, finds its historical and meaningful ground in the memorial act of the Jewish Passover, and if that nexus point is the decisive illustration of a necessary "spiritual communion between Israel and the church"—that is, that "worship by Christians is the participation of Gentiles in the worship of the Jews"[87]—then to sacramentalize the Lord's Supper is to render it incomprehensible in light of its historic origins in Passover and thus sunder the Jewish-Christian continuity that the meal is in fact intended to describe.

Clearly, Barth's final rejection of sacramental theologies of the Eucharist was consistent with his published views from the 1940s, if nonetheless more stridently expressed. Further, his grounding of his own eucharistic theology in *exegesis*—"Bible study is necessary whenever a church is open to . . . rediscovering the meal instituted by Jesus Christ"—was a common thread across all three publications, from 1945 through to 1986. But in basing his rejection of sacramentalism in his commitment to Jewish-Christian solidarity, Barth was introducing a distinctive new element into the conversation that drew upon arguably his life's greatest work. It is to this that we now turn our attention in this final section of the book.

---

[86]Barth, *Rediscovering the Lord's Supper*, 27.

[87]Barth, *Rediscovering the Lord's Supper*, 26-27.

JEWISH-CHRISTIAN RELATIONS

In an oft-quoted letter of 1967 to F.-W. Marquardt, Karl Barth noted that his own visceral and "irrational aversion" toward Jews was thankfully not to be found in his sons.[88] It is a matter of continuing debate whether in criticizing himself in this way, Karl was being unnecessarily harsh or was rather finally owning up to his anti-Jewish shortcomings. The fact that Yad Vashem, in bestowing upon the Protestant pastor Hans Schaffert the title of "Righteous Among the Nations," noted that his "feelings of solidarity toward the Jews started during the days he studied theology with Prof. Karl Barth in Basel," suggests that the elder Barth's self-criticism was not as justified as he seems to have thought.[89] In any event, we are left with a father's assessment of his sons that paints them in a much more favorable light. But if Karl perceived himself wrongly in this matter, was he also mistaken about his children? In particular, what were the overall contours of Markus's engagement with Jews and with Jewish-Christian relations?

It was seen earlier that when Markus Barth decided in 1972 to return to Basel, he did so bearing the extraordinary description from Guido Kisch of being one of the genuine "*chaside omit ha-olam*" of the time.[90] This, however, was not the only honor bestowed upon him in recognition of his many contributions to Jewish-Christian dialogue over the years. In January 1994, Barth received word from the Citizen Ambassador Program that he had been selected to be part of a Jewish Studies delegation to Russia, Poland, and Hungary that was due to take place in June of the same year. It seems that he had not applied himself for this opportunity—indeed, that would have been highly unlikely given his rapidly deteriorating health and his acceptance of the limitations that this now placed upon him. Rather, he

[88]K. Barth to F.-W. Marquardt, September 5, 1967, in *Letters, 1961–1968*, ed. J. Fangmeier and H. Stoevesandt, trans. G. W. Bromiley (Grand Rapids, MI: Eerdmans, 1981), 262.

[89]See the encomium published by Yad Vashem for Hans Schaffert following his recognition in 1967 as a "Righteous Among the Nations." https://righteous.yadvashem.org/?search=schaffert&searchType=righteous_only&language=en&itemId=4017355&ind=0. Alongside Schaffert, three other people, whose actions during World War II on behalf of Jews were so courageous that they have been honored by Yad Vashem as being "Righteous Among the Nations," are also acknowledged by Yad Vashem as having been significantly influenced by Karl Barth. They are Charles Westphal, Ruth Wendland, and Helene Jacobs.

[90]The term used by Kisch means "the righteous ones of the nations of the world."

had been "selected to receive this invitation because of [his] activity within the field of Jewish Studies."[91] As early as September 1962, in fact, Barth had been invited by Stephen Schwarzschild to speak to the Massachusetts Board of Rabbis on the topic of Jewish-Christian dialogue.[92]

There is, in other words, little doubt that Markus Barth was a genuine pioneer—at least from the Christian side—of Jewish-Christian dialogue at a time that, when he was most active in it, the field was still in its infancy.[93] As Randi Rashkover has rightly observed, "Markus Barth's work"—and notably, she also includes Karl's work in this assessment—"can be appreciated as a tireless effort to exegetically re-order Jewish-Christian relations."[94] Rashkover's comment highlights a point that has already been made: that Barth's sense of solidarity with the Jewish people was the fruit not merely of a humanistic impulse but of sustained reflection on the witness of Scripture. Nevertheless, as previous episodes through this book have illustrated, Barth's *actual* relations with Jews, not least his engagement with the State of Israel, were characterized by frequent and often censorious critique. Again, as Rashkover puts it—and again, much like the case with Karl—there is a certain tension within Markus Barth's paradigm for Jewish-Christian dialogue "between rhetoric and action, culture and practice" that combines to "put his own discourse about the brotherhood of Christians and Jews into crisis."[95] In this final section of the book, then, we will seek to survey some of Markus's engagements with Jewish-Christian dialogue and to identify those points of progress and those points of tension.

Personal relationships. In the first instance, it is helpful to note that throughout his adult life, Markus had a good number of close relationships with Jews. His father was often, and wrongly, accused of having only a

[91]Letter to M. Barth, January 10, 1994. MBMC. Series II. Correspondence. Box 4 (1990s).

[92]S. Schwarzschild to M. Barth, September 1962. MBMC. Series II. Correspondence. Box 8, file 310.

[93]Post-Holocaust Jewish-Christian dialogue was initially driven by the churches through the 1960s–70s. Only from the 1980s did it become part of critical inquiry within the academy. R. Rendtorff, "Der Dialog hat erst begonnen," in *Christen und Juden im Gespräch: Eine Bilanz nach 40 Jahren Staat Israel*, ed. G. Manfred et al. (Regensburg: Verlag Friedrich Pustet, 1989), 41-55; also K. H. Holtschneider, *German Protestants Remember the Holocaust: Theology and the Construction of Collective Memory* (Münster: Lit Verlag, 2001), 37.

[94]Rashkover, "Markus Barth," 263.

[95]Rashkover, "Markus Barth," 263-64.

theoretical understanding of Jewish people. Emil Fackenheim and Friedrich-Wilhelm Marquardt are just two commentators who leveled such charges against him. For Fackenheim, Karl Barth made only "a few attempts to speak to Jews toward the end of his life—when . . . it was too late."[96] Marquardt was just as scathing, claiming that for Karl, Jews existed "as mere forms of our perception and the stuff of our alienated consciousness," but with no independent reality.[97] I have sought elsewhere to show that such accusations against the senior Barth are simply false.[98]

In any event, it has never been possible to make such claims about Markus, as his personal and professional relationships with Jews were always important to him. This has already been demonstrated in earlier chapters in, for example, his housing of the Eisenstadts in the Bubendorf vicarage, following their escape from Nazi-occupied territories, as well as the Barth family's warm relations with their Jewish neighbors in Chicago.

There were also significant relationships with key members of America's Jewish communities. From the early 1960s through to the final years of his life, Barth was in regular contact with leading Jewish intellectuals and teachers. Not least among them were Abraham Heschel, Jacob Taubes, Stephen and Henry Schwarzschild, Emil Fackenheim, Michael Wyschogrod, and Zalman Schachter. However, while these relationships were generally warm, not all were consistently cordial. Indeed, perhaps one of the characteristics of Barth's friendships with Jewish colleagues was their volatility.

Wyschogrod and Fackenheim, for example, both had close friendships with Barth in the early to mid-1960s, which were later soured by theological and political disagreements. With Wyschogrod, the argument initially concerned their opposing views on America's involvement in the Vietnam War before turning heatedly to the rights and wrongs of the Israel-Palestine conflict. With Fackenheim, the argument was more strictly theological. For him, "Auschwitz"—as symbol and reality—was such a theologically

---

[96]E. Fackenheim, *To Mend the World: Foundations of Post-Holocaust Jewish Thought* (New York: Schocken, 1989), 284.

[97]F.-W. Marquardt, *Die Entdeckung des Judentums für die christliche Theologie: Israel im Denkens Karl Barths* (Munich: Christian Kaiser Verlag, 1967), 316.

[98]See, for example, M. Lindsay, *Barth, Israel and Jesus: Karl Barth's Theology of Israel* (Abingdon: Routledge, 2016), 26-35.

rupturing event that it had, necessarily, to be the overriding theological criterion and datum for both Judaism and Christianity. As he put it to Barth, "From a Jewish standpoint . . . the very first condition of Jewish-Christian dialogue . . . is Christian recognition of a still-living bond between God and Israel; and that a Christian who does give this recognition cannot by-pass the scandal of the particularity of Auschwitz."[99] That is, only by acknowledging the hermeneutical priority of the Sho'ah to modern Jewish *and Christian* faith could Jewish-Christian dialogue be possible. Barth, on the other hand, while acknowledging the existential trauma of the Holocaust, wanted still to be able to prioritize a Christian belief in resurrection hope.[100] As he lamented to the Canadian theologian David Demson, "Defiance rather than hope is the Leitmotiv of [Fackenheim's] thought. . . . [He] appears to live more from the great enemy, and correspondently: from negation, than from the source of hope."[101]

With both Wyschogrod and Fackenheim, at least part of the disagreement had to do with determining what constituted the proper attitude toward Israel. Barth perceived that a Jewish prioritization of Auschwitz, such as he saw exemplified in Fackenheim and Wyschogrod, was being used to justify militaristic Zionism, with the administrations of Golda Meir and Menachem Begin being particularly guilty. "[Al]most all Jews," he said, somewhat intemperately, "are becoming Zionists and are doing this not without the great danger of endorsing Nazi-like features of blood and soil, nationalistic and militaristic thinking of infamous memory."[102] Repudiating the claim that Israel was in a fight for its survival, Barth declared during a public forum in February 1970, "That is what I heard Hitler say in the 1930s."[103] There was no doubt, said Barth, that Israel had a legitimate claim to the land on which it was situated. Nevertheless, its tenure should be as

[99]E. Fackenheim to M. Barth, April 21, 1967. MBMC. Series II. Correspondence. Box 13, file 389.

[100]For details, see my two articles: "Jewish-Christian Dialogue from the Underside: Markus Barth's Correspondence with Michael Wyschogrod (1962–84) and Emil Fackenheim (1965–80)," *Journal of Ecumenical Studies* 53, no. 3 (2018): 313-47; and "Jewish-Christian Dialogue in Review: Markus Barth's Correspondence with Emil Fackenheim (1965–1980)," *Journal of Reformed Theology* 14, no. 3 (2020): 246-62.

[101]M. Barth to D. Demson, August 13, 1979. MBMC. Series II. Box 25, file 601.

[102]M. Barth to N. Porteous, July 15, 1969. MBMC. Series II. Box 16, file 427.

[103]B. Wilcox, "Inter-communication Critical, Says Rabbi," *Miami News*, February 5, 1970, 32.

"steward" not "possessor," with a responsibility of care and protection for *all* who lived there, and not only Jews.[104]

Barth was adamant that such criticism of Israel was not only justified, but indeed required by Christianity's kinship with the Jewish people. Christians, he said, "shall bear witness to our solidarity with our suffering brother in a helpful manner only when we have the courage to express a critical solidarity."[105] Insofar as these sorts of comments ultimately shattered many of his Jewish friendships, it is worth exploring in some detail what Barth's theology of Israel actually was.

The state of Israel. The start of Barth's academic career coincided neatly with the establishment of the state of Israel in 1948. From that time on, the nature and reality of Israeli politics and its international relations remained central to his work, his writing, and his sense of vocation. However, though he was a committed and passionate supporter of Israel, he was by no means an uncritical one. As he put it in *The People of God*, "Despite Jewish misgivings, a Christian should be permitted to view critically the policies of the Israeli right wing parties and of the 'hawks,' the cruel and damaging practices of the occupation regime in the annexed and occupied territories."[106] Indeed, so dismayed did he become by Israel's suppression of Palestinian rights that, in 1973, he met with Yassar Arafat to discuss what might be done to bring about peace.

Emerging from his reflections during this time came two of Barth's most provocative lectures, "Jesus the Jew" and "Israel and the Palestinians." Delivered during 1973–1974, he sought in them to balance his commitment to Israel's legitimacy, on one hand, and his zeal for Palestinian freedoms on the other. He was especially critical of the 1950 Law of Return,[107] and Israel's perpetual search for "secure borders," both of which were, he said, justifiably regarded by Palestinians as real and present threats to life, dignity,

[104]B. Wilcox, "Church Council Might Back Israelis' Rights in Mideast," *The Miami News*, February 4, 1970, 8.

[105]M. Barth, *Jesus the Jew*, trans. F. Prussner (Atlanta: John Knox, 1978), 93.

[106]M. Barth, *The People of God* (Sheffield: JSOT Press, 1983), 70.

[107]Passed unanimously by the Knesset on July 5, 1950, the Law of Return grants to any person with one or more Jewish grandparent, and their spouse, the right to relocate to Israel and acquire Jewish citizenship.

and property.[108] While prepared to acknowledge that Palestinian activists sometimes engaged in terrorism, Barth insisted that such activists were themselves almost invariably "people who have been victims of exerted violence."[109] Perhaps not surprisingly, such criticism of Israel, and seeming justification of Palestinian terrorism, caused some commentators to turn against him in barely contained anger. Whereas previously Barth had frequently been "reviled as a hard-boiled Zionist" for allegedly misusing the Scriptures to bestow upon Israel "an undeserved halo,"[110] now he found himself the target of undisguised hostility from the Jewish side. For Zwi Werblowsky, for example, Barth's academic and public commentaries on Israeli policies made him one of those friends "from whom [may] God protect us." In the rabbi's opinion, Barth's criticism of Israel disqualified him from being a "moral partner in any dialogue, since after such obscenity no communication is possible."[111]

And yet, in spite of his often harsh criticism, and despite the equally hostile repudiations of his views by some Jews, Barth's last word on the state of Israel remained, like his father's, a resounding "Yes." "We believe that the Jew Jesus Christ and the solidarity of all members of the one (Old and New Testament) people of God call upon all Christians . . . to give unconditional support to the Jewish *people*, both in its dispersion and in the State of Israel."[112] In view of Barth's criticisms of Israeli politics and military

---

[108]Barth, *Jesus the Jew*, 59-60.

[109]Barth, *Jesus the Jew*, 70-71. He specifically singled out, as examples of such "exerted violence," the atrocities committed in 1948 at Deir Yassein by the Jewish Irgun and the "Lehi Group," in which 107 Palestinian villagers were massacred, and the assassination of Palestinian leaders in Beirut by the Israeli military. As the final revisions to this book were being made, Hamas militants raided southern Israel on October 7, 2023, killing approximately 1,200 people, predominantly Israelis, in what was the biggest loss of Jewish life in a single day since the Holocaust. In response, Israel launched a massive air and ground offensive in Gaza, ostensibly to destroy Hamas, but—according to many commentators—in fact to "ethnically cleanse" Gaza of all Palestinians. Much of Barth's language in these two lectures from 1973–1974—his rejection of Israel's claim to be acting purely in self-defense, and his assertion that "brutal violence by terrorists . . . is provoked by prior use of naked power"—has been repeated in the aftermath of the October 7 massacres. It is probable, in my view, that had he been alive, Barth would have censured Israel in 2023 in precisely the way he did in the early 1970s and would have attracted precisely the same ire from the pro-Israel side.

[110]M. Barth, *Jesus the Jew*, 43.

[111]Z. Werblowsky to M. Barth, May 4, 1975. MBMC. Series II. Box 22, file 553.

[112]Barth, *Jesus the Jew*, 95.

strategies, it can legitimately be asked why he nonetheless felt compelled to make this affirmation. The answer lies, in part, in his understanding of how one ought to define the biblical and post-biblical people of Israel in relation to God's covenant community.

The people of Israel and the people of God. The church has consistently claimed monopoly ownership of, and identification with, the term *people of God*. The late Franklin Littell put it neatly when he said that "the cornerstone of Christian Antisemitism is the superseding or displacement myth . . . that the mission of the Jewish people was finished with the coming of Jesus Christ, that 'the old Israel' was written off with the appearance of 'the new Israel.'"[113] Even after the Sho'ah, Roman Catholicism was perpetuating this view by speaking, in *Lumen Gentium*, of the church as "the new Israel."[114]

Yet it was precisely the Sho'ah that compelled a reconsideration of the place and role of post-biblical Israel within Christian imagination and theology. As we have seen in an earlier chapter, Markus Barth was in the early forefront of this reappraisal. A founding member in 1969 of the Christian Scholars' Group on Jewish-Christian Relations, Barth was intimately involved in the drafting of the 1973 "Statement to Our Fellow Christians," which set forth fourteen propositions concerning the rightful Christian understanding of Jews, Judaism, and the state of Israel.[115] Among the more theologically provocative propositions was the third, which stated, "The singular grace of Jesus Christ does not abrogate the covenantal relationship of God with Israel. . . . In Christ the church shares in Israel's election *without superseding it*."[116]

---

[113]F. H. Littell, *The Crucifixion of the Jews: The Failure of Christians to Understand the Jewish Experience* (Macon, GA: Mercer University Press, 1986), 2.

[114]Vatican Council II, *Lumen Gentium*, Dogmatic Constitution on the Church (November 21, 1964), II.9.

[115]"Statement to Our Fellow Christians," Christians Scholars' Group on Jewish-Christian Relations, 1973. Cited in Littell, *Crucifixion of the Jews*, Appendix A, 134-40. The Christian Scholars' Group on Jewish-Christian Relations was first convened by the Faith and Order Commission of the National Council of Churches. The Secretariat for Catholic-Jewish Relations of the National Conference of Catholic Bishops, and the National Conference of Christians and Jews were also involved periodically in co-sponsoring the group's activities and research. Since 2002, the group has partnered with the Center for Jewish-Christian Learning at Boston College.

[116]"Statement to Our Fellow Christians," in Littell, *Crucifixion of the Jews*, 135. Emphasis added.

Of course, Barth never minimized the significance of the church in the electing will of God. In the words of the 1973 statement, Barth affirmed with his cosignatories that "in Christ the church shares in Israel's election," with Gentiles now "numbered among Abraham's 'offspring' and therefore fellow-heirs with the Jews."[117] Similarly, in *The Broken Wall*, Barth insisted that the church is the "first-fruit of God's revelation."[118] "The church and those in the church *are God's house* and belong to the commonwealth ruled by God in the same political sense that is characteristic of Israel's belonging to God."[119]

There is thus no doubt in Barth's mind that to speak of "the people of God" must mean to speak of the church. But he was equally clear that the church's identity as the "people of God" is only ever conditional, secondary, and fragmentary. That the church is a community of people made alive to God in Christ must be considered in light of the fact that "a house and temple . . . already existed *before* there was a church. . . . God *had* a household and a people for the revelation of his grace and glory, *even Israel*."[120] This is not in itself, of course, a novel insight, nor even a particularly philosemitic one. Even the strongest advocates of supersessionism accept that the church's place in God's covenant was chronologically second, even if not providentially so.

But Barth goes beyond simply stating the obvious point that Israel came before the church in history. He consistently insisted, rather, that it is the very historical primacy of Israel that secures its continuing election, and the church's subsequence that renders it conditional. It is not, argued Barth, the Jews' place within the household of God that is in question. "What is problematic, however, is the name, the claim, the existence of the church. Is this (in its majority Gentile) body really the people of God? The certain answer is: only when incorporated in the people elected forever."[121]

When the church forgets that it lives only by this secondary and fragmentary incorporation and instead places its emphasis, as Paul does in

---

[117]"Statement to Our Fellow Christians," articles 1, 3. Cited in Littell, *Crucifixion of the Jews*, 134-35.
[118]Barth, *Broken Wall*, 90.
[119]Barth, *Broken Wall*, 103. Emphasis added.
[120]Barth, *Broken Wall*, 119. Emphasis added.
[121]Barth, *People of God*, 53.

Ephesians, on the "growth and building of the One, Holy Apostolic, Catholic Church," then that very church—this *conditional* people of God—takes on a "strange, dangerous, and unfriendly" aspect, particularly toward those whom it deems to be at its margins.[122] And perhaps not surprisingly, the one people by whom the church's own conditional incorporation is supported, the Jews, have been not infrequently the most marginalized and therefore the most endangered by the church's expansion.

As has been commented upon repeatedly through this book, Barth's response to the church's misplaced arrogance was to remind it of the actuality of reconciliation that, through the hermeneutical lens of Paul's Ephesians letter, takes shape most authentically and necessarily in the reconciliation of Jews and Gentiles. "The whole work of Christ," says Barth, "is not only related to, but *consists of* the breaking down of the dividing wall between Jews and Gentiles. We observe that it is *not* related, primarily, to the partition between races and classes, nations and neighbours, ages and cultures."[123]

While all sorts of other social, ethnic, gender, and economic relationships are relativized by Christ, there "is no substitute for that unique peace" between Jews and Gentiles, and which is in itself "the source from which peaceful co-existence at all levels of life is to be drawn."[124]

But what of the attitude of Jews toward Christ? If the church's identity as God's people is to be viewed only through the lens of Israel's prior and continuing election, is Israel's identity as the people of God similarly relativized by the non-acknowledgment of Jesus as the Jewish Messiah? Are Jews, therefore, also rendered the people of God in only a fragmentary and conditional fashion? To this, Barth responded with a categorical, "No!" Jews remain members of God's household regardless of their attitude to Christ and even God. Regardless of what Israel did and does with its election, regardless of its behavior, attitude, obedience, or disobedience,

> Nothing can wipe out the privilege and function of Israel. Even the faithlessness of Israel cannot nullify God's faithfulness. . . . The Israel of which

---

[122]Barth, *Broken Wall*, 19.
[123]Barth, *Broken Wall*, 116. Emphasis added.
[124]Barth, *Broken Wall*, 117.

> Paul speaks in Ephesians is therefore Israel in whatever attitude and attire it meets our eye or confronts our ways. It is the Old Testament people and the Jew of to-day, the true worshippers and those who, with the help of a disciple of Christ, and of a Gentile judge and his soldiers, crucified the "king of the Jews." By God's election to be his child and servant, Israel has character that is indelible.[125]

Clearly for Markus, the primacy of Israel's election remains even to this day. And so, whereas the church has traditionally understood Jewish acceptability before God as being dependent upon the extent to which each individual Jew enters the life of the Christian community, Markus Barth saw it in entirely the opposite way around: the church's acceptability before God is dependent upon her attitude toward Israel. That is why he insisted that the only true test of the sincerity of any political or religious movement, including the church, is the way it treats the Jews.[126] As he put it in *The People of God*, "[In] the relationship [of Christians] with Jews their relation to Jesus Christ is verified or falsified."[127]

> The church . . . has no right to let herself be called "body of the Messiah (or, of Christ)," nor call herself "people of God," unless she recognizes and acknowledges that she is participating in the history and community of the Jews. . . . He who would want to have peace . . . without community with the people of which Jesus is a native son, would separate himself from salvation.[128]

Unfortunately, the souring of Barth's friendships with many of his Jewish interlocutors was not least because they believed him in his criticism of Israel to be guilty at precisely this point. In Michael Wyschogrod's words, to "sit in judgment over Israel . . . is a very dangerous enterprise." There could, he said, be no room for such self-righteousness on the part of anyone who confesses

---

[125]Barth, *Broken Wall*, 122. See also Barth, *Jesus the Jew*, 27. One cannot help but see in this passage a remarkable similarity to Karl Barth's affirmation in *CD* III/3 that, in spite of all infidelity and oppression, the Jews have continued to survive. "The Jews can be despised and hated and oppressed and persecuted and even assimilated, but they cannot really be touched. . . . They are the only people that necessarily continues to exist, with the same certainty that God is God, and that what He has willed and said and done according to the message of the Bible is not a whim or a jest, but eternally in earnest." K. Barth, *CD* III/3, 218-19.

[126]Barth, *Broken Wall*, 118.

[127]Barth, *People of God*, 49.

[128]Barth, *People of God*, 47.

Christ and who purportedly recognizes the inextricable bond between Jesus and Israel. "The face of the living Jew is the closest you will ever get in this life to seeing the face of your Lord. . . . If you separate yourself from the consensus of this people, you are separated from your Lord. . . . If your morality leads you to the hurting of Jews, it is not the morality of your Lord."[129]

Certainly, Barth's preparedness to offer stinging rebukes of Israel's posture toward its neighbors was provocative and worded, on occasion, with intemperate vigor. Nevertheless, and notwithstanding his lapses in rhetorical and linguistic judgment, it would be wrong to characterize him as anything other than *wanting* to be ardently on the side of both Israel as a state and his Jewish friends. As he worded it as early as 1959, "Unless we do all in the conviction that Israel . . . is here to stay, we deny and fight the election of the gracious God."[130]

For Barth, as for very few other Christian theologians of his generation, the Jewish-Christian relationship had to be conceived as a "conversation" between equals. "No access is open, no Holy Spirit is available and operative, that would admit either one of the two *without the other* to the throne of grace."[131] While similar pronouncements became more common from the 1980s, Barth saw the theological necessity of such a conviction long before most and worked tirelessly to advance it. Were this to have been the single contribution that Markus Barth made to twentieth-century Protestant theology, it would have been, insofar as he made this claim only fourteen years after the Holocaust, vitally important. That he provided so much more—in New Testament studies, in the formation of pastors, and in the constant striving for theologically grounded justice and equity—grants him a rare place in modern theological history.

---

[129]M. Wyschogrod to M. Barth, January 1, 1975. MBMC. Series II. Box 21, file 545.

[130]M. Barth, "Reflections on US Foreign Policy," *Christianity and Crisis* 17 (October 14, 1957): 134.

[131]Barth, *Broken Wall*, 124. Emphasis added.

EPILOGUE

There is little doubt that the broad field of "Barth studies" has flourished over the past three decades. Much of the energy has been generated by the "usual (institutional) suspects"—in particular, Princeton Theological Seminary, its Center for Barth Studies, and also some of the Scottish universities, in which there has been a recently renewed interest—as well as by the (somewhat unfortunately) hot-headed prosecution of various long-standing debates. Among the latter, one would immediately think of Karl Barth's doctrine of election, the implications of the same for his understanding of Christology and the triune being of God—the notorious McCormack-Hunsinger-Molnar debate—as well as the still-controversial matter of his theological understanding of the Jewish people. The entire field of inquiry is also now genuinely global and interdisciplinary, with postcolonial/anticolonial critiques (J. Cameron Karter, Rothney Tshaka), interfaith studies (Jennifer Rosner, Joshua Ralston), and gender theologies (Faye Bodley-D'Angelo, John Blevins, Hanna Reichel) bringing Barthian scholarship into active and fruitful dialogue with global South, non-Christian, and other previously marginalized voices. And if in the mid-2000s the task was to think "with Barth but beyond Barth,"[1] the 2023 Barth conference at Princeton—"Barth and the Political"—demonstrated the increasing move within at least some scholarly circles to think "with Barth but *against* Barth."

[1]See for example, G. Thomas, R. R. Brouwer, and Bruce McCormack, eds., *Dogmatics After Barth: Facing Challenges in Church, Society and the Academy* (Leipzig: CreateSpace Independent Publishing Platform, 2012).

Nonetheless, and for entirely understandable reasons, "Barth studies" has hitherto been engaged solely with the life, legacy, and contribution—to theology, church, and civil society—of *Karl* Barth. With the notable exception of the 2018 Markus Barth Symposium at Princeton Theological Seminary, the work of the "other Barths"—one should think here not only of Markus but also at least of Christoph—has been sorely neglected.

One can hardly be surprised by this. Few theologians since the Reformation have had as voluminous a literary output as Karl, or as wide and enduring an influence as him—across Roman, Orthodox, and Protestant traditions, as well as in various national and international political debates. As someone who has been enmeshed within those studies for nearly thirty years, I can hardly complain about this emphasis! And indeed, I do not. It is a scholarly focus that has been both justified and extraordinarily fruitful, not least of all for the churches in whose service Karl Barth always knew himself to be.

However, now that we are fifty-five years beyond his death, it seems timely to expand the scope of Barth scholarship so as to more intentionally consider the contributions of some of the lesser-known Barths. In this book, the aim has of course been to explore in some detail the life and legacy of Karl's eldest son—and probably the most recognizable of these other Barths—Markus. But as I have already suggested, there is work to do also on Christoph—both in terms of his Old Testament scholarship as well as his role as a theological teacher within majority-Muslim Indonesia—and perhaps also some updated scholarship on Karl's father, Fritz. Certainly, Markus's children would contend that Rose Marie similarly deserves greater recognition for her own ministry, as well as for the assistance she provided to Markus in his work. As someone who undertook her own theological studies, Rose Marie—not entirely unlike Charlotte von Kirschbaum—typed, checked, and corrected Markus's manuscripts, offering her own critical suggestions along the way, and participated fully in the regular "open evenings" that were such a feature of Markus's pedagogy from Dubuque onward. It was also Rose Marie who kept Markus abreast of the major developments in, and commentary upon, the civil rights struggle in the US and the debates about America's involvement in Vietnam. While

I have attempted to note some of these contributions of hers throughout the book, nevertheless the book does not tell her story. It is, however, a story worth telling—by someone else.

In any event, if this book has done just one thing, I would hope that it has demonstrated that "Barth studies" ought no longer simply be restricted to Karl, no matter how imposing a figure he is, and surely deserves to remain. If I can venture an analogy, no one would decry Basil of Caesarea's towering influence or his recognition as a doctor of the church. And yet his younger brother, Gregory of Nyssa, is now also widely acknowledged as a highly significant theologian in his own right, despite the fact that he received precious little scholarly attention until the middle of the twentieth century. Studies of the Cappadocian Fathers may well continue to be dominated by engagement with Basil (and also, of course, Gregory of Nazianzus), but "the other Gregory"—while neither "Great," nor a doctor of the church—has become an indispensable part of that story. In the same way, Markus deserves to be an indispensable part of the Barth story; he is, if you will, "little Gregory" to Karl's "Basil."

Perhaps the analogy is poor, but the point, I hope, is well taken. While Karl Barth's own theological work will and should rightly continue to be an area of intense debate and scrutiny within both academy and church, one need not engage primarily with him in order to be fruitful within "Barth studies" more broadly. Quite aside from whatever gems might be discoverable in the legacies of Fritz, Christoph, and even Rose Marie, there is a significant amount of further research into Markus Barth's life and theology still to do. As I said at the start of this book, others may—and should—narrate Markus's life, and even exegete his theology, differently, by dressing him in (as Mark Twain would have it) different "clothes and buttons." To do so—to interpret him other than as I have done—is the stuff of scholarship, and greatly to be desired. It is my hope that this book stimulates such interest and scholarly engagement, and in so doing helps widen the vision of "Barth studies" beyond its traditional limit.

Appendix

MARKUS BARTH'S COURSE REGISTER, 1973–1986

(according to the official course register from the University of Basel)

SUMMER SEMESTER 1973

- Lectures: Galatians
- New Testament seminar: Problems in the Epistle of James

WINTER SEMESTER 1973–1974

- Lectures: Introduction to the History and Theology of the New Testament (open to students from all faculties)
- Preliminary seminar: Selected texts from the Synoptic Gospels
- Practical assessment: Hymns in the New Testament

SUMMER SEMESTER 1974

- Lectures: Church, Cultus, and Cosmos (Interpretation of Colossians)
- Seminar: The Nature of the Sermons (according to the discourses in the Book of the Acts)
- Practical assessment: Recent Research on Paul

WINTER SEMESTER 1974–1975

- *Taught during Barth's first term as faculty dean*
- Lectures: The Revelation of John
- Preliminary seminar: Passion Narratives
- Colloquium on Apocalyptic

SUMMER SEMESTER 1975

- *Taught during Barth's first term as faculty dean*
- Lectures: Theology of the Resurrection: Exegesis and Dogmatics (with Prof. Heinrich Ott)
- Lectures: Pauline Ethics (with lecturers from the Catholic Theological Faculty from Lucerne)
- Seminar: Politics and the Kingdom of God

WINTER SEMESTER 1975–1976

Not listed

SUMMER SEMESTER 1976

Not listed

WINTER SEMESTER 1976–1977

Not listed

SUMMER SEMESTER 1977

- Seminar: New Testament Homiletics (with Prof. Eduard Buess)
- Seminar: Meals and the Lord's Supper in the Lukan Texts
- Practical assessment: Problems in New Testament Theology

WINTER SEMESTER 1977–1978

Not listed

SUMMER SEMESTER 1978

Not listed

WINTER SEMESTER 1978–1979

- Lectures: The Gospel of John
- Seminar: New Testament Homiletics (with Prof. Eduard Buess)

SUMMER SEMESTER 1979

- Seminar: Wisdom in the Old and New Testaments (with Prof. Ernst Jenni)
- Seminar: Christ, Humanity, and Nature in the New Testament
- Practical assessment: Text-Critical Studies

WINTER SEMESTER 1979–1980

- Lectures: Introduction to the New Testament (History and Theology)
- Practical assessment: Short readings from the Septuagint and New Testament texts on the theme "Promise and Fulfilment"

SUMMER SEMESTER 1980

- Lectures: Pauline Ethics
- Seminar: The Letters of James and 1 Peter
- Colloquium on Pauline Ethics and the New Pauline Studies
- Practical assessment: Studies on the Revelation of John

WINTER SEMESTER 1980–1981

- Lectures: The Gospel of Mark
- Preliminary seminar: Speeches in the Book of the Acts
- Colloquium on the Gospel of Mark lectures
- Seminar: New Testament and Systematic Theology (with Jan Milič Lochman): The Confession of the Divinity of Christ

SUMMER SEMESTER 1981

- Lectures: Galatians
- Seminar: Christ-hymns
- Practical assessment: The Old Testament in the New
- Colloquium on the Galatians lectures

WINTER SEMESTER 1981–1982

Taught during Barth's second term as faculty dean

- Lectures: Introduction to the New Testament (History and Theology)
- Revision course: Introduction to the New Testament
- Lectures: The Gospel of Luke

SUMMER SEMESTER 1982

Taught during Barth's second term as faculty dean

- Lectures: The Lord's Supper in the New Testament
- Practical assessment: Freedom, Service and Work in Philippians

WINTER SEMESTER 1982–1983

- Lectures: Hebrews
- Preliminary seminar: Methods of Interpretation
- Practical assessment: Baptism in the New Testament
- Colloquium on the Hebrews lectures

SUMMER SEMESTER 1983

These were Barth's scheduled classes, but as noted in chapter 7, he had forced to take medical leave due to very high blood pressure, and had in fact spent six weeks in the hospital.

- Lectures: Authority and Interpretation of the Bible
- Seminar: Law and Ethics in Paul
- Revision: New Testament Bible Studies

WINTER SEMESTER 1983–1984

- Lectures: Introduction to the New Testament
- Preliminary seminar: Steps to Interpretation
- Practical assessment: Biblical Texts on the Lord's Supper

SUMMER SEMESTER 1984

- Lectures: The Gospel of John
- Seminar: The Belief of Paul
- Colloquium on the Gospel of John lectures
- Practical assessment: Text-critical studies

WINTER SEMESTER 1984–1985

- Lectures: Romans (chapters 9–16)
- Colloquium: Legal Issues from Theological and Legal Perspectives (with Dr. Jur. Detlef Krauss)
- Short lecture: The Revelation of John

SUMMER SEMESTER 1985

Not listed

WINTER SEMESTER 1985–1986

Markus Barth was from now on listed as an emeritus.

- Lectures: Introduction to the New Testament I (Gospels, Acts and Revelation)

BIBLIOGRAPHY

PRIMARY SOURCE MATERIAL: MARKUS BARTH

In addition to published works, two collections of unpublished letters and papers from Markus Barth's literary estate have been used throughout the text. They are, with abbreviations:

MBMC Markus Barth Manuscript Collection, held as part of the Special Collections in the Wright Library at Princeton Theological Seminary.

MBL Markus Barth (Lindsay) Collection, held by the author, in mixed digital and hardcopy format.

"Versuche zur Lösung der soziale Frage aus vormarxistischer Zeit: Eine auszugsweise Darlegung des utopischen Sozialismus der Zeit 1800–1800." Unpublished booklet, 1933.

"Der politische Friede in der Botschaft der Kirche." *Zentralblatt des Schweizerischen Zofingervereins* 78 (1937–1938): 133-37.

Das Abendmahl: Passamahl, Bundesmahl und Messiasmahl. Theologische Studien 18. Zürich: Evangelischer Verlag, 1945.

Der Augenzeuge: Eine Untersuchung über die Wahrnehmung des Menschensohnes durch die Apostel. Zollinkon-Zurich: Evangelischer Verlag, 1946.

"Gemeindeaufbau in biblischer Sicht." *Kirchenfreund: Blätter für biblisches Bekennen in der Kirche* 81, no. 6 (March 1947): 81-85.

"Jesus Christus, der grosse Hohepriester des neuen Bundes." *Kirchenfreund: Blätter für biblisches Bekennen in der Kirche* 83, no. 6 (June 1949): 145-50.

Die Taufe—Ein Sakrament? Ein exegetischer Beitrag zum Gespräch über die kirchlicher Taufe. Zurich: Evangelischer Verlag, 1951.

"Um eine Verfassung der Reformierte Kirche in Baselland." *Reformierte Kirchenzeitung* 17/18, September 1, 1951.

"Vorwort." In M. Niemoeller, *Der Christen Weg Zwischen Ost und West*. Riehen: Schudel, 1952.

"The Mission and Misery of Europe's Churches." *The Christian Century*, November 11, 1953.

"For Criminals Only." *The Divinity School News* 23, May 1, 1956.

"Reflections on Another Doctrine." *Comprendre* 17/18 (March 1957): 1-7.

"A New Man Is Born." *The Reformed Review* 10, no. 3 (April 1957): 1-10.

"Give the King Thy Justice, O God." *The Pulpit* 28, no. 7 (July 1957): 6-7, 21-23.

"Introduction to Demythologizing." *Journal of Religion* 37, no. 3 (July 1957): 145-55.

"Reflections on US Foreign Policy." *Christianity and Crisis* 17, October 14, 1957.

"Baptism and Evangelism." *Scottish Journal of Theology* 12, no. 1 (March 1959): 32-40.

"The Preacher and the Authority of the Bible." *Foundations: A Baptist Journal of History and Theology* 2 (July 1959): 230-34.

The Broken Wall: A Study of the Epistle to the Ephesians. Valley Forge, PA: Judson, 1959.

"The Church and Israel in Paul's Epistle to the Ephesians (A Summary)." *The Student World* 52 (1959): 68-80.

"Israel und die Kirche im Epheserbrief." *Stimme der Gemeinde* 11 (1959): 561-66.

"Israel und die Kirche im Brief des Paulus an die Epheser." *Theologische Existenz heute* 75 (1959): 1-46.

"Marriage Is Not the Chief End of Man." *Social Progress* 50, no. 4 (February 1960): 5-7.

"The Blake Proposal: Pool of the Rich or Pilgrimage of Servants?" *McCormick Quarterly* 15, no. 3 (1962): 3-8.

"The Freedom of God." In *The Empirical Theology of H. N. Wieman*, edited by R.W. Bretall, 288-98. New York: Macmillan, 1963.

"Conversion and Conversation: Israel and the Church in Paul's Letter to the Ephesians." *Interpretation: A Journal of Bible and Theology* 17, no. 1 (January 1963): 3-24.

With V. H. Fletcher. *Acquittal by Resurrection*. New York: Holt, Rinehart & Winston, 1963.

"Salvation from the Jews?" *Journal of Ecumenical Studies* 1, no. 2 (1964): 323-26.

"Developing Dialogue Between Marxists and Christians." *Journal of Ecumenical Studies* 4, no. 3 (1967): 385-405.

"Jesus, Paulus und die Juden." *Theologische Studien* 90. Zürich: EVZ, 1967.

"Rechtfertigung." In *Theologische Studien* 90. Zürich: EVZ, 1969. ET: *Justification: Pauline Texts Interpreted in the Light of the Old and New Testaments*. Trans. A. M. Woodruff III. Eugene, OR: Wipf & Stock, 1971.

"Review of B. Childs, *Biblical Theology in Crisis?*" *Interpretation: A Journal of Bible and Theology* 25, no. 3 (1971): 350-54.

Ephesians: Introduction, Translation, and Commentary on Chapters 1–3. Anchor Bible 34. New York: Doubleday, 1974.

Ephesians: Translation, and Commentary on Chapters 4–6. Anchor Bible 34A. New York: Doubleday, 1974.

Jesus the Jew. Translated by F. Prussner. Atlanta: John Knox, 1978.

The People of God. Journal for the Study of the New Testament Supplement Series 5. Sheffield: JSOT Press, 1983.

"Traditions in Ephesians." *New Testament Studies* 30, no. 1 (1984): 3-25.

"The Letter of Paul to the Ephesians." In *The Oxford Companion to the Bible*, edited by B. Metzger and M. D. Coogan, 185-89. Oxford: Oxford University Press, 1993.

With H. Blanke, and A. Beck. *Colossians*. Anchor Bible 34B. New York: Doubleday, 1994.

With H. Blanke. *The Letter to Philemon: A New Translation with Notes and Commentary*. Eerdmans Critical Commentary. Grand Rapids, MI: Eerdmans, 2000.

Israel and the Church: Contribution to a Dialogue for Peace. Eugene, OR: Wipf & Stock, 2005.

Rediscovering the Lord's Supper: Communion with Israel, with Christ, and Among the Guests. Eugene, OR: Wipf & Stock, 2006.

SECONDARY SOURCE MATERIAL

Anderson, C., and B. L. McCormack, eds. *Karl Barth and the Making of Evangelical Theology: A Fifty-Year Perspective*. Grand Rapids, MI: Eerdmans, 2015.

Balthasar, H. U. von. *Karl Barth: Darstellung und Deutung Seiner Theologie*. Koln: Jakob Hegner, 1965.

Barnett, V. *For the Soul of the People: Protestant Protest Against Hitler*. New York: Oxford University Press, 1992.

———. "Bonhoeffer and the Conspiracy." In *The Oxford Handbook of Dietrich Bonhoeffer*, edited by P. Ziegler and M. Mawson, 65-76. Oxford: Oxford University Press, 2019.

Barth, K. *Evangelical Theology: An Introduction*. Grand Rapids, MI: Eerdmans, 1963.

———. *Gesamtausgabe*. Edited by Hinrich Stoevesandt, Hans-Anton Drewes, and Peter Zocher. 56 vols. Zurich: TVZ, 1971–2022.

———. *The Heidelberg Catechism for Today*. Translated by S. C. Guthrie. London: Epworth, 1964.

———. *Karl Barth–Rudolf Bultmann Briefwechsel, 1922–1966*. Edited by B. Jaspert. Zurich: TVZ, 1994.

———. *Letters: 1961–1968*. Edited by J. Fangmeier and H. Stoevesandt. Edinburgh: T&T Clark, 1981.

———. "Nein! Antwort am Emil Brunner." *Theologische Existenz heute* 14 (1934): 1-63.

———. *Revolutionary Theology in the Making: Barth-Thurneysen Correspondence, 1914–1925*. Translated by J. D. Smart. London: Epworth, 1964.

———. *The Teaching of the Church Regarding Baptism*. Translated by E. Payne. London: SCM Press, 1948.

———. *The Theology of the Reformed Confessions*. Translated by D. L. Guder and J. J. Guder. Louisville, KY: Westminster John Knox, 2002.

———. "Wünschbarkeit und Möglichkeit eines allgemeinen reformierten Glaubensbekenntnisses." In *Die Theologie und die Kirche*, vol. 3, *Gesammelte Vorträge*. Munich: Christian Kaiser, 1928.

Barth, R. M. "Zum Geleit." In R. Köbler, *Schattenarbeit: Charlotte von Kirchsbaum—Die Theologin an der Seite Karl Barths*. Cologne: Pahl-Rugenstein, 1987.

Bergen, D. *Twisted Cross: The German Christian Movement in the Third Reich*. Chapel Hill: University of North Carolina Press, 1996.

Blake, E. C. "A Proposal Toward the Reunion of Christ's Church." In K. Watkins, *The American Church that Might Have Been: A History of the Consultation on Church Union*. Eugene, OR: Pickwick, 2014.

Bonhoeffer, D. *Discipleship*. Vol. 4 of *Dietrich Bonhoeffer Works*. Edited by G. B. Kelly and J. D. Godsey. Translated by B. Green and R. Krauss. Minneapolis: Fortress, 2001.

Brauer, J. "In Memoriam: J. Coert Rylaarsdam." *University of Chicago Chronicle* 17, no. 16. May 14, 1998.

Busch, E. *Glaubensheiterkeit: Karl Barth—Erfahrungen und Begegnungen erzählt von Eberhard Busch*. Neukirchen: Neukirchener Verlag, 1994.

———. *Karl Barths Lebenslauf*. Munich: Christian Kaiser Verlag, 1975. ET: *Karl Barth: His Life from Letters and Autobiographical Texts*. Translated by J. Bowden. Grand Rapids, MI: Eerdmans, 1994.

Byron, J. "Review of *Philemon*." *Journal of Biblical Literature* 121, no. 2 (2002): 383-86.

Clements, K. *Bonhoeffer and Britain*. London: Churches Together in Britain and Ireland, 2006.

Cochrane, A. C. *Eating and Drinking with Jesus: An Ethical and Biblical Enquiry*. Louisville: Westminster, 1974.

Come, A. B. "The Occasion and Contribution of the Confession of 1967." *Journal of Presbyterian History* 79, no. 1 (2001): 59-71.

Congdon, D. W. *The Mission of Demythologizing: Rudolf Bultmann's Dialectical Theology*. Minneapolis: Fortress, 2015.

Cornell, G. W. "Religious Play Said Still Anti-Semitic." *The Berkshire Eagle*, May 16, 1970.

DeCou, J. "The First Community: Barth's American Prison Tours." In *Karl Barth and the Making of Evangelical Theology: A Fifty-Year Perspective*, edited by C. Anderson and B. L. McCormack, 67-87. Grand Rapids, MI: Eerdmans, 2015.

Dickinson, C. "Markus Barth and Biblical Theology: A Personal Review." *Horizons in Biblical Theology: An International Dialogue* 17, no. 2 (1995): 96-116.

Dorrien, G. *The Making of American Liberal Theology: Crisis, Irony, and Postmodernity, 1950–2005*. Louisville: Westminster John Knox, 2006.

Drewes, H. A. "Intellectual and Personal Biography III: Barth the Elder (1935–1968)." In *The Oxford Handbook of Karl Barth*, edited by P. D. Jones and P. Nimmo, 52-68. Oxford: Oxford University Press, 2020.

Enns, J. *Saving Germany: North American Protestants and Christian Mission to West Germany, 1945–1974*. Montreal: McGill-Queen's University Press, 2017.

Filson, F. "Review of *Die Taufe—Ein Sakrament?*" *Theology Today* 10, no. 1 (April 1953): 130-31.

Flesch-Thebesius, M. "Nelly Barth." In *Ich bin was Ich bin: Frauen neben grossen Theologen und Religionsphilosophen des 20. Jahrhunderts*, edited by E. Rohr, 223-46. Gütersloh: Gütersloher Verlagshaus, 1997.

Flood, D. R. *Rape in Chicago: Race, Myth, and the Courts*. Urbana-Champagne: University of Illinois Press, 2012.

Gaitens, R. J. "Pros and Cons of the Confession." *Pittsburgh Post-Gazette*, January 7, 1967.

Gowan, D. E. "In Memory of Markus Barth: A Personal Note." *Horizons in Biblical Theology: An International Dialogue* 17, no. 2 (1995): 93-95.

Harries, R. *After the Evil: Christianity and Judaism in the Shadow of the Holocaust*. Oxford: Oxford University Press, 2003.

Hennecke, S. "Biography and Theology: On the Connectedness of Theological Statements with Life on the Basis of the Correspondence Between Karl Barth and Charlotte von Kirschbaum (1925–1935)." *International Journal of Philosophy and Theology* 77, no. 4-5 (2016): 324-36.

Hepburn, A. "Reconciliation and the Work of Herbert Sulzbach." *Kirchliche Zeitgeschichte* 25, no. 1 (2012): 180-95.

Heppe, H. *Reformed Dogmatics: Set Out and Illustrated from the Sources*. Translated by G. T. Thomson. London: Allen and Unwin, 1950.

Herskowitz, D. "Karl Barth and *Nostra Aetate*: New Evidence from the Second Vatican Council." *Journal of Theological Studies* 72, no. 2 (2021): 843-74.

Hockenos, M. D. *Church Divided: German Protestants Confront the Nazi Past*. Bloomington: Indiana University Press, 2004.

———. "Martin Niemoeller in America, 1946–1947: A Hero with Limitations." *Contemporary Church History Quarterly* 18, no. 2 (2012): https://contemporarychurch-history.org/2012/06/conference-paper-martin-niemoeller-in-america/.

Hunsinger, G. "Sacraments." In *The Oxford Handbook of Karl Barth*, edited by P. D. Jones and P. T. Nimmo, 451-66. Oxford: Oxford University Press, 2019.

Jenkins, P. *The Great and Holy War: How World War One Became a Religious Crusade*. New York: HarperCollins, 2014.

Jüngel, E. *Barth-Studien*. Zurich: Benziger 1982.

Käsemann, E. "Review of *Der Augenzeuge*." *Theologische Literaturzeitung* 73, no. 11 (1948): 665-70.

Kershaw, I. *Hitler, 1889–1936: Hubris*. London: Penguin, 1998.

Kuhn, T. K. "'McCarthy-Schwierigkeiten.' Der Streit um Helmut Gollwitzer als Nachfolger Karl Barths 1961/62." *Basler Zeitschrift für Geschichte und Altertumskunde* 109 (2009): 53-102.

Lindsay, M. R. *Barth, Israel, and Jesus: Karl Barth's Theology of Israel*. London: Routledge, 2016.

———. "The Identity of the People of God: Israel and the Church in the Theology of Markus Barth," *Colloquium* 43, no. 1 (2011): 3-16.

———. "Jewish-Christian Dialogue from the Underside: Markus Barth's Correspondence with Michael Wyschogrod (1962–84) and Emil Fackenheim (1965–80)." *Journal of Ecumenical Studies* 53, no. 3 (2018): 313-47.

———. "Jewish-Christian Dialogue in Review: Markus Barth's Correspondence with Emil Fackenheim (1965–1980)." In *Journal of Reformed Theology* 14, no. 3 (2020): 246-62.

MacLachlan, D. "Like Son, like Father: Reflections on the Influence of Markus Barth on Karl Barth's Thinking About Baptism." *Journal of Reformed Theology* 14, no. 3 (2020): 183-98.

Maring, N. "Is Baptism a Sacrament? Review of *Die Taufe—Ein Sakrament?*" *Foundations* 3, no. 1 (January 1960): 74-83.

Mayne. R. *In Victory, Magnanimity, in Peace, Goodwill: A History of Wilton Park*. London: Frank Cass, 2003.

McCormack, B. L. *Karl Barth's Critically Realistic Dialectical Theology: Its Genesis and Development, 1909–1936*. Oxford: Clarendon, 1997.

Meland, B. E. "The Student-Faculty Spring Conference." *The Divinity School News* 23, no. 3. August 1, 1956.

Moltmann, J. *A Broad Place: An Autobiography*. Translated by M. Kohl. London: SCM, 2007.

Moule, C. F. D. "Review of *Philemon*." *Journal of Theological Studies* 52, no. 2 (2001): 821-24.

Mumma, R. E. "The Presbyterian Confession of 1967." *The Harvard Crimson*, July 14, 1967.

Nimmo, Paul. "Markus Barth on the Lord's Supper." *Journal of Reformed Theology* 14, no. 3 (2020): 199-228.

Novak, D. "Hunsinger's *Karl Barth: Post-Holocaust Theologian?*" *Studies in Christian-Jewish Relations* 14, no. 1 (2019): 1-3.

Osiek, C. "Review of *Philemon*." *Biblica* 83, no. 2 (2002): 293-96.

Plant, S. "When Karl met Lollo: The Origins and Consequences of Karl Barth's Relationship with Charlotte von Kirschbaum." *Scottish Journal of Theology* 72, no. 2 (2019): 127-45.

Postert, A. "German Youth Between Euphoria and Resistance: Political Coercion and the Coordination of German Youth." In *From Weimar to Hitler: Studies in the Dissolution of the Weimar Republic and the Establishment of the Third Reich, 1932–1934*, edited by H. Beck and L. E. Jones, 366-93. New York: Bergahn, 2019.

Ramm, B. *After Fundamentalism: The Future of Evangelical Theology*. San Francisco: Harper & Row, 1983.

Rashkover, R. "Markus Barth: The Jews Are Our Brothers." *Journal of Reformed Theology* 14, no. 3 (2020): 263-79.

Rogers, J. B. "Biblical Authority and Confessional Change." *Journal of Presbyterian History (1962–1985)* 59, no. 2 (1981): 131-60.

Röthlisberger, E. *Gerty Pestalozzi-Eidenbenz: Ein Leben 1893–1978. Tagebücher und Briefe*. Brugg: Keller Druck, 1993.

Schlagenhaufen, F. "Review of *Der Augenzeuge*." *Zeitschrift für katholisches Theologie* 69, no. 2 (1947): 235-38.

Scholder, K. *The German Churches and the Third Reich*. Vol. 1, *1918–1934*. Translated by J. Bowden. Philadelphia: Fortress, 1988.

Selinger, S. *Charlotte von Kirchsbaum and Karl Barth: A Study in Biography and the History of Theology*. University Park: Pennsylvania State University Press, 1998.

Shumway, K. "Our First 125 Years." In K. Shumway, C. Andrews, and J. Bryant, *A Century and a Quarter with the First Baptist Church of Chicago*. Chicago: Chicago First Baptist Church, 1958.

Small, J. D. "The World of the Bible—Always Strange, Always New: Markus Barth as a Teacher." *Journal of Reformed Theology* 14, no. 3 (2020): 169-82.

Spinks, B. *Reformation and Modern Rituals and Theologies of Baptism: From Luther to Contemporary Practices*. Aldershot, UK: Ashgate, 2006.

Stohr, C. "Trading Gains: New Estimates of Swiss GDP, 1851–2008." London School of Economics Working Papers 245, June 2016.

Stringfellow, W. and A. Towne. *The Bishop Pike Affair: Scandals of Conscience and Heresy, Relevance and Solemnity in the Contemporary Church*. Eugene, OR: Wipf & Stock, 2007.

Tietz. C. *Karl Barth: A Life in Conflict*. Translated by V. Barnett. Oxford: Oxford University Press, 2021.

———. "Karl Barth and Charlotte von Kirschbaum." *Theology Today* 74, no. 2 (2017): 86-111.

Tillich, P. *Berliner Vorlesungen III (1961–1958)*. Edited by E. Sturm. Berlin: De Gruyter, 2009.

Torrance, T. F. "The Atonement and the Oneness of the Church." *Scottish Journal of Theology* 7, no. 3 (September 1954): 245-69.

Twain, M. *Autobiography of Mark Twain*. Vol. 1, *The Complete and Authoritative Edition*. Edited by H. E. Smith. Berkeley: University of California Press, 2010.

Van Til, C. *The Confession of 1967: Its Theological Background and Ecumenical Significance*. Phillipsburg, NJ: P&R, 1967.

Weitzel, T. "The Town Crier." *Chicago Daily News*, April 25, 1956.

West, C. "Review of M. Barth and V. H. Fletcher, *Acquittal by Resurrection*." *Theology Today* 22, no. 1 (April 1965): 148-49.

Williams, R. *Christianity in Poetry and Polity: Some Anglican Voices from Temple to Herbert*. Oxford: SGL, 2004.

Ziegler, P. "Remembering Markus Barth: A Biblical-Theological Existence—An Introduction." *Journal of Reformed Theology* 14, no. 3 (2020): 229-45.

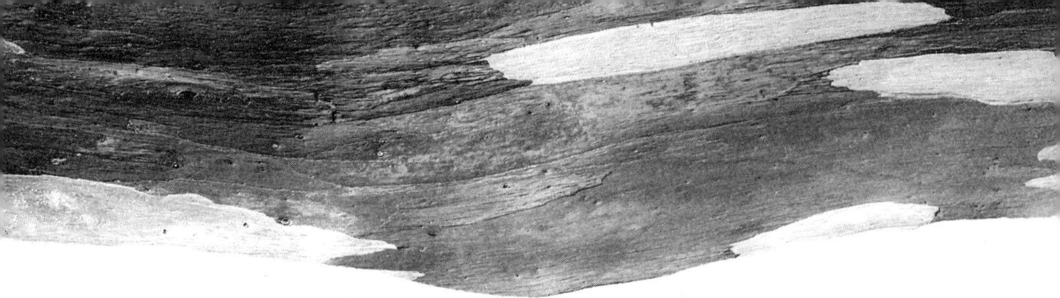

NAME INDEX

SUBJECT INDEX